Unless otherwise noted, all scripture references are taken from The Holy Bible, The New International Version, Copyright © 1978 by New York International Bible Society Publishers. Used by permission.

Vertical Reality

©1997 by Christ Church Publishing

ISBN 0-9642487-5-1

<u>All Rights Reserved</u> No portion of this book may be reproduced, stored in a retrieval system, or transmitted in any form or by any means—electronic, mechanical, photocopy, recording, or any other—except for brief quotations in printed reviews, without prior permission of the publisher.

Cover Design by Roseanne Hallstrom, with Olivier Melnick. Illustration by Paul Graves.

Appreciation

There are many people I would like to thank for their participation in making this book possible.

Thanks to my wife Marcy, whose encouragement to print the original bulletin covers was the origin of this devotional. Marc, you are the best.

Thanks to Wendy, Simon and Grandma Eadie for the countless hours of typing and retyping. Your servants' hearts are greatly appreciated.

Thanks to Barney, Dudley, David, Brian and Bob for their willingness to edit on such short notice. Your theological advice has been of tremendous help.

Thanks to Roseanne for the incredible ability to translate my heart in picture and design. You have carried my heart for over 25 years and I will forever be grateful. Thanks also to Paul Graves for the cover illusration.

Thanks to Andrew and Dana for your prayer covering. Without prayer, this project would have never been completed.

Thanks to the elders and family at Christ Church Kirkland who have read the devotionals over the years and have diligently put them into practice. You have made pastoring a joy.

Dedication

This book is dedicated to the men who have influenced my life the most. Long before mentoring was popular, they were there. They were there to train me and equip me, but most of all, they were there to be an example of how to radically pursue Jesus Christ and seek His Kingdom first.

I dedicate this book to James T. Hamann who has been my spiritual father from the beginning. For nearly twenty five years now he has poured his life into me and has been a godly example of devotion, perseverance, integrity, relationship, abandonment and more. Like Paul to Timothy, he took time to know me, expressed his love to me and instilled in me the confidence to go on.

Thanks Jim, for leading me in the way and for loving Jesus the way you have. You and Phyllis have influenced the lives of thousands and you have profoundly touched mine. I will be forever grateful.

I dedicate this book to Dennis Peacocke who has been like an older brother and a spiritual coach. Dennis' example of manliness and Kingdom pursuit has challenged me, provoked me and deeply encouraged me to want more. His pursuit of the Kingdom of God has re-centered me and his teaching on spiritual warfare has equipped me and prepared me for the purposes of God.

Thanks Dennis for being a credible example of a husband and father. You have drawn Jesus out of me and inspired me to go deeper. Your footprint has been left in my life and I will never be the same. I will be forever indebted to you and Jan.

I dedicate this book to Barney Coombs who has been like a favorite uncle. Over the years Barney has come in and out of my life at the most strategic times. His example of multiplying one's talents has been seen by all.

Thanks Barney for your pastoral heart. You have saved me from much and have pressed me for excellence. The love you and Janette have demonstrated means alot.

Norm Willis
Kirkland, Washington

Forward

My father once told me, "Much of your life will depend on the people you hang around." As I look back on fifty years now, I can see the wisdom in those words. I have been especially blessed to hang out with some choice saints throughout the years. I have also spent time around some who smelled too much like the world's system to be healthy.

I like being around Norm Willis. He smells right. No stench of self-righteousness or shallow religion; no pretense or facade; but a man who is not afraid to be an incarnation of Jesus' life in a community of faith. There is the refreshing scent of restful integrity. I find myself wanting to hear what he says, know what he is thinking, and see things the way he sees them.

There are some great saints I would love to talk with, but not everyday (if you know what I mean). I have found Norm easy to know. He speaks from a father's heart and a pastor's wisdom. When we visit, time flies and I am never ready to stop.

It would be a real and precious privilege to spend time everyday with Norm. I know my days would be brightened and my life would be fuller, but that is impossible with his responsibilities and mine . . . but what if I could spend time reading his thoughts on the important things?

I am thrilled that Norm has taken the time to offer us this opportunity. I know it is a sacrifice to get all this material in a form that would bless us. He has done it and I am grateful.

I am still trying to practice my father's advice. I choose to spend time with those who raise my standards and encourage my efforts. I will spend time with Norm Willis.

Dudley Hall
President of Successful Living Christian Ministries

INTRODUCTION

The future is now. The technological age is rapidly bringing us things that were once science fiction fantasies. Computer induced reality is no longer a thing of the future; it is experienced every day in what is called "Virtual Reality." As real as self-induced realities may seem, they are void of the ability to produce change. Though virtual reality may offer entertainment value, it will never bring us into the fullness of God's desire or build our lives upon the rock of eternal truth.

Sons and daughters of God are those who build their lives upon the rock-solid foundation of vertical reality. Vertical reality is life based upon relationship with our Heavenly Father. Standing diametrically opposed to anything self-induced, a person committed to vertical reality says, "My life is not my own. Consequently, my direction, decisions and destiny will come forth out of relationship with Father."

The way of the Kingdom is not the way of self-determination. Progress in the Kingdom of God is achieved through our abiding relationship with Christ. God's command to the priests in Leviticus 6:9-13 was "... *the fire must be kept burning; it must not go out. Every morning the priest is to add firewood ... the fire must be kept burning on the altar continuously; it must not go out."* As with the priest, our relationship with Jesus must be continuous. The intimacy Christ desires and the intimacy we need are not something that can be maintained on a weekly basis. Every morning we can add to the fire. Moment by moment we can turn our focus to the awareness of God's abiding presence. In His presence we are transformed and become the people of His desire.

Vertical Reality is written as a daily aid to our time in Father's presence. Beginning with Christ as our center, it seeks to rearrange any perspective that is orientated in self and change that orientation to Christ. Man's continual challenge is to turn away from himself and view life from a Kingdom perspective rather than a self-centered one. Each day this devotional looks at a different subject and challenges our perspective of it. *Vertical Reality* seeks to bring the reader before the standard of God's Word and allow the power of the Word through the Holy Spirit to be the changing agent.

૪૩૪૦

January 1st

FORCEFULLY ADVANCING

"From the days of John the Baptist until now, the Kingdom of Heaven has been forcefully advancing and forceful men lay hold of it"
Matthew 11:12

The Kingdom of God is on a forceful advance. The nature of God's Kingdom is progressive. There is nothing static about the Kingdom of God. For nearly 2,000 years, believers of nearly every tribe, nation and tongue have prayed, *"Thy Kingdom come"* and come it has. The Kingdom of God comes and it keeps coming. It forcefully advances, giving way to no one or to no thing. It is marching, it is moving onward and upward. The Kingdom of God is on a forceful advance. It is taking dominion over darkness and buying back captives from the kingdom of self.

That the Kingdom of God will advance is God's doing. That it will advance in us is our doing. We must give careful attention to the Kingdom's advance in our own lives lest it advance everywhere else but in us. The forceful advance of the Kingdom must begin in our own personal lives. It advances in us turning us from self-centered individuals seeking our own way into Christ-centered individuals seeking first the Kingdom of God.

A literal translation of Matthew 11:12 is *"But from the days of John the Baptist until now, the Kingdom of Heaven is taken by violence and the violent seize it."* For many, having violence in a Bible verse is a contradiction of terms. Contemporary thought has schooled us in a pacifistic mentality of the Kingdom, but the Bible does not teach pacifism in regard to our pursuit of the Kingdom. To seek after God, we must be violent, energetic, forceful people. This is not the violence of behavior, but the violence of pursuit. To be violent in our pursuit is to deal forcefully with attitudes of apathy and passivity. To be violent in our pursuit means to act on and not be acted upon. It means we seize what we see to be the will of God, not waiting for it to magically seize us.

Are you on a forceful advance? Has the violent pursuit of the Kingdom of God been made real to you? Jesus Christ did not die a violent death so we could live a passive life. It is time to declare war on apathy and begin to march in step with the forceful advances of the Kingdom of God.

January 2nd

SELLING ALL

"The kingdom of heaven is like a treasure hidden in a field. When a man found it, he hid it again, and then in his joy went and sold all he had and bought that field"
Matthew 13:44

We can thank the Lord that this man knew nothing of contemporary creative finance. If this parable were written from the perspective of present trends, it would have the man financing the field, then renting it out to another in order to maximize his return on investment. But the Kingdom of God is a field that cannot be bought as a rental. This is a field that requires "owner occupancy." You cannot purchase this field with zero-down financing and then let someone else live there in order to make your payments. No, this field requires that you joyfully sell all you have, then come back and purchase the field.

My encouragement is for us to conduct a "title search" of our field and see whether or not there is anything yet owing or some other kind of lien held against it. In order for us to buy the field, Jesus said we must sell all we have. So in order for us to own the title deed of this property, we must first sell all of our fears. Fear has no place in the Kingdom of God. The treasure requires that we sell all of our securities and find our security only in Him and that which He directs us to do. To buy this field, we must sell the control of our own future and trust in Him with all of our heart by seeking His Kingdom first. To "joyfully sell all" means we sell every desire for any other field and maintain a single eye for the field that contains the Kingdom of God.

The Kingdom of God, and this Kingdom alone, is the only thing that will satisfy and give life ultimate meaning and purpose. But be certain this is a Kingdom that will require all.

CSSO

January 3rd

FRUIT THAT REMAINS

"You did not choose Me, but I chose you and appointed you to go and bear fruit - fruit that will last"

John 15:16

With much concern, we witness trends sweeping through the church that promise tremendous results and do, in fact, make good on their promises, only to see the fruit of their promises short-lived. Like fad diets, the results are quickly achieved, but because there is no lifestyle change, you soon revert back to your original condition, plus some.

Perhaps the area most clearly illustrated is that of church growth. With much compromise of biblical standards and void of the cross, we have seen churches sell the gospel of "easy believism" in order to accelerate their growth. As a result, we have seen the emergence of professing Christians who have little or no understanding of obedience, holiness, commitment, surrender and a multitude of other characteristics so vital to the fullness of the Gospel.

Though the standard has been reduced, the proponents of this philosophy have pacified themselves with the fact that their churches are growing, with an ends justify the means approach, they have taken great delight in their unprecedented growth.

Recent studies, however, would reveal that this fad, like all others, was also short-lived. Baby boomers have been returning to church in record numbers; that is until a year ago. Since then, according to George Barna, a noted church statistician, the percentage has actually dropped five percent. Barna explains that because of our "limited sacrifice span," the cost of staying far outweighed the potential benefit; so consequently, hundreds of thousands are exiting.

Bait determines the type of fish you catch. When you bait with self-centered, no-cost promises, you catch self-centered, unwilling-to-pay fish. They remain until the perceived benefit is exhausted, then they are off to the next promised fad.

Fruit that remains is His goal. It may not promise off-the-chart results, but I will stick with the biblical standard and hold myself and those who are to come to the transformation of the inner man.

January 4th

GET READY

"Go through the camp and tell everybody, 'Get your supplies ready'"
Joshua 1:11

It is not easy to pack up and move a nation. You do not just wake up one day and decide you are going to move an entire nation. Movement of this magnitude requires tremendous planning and foresight. For three days the children of Israel readied themselves for the journey.

Sometimes moving the church is as difficult as moving a nation. It does not happen overnight and it does not happen without a lot of work. Sustained movement requires vast preparation. It requires the preparation of heart. It requires the preparation of vision. It requires the preparation of resources. Preparation is essential to purposeful movement.

As we face the new year, it is Father's desire to move us deeper into His purpose and intent for our lives. The new year will bring with it new visitation. New visitation will require new expectation. Joshua's exhortation to the people is ours as well: *"Get your supplies ready."* It is time to get our supplies ready for the habitation of God.

What are the supplies God has given you that must be prepared? Perhaps they are gifts that have been given you that must be prepared. Perhaps they are gifts that have been given that are lying dormant. Maybe it is a ministry that he has called you to, but fear has kept you from functioning. Perhaps it is something you must lay down in order to be properly prepared.

Preparation is first a matter of the heart. We must first get our hearts ready before we work on our actions. Internal preparation comes before external. Anticipation sets the stage for God's coming. If we do not expect Him to come, He probably will not. But, when expectation is high and we come with hearts full of anticipation, we experience His moving.

The Word of the Lord is "GET READY." Make whatever arrangements needed in order to be properly postured at God's coming. Prepare your heart and your mind. Prepare your expectation. God is doing a new thing.

January 5th

THE POWER OF CORPORATE PRAYER

"How could one man chase a thousand, or two put ten thousand to flight unless their Rock had sold them, unless the Lord had given them up?"

Deuteronomy 32:30

For what will the church age of the '90s be remembered? As the '70s brought the Jesus People explosion and the Charismatic renewal, what will the hallmark of the '90s be? Will it be the growth that came through discipleship and shepherding? Will it be the influx of new believers through power evangelism and signs and wonders? Will it be the structuring of the body through the identifying of Ephesians' chapter four gift ministries?

As vital and dramatic as each one of these moves has been, I believe there is one other that stands apart from the rest—one sovereign move of the Holy Spirit that history will prove to be a divine visitation for which the '90s will be remembered. A sovereign visitation, yet one which comes without fanfare and blazonry. Its subtlety is in the fact that its results are not often realized until years later. The visitation I am referring to is the sovereign move of corporate prayer. Without question, we are experiencing the greatest prayer movement in living memory. Men, like Larry Lea and David Young Cho, have been used mightily of the Lord to restore a biblical emphasis on the importance of corporate prayer.

Corporate prayer is the uniting of the local church for the purpose of intercession and spiritual warfare. It is different from other equally important forms of prayer in that it requires the gathering of the body of Christ. We are told in Deuteronomy 32:30, *"One will chase a thousand and two will put ten thousand to flight."* As grateful as we are for the power to put a thousand to flight, our goal is to chase ten thousand. C. Peter Wagner, the noted expert on church growth, writes, "The spread of the Kingdom of God occurs when Christians are revived and that revival is released through corporate prayer." Our need for revival is great. God's desire to give us revival is even greater. Corporate prayer is the key to unlock that desire.

☙❧

January 6th

THE PRAYERS OF DESPERATION

"The prayer of a righteous man is powerful and effective"
James 5:16

There they were gathered together. Peter was there, as were James and John and the eight others. The Scriptures tell us *"They all joined together constantly in prayer, along with the women and Mary."* (Acts 1:14)

I am sure this was not a prayer meeting full of faith and great expectation. In fact, they were probably a bit dejected. After three years with the Lord, now they were alone. The responsibility of all the training and preparation weighed heavily on their shoulders. It was now their move. The destiny of eternity was weighed in the balance. Would they follow through or would they retreat in fear and apprehension?

Sometimes you just pray. At other times, you are driven to pray. This was one of those times. These were not simple prayers. They were *"constantly in prayer."* This was true intercession. Deep calling unto deep, and it ushered in one of the greatest revivals history has ever known. Could we ever expect that kind of visitation again? Did Father do what He did at Pentecost just to get things started, or was it representative of how desperately He desires to visit this Earth?

History bears witness to the latter. Pentecost was but a representation of what happens when people will give themselves constantly to the prayer of revival.

The prophet Joel prophesied and the apostle Peter repeated this: *"In the last days, God says, 'I will pour out My Spirit on all people.'"* Though this prophecy was fulfilled in part at Pentecost, it was not fulfilled in its entirety. Joel promised God's Spirit would be poured out on all people. Pentecost gave the Spirit to just the Jew. There is another outpouring yet to come—an outpouring reserved for the last days that, I am sure, will be preceded as it was with the first, with those *"joining together constantly in prayer."*

Revival tarries because of the prayerlessness of the church. The prayer of revival is a prayer that makes the kingdom of darkness shudder in fear. Let us give ourselves constantly to such a prayer.

January 7th

A HEART OF WISDOM

"Teach us Lord to number our days that we may gain a heart of wisdom"

Psalm 90:12

What a goal! The ability to go through life and come through to the other side having gained a heart of wisdom. With every day that passes, we should be able to see the increase of wisdom and understanding into the ways of God.

There are two ways to gain wisdom. There is a wisdom that comes from hindsight, and there is a wisdom that comes from foresight.

Hindsight is the wisdom that is gained by experience. Having gone through life's events and using them before they use us, we are able to translate those events into wisdom. When all is said and done, experience is the best teacher. The wisdom gained from experience is a wisdom with character. That is, it is well rounded, balanced, humble and easy to fellowship. Wisdom that is void of experience tends to be proud, cocky and self-centered.

There is also a wisdom to be gained in foresight. This is the wisdom that comes when we have taken the time to anticipate the heart of God and by the empowering of the Holy Spirit, discern His will for our future.

May I challenge you to let this year become a year of foresight. It is always wise to learn from experience, but if through foresight we can spare ourselves some of those experiences, let us do it. Why not ask the Holy Spirit for discernment in regard to family, work, ministry and your personal relationship to Christ? Ask Him for the ability to anticipate His next move, then learn to prepare your heart for its coming.

January 8th

THE SOURCE OF KNOWLEDGE

"The proverbs of Solomon . . . for the attaining of wisdom and discipline, for acquiring a disciplined and prudent life, doing what is right and just and fair; for giving prudence and discretion to the young . . ."

Proverbs 1:1-4

*W*estern thought and education have been built upon the foundation of rationalism and reason. Its focus has been the academic development of the mind with little concern for the formation of the character. Believing morals to be strictly a personal matter that cannot be legislated, Western thought has diefied the mind and made it the grid that validates all else.

In contrast, biblical thought has quite a different perspective. Believing internal character to be the key to knowledge, it subjects the mind of man to the Spirit of God and validates all knowledge through the grid of the Holy Spirit. Wisdom and knowledge are then substantiated by such qualities as prudence, discretion, discernment and discipline, which are qualities of man's heart and spirit, not his mind.

How are your children being educated? Is the philosophical base of their education built on the foundation of the Holy Spirit, or is it built on the philosophical base of reason and rationalism? Is their education giving them a biblical world view or is it reinforcing a humanistic one?

These questions are answered by determining who is the source of their education. In order for the foundation of their education to be built on the foundation of the Holy Spirit, the Holy Spirit must be the source of their instruction. If the human teacher is their source, the best you can expect is human wisdom. While that may or may not be academically sound, it will never produce the quality of character that the Word of God requires.

Raising up a generation that will do exploits for God will require an education *"taught by the Holy Spirit, expressing spiritual truths in spiritual words."* (I Corinthians 2:13) Educating our children in this world's system is a form of Russian roulette and, let us face it, all of them are far too important to take that chance.

January 9th

THE POSSIBILITY OF THE IMPOSSIBLE

"Who through faith conquered kingdoms, administered justice and gained what was promised; who shut the mouths of lions"

Hebrews 11:33

Could this be the season for you to gain what was promised? What you always believed was impossible, is possible . . . for all things are possible to those who believe. This is the year to:

- ➤ Comprehend the Incomprehensible
- ➤ Know the Unknowable
- ➤ Believe the Unbelievable
- ➤ See the Unseeable
- ➤ Do the Undoable

Right now that "nay saying spirit" within us all is saying, "Yeah, yeah, yeah . . . You'll never accomplish it. You'll never believe it. You'll never possess it." It is about time we all declare war on that unbelieving spirit and step out to trust God at His Word. The only thing between us and possessing that which has been promised, is faith.

"Who through faith . . . gained what was promised."

Abraham, Moses, Noah, Rahab . . . we call them the "Heroes of the Faith." What distinguished them as heroes was simply their faith. They had pursued and laid hold of that quality which enabled them to believe the unbelievable and possess the unpossessable.

The possibility is the same for you and me. Faith and unbelief are both choices of the will. Why not choose faith and step into the realm of heroes and walk the paths of the ancients who were commended for the faith?

☙❦❧

January 10th

LIMITLESS LOVE

"This is love: not that we loved God, but that He loved us and sent His Son as an atoning sacrifice for our sins"

1 John 4:10

Love is such an often used word. We love ice cream and we love baseball. We love a vacation and we love the family dog. We love so many things, but be assured that when the Scripture speaks of God loving us, this is love of a different kind.

The love God has for us is beyond description. Try as we might to describe it in our finite understanding, we can not. Even if we possessed superior knowledge and infinite vocabulary, we would still fall short of describing the majesty of His love.

Some time ago, I had the misfortune of performing a funeral for a stillborn baby. You can imagine the grief that this mother and father felt as they buried their boy. Hopes, dreams and wishes snatched from them in a moment of tragedy.

As I felt just a small piece of their pain, I could not help but think of the love of our Father who did not just experience the loss of His Son. He willingly gave His Son as an atoning sacrifice. Nobody took Jesus from Him; He gave His only begotten Son. Love of this magnitude is unfathomable.

You would think that love of this degree would be all that was needed to convince someone of God's righteous intention and of our tremendous need. But, unfortunately, it is not. We read, *"He came to His own and His own received Him not."* Imagine after that degree of sacrifice to be spurned and rejected by those to whom you so sacrificially gave.

If you have never experienced Father's limitless love found in Jesus Christ, I invite you to do so. Jesus said, *"I am the way and the truth and the life. No one comes to the Father except through me."* (John 14:6) His death was so we might have relationship with God. A relationship which comes by the confession of sin and the accepting of Christ's atoning sacrifice.

January 11th

LOOKING DOWN

"And God raised us up with Christ and seated us with Him in the heavenly realms in Christ Jesus... "

Ephesians 2:6

*H*ow we stand in life depends on where we sit. The positions we take in life are determined by where we see ourselves in relation to the eternal. Our placement determines our position. If we see ourselves seated in the Heavenly with Christ, that Heavenly placement must cause our positions in life to line up accordingly.

To be seated with Christ means to *"set our hearts on those things which are above."* (Colossians 3:1) This is a purposeful determination to give our hearts and minds over to what His placement determines. Though our feet are on Earth, our minds and hearts must be in the Heavenlies where we receive direction and transformation.

In the late `70s, Jimmy Owens sang a song that said, "Keep looking down; you are seated in the Heavenlies." This line played on the familiar phrase, "Keep looking up." When we see by revelation the truth of our placement in Christ, we understand clearly the significance of, "Keep looking down, you are seated in the Heavenlies." Looking down is simply the understanding that we must look at the things of this Earth from Heaven's viewpoint. We must look to the temporal from the perspective of the eternal. This viewpoint gives us a fresh focus on life. It takes us from the central position by which all is judged and places Jesus Christ there. With Christ in the center, man's point of view is eternally changed and changed for the eternal.

So keep looking down; we are seated in the Heavenlies. From where we are sitting, we can stand tall.

☙❦☙

January 12th
NEW DEFINITIONS AND NEW BOUNDARIES

"Peter saw heaven opened and something like a large sheet being let down to earth by its four corners. It contained all kinds of four-footed animals, as well as reptiles of the earth and birds of the air. Then a voice told him, 'Get up Peter. Kill and eat'"

Acts 10:11-13

*V*isitation sounds so romantic until it comes. The visitation of God seldom comes to us as we expected it to. We expect the clean and easy, and God often sends the mixed and confusing. We expect it to come in announcement and fanfare, but it usually comes shrouded in mystery and wrapped in mixture.

So it was with Peter. Peter had experienced some dramatic visitations of the Holy Spirit's power. The days prior had brought powerful healings, angelic visitations and divine encounters. Now he found himself in the midst of another one, but this one was unlike the rest. As he saw a sheet being let down from Heaven, it was full of the clean and the unclean. It was not the mixture that startled Peter, for mixture is a way of life. There will always be mixture in visitations as long as the human element participates with the divine. What startled Peter was the command to, *"Get up. Kill and eat."* The fact that Peter was commanded to participate in spite of the mixture was most confusing to him. No unclean thing had ever passed his lips, but God was doing a new thing. New definitions were being written, and new boundaries were being formed.

In any visitation of God, there will be mixture. Wherever we mix God's intention with man's desire, zeal, flesh, ignorance, etc., we are bound to come up with the clean and the unclean. Though mixture is never desired, its presence does not negate the visitation. Perhaps the limitations we have put on God are no longer. Visitation requires flexibility. When God comes to play, He comes to play as Captain.

⊗

January 13th

SAYING WHAT YOU THINK

"I tell you the truth, if you have faith as small as a mustard seed, you can say to this mountain, 'Move from here to there' and it will move"

Matthew 17:20

Jesus never told us to think our way through obstacles. He told us to speak to them and command their removal. Yet, it would appear by our actions that He said think because most of us spend far more time and energy thinking about them than we do speaking to them.

Would this be true of you? Are you a thinker or a sayer? Thinking certainly has its place. We use our thinker to determine many things, but once anointed thinking has fulfilled its course, it is time to speak. The power is in the spoken word, not the mental thought. Thoughts left unspoken have a way of turning into speculations and vain imaginations. Anointed thoughts which are then spoken become mountain movers and stronghold destroyers.

Our adversary has worked hard to silence the church. He has silenced much of the church world in praise. But Jesus told us if we did not cry out the rocks would. He has silenced much of the church world in prayer. Though silent prayer may be effective when praying to God, it most certainly is not effective in the binding of principalities and powers and the loosing of satanic strongholds. Why, might you ask? For the simple reason that principalities, powers, strongholds, demons or any other adversary of darkness are unable to read our minds or discern our thoughts. God alone is capable of that. So in order for them to be brought down as with the mountain, we must speak to them. Moses did not think the Red Sea to part; he spoke to it and it parted.

Father has given us power in our words. When it comes to praise, worship and intercession, let us use them as we have been instructed. Let us, with our voice, speak to the situation rather than think to it.

January 14th

A SPIRITUAL HOME

"You also, like living stones, are being built into a spiritual house"
1 Peter 2:5

Anyone who has ever built or been involved with building a house knows it is not an easy process. Much to my disappointment, when the lumber package came from the lumberyard, the boards were not pre-cut nor were they numbered. This meant that in order for those individual boards to be built into a house, each one would have to be cut, nailed and even hammered. Sometimes the wrong board was used and the fit was not acceptable, so the process started over again.

Fortunately for us, as we went through this process, we were not working with living boards. For if we were, when they found out that the process included cutting, nailing and hammering, they might have crawled away in search of a new home.

A local church is not made of dead boards, but of living stones. The difficulty lies in the fact that when Father sent us the "stone package" to build this spiritual house, they too are not pre-cut or numbered. So, in order for this house to be built, each and every stone must be chipped and chiseled to fit into place.

Placement in the local church is not an easy process. Our enemy knows that our unity together is the simple, greatest proof of Christ's validity. (John 17) So, he does everything within his power to hinder the realization of unity. He knows, also, that until the body comes together *"bone to bone and rises to an exceeding great army"* (Exodus 34), Father's purposes for this Earth will not be realized. He knows that until the individual is placed properly in the body, there is not the correct flow of nutrition and life. So, he will use everything at his disposal to prevent the living stones from being built together.

We must become wise to our enemy's tricks. As God leads us to a local body, be assured that our placement with Him will come with much warfare and difficulty. We are in need of cutting and chiseling in order to assume the proper fit. Let us stand firm and resist the devil's schemes to prevent the coming together of the body of Christ.

January 15th

A BIBLICAL PHILOSOPHY OF WORK

"For we are God's workmanship, created in Christ Jesus to do good works, which God prepared in advance for us to do"

Ephesians 2:10

Someone has said, "Work is a necessary evil on the highway to pleasure." It is tragic to listen to the common man's philosophy of work. Reading through a book of quotes, I came across a few that reveal the attitude many carry in response to work:

- WORK: "drudgery in disguise"
- WORK: "exercise continued to fatigue"
- WORK: "something that must be done whether you like it or not"

It is only a society captivated by pleasure and ease that would hold such a negative perspective of work. In contrast, let us look at a few verses that explain the philosophical perspective the Word of God holds in regard to work:

- *"We must do the work of Him who sent us."* (John 9:4)
- *"He will test the quality of each man's work."* (I Corinthians 3:13)
- *"If a man will not work, he shall not eat."* (II Thessalonians 3:10)

Webster defines work as "sustained physical or mental effort to overcome obstacles and achieve an objective or result." I would place the emphasis here on sustained. Anyone can begin a work, but there are few who sustain it to its completion and desired end. One of the characteristics that distinguished Jesus from the rest was His ability to persevere and endure. Jesus said that His Father was always at work, and He too, knew of that perpetual motion.

Work is a godly characteristic. To embrace a positive work ethic is to embrace an aspect of God's image. Work is the channel through which the Kingdom of God takes root in this Earth. If you have yet to find your place of employment, the body of Christ needs you. Without your gifts in operation, the body of Christ is incomplete, and the one who is doing your task is misplaced. So let us put away an unredeemed perspective of work and embrace a Kingdom work ethic.

January 16th

LOOSE LIPS

"Deliver me from my enemies, O God; protect me from those who rise up against me. Deliver me from evildoers and save me from bloodthirsty men"

Psalm 59:1-2

*W*e are told in the introduction of Psalm 59 that this Psalm was to be sung to the tune of "Do Not Destroy." The enemy's intent is to destroy. His means of attack are careless and ruthless words spoken by loose lips. David's enemies were not just those out to kill him, but also those who were out to slander him, for they understood that if they could discredit the man, they could destroy his message.

The focus of satanic attack in the body of Christ is the destruction of relationship and the discrediting of leaders. As long as he can hinder the unity of Christ's body, he can hinder the fulfillment of all things as spoken of in Acts 3:21. His chosen weapons of attack are words.

"See what they spew from their mouths—they spew out swords from their lips and they say, 'Who can hear us?'" (Psalm 59:7)

As long as those words are swords, it is God's desire that no one hear them. Yet, often armed with self-pity, they go in search of someone willing to hear their case and take up their offense. Sympathy toward evil is a snare to be avoided at all costs. Samson was sympathetic toward Delilah and it led to his destruction. Eli was sympathetic toward the evil of his sons and it led to his destruction and the death of his sons. Beware of words wrapped in the clever deceit of self-pity. They will draw you in and force you to formulate opinions without giving you a clear perspective.

In the end, God is the final judge and the defense of the innocent. *"God will go before me and will let me gloat over those who slander me . . . For the sins of their mouths, for the words of their lips, let them be caught in their pride."* (Psalm 59:9,12)

But, let us be caught with clean lips and words of unity and support.

January 17th

STRATEGIC INFILTRATION

"Now the serpent was more crafty than any of the wild animals the Lord God had made"

Genesis 3:1

The saying goes, "If you can't beat 'em, then join 'em." If there is anything our enemy knows for sure, it is the fact that he cannot beat the church. The victory of Calvary assured us of that fact. But, this did not stop our adversary. It merely changed his strategy. Now, instead of trying to beat us, he simply joins us, and from that posture he seeks to redefine our purpose and intent of mission.

The result of this redefinition has given us some rather sober realities and has caused most of the church world to adopt unsound biblical presuppositions, such as:

> ➤ The kingdom of darkness has a rightful co-existence with the Kingdom of God.
> ➤ The kingdom of darkness is too powerful on Earth to be shattered.
> ➤ The Kingdom of God is a future Kingdom and not currently related to this Earth.
> ➤ The power of the Kingdom of God is only personal, not corporate.

These presuppositions have caused us to retreat in battle, and instead of *"occupying until He comes,"* we have focused on Heaven and the eternal reward that awaits us. But, recently the word of the Holy Spirit has been blowing once again, and the church is arising in this final hour to rediscover her call and restore her purpose. This restoration is causing us to see:

> ➤ The kingdom of darkness has no legitimate place in Heaven nor on Earth.
> ➤ Satan was stripped of his power at Calvary and his kingdom is beatable.
> ➤ Though the Kingdom of God is future, it is also now and among us.
> ➤ The power of the Kingdom of God belongs to the body of Christ, and it is a relevant power.

These realities cause us to see that Jesus Christ is now the Earth's rightful King. Calvary won Him that, not the second coming. It all begins at the cross and resurrection, and is not awaiting the second coming. The second coming confirms and consummates, but Calvary initiates. This means we can now walk in victory and experience the joy of the overcomer.

❧❦

Pause for thought:

How do you see the government of Jesus' Kingdom in your life? Do you believe we do not have to let any other thing take precedence over the Kingdom of God being manifest in our life?

January 18th

REST ON THE RUN

"... I press on to take hold of that for which Christ Jesus took hold of me ... I press on toward the goal to win the prize ..."
Philippians 3:12,14

If you are not going forward, you are falling backward. Human reasoning says there is neutral or static ground. We comfort ourselves with the justification that there is a rest ground which we need. Though we acknowledge a need for rest, we see that according to Hebrews 4, Jesus Christ is the believer's rest.

The apostle Paul seemed to make no provision for a static, restful place in his pursuit of Christ. The apostle was always pressing on. He was always reaching for more, desiring more, giving more of himself in abandonment to Jesus Christ. This attitude was not limited to the super apostles. According to the editor of the *Theological Word Book of the Old Testament*, there was no provision in the Hebrew language for static thought. The thought of being static in behavior and practice was alien to the Hebrew mind. In fact, it was so alien that there was never provision made in their language for the concept. The Hebrew language apparently does not have the words that can express the concept of being static. It is this mentality that Paul brings into his pursuit of Jesus Christ. No room for static pursuit. No room for stopping to rest. It seems to be in Paul's mentality and the mentality of the Hebrew mind, that the believer in Jesus Christ finds his rest on the run.

When believers find their rest in Christ, they are renewed on a continual basis. This does not mean that we never make provision for physical rest. It simply means that as we daily abide in Christ, we are continually renewed. Consequently, if we take a day off from Christ, rather than coming back rested, we return fatigued because we cut ourselves off from our rest source. Daily steps of obedience to Jesus Christ provide rest. As we abide in Christ, pressing on toward the goal of our high calling, we are renewed daily and enter into deeper levels of rest.

Deepen your devotion to Christ, and you will find your rest on the run.

January 19th

UNSPOKEN PROFANITY

"Do not misuse the name of the Lord your God, for the Lord will not hold anyone guiltless who misuses his name" Exodus 20:7
"Do not swear falsely by My name and so profane the name of your God"

Leviticus 19:12

Are you guilty of profanity? Before you so quickly answer "no," perhaps you should look at profanity from a slightly different perspective. "Profane" means to treat that which is holy as if it were common. It is to make the sacred familiar and treat the hallowed as if it were public. Profanity is not just coarse speech. One can be guilty of profanity in the midst of a worship service. One can be uttering words of a prayer, but if their heart is not right, the prayer can become profane.

Man looks at the outward appearance, but God looks at the heart. As man focuses on the outward and majors on the profane words that have been spoken, God looks at the heart and judges on the basis of what He sees, not just what He hears. Though He may not hear profanity spoken, He is more concerned with the profane actions that make the holiness of what He is doing common and unhallowed.

Profanity works hand in hand with religion. When a people lose their personal intimacy with Christ, they resort to empty forms and ritualistic traditions. These forms and traditions are without the presence of God. Consequently, they are dead and unholy. As man continues to go through the motions and calls it Christianity, he embraces a profane thing and worst of all, presents a profane thing to those in need of Christ. The forms make Christianity common and rob it of the presence of God that draws people in and awakens their eternal destiny. The common and unhallowed will never draw anyone. The unsaved already have that. What the unsaved need to see is that which is holy, hallowed and unique.

By sanctifying God in our hearts, we keep Him, and the wonder of what He is doing, holy. As we set Him apart, we keep ourselves from viewing Him as something that is common. By hallowing Him and His works, we give Him His place of honor and keep His distinction from us clearly seen.

✥

January 20th

NON-PROFIT OR FOR PROFIT

"Why spend money on what is not bread and your labor on what does not satisfy"

Isaiah 55:2

Where are you being spent? We usually do not think of ourselves as a commodity to be traded, but the truth of the matter is this: We do spend our lives on that which is most important to us. Some spend their lives in the pursuit of pleasure—cars, boats, homes, hobbies, etc., all in the pursuit of trying to make themselves happy. Others spend their lives building their careers in pursuit of the American dream of financial independence.

This desire is God-given though the focus is often diverted. The spirit of Father is the spirit of reproduction. We were created in His image and given the command to multiply and replenish the Earth. To be like Him, we need to multiply ourselves in others and spend our lives on replenishing that which has previously been spent. A consuming spirit is not one born from above, but rather one born of this world.

We want to declare that the church is no longer a non-profit organization. Though the state has given us that classification, we want to state boldly and unashamedly, we exist to make a profit. If our investment in the lives of others is not multiplied, then we have failed miserably. Let there be no mistake, our profit will not be measured in dollars and cents, but rather in the spiritual reproduction in others what Father has invested in us.

Corporations have what they call their "R.O.I." This stands for Return On Investment. We believe Father is looking for the R.O.I. He has created us in His image and equipped us to do His will. Now He is looking to see what type of return He will get on His investment.

We are challenged to spend our lives on the Kingdom of God and the pursuit of Father's purposes. This is an investment that carries a money-back guarantee.

ଓଦ୍ଧଠ

January 21st

MACHINE OR MAN

"Endure hardship as a good soldier of Christ Jesus . . ."
II Timothy 2:3

General Patton said, "Wars are fought with weapons, but they are won by men. It is the spirit of men who follow and the men who lead that gain victory."

How easy it is to put our confidence in the machine rather than the man. Though the Pentagon may spend millions on a plane, it all comes down to the spirit and capabilities of the one who flies it. Fatigue, fear and a multitude of other potential destroyers can cause a multi-million dollar machine to be no more effective than a $2.98 G. I. Joe Flyer.

Paul, writing to his son, Timothy, encourages him to *"Endure hardship like a good soldier of Christ Jesus. No one serving as a soldier gets involved in civilian affairs."* (II Timothy 2:3,4) It is the spirit of men who follow and the men who lead that gain victory. Paul understood this truth. There is no question that the army of God has the most effective war machine ever invented. It is a fact that we possess more power and more authority than any of our enemies. The weapons with which we war are not carnal but they are mighty, capable of pulling down strongholds. Though this war may be won in the realm of power and authority, it can be lost in the realm of endurance and commitment. The army of God will not lose this battle because of the lack of power and authority. Those who lose will do so only because of the weakness of spirit and the distraction of focus.

"Endure Hardness." Living in the combat zone does not promise to be a holiday. To carry the mantle of war is to live in the continual shadow of the battle. But be it certain, if our endurance will wax, Satan's tolerance will wane. Remember the promise is to those who "endure to the end."

"Civilian Affairs." Who is "minding the store?" We are told that Father came looking to see who was "minding the store," and He found we were all involved in civilian affairs. These past years He has been calling us out of civilian pursuits and thrusting us back into the family business in order that we may complete that which Jesus began.

Let us war like it is a privilege, not an obligation.

January 22nd

HAVING OUR CAKE AND EATING IT TOO

"But many who heard the message believed, and the number of men grew to about five thousand"

Acts 4:4

The blessings of the early church's growth brought with it an interesting challenge. It was basically pretty easy when it was just Jesus and the twelve. Oh sure, they had their relational challenges and their sibling rivalries, but working those challenges through with only twelve was relatively easy. Imagine the dynamic that took place when the twelve grew to 120 in the upper room, then shortly thereafter they grew to 3,000, then not long after that they reached 5,000.

The intimacy of the twelve, the camaraderie of 120, was soon swallowed up by 5,000. Or was it? The Scriptures seem fairly clear that what they experienced as a few, they now experienced it in the many. Acts 4:4 tells us the number of men reached 5,000. We can conservatively estimate that if each man had one wife and two children, the church numbered approximately 20,000 people. Yet, we read in Acts 4:32 that all the believers were of one heart and of one mind. It goes on to say that among the 20,000, there were some who were needy, for from time to time people would sell their homes and give the proceeds to the apostles so they could distribute the funds as needs arose.

If the church is built according to Kingdom principles, we need not sacrifice family intimacy in order to grow, providing we have a mind set for both. Some will say we want to remain small in order that we might enjoy the intimacy of family we are currently experiencing. While this is a noble desire, it disregards the Great Commission and compassion for the lost. On the other hand, another might say we do not have time to build family, for thousands are dying without Jesus every day. This, too, is noble, but it disregards the basic building block of Kingdom existence i.e., family.

The Lord would say to us we do have time, and we will have both, intimacy and size, family and growth, equipping and evangelizing. God is willing. The only thing that would prevent either is our limited perspective and desire for only one.

January 23rd

LIFE SAVERS

"But you will receive power when the Holy Spirit comes on you; and you will be my witnesses in Jerusalem, and in all Judea and Samaria, and to the ends of the earth"

Acts 1:8

How handsome he looked in his red lifeguard trunks. His tanned, muscular body would lead one to believe that his life-saving techniques had been perfected in toilsome hours of training. His lifeguard tower was an architectural wonder. The wood was of finest quality and the design was a piece of art.

So why did she drown? He saw it all, he heard the screams and saw the panic of those wondering where the lifeguard was who had been trained for such a time as this. But, in the moment of despair, his true condition was revealed. Though he was handsome and tan, though his tower was pleasing to the eye, he did not know how to swim. He would be hard pressed to save himself, let alone the life of one in pending doom.

You need not look too far to see the similarities of this story and the church. Designed of God to be a life saving institution, yet many would be hard pressed to save themselves. Outwardly, it all looks good. Nicely designed churches and smiles from ear to ear, but could we perform our task in the moment of despair? Have we fulfilled our call in the face of need? Have you ever saved the life of one going down in the waters of despair?

The lifeguards are in need of swimming lessons. The cries of those who have drowned on the beaches are being heard across the land. The cry of Him who calls, says, "Get down off your towers and into the water, for only in the water of people's lives will you learn the art of lifesaving."

Lifesaving is not an art reserved for the privileged few. It is the responsibility of all who have been called by His name. It is your responsibility and it is mine.

May the cries of those drowning call us off the tower and into the waters of training.

January 24th

WITHOUT A VISION, THE PEOPLE . . .

"Where there is no revelation, the people cast off restraint"
Proverbs 29:18

So much could be said about what a people with a vision do. The Bible says people without a vision cast off restraint. (Proverbs 29:18KJV) Motivators tell us people without vision accomplish nothing. Leaders tell us people without vision only follow but never lead.

Vision is a means of attainment. Long before one realizes their accomplishment, they pursued their vision. Vision was that thing that kept them going, where all else said stop. Vision was the very thing that mapped out the steps of accomplishment.

Vision is what God gives a church that is willing to rise to the full challenge of commitment, as revealed in the Scriptures. Vision is that which the Holy Spirit allows a church to see in relation to God's purpose for them. Upon being obedient to what they see, momentum is created, resulting in spiritual advancement. Vision is seeing into the future from God's perspective and believing He will allow you to attain what you see.

Vision that is pursued with abandonment generates power. Each level of vision realization requires a new level of personal abandonment. Is a new level of realization presently before you? If so, to step into that level and walk in its realization will require a deeper level of abandonment, abandonment that is expressed through obedience, trust, risk, faith and action.

Without a vision, people are people. But, with a vision, people become world changers. With a vision, people make a difference.

January 25th

COVENANT RELATIONSHIPS

"From him the whole body, joined and held together by every supporting ligament, grows and builds itself up in love, as each part does its work"

Ephesians 4:16

Covenant relationship is perhaps the most misunderstood principle in the body of Christ today. Ignorance, zeal, fear and willfulness all blend together to keep the reality of covenant in our relationships from coming to a functional place. A covenantal relationship is simply the reality that God joins members of the body together and then gives them definite terms by which they are to conduct their relationship.

To the Hebrew mind, covenant was a given. The Hebrews were a covenant people. They had in their possession the old covenant. Ingrained in their minds from youth were the blessings of obeying the covenant and the suffering of curses, if broken. But to the American mind, it is not so. We are the people who are burned in litigation and broken contracts because the principles of covenant keeping have not been ingrained into our thought and practice. For many, relationships are expendable and their word to be broken, if inconvenient.

In the midst of this American mind set, God is desirous of renewing our minds and instilling into our behavior the principles of relational covenant. These principles will carry us through the storms of adversity and bring us through the other side, walking together and enjoying our friendship.

How important are relationships to you? Not just husband and wife, parents and children, but friendships as well. When you compare them to your priority list, where do they line up? Below jobs? Below earthly pursuits? Below the pursuit of pleasure? If so, you have prioritized the temporal above the eternal. Relationships are a wealth we will take with us. How those relationships will play out in Heaven, I do not know, but that Heaven is structured in family is certain, for Paul speaks to us in Ephesians 3:15 about the families of Heaven.

I encourage you to examine your relational wealth and make an investment in covenant.

January 26th

WHEN SILENCE IS THE BEST DEFENSE

"The high priest stood up and said to Jesus, "Are you not going to answer? What is this testimony that these men are bringing against you?" But Jesus remained silent"

Matthew 26:62, 63

But Jesus remained silent. Why? From the human perspective, it seemed such a waste. Perhaps with just a simple explanation, the whole matter could have been resolved. A few words with a miracle or two thrown in and Jesus would have been free, but Jesus remained silent.

"Joseph's master took him and put him in prison." (Genesis 39:20) No record is given of Joseph's defense. The writer considered it not important enough to record, or perhaps it was not recorded because there was none. Imagine it—thrown into prison without a defending word. The loss of position and pride when chances had it a word of explanation and defense could have explained the whole story and revealed the real culprit. But Joseph, like Jesus, remained silent.

Was their silence limited to their particular circumstance, or do we see a covenantal principle in operation?

I believe we are seeing more than limited circumstances. I believe we are seeing the application of a covenantal principle of relationship. Understanding that covenant is made and broken with a word, it is sometimes covenantally prudent to withhold truth so as to protect the integrity of relationship. If a word would save face and reputation but dishonor relationship and position, it is perhaps best to remain silent and let the Holy Spirit sort out the results.

It is here that true motivation is revealed. Principle or reputation. Integrity or the saving of one's self. If it worked for Jesus and Joseph, then perhaps it is the way for us as well.

※

January 27th

WHEN REBELS STUMBLE

"... The ways of the Lord are right; the righteous walk in them, but the rebellious stumble..."

Hosea 14:9

Have you ever been snared by the thought, since someone is stumbling over what you believe, it must therefore be wrong? How often have we listened to a negative report about what someone is doing and without going to the source, concluded what they are doing is indeed wrong?

The prophet tells us in this passage that the same truth will progress one in "the way" and cause the other to stumble. The way does not change. The only difference between the two is the condition of each person's heart. The one, the Scripture says, is righteous, while the other is rebellious.

Unfortunately, the *"rebellious"* here are not limited to those outside the covenant. More often than not, those who rebel from the way are our own brothers and sisters, who for one reason or another, were unwilling to embrace the way designed for them. Consequently, they rebelled.

If that were the end of the story, it would be a little easier to digest, but all too often those who do rebel do not see the burden of their own responsibility and instead blame it on others. The guilty become "that church," "those elders," "that pastor," "my husband," "my wife." Everything seems to be just fine with those who are being accused, but to listen to those who are doing the accusing, you would think God is about to release the seven plagues on them at any minute.

Let me offer you a piece of advice Though there is a measure of truth in every critic's accusation, if someone gives you a negative report, check the heart of the one reporting. If it is motivated in rebellion, recognize they are stumbling over truth, not error.

When you see a rebel stumble, do not sell the truth, but bless the Lord you are standing in "the way" and pray for the one who has stumbled off course.

◊

January 28th

MANY PARTS, BUT ONE CONSCIOUSNESS

"The body is a unit, though it is made up of many parts; and though all its parts are many, they form one body. So it is with Christ"
I Corinthians 12:12

"*So it is with Christ.*" We are like the functioning of a body. We are made up of many parts with diversity of functions. Though some of my bodily parts may look the same, they fulfill different bodily tasks. My two hands have the same outward appearance, but one is capable of writing legibly and the other is not. One is able to grip a ball and throw it with a reasonable level of accuracy and the other is not. So it is with the body of Christ. Outwardly, many may have the same appearance, but all possess certain abilities that distinguish them from the rest.

Unity in diversity is the hallmark of the body, for though the body is made up of many parts, it possesses only one consciousness. That is, the arm thinks in harmony with the hand, and the legs function in harmony with the feet. This harmony of thought does not, in any way, take away from their uniqueness of design or diversity of function. It simply illustrates the fact that, though they all have a significant function, their effectiveness is determined by their equal submission to the head.

Though the body of Christ is made up of many parts, we are designed to have only one consciousness. All of us possess unique personalities and function in the diversity of execution, but we are created by God to operate in submission to the head, i.e., Jesus Christ. This mutual submission to the head allows for the harmony of consciousness.

Though that might sound "New Age" to some, it is simply the acknowledgment that in the church body, He is Lord and it is His desire to unify the members of His body and enable them to think as one. Or as the apostle Paul put it:

"I appeal to you, brothers, in the name of our Lord Jesus Christ, that all of you agree with one another so that there may be no divisions among you and that you may be perfectly united in mind and thought." (I Corinthians 1:10)

January 29th

SEEING THROUGH SPIRIT EYES

"From now on know no man after the flesh" II Corinthians 5:16

How hard it must have been for those who watched the Christ child grow to one day accept the reality that He was the promised Messiah. After all, they had watched Him as He *"learned obedience."* (Hebrews 5:8) They had witnessed the awkward stages of adolescence. They remembered all too well the calamity of childhood. He had played with their children. Toys had been broken. Milk had been spilt. After all, does not everybody know, prophets do not grow up from little boys?

The challenge that is constantly before us is the ability to see one another through the eyes of the Spirit, not through the eyes of flesh. That is, the choice to focus on the treasure in the earthen vessel, giving allowance for the vessel itself. The flesh can be so deceptive. It will cause us to excuse our own earthliness while we criticize others for theirs. Jesus recognized their problem when He instructed us not to look at the speck of sawdust in our brother's eye while we ignore the plank in our own. (Matthew 7:3) To see each other through Spirit eyes is to see them as Jesus sees them. It means to see them complete, to see the real them, who they are in Christ, not who they are in their shortcomings and flaws.

This is a truth that is magnified in our children, as we see them running the halls, hitting each other and stealing one another's toys. As we fulfill our duty in the nursery changing dirty diapers, how easy it is to forget that these youngsters may one day be our apostles and prophets. To see through the eyes of the Spirit is to realize that great men and women of God all began even as our children have begun. Every general in God's army has begun from the same place. The starting point is unredeemed flesh. From there everyone must learn obedience even as Jesus did.

To see through Spirit eyes is to acknowledge that prophets do grow up from little boys, do not they?

January 30th

CHANGE

"I tell you the truth, unless you change and become like little children, you will never enter the Kingdom of Heaven"
Matthew 18:3

Change is a law. Change is a principle that you can count on. It has come and it will come. Whether we like change or not, change happens. In the Kingdom of God, change is a virtue. It is also selective. Change comes, but change only comes to you if you are willing to embrace its results. This is why change often appears to be arbitrary. Some change and some do not. It is not change that produces change in us. What produces change in us is our response to the change that comes.

God called Israel a stiff-necked people because they were a people of resistance. They refused to change. When we resist God's desired change, we develop attitudes of obstinacy and stubbornness. Change is the only way into the Kingdom of God. Change is the only way into progressive stages of maturity in our Christian walk. In this Kingdom, change is constant. When you cease to change, you cease to grow.

The change God desires is not just the change of circumstances. He desires the change of you. Someone aptly said, "Everyone thinks of changing the world, but no one thinks of changing themselves." Those who can not change mind or practice will not be able to change the world.

"Unless you become like little children you will never enter the Kingdom of Heaven." (Matthew 18:3) Quite obviously, Jesus was not addressing physical change. I am an adult and can never again become a child. Jesus was not addressing what we are, but who we are. Though what I am is fixed, who I am must remain in a state of constant change. We must be in a state of continual transformation into the image of Jesus Christ. It is this attitude of change that keeps us child-like and qualified to enter the progressive stages of God's Kingdom.

In all the changing, have you changed? Do not settle for just the change of circumstances. In all the changing, change you.

January 31st

THE RELATIONSHIP BETWEEN UNITY AND WORSHIP

"Therefore, if you are offering your gift at the altar and there remember that your brother has something against you, leave your gift there in front of the altar. First go and be reconciled to your brother, then come and offer your gift"

Matthew 5:23,24

In these verses, Jesus clearly establishes an inseparable relationship between unity and our worship. Yes, worship is directed toward God alone, but worship is more than just the act of singing. Worship involves the whole man. By virtue of the whole man being involved, man's relationships become an integral aspect of his worship.

Man's philosophy of independence has brought him to a place where only his relationship to God matters. Independent and compartmentalized thinking has developed in us the mentality that our relationships to our fellow men have little or no bearing to our relationship with God. Though modern thinking may support this philosophy, the Bible does not. In verse 21-22 of this chapter, Jesus elevated relationship to such a paramount place that he said if you even as much as call your brother a fool, you will be in danger of going to hell. This issue was so important to Jesus that He commanded us to *"Leave your gift in front of the altar and go and be reconciled to your brother, then come and offer your gift."*

In John 17:22, Jesus further establishes this relationship. He says, *"I have given them the glory that you gave me, that they may be one as we are one."* As we enter into the act of worship, we are telling God in our own words who we see Him to be. After hearing those words of adoration, He responds back to us by allowing us to experience His glory. His glory is not given to us for feelings alone. He gives us His glory in order that we might be unified. In the coming of His glory our own independent ways are broken down and our desires are reshaped to conform with divine desire. God's glory transforms us, and in that transformation our lives are unified together into a living demonstration of Christ's prayer.

Are you at odds with your brother? Perhaps it is time to leave your gift and go and reconcile with your brother.

February 1st

SELF

"Do nothing out of selfish ambition or vain conceit, but in humility consider others better than yourselves. Each of you should look not only to your own interests, but also to the interests of others"
Philippians 2:3-4

SELF, SELF, SELF. Since the fall, man has been cursed with an inordinate preoccupation with self. Man's drive is to do something for himself, with himself or to himself. The promoting of self is the basic drive of humanity. It has been this way throughout the ages.

Greece said:	"Be wise, know yourself."
Rome said:	"Be strong, disciple yourself."
Religion says:	"Be good, conform yourself."
Hedonism says:	"Be sensuous, enjoy yourself."
Education says:	"Be intelligent, expand yourself."
Psychology says:	"Be confident, assert yourself."
Materialism says:	"Be satisfied, please yourself."
Pride says:	"Be superior, promote yourself."
Asceticism says:	"Be lowly, suppress yourself."
Humanism says:	"Be capable, believe in yourself."
Legalism says:	"Be pious, limit yourself."
CHRISTIANITY SAYS;	"BE FREE, DIE TO YOURSELF."

The Kingdom of God is a backward Kingdom. The way up is the way down. The way to find yourself is to lose yourself. Jesus never made self the focus of our pursuit. In fact, He said if we cared to follow Him, we would have to deny ourselves. In the denying of self, we discover Jesus, and in that discovery, we are set free.

The answer to being consumed with self is serving others. Paul said, *"Do nothing out of selfish ambition."* That includes everything. If, in humility, we can consider others better than ourselves, we can deal a death blow to the preoccupation with self.

Do something kind for someone today. Look for a specific gesture of service that denies self and serves others.

February 2nd

BROUGHT OVER

"May you give thanks to the Father who . . . rescued us from the power of darkness and brought us over into the Kingdom of His beloved Son"

Colossians 1:13 (Barclay)

Salvation is more than an after-life experience. To be saved involves more than just going to Heaven. To be saved means that we are saved from one Kingdom and have been *brought over* into another. The work of Jesus Christ not only secured for us a place with Him in eternity, it transferred our daily allegiance from the kingdom of darkness over to the Kingdom of God.

In the ancient world, when one empire was a victor over another, it was the custom to take the population of the defeated country and transfer it lock, stock and barrel to the conqueror's land. This was how empires were built. It is from this custom Paul writes when he says we have been *brought over* from the power of darkness into the Kingdom of His beloved Son.

The Kingdom of God is an empire Jesus Christ conquered over the kingdom of darkness. Now He goes in search of His subjects. Those who hear His call are not only prepared for eternity, but are *brought over* into the daily recognition of the governing reign of Jesus Christ. We no longer live for ourselves. We have been *brought over* and now our wills have been purchased and have been yielded to the will of the Kingdom.

Once we have been *brought over*, what belongs to the reigning Kingdom belongs to us. Paul says, as a result of the transfer, we now have light instead of darkness, freedom instead of slavery, forgiveness instead of condemnation, and the power of God instead of the power of Satan. This is the inheritance the apostle speaks of: the inheritance of God's "dedicated people."

Have you made that dedication to the Kingdom of God? Have you come over since you were saved? It is possible to be saved and never make the governmental transfer. If that is you, God's desire is for you to yield the governmental decisions of your life over to Jesus Christ. In so doing you will be *brought over* and qualified to partake of the inheritance of God's dedicated people.

February 3rd

WHEN TRUTH IS BLACK AND WHITE

"You shall know the truth and the truth shall set you free"
John 8:32

Either, or—or and, and both? Most of us like to have our lives and thoughts in nice organized boxes. When issues are black and white, they are much easier to understand. When we can easily categorize an issue as black or white, it enables us to formulate a conviction on it. The only problem is, issues are not always black and white. This does not necessarily mean they are grey. Sometimes issues in God are both. We want them to be either this way or that way, but God in His sovereignty often makes them both this way and that way.

Is Jesus the Lion of Judah or is He the Lamb who takes away the sins of the world? It would make it far easier for us to understand if He was either lion or lamb but the truth of the matter is He is both lion and lamb. To press Him into Jesus the lion box or Jesus the lamb box would eliminate half of His descriptive function. It is the ability to see Him as "and, and both" that opens us up to the fullness of who He is.

Because truth oftens dwells in the "and, and both," you can find Scripture to support each side and seemingly contradict itself. In fact, they are a contradiction if we only see "either or." Often people come with a list of Scripture to point out a perceived error. With great conviction, they recite verse after verse to support their conclusion. No sooner have they left than others come with what seems to be the antithesis of what the first one said, and they too have their list of verses to support their view. Confusion would reign supreme if we did not see truth being the embodiment of "and, and both."

One verse tells us to rest, another tells us to make every effort. One verse says Christ is the only mediator between God and man, another verse says to obey those who have the rule over you. One verse says that we need only the Holy Spirit to teach us, another verse tells us God gave the five-fold gifts to equip the saints. Truth is found in the ability to see the balance of truth. This is not to say there are not biblical absolutes that stand alone, for there are. Diety of Christ, inerrancy of the Word, Lordship of Jesus. These need not be balanced for they are absolute. Let us be careful in our application of truth that we are not throwing out one side in order to promote the other.

February 4th

THE DIVINE LEARNING PROCESS

"But when he, the Spirit of truth, is come, he will guide you into all truth"

John 16:13

Jesus is the truth. Jesus does not just teach truth, but He is the truth. Since He is the truth, then He is the goal of our learning. Learning is accomplished only as Christ is the goal of our learning. Learning is accomplished only as Christ is unveiled in us and we become fashioned in His likeness.

The process of divine learning begins with receiving information. As the word of God is received, the mind and spirit are informed. Now the Holy Spirit has something to work with as He guides us into truth; the information we have received becomes illumination. The Holy Spirit shines His light on the truth, and we begin to see and understand as never before. As the light dawns, we move into revelation. The truth has moved from our heads to our spirit and has become a living word. This results in inspiration. Now we begin to sense a new desire to obey the word. We find ourselves responding in new levels of joy. As we walk in obedience to the revelation we have received, we step into realization. This is the stage where we are changed. Others begin to sense something new about us. The veil of flesh that has concealed Christ begins to fall away, and the character of Jesus is more consistently seen. As this stage continues, it leads us into transformation where we are transformed into the very likeness of Christ and become His hand extended to a world in desperate need of an authentic representation.

The process of truth is not complete until transformation has taken place. To be like Him is the goal of our knowledge. It is never enough to be just informed without becoming transformed. As you open yourself up to intimacy with the Holy Spirit, He will guide you through the process.

February 5th

THE COST OF PLAYING IT SAFE

"Therefore I advise, leave these men alone! Let them go! For if their purpose or activity is of human origin, it will fail. But if it is from God, you will not be able to stop these men; you will only find yourselves fighting against God"

Acts 5:38-39

Though Gamaliel displayed a tremendous amount of wisdom during that moment, his foolishness possibly overtook him in the end. The wisdom of the moment said, "Play it safe, watch and see." Playing it safe can be an effective strategy for the moment, but sooner or later one has to make a decision. No record is ever made of Gamaliel making a decision to follow Christ. It appears that the Holy Spirit was working on his heart, for he was the only member of the Sanhedrin willing to free the apostles. But, did Gamaliel ever risk acting on what he saw take place, or did he take his "play it safe, watch and see" attitude with him to the grave?

Religion is a crippler. Religious preconceptions blind you from seeing the obvious. Why couldn't the Sanhedrin see the hand of God working in the lives of the apostles? A known crippled beggar was dramatically healed. Under a guarded jail, the apostles miraculously disappeared. One would think that these signs and wonders would be convincing enough for them to see the obvious, but their religion blinded them from the obvious and caused them to miss the very thing they sought.

What about us? Before we point the finger of judgment at the Sanhedrin, let us examine our own lives. We have cried for more. We have longed for a visitation. We have asked for a fresh visitation, but when it comes, will we play the "watch and see" game? In the beginning, safety can be wise, but remember the purposes of God live in the land of risk. Sooner or later safety must be replaced with risk, if we intend to experience the visitation of the Lord.

February 6th

FRESH SUPPLY

"But if I say, 'I will not mention Him or speak anymore in His name,' His Word is in my heart like a burning fire, shut up in my bones. I am weary of holding it in"

Jeremiah 20:9

Weariness has hit the body of Christ in epidemic proportions. Everywhere people speak of being tired and weary. It seems that for many, their strength has run out, their joy has departed, and weariness has become a way of life.

Though weariness is war-time reality, it is not part of the normal Christian life. Weariness is not a fruit of the Spirit nor is it a Christian virtue. Weariness is a tactic of the enemy used to wear God's people down and ultimately to eliminate them from the fight.

Weariness is only a symptom of separation. Once we are separated from the daily, consistent presence of Jesus Christ, weariness is the result. In His presence, we find a fresh supply of strength and grace. In His presence, we find a fresh supply of fuel and enablement.

Once we are cut off from the source and resort to living on our own, weariness is the result. The psalmist said, *"My heart grew hot within me and as I meditated, the fire burned."* (Psalm 39:3) As we meditate in His presence, the fire is rekindled. A fire left to itself without fresh supply will soon burn out. Daily devotion in the presence of Jesus Christ keeps the fire alive with fresh supply. It keeps the fire burning hot, consuming impurities and anything else not consistent with who we are in Christ. When the fire grows cold, we must stoke it and add a fresh supply of wood. We do that by re-establishing daily devotion. Some would think that as we mature in Christ, it takes less time to refuel. The truth is, it takes more. The more we mature in the Lord, the more it takes to keep the fire burning. As the fire burns, it gets hotter. The hotter it gets, the more it consumes. If less fuel is given to the fire, the fire cools down and soon weariness sets in. You are never too mature for the presence of God. A passion for His presence is the remedy for weariness.

February 7th

THE REALITY OF REVIVAL

"In the last days, God says, 'I will pour out my Spirit on all people'"
Acts 2:17

Revival can be a romantic concept, but a confusing reality. To talk revival is quite encouraging. Very few ever react to the concept. It sounds so nice: visitation, outpouring, harvest. But when the reality of those hit the church, the romance soon dissipates. What we so eagerly desired now means work. The visitation we so eagerly anticipated often comes in a manner we did not expect. Revival involves change and change often means fear. The usual is replaced with the unusual, the expected with the unexpected. When God comes in revival, He comes with His own agenda, and He does not come asking our permission.

Though birth begins with romance, it does not stay there for long. The intimacy that produced the birth is soon replaced with morning sickness and the reality of a nine month term. During the birth process the woman screams in pain with no recollection of the romance that began this process. If the natural way, she would most likely quit in the peak of pain and stop the process, but that option is not available. Soon after the child is born, the pain is forgotten and the romance returns.

So it is with the process of revival. As the Holy Spirit comes, He moves outside the scope of our limitations. Sometimes He does things that are not respectable according to our standards of respectability. As it was on the day of Pentecost, people can even give the appearance of being drunk. When the Spirit comes in power, He often insults the natural mind. This is why Paul exhorts the Corinthians saying the natural mind sees the things of the Spirit as foolishness, unless they are spiritually discerned.

As revival comes and our prayers are heard, remember that God's ways are not our ways.

February 8th

MANY FILLINGS

"Elisha said, 'Go around and ask all your neighbors for empty jars. Don't ask for just a few'"

II Kings 4:3

When it comes to the visitation of God, a little dab will not do you. When God is manifesting His presence, we need to get all we can possibly receive. Elisha knew God's intention to bless the widow woman. So he instructed her to go and get as many jars as she possibly could, so she would not have to settle for a little blessing, but could receive an abundant one. As long as the widow woman had jars, the oil continued to flow, but as soon as she ran out of jars, the oil stopped.

We are the vessel that contains the presence of the Lord. God's desire is to fill us up. We must not ask for just a few fillings, but get as many fillings as we possibly can. As long as we continue to come postured in desire, the oil will continue to flow. But as soon as our desire is full, the oil will cease. When the oil ceases to flow, the presence of God becomes a thing of the past.

God's desire is to come to us in His fullness. He desires to come in power. When He comes in power we can expect laughter, weeping, ecstasy, awe, shaking, falling down, deliverance, supernatural gifts and more. As God begins to manifest Himself in this manner, we wait to be sure we are postured in such a way as to receive all He desires to give. As opportunities come for prayer, we want to be sure we make ourselves available for each prayer opportunity so God will have the chance to fill our vessel, even if it was just filled last time.

Let us not limit the desire of God. As long as God is pleased to answer prayer and manifest His presence, let us take the opportunity for our vessels to be filled.

൞

February 9th

TURNED OVER BY GOD

"This is how my Heavenly Father will treat each of you unless you forgive your brother from your heart"

Matthew 18:35

At first this verse does not look all that alarming. It could be read as just another promise by Jesus of care from our Heavenly Father. But, if we read it in the context it was written, we understand it to be a verse of severe warning and pending judgment unless we forgive those who have hurt us.

The parable of the unmerciful servant ends with the master turning the servant over to "torturers" until he could repay the debt. The master's first response to the servant was mercy. He forgave the massive debt the servant owed him. The master responded in anger and put the unmerciful servant in jail. With the parable concluded, Jesus said, *"This is how my Heavenly Father will treat each of you unless you forgive."* The parable was a fictitious story, but the conclusion was a promise. If we do not forgive, our Heavenly Father turns us over to a "jailer" who tortures us with the consequences of unforgiveness.

The decision to withhold forgiveness removes God's covering from our lives and opens us up to the torturous experience of resentment, bitterness, hate, envy, jealousy and spite. Like black hooded henchmen, these servants of evil torment and keep us enslaved to those who did us wrong. Forgiveness frees us from the torturers and opens the prison doors of resentment, bitterness and the rest.

Often we say the wrong done to us is too great to forgive, the pain too deep to forget, but the pain we feel is not the pain of the wrongful act. The wrongful act is covered by the blood of Christ. The pain we feel is the torturous pain of unforgiveness. As we choose to let go of unforgiveness, we are set free from the prison of pain that unforgiveness brings. As we make that choice, the power of redemption is released enabling us to forget our offender and embrace the freedom of God's mercy. Since we have received the maximum in mercy, let us never expect justice from others. Mercy triumphs over judgment.

February 10th

AN UNDIVIDED HEART

"Create in me a pure heart, O God"
Psalm 51:10

The Word of God is limited by the heart of man. God is not limited in capacity. He is capable of doing anything, because nothing is impossible with God, but, there are many things God is not able to do, for He is hindered by the uncooperative heart of man.

This truth is clearly illustrated in the lives of Moses and Peter. God could miraculously bring water out of a rock, but He could not make Moses patient. Jesus was able to heal Malchus' ear, but He could not automatically change Peter's heart and remove the violence and hatred that was in it. It was simple for God to perform miracles in the realms of the material or physical because everything in creation obeys His command. Since the natural and physical realms are already yielded to Him, miracles are simple and consistent, but the heart of man is not fully yielded to our Creator. Therefore, as Moses and Peter, we can witness the physical miracle, but never experience the personal one.

The greatest miracle in life is the miracle of a changed heart. Often we pray for physical healing or the miraculous change of physical circumstances. Soon, we are overcome with frustration and doubt, perceiving that God has not answered our prayer. But, in reality, He has been performing the greatest miracle of all. He has been using the circumstances we want changed to change our heart. Yes, the miracle is happening, but not the kind of miracle we were looking for. Many times God seeks to change the heart before He alters the physical. He is using the very thing we want changed to change us, and in the changing of us, we discover the greatest miracle of all.

Perhaps the greatest miracle of all is the miracle of an undivided heart. That is, the miracle of having our hearts so turned toward Jesus that we no longer want our own way, but only His. May our prayer be as King David's, *"Give me an undivided heart."* (Psalm 86:11)

A heart that is wholly united will most certainly see the miraculous.

February 11th

SERVING BEYOND OURSELVES

"It was revealed to them that they were not serving themselves but you"
1 Peter 1:12

The prophets of old lived beyond themselves. Under the inspiration of the Holy Spirit, they were permitted to see into things that caused them to sow their lives for the purposes of the generations to come. Their serving did not begin and stop with themselves; they made decisions and sowed actions that continue to serve the generations today.

Serving beyond ourselves requires revelation. It requires a progressive vision that is ever expanding. Some people have no vision; consequently, they can not even serve themselves. Enslaved by sin, they are not even good for themselves. They remain in the vicious circle of self serving, never getting beyond themselves. Serving beyond ourselves requires a vision bigger than ourselves. Having a vision for the generations to come releases the faith necessary to leave behind an investment that will continue to pay dividends well into the future.

King David served the purposes of God for his generation and then he died. Though he died, his investment continued. David had a vision beyond himself. He was not serving himself, but serving us even though he had no concept of who we were. David's vision, for the generations to come, established a spiritual trust. Though he is gone, his investment still continues to pay dividends thousands of years later.

God's desire is to move us beyond ourselves in order that our lives will continue to produce fruit in others after we are gone. His desire is to give us a vision for the coming generations that will enable us to sow beyond ourselves into the lives of those to come. There are books to be written and songs to be sung. There are gifts to be developed and ministries to be born. There are decisions to be made and lives to be changed.

Has it been revealed to you that you are not serving yourself? Pray that God will grant you a vision for the generations to come. Then sow that vision in daily obedience to what you see.

※

February 12th

THEOLOGY OF A LESSER GOD

Their gods are gods of the hills. That is why they were too strong for us. But if we fight them on the plains surely we will be stronger than they"
I Kings 20:23

The officials of King Aram thought they had discovered the weakness of Jehovah. They were convinced that Jehovah was a God of the mountain tops and if they could fight in the valley, the victory would be theirs. For one year, they mustered an army to fight Israel in the valley, only to discover that God is God, whether He be on the mountain or in the valley. God's power is inherently within, and it is not dependent upon location or circumstance.

The church is often inflicted with this Aramean spirit. Often the accusation comes to us that our God is the God of the mountain tops, but not in the valleys. As a result of this accusation, many may have developed a theology of a lesser God when things are different. As long as things are going well, God is sovereign, but when circumstances turn bad, God becomes lesser and we are on our own.

The God we serve is no lesser in the valley than He is on the mountain top. God is God wherever He is, and He is God wherever we are. It is in the valley times of our life that He desires to manifest His life-changing power and prove Himself to us. It is for this reason we must never bring God into accusation when we are in the valley of difficult circumstances. These are the times when we need God on our side. We must never neutralize God's power through accusation.

God loves to demonstrate His redemptive power in the valley. Are you in the valley of difficulty? Call out to Him now and see His deliverance.

"I will deliver this vast army into your hands and you will know that I am the Lord." (I Kings 20:28)

February 13th

THE COMPLETE JESUS

"Jesus answered, 'I am the way, the truth and the life'"
John 14:6

Do you follow the complete Jesus or just a part of Him? Is it just Jesus the LIFE you know, or do you know Him as the TRUTH and the WAY? Have you accepted Jesus the TRUTH, but fallen short of embracing Him as the WAY and the LIFE?

To follow Jesus is to follow the complete Jesus, not just a part of Him. To follow Him begins with following Him in the WAY. Many believe Him to be the TRUTH, but stop short in following the predetermined course that Jesus has established. To be the WAY means that He is the predetermined method. He is the master who establishes the course and then calls His followers to walk in His footsteps on that path. It means we forsake our WAY and willingly give our wills over to the One who is the WAY. Not only is Jesus the WAY, He is the TRUTH, meaning the predetermined WAY He chose is a truthful WAY. Everything about it is inherently true. It does not just contain TRUTH, but it is TRUTH. But, to believe Him to be true, but not embrace Him as your WAY, is to settle for a part of Jesus.

Not only is Jesus the WAY and the TRUTH, but He is also the LIFE. He is what makes LIFE vital and full of purpose. In being the LIFE, He breathes vitality and significance into the TRUTH and the WAY. Many are attracted to Jesus the LIFE because of the significance He offers, but to focus on the LIFE without mixing it with the TRUTH and the WAY is to miss the fullness of who He is, and in so doing never become all He has intended us to be.

Embrace the complete Jesus. Allow Him to give your LIFE significance, to establish you on the TRUTH and to change your WAY for His.

February 14th

THE POWER TO REPRODUCE IS IN THE FRUIT

"They claim to know God, but by their actions they deny him"
Titus 1:16

It has often been said, "Actions speak louder than words." This is especially true when it comes to witnessing. Evangelism is first demonstration before it is proclamation. People must see Jesus in us before they hear Jesus from us. When they are attracted to the Jesus in us, we can be sure they are seeing the real thing.

Sometimes our efforts in evangelism are fruitless because we seek to lead people into religion, not Christ. We see their need and offer them a set of rules and regulations rather than the love of Jesus. People must encounter the love of Jesus before they will forsake their love for sin. Often we seek to convert our family and friends into our particular church structure. Though it is essential to love our church, our church structure is not the power of God unto salvation.

To be effective in our efforts of evangelism, we must first make sure our own conversion is real. To lead others to Christ, we must first give ourselves to Him in fullness. Secondly, we must bear the fruit of love and humility. The seed of reproduction is in your fruit. The knowledge of good and evil or legalistic laws do not carry the miracle of reproduction. The miracle of reproduction is inherent in the seed, and the seed is in the fruit. To see others come to Christ, we must demonstrate the fruit of the Spirit. We must show them the life before we tell them the way.

Do you desire to see your loved ones come to Christ? Then walk in the fruit of the Spirit. Attraction is found in the fruit. The seed of reproduction is planted by kindness, joy, love, peace and patience. In seeing the fruit, they will see Jesus in our actions and will testify to His reality.

February 15th

DENYING SELF

"If anyone would come after me, he must deny himself"
Matthew 16:24

Why did Jesus have to make this matter so personal? It would have been much easier if we had to deny things we did not like such as school, work, bad food or income taxes. But, to deny oneself is to make the issue of consecration quite personal and much more difficult.

To deny oneself stands in direct opposition to the American way. We have been schooled to believe that individuality and independence are virtues, not liabilities. From the time of our youth we are trained by the world to think independently and act independently. But this is not what Jesus taught us to do. Jesus did not teach independence or individuality of self. He taught the denial of self and the embracing of God's governmental way—a government that conforms our individuality into Christlikeness. Christ taught us to lose ourselves, not train ourselves to be independent. The very description of us being a body reveals a picture of interdependence. It reveals many members who possess their own unique identity and function, but are still completely dependent on each other for life and fulfillment of function.

Independence separates and isolates. God's desire is to tear down the walls of isolation and make His people a body—dependent upon and supportive of each other. Interdependence is not an admission of weakness, but an acknowledgment of divine design. To acknowledge our interdependence is to multiply our strengths, for when we are joined to one another we possess the strength of the whole, not just the isolated part.

Have you denied yourself since coming to Christ? Our right to ourselves was crucified on the cross. Let it die in exchange for Christ.

February 16th

YEAH-BUTS & RATIONAL LIES

"But they all alike began to make excuses."
Luke 14:18

Man is a genius when it comes to making excuses. The utter creativity of the human mind is miraculously released when faced with the need of an excuse. Every creative instinct given is immediately released to dream up an escape and find a "rational-lie." Excuse making has been elevated to the level of an art form.

Accommodation to religion and worldliness has raised a generation of "yeah-but-ers." Every expectation of God is met with a yeah-but. Commands are read and interpreted as suggestions with the justification of a "yeah-but, in this day and age that could never be done." Absolutes are eliminated with the "rational-lies" of "yeah-but, we must take into account the culture of the day."

"Yeah-but-ers" are "rational-liars." A "yeah-but-er" can rationalize any accommodation and even provide a few good verses out of context to support their rational-lies. The heart is deceitfully wicked and can rationalize almost anything the mind wants. This is why it is so critical that we embrace the process of the renewing of our minds. As our minds are renewed, we are able to discern the yeah-buts when they come and prevent the rational-lies.

Once we enter the realm of the yeah-buts, grace is forfeited. Grace is supplied to those willing to face the just requirements of God's expectation. When there is the willingness to embrace His way, God lavishes His grace in abundant supply. When His way is excused through yeah-buts and rational-lies, grace is forfeited. "Yeah-buts" and "rational-lies" remove the supernatural element from our Christian walk. A willingness to face God's desire acknowledges our weakness and inability. In the face of weakness, His strength is supplied. His strength empowers us to do the supernatural acts of God. But to excuse our weakness and rationalize our inability leaves us on our own, void of God's power.

Grace or "yeah-buts?" God's strength or "rational-lies?" The choice is ours, but the two do not dwell together.

◈

February 17th

OFFEND THE MIND

"Aware that his disciples were grumbling, Jesus said, 'Does this offend you?'"

John 6:61

Does it surprise you that even Jesus offended those who followed Him? It is interesting to note that not only did Jesus offend those who followed, but in the face of the offense He did nothing to try to appease those who were offended.

The Greek word translated "offend" is the word "skandalizo," from which we get the word "scandalize." The word means to cause a person to begin to distrust and desert one whom he ought to trust and obey.

The teaching, that Jesus had just delivered, scandalized many and as a result, the Scriptures say, *"from this time on, many of His disciples turned back and no longer followed Him."* (John 6:66) Upon their leaving, Jesus never went after them or changed His message to secure that place of those still with Him. Jesus understood the principle that an offended mind only reveals a divided heart. He understood that offenses are to be expected. Those who understand the principles of covenant will embrace the truth of God's Word and see the matter reconciled. But those with divided hearts will begin to distrust and, if left unresolved, will soon desert those they ought to trust and obey.

Are you carrying an offense? Has something been said that brought offense to your mind? If so, perhaps it was permitted to reveal your heart. Allow the Holy Spirit to reveal the condition of your heart and see if it is you that must humble yourself and make the change.

ᚼ

February 18th

SHADOW OR SUBSTANCE

"Don't let anyone judge you by what you eat or drink or with regard to a religious festival, a New Moon celebration or a Sabbath day. These are a shadow of the things that were to come; the reality, however, is found in Christ"

Colossians 2:16-17

Two thousand years later and mankind is still consumed with shadows and suspect of substance. Man will travel miles in search of a shadow, all the while denying the very substance he has known all his life. Jesus Christ could not possibly be the substance, he reasons; that would be too simple and in fact a bit foolish. But God has chosen the foolish things of this world to confound the wise. He takes great delight in shrouding truth and foolishness in order that He might reveal the wisdom of His plan.

Paul's focus to the Colossians was the fullness of Jesus Christ. He was writing to establish the fact that Jesus was the fullness of God in bodily form and He gave His life as a ransom for us that we might be given that same fullness. Having argued his case for Christ's fullness, Paul contrasts Jesus to the emptiness of ritualism, legalism, mysticism and ceremonialism. He argues that all of these were mere shadows of what was to come, but the substance of what they pointed to was the person of Jesus Christ.

Deception has changed little in the past two thousand years. A quick glance at contemporary man tells us he is still consumed with the shadow. The religious man is consumed with ritualism, legalism and ceremonialism. Humanism is full of new age mysticism and discreet pantheism. Currently we are even seeing a resurgence of angelic icons. Man, outside of Christ, is trapped in the same patterns trying to fill up his emptiness. But none of these shadows are capable of adding one ounce to the emptiness we experience outside of Christ.

Jesus Christ is the fullness that fills our emptiness. Security will not fill us. Peace will not fill us; neither will property, purpose or belonging. Outside of Christ, these are but shadows that point us to the fullness. In Christ we find the fullness of them all condensed into one person.

CB80

February 19th

PRACTICE HOSPITALITY

"Share with God's people who are in need. Practice hospitality"
Romans 12:13

Well, you can not be much more direct than that. The apostle Paul laid the responsibility in front of them as plainly as could be. The people of God are to be hospitable people.

Webster defines hospitality as: 1) given to generous and cordial reception of guests, 2) offering a pleasant or sustaining environment. I think for too long, we have relegated hospitality to the realm of the gifted. Though it is a gift that is perfected by some, it is also a responsibility that is to be practiced by all. It is not by mistake that Paul chose the word practice. For some, it requires just that. Providing a pleasant environment does not come to them naturally, so they must practice in order that they might present that generous reception. Others have the ability to be hospitable; they just do not take the time even though we are commanded to do so.

Our home can be one of the greatest sources of blessing we have if we allow it to become a vehicle of hospitality. In the physical realm, we are witnessing a dramatic increase of "home births." These are babies born in the comfort of homes versus the sterility of hospitals. I am believing God for some home births in the spiritual realm. That is, spiritual babies being born into the Kingdom as a result of you and me opening our homes as dwellings of blessing.

When was the last time you had someone in your home? Can I encourage you to practice hospitality? As we enjoy church growth, we must do so with the awareness that these precious people also need to be in our homes. It is not enough just to talk to them in the institution. We must also fellowship in the environment of our own homes.

Why not ask someone today?

~~~

February 20th

I DON'T UNDERSTAND

"Though it cost all you have, whatever else you get, get understanding"
Proverbs 4:7

I just don't understand. I don't understand why they do the things they do. I don't understand why they think the way they think. Perhaps most importantly, I don't understand why they are not just like me. In spite of my lack of understanding, they are still my family and the place God chose to bring me into this world.

Though understanding is essential, it is not supreme. Though it is vital, it is not the basis of our placement. Placement is based on sovereignty and relationship, not knowledge or understanding.

Proverbs reveals that understanding is a costly commodity, and like anything else of tremendous value, it is purchased over a long period of time. Like an expensive set of china, you purchase it one piece at a time as your budget allows. Most are able to accept this reality in terms of earthly possessions, but when it comes to spiritual understanding, they feel a compulsion to know it all and know it now. Though this is a noble desire, it can be a destructive one as it gives the devil a foothold of accusation.

Be it understood, understanding is essential, but it is acquired over a long period of time. You may not understand everything; that is okay. It will come in time if you give yourselves to it. Understanding is very costly and it is purchased in installments and often, between each installment payment, there is a time of confusion or misunderstanding. This confusion is designed of God to bring us into deeper dependency on Him and relationship to Him.

☙❧

February 21st

THE DEATH TREATMENT

"Make every effort to keep the unity of the Spirit through the bond of peace"

Ephesians 4:3

There is a saying in some countries that says, "If you don't die from your disease, you will from the treatment." I am afraid that this play on words has come home to roost. We are currently facing a condition in the body of Christ where many more are dying from the abusive treatment than from the so-called disease. Is it speaking in tongues or breaking fellowship with those who do?

The question comes down to this: What damages the body of Christ most, suspected doctrinal error or breaking fellowship over beliefs not essential to salvation?

I submit to you that breaking fellowship is far more grievous than the suspected error. Assumed doctrinal error has never broken fellowship between God and man. If it had, I am afraid at one point or another, we would all have been rather lonely. If it does not break fellowship with God, then it should never be allowed to break fellowship between His children.

This is not an appeal for us to forsake all convictions. It is simply an appeal to cease making one's opinions and beliefs on nonessentials the basis of our unity and fellowship. It is an appeal for the body of Christ to realize, once again, that knowledge and right thinking are not supreme. Relationship is far more important to God and the realization of His purposes than correct thinking on non-essential matters. The thing Scripture tells us that God hates is the sowing of discord among the brethren. In God's sight, the greater wrong is allowing opinions and beliefs to become a breach of fellowship between members of the same family.

The burning passion of John 17 was the oneness of Christ's body. To be like Him is to give ourselves, spirit, soul and body to the realization of that oneness. Yes, there are those with "diseased" thinking. We have met "those" and they are us. So, let us make sure our treatment will heal, not divide and destroy.

February 22nd

THE MINISTRY OF RECONCILIATION

"All of this is from God who reconciled us to himself through Christ and gave to us the ministry of reconciliation: That God was reconciling the world to himself in Christ not counting men's sins against them. And he has committed to us the message of reconciliation"

II Corinthians 5:18-19

Let it never be said again, "I have no ministry." The apostle Paul makes it perfectly clear that we all have a ministry born of God. That ministry is this: We are all ministers of reconciliation. Ministers with a message. The message that we have been ordained to carry and anointed to speak is the message of reconciliation.

The Greek word for reconciliation means to change from enmity to friendship. Think of it: We have been given the power and the ability to change man's relationship with God from a relationship of enmity to one of friendship, from a relationship of strife and that of an outsider to one of peace and a member of God's own household.

This is an awesome task, but it is one that we do not carry on our own. II Corinthians 5:20 says God is making His appeal through us. The ministry of reconciliation is simply making ourselves available as channels for Father to make His appeal to those separated and living in enmity.

Sometimes this ministry has its application on a horizontal level as well. Sometimes those in need of reconciliation are brother to brother, sister to sister. It is to these, Father seeks to make His appeal through us.

The words to the message of reconciliation are the words of love. Without love there is no reconciliation. Love is the oil that Father uses to soften the hardened heart and break down the walls of defense.

So with opened eyes, let us minister Father's love and become agents of reconciliation.

ଔଃଔ

February 23rd

WHEN HE WHO IS IN, COMES ON

"But you will receive power when the Holy Spirit comes on you"
Acts 1:8

He who dwells within us also desires to *"come on"* us. When we are born again, the Holy Spirit is given to us as an earnest guarantee of Father God's future intention. He is given as a guarantee that Father will complete the work that He has begun and bring us into the fullness of our created purpose. The indwelling presence of the Holy Spirit continually guides us, teaches us, comforts us and becomes for us all we need to become the sons and daughters of God.

As we look to the Scriptures, we see that the Holy Spirit who dwelled within also "came on" at various times for specific reasons. We read in John 20:22 that Jesus breathed on the disciples and they received the Holy Spirit. Just a few days later He told them to go to Jerusalem and wait until the Holy Spirit came on them in power. Seeing the task of evangelism before the disciples, Jesus knew that they would be in need of divine power to equip them for the specific task that stood before them.

Though the indwelling presence of the Holy Spirit is an earnest guarantee of our inheritance, it is not the complete power equipping us for Kingdom responsibility. It is the manifest presence of the Holy Spirit that comes on us in power that equips us to do the works of the Kingdom of God. Though the disciples had the indwelling presence of God, they needed the manifest presence of God as well to become the witnesses God intended them to be. So they went to Jerusalem to wait.

Waiting on God postures us to receive the manifest presence. As we learn to wait and posture ourselves in expectation, we can anticipate the Holy Spirit who dwells within, also "coming on," empowering us to accomplish what God desires.

February 24th

MAKING PROVISION FOR FAILURE

"I urge you to live a life worthy of the calling you have received. Be completely humble and gentle; be patient, bearing with one another in love. Make every effort to keep the unity of the Spirit"
Ephesians 4:1-3

It is the strength of the family bond that enables its members to stick together through times of testing and disagreement. While growing up, brothers and sisters often have sharp disagreements and at times heated arguments. But because they are family, they bear with one another in love. They were family before the fight and they are still family after.

Imagine what the church would be like if it did the same. Imagine where we would be if in the midst of disagreements and concern, the members made every effort to keep the unity of the Spirit.

Have you made provision in your thinking for relational failure? Though we do not plan for others to fail, forbearance makes provision for them if they do. Forbearance is that virtue in us that says, in the face of failure, "Though you have failed, you are still family and family sticks together."

Without the quality of unity, the church is relegated to the status of a club where membership is based on performance. What separates the church from all other man-made institutions is the fact that the joining of its members is not based on performance, but God's sovereign choice. Unfortunately, in the face of failure or unmet expectations, we often forget who joined the members together. Members often change churches, not because God moved them on, but because they were no longer satisfied with the pastor, the people, or the program.

Making provision for failure requires that we be completely humble. Humility enables us to see the log in our own eye before we question the speck in our family's eye.

Is there someone you need to exercise patience with? Are there those whom the Lord is asking you to forebear? *"If someone is overcome with a fault, be spiritual and restore them and in so doing preserve the unity of the Spirit."* (Galatians 6:1)

February 25th

TAKING SUSPICION CAPTIVE

"The weapons we fight with are not the weapons of this world. On the contrary, they have divine power to demolish strongholds. We demolish arguments and every pretension that sets itself up against the knowledge of God and we take captive every thought to make it obedient to Christ"
II Corinthians 10:4,5

Taking every thought captive is the first principle of war. We do not wage war as this world does. We do not fight flesh and blood as the armies of the world do. Our battle is a battle of words and thoughts that formulate strongholds and keep God's people captive—captive to thoughts, vain imaginations, and speculations that are unfounded and have no basis for truth, which nevertheless become strongholds.

Strongholds are seldom based on facts. Usually they are based on lies and speculations that are left unattended and over time are accepted as true. The enemy of our soul seeks to tear God's people apart. Understanding that unity is a direct answer to Christ's prayer of John 17, he seeks to divide what Father desires to join together. Suspicion, accusation and wrong conclusions are his tactics of choice. Suspicion opens the doorway to accusation. The enemy sows a seed of suspicion about a person or a church and soon rumor and accusation run rampant. The unfounded accusations cause one to form certain presuppositions about those under suspicion. Those presuppositions cause one to draw conclusions, and conclusions necessitate certain decisions. Often the decisions are to discredit, reject and warn others to stay away from those under suspicion. The tragedy is that the entire process was based on speculation orchestrated by Satan to divide God's people so he can accuse Christ of not being powerful enough to unite His own family.

People often move from suspicion to decision having never talked to the person toward whom the accusation was directed. For the sake of unity, let us put this practice aside and recognize the author behind the lies. As family, let us recognize the war we are in and make every effort to preserve the unity of the Spirit.

☙❧

February 26th

THE CANNIBALISM OF SELF

"Do not repay anyone evil for evil...vengeance is mine says the Lord"
Romans 12:17,19

Though cannibalism is looked upon with disgust in the natural world, it has become quite acceptable in the spiritual. Through gossip, slander, bitterness and strife, we feed upon ourselves with carnivorous appetites.

"Of the seven most deadly sins, anger is probably the most fun. To lick your wounds, smack your lips over grievances long past, roll your tongue, the prospect over bitter confrontations still to come, savor to the last toothsome morsel both the pain you are given and the pain you are giving back is a feast for a king. The chief drawback is that what you are wolfing down is yourself. The skeleton at the feast is you." *Fredrick Bucchner.*

Perhaps the reason the body of Christ has become so emaciated is due to its cannibalistic practices of conflict resolution. The fleshly reactions of an uncontrolled soul have caused us to react in such a way that has led to our own personal consumption. As a skilled maitre d', the devil has garnished our plate with artistic design and then as the choir sang softly, we served us ourselves.

Vengeance is God's. Let us put away the cannibalistic tendencies of bitterness, anger, strife and discord. Let us turn the tide and serve the devil on a platter, by embracing the higher way of humility, unity and love. "LOVE NEVER FAILS." (I Corinthians 13:8) It will not fail you and it will not fail whatever your circumstances might be.

February 27th

SPIRITUAL PLACEMENT

"You also, like living stones, are being built into a spiritual house"
I Peter 2:5

Anyone who has ever built or been involved with building a house knows it is not an easy process. Much to my disappointment, when the lumber package came from the lumber yard, the boards were not pre-cut nor were they numbered. This meant that in order for those individual boards to be built into a house, each one would have to be cut, nailed and even hammered. Sometimes the wrong board was used and the fit was not acceptable so the process started all over.

Fortunately as we went through this process, we were not working with living boards. For if we were, when they found out that the process included cutting, nailing and hammering, they might have crawled away in search of a new home.

Christ's church is not made of dead boards, but of living stones. The difficulty lies in the fact that when Father sends us the "stone package" to build this spiritual house, they too are not pre-cut or numbered. So, in order for this house to be built, each and every stone must chipped and chiseled to fit into place.

Placement in the local church is not an easy process. Our enemy knows that our unity together is the simple, greatest proof of Christ's validity (John 17), so he does everything within his power to hinder the realization of unity. He also knows that until the body comes together, *"bone to bone and rises to an exceeding great army"* (Exodus 34), Father's purposes for this Earth will not be realized. He knows that until the individual is placed properly in the body, there is not the correct flow of nutrition and life. So he will use everything at his disposal to prevent the living stones from being built together.

We must become wise to our enemy's tricks. As God leads you to a local body, be assured that your placement will come from much warfare and difficulty. We are in need of cutting and chiseling in order to assume the proper fit. Let us stand firm and resist the Devil's schemes to prevent the coming together of the body of Christ.

February 28th

CARNALLY MINDED

"And I could not speak to you as spiritual but as carnal, even as babes in Christ . . . for you are yet carnal, for there is among you envying and strife and divisions, are you yet carnal and walk as men?"
I Corinthians 3:1-3

How easy it is to be squeezed into the patterns of this world and find ourselves thinking carnally rather than spiritually. To think carnally simply means that our thought process is governed by natural thinking rather than the Spirit and The Word. To be carnally minded is a subtle thing because it has more to do with attitudes than it does actions. Though attitudes are easy to discern, they are often so slippery it is difficult to determine the course for correction.

The scriptures use three words to describe the fruit of a carnal mind:

➢ ENVY: This is an attitude that speaks of the covetousness in one's heart that produces a feeling of displeasure when witnessing or hearing of the prosperity of another. In its worst sense, envy seeks to deprive another from what they have and desires to have the same for themselves.

➢ STRIFE: This is evidence of a contentious spirit, one motivated by quarreling and the drive to debate every issue. It is the spirit of those in I Corinthians 1:11-13 that prompted the Corinthian believers to divide into factions, those for Paul and those for Apollos.

➢ DIVISIONS: This word means, a standing apart from. Its root is the word, asunder. It has to do with the cutting of family ties or the standing apart from family identity. To break the word into syllables, it simply means 1) di 2) vision (direction). It means to secretly or openly carry a vision other than that of the family. This vision may be an appropriate vision; it is just not the family's vision.

The apostle Paul's answer to the carnally minded man is to acknowledge Christ's ownership of our lives (I Corinthians 3:23) and thereby put off being governed by natural and embrace spirit-controlled thinking.

March 1st

OBLIGATED TO JESUS

"But Daniel resolved in his heart not to defile himself"
Daniel 1:8

In an accommodating system, Daniel stood as a person of contrast. Nebuchadnezzar's goal was the compromising of Daniel's identity. He could remain a Jew on the outside. After all, there was nothing the king could do to change that, as long as he became Babylonian on the inside. The king's strategy was simple. Obligate him with the royal food so as to pacify him with the good life. Daniel perceived the king's tactics and resolved not to obligate himself to anything the king would offer.

The enemy of our soul has no new tricks. The same tricks of deceit he used on Daniel, he seeks to use on us. His strategy is obligate. He seeks to lure us into seemingly good situations, but they are situations that obligate us. As a result, he has a hook in us that could possibly lead to our failure. Perhaps it is a promotion that comes with the requirement of working Sundays. Obligation to the job puts the career above fellowship and equipping and soon it is intimacy with Christ that is lost.

"You shall have no other gods before me." (Exodus 20:3) God's intent is that we would obligate ourselves to no one but Him. We have been bought with a price and are already obligated to Him. To protect that obligation, Daniel resolved.

How big is your sphere of resolve? What have you resolved in regard to movies, drinking, dating, music or speech, friendship and working Sundays? Resolve is simply this: You predetermine a set of standards that will determine your behavior when you face the fray. The time to decide behavior is before the temptation, not during or after.

"Those who know their God will firmly resist." (Daniel 11:32) It is our knowledge of Christ that gives us the ability to resist. As we know Him better, we begin to gain a greater understanding of our identity and purpose. As we know Him, our love for Him increases. Our love for Christ, mixed with a clean vision of our identity and purpose, is sin's greatest deterrent.

March 2nd

SUCCESS OR EXCELLENCE

"Do not conform any longer to the pattern of this world, but be transformed by the renewing of your mind"

Romans 12:2

What price success? How far are you willing to go? Must success come at the price of compromise? These and other questions can only be answered based upon how one defines success. It is one's criteria of success that determines what they must do to achieve it.

The patterns of this world define success from a completely different set of criteria. The world asks how much, how big, how many, what did it cost? But the Scriptures do not take these matters into account when they evaluate success. In fact, the Scriptures do not even stress success as we know it. They put the emphasis upon excellence rather than success. Real success is not getting the desired results whatever the cost. Success is not defined in terms of prosperity, power, prominence, popularity or any other worldly pattern. Real success is doing the will of God regardless of the consequences.

Truth places the emphasis on excellence rather than success, for excellence addresses the character, whereas success addresses the external. From the world's point of view, a person can be characterized as successful even if his character and motivation is askew. They may have the biggest and the best, but if the internal issues of character and right standing before God are not brought into alignment, they are not successful.

To move away from the patterns of this world is to begin to pursue excellence rather than success. Excellence means it has been done with integrity. Excellence means it is been done with honesty. Excellence means it has been done without relational offense, or if offense occurred, it has been resolved. Excellence means it has been done through the inspiration of the Holy Spirit with an eye toward Christ receiving the glory, not us.

How far am I willing to go? As far as it takes for me to stand before God in excellence and bring Him glory.

March 3rd

WHAT THEY SEE IS WHAT WE GET

"Treat your servants in accordance to what you see"
Daniel 1:13

Not only was this a request of Daniel, it is also a spiritual principle. The world and those around us treat us according to what they see. If they see us being harsh and judgmental, they will treat us harshly, whereas if they see us being loving and compassionate, they will treat us with love.

"Natural thinking" says, "Become like the world in order to win them to Christ." The mind reasons that if we are too different, they will think us strange and alienate us. "Kingdom thinking" says, "Be a contrast to the world so as to provoke them to repentance." If the world treats us in accordance to what they see and they see no apparent difference, they will treat us like themselves. Whereas, if they treat us according to what they see and they see a godly contrast, it will provoke them to interest and inquiry.

When I was saved, it was someone who was completely opposite to me that had the most impact on my life. I was bankrupt socially and tired of the "scene." I wanted change, not more of the same. So, as I began my search, I looked for my opposite because I no longer liked what I represented.

"COMPARE OUR APPEARANCE" (Daniel 1:13). Comparison is God's means to awaken wonder that leads to inquiry.

As the world compares themselves to those of the Kingdom, they must see a contrast in character, honesty, kindness, joyfulness, love, hope and peace. As they compare, they must see a contrast in appearance, modesty and honor. As they compare, they must see a contrast in discipline, order, cleanliness and personal government.

March 4th

A SPIRIT OF WILLINGNESS

"Your troops will be willing on your day of battle"
Psalm 110:3

*I*t is nearly an impossible task, but it is the way the purposes of God have ordained. Build an army, but build on the basis of willingness and "volunteerism."

Most armies are built on the basis of threat and consequence. Orders are given by commanding officers, and if the order is not obeyed, the consequent punishment is handed out ranging from kitchen duty to court martial.

It is not so in the army of God. Though the expectation is the same, if not higher, the tactics are quite different. The army of God replaces the commanding officer with a servant leader. Orders are replaced with appeals and the punishment of infractions are left to God.

Yes, it is nearly an impossible task, but God has provided a way. The way God has ordained for His army to succeed is through the spirit of willingness. If the people are willing, orders are not necessary. If the people are willing, servant leadership is enough. If the people are willing, the battle is won.

Israel, in the wilderness, is the tragic story of an unwilling people. Time and time again, Moses sought to lead the people, but they were unwilling to follow the man of God. Their stubbornness won them the dubious title of being a stiff-necked people. Unwilling to yield, unwilling to follow, their stubbornness prevented their generation from entering the land that God had promised.

In the world, a willingness to yield to another is a sign of weakness, but in the Kingdom of God, it is a virtue. God seeks those who are willing to follow, those willing to follow Him and willing to follow His delegated ones. Perhaps it is time for a willingness check. For the sake of this army's success, let us grow in our expression of willingness.

March 5th

MISSIONS AWARENESS

"But you will receive power when the Holy Spirit comes upon you and you will be my witnesses ... to the ends of the earth"

Acts 1:8

What is your concept of missions? What is your image of a missionary? What should the missions program of the local church look like?

In order to sustain the blessing of God, every individual and local church will at some point have to adequately resolve these questions. Father's heart involves the nations. He is not American, nor is He limited to any other ethnic or geo-political boundary. The nations are the Lord's, and as He prospers a given congregation, it is imperative that they begin to develop a world perspective.

A missions program must be more than an isolated meeting every three years. A missionary is not someone who could not succeed at home. A heart for the nations must be a vital aspect of every believers life.

Consider these statistics as you evaluate your missions philosophy:

- Of the 20 largest churches in the world, only one is in America.
- New churches are planted every week in Africa and Asia alone.
- People are becoming Christians in Latin America three times faster than the growth rate of the entire population.
- 40% of Africa's population is Christian.
- In 100 AD, there were 416 non-Christians to every Christian in the world. In 1989, there were seven non-Christians to every Christian in the world. By the end of this century, with the present growth rate of Christianity around the world, this will be reduced to three to one.
- There are approximately 85,000 missionaries in the world. There are approximately 485,000 Avon ladies in America and approximately 750,000 Amway distributors in America.
- The average Christian in North America gives less than 2% of their annual income to any religious organization.
- There are still 13,000 ethnic groups in the world that have no missionary, no church and no Scripture in their language.
- North American churches possess 95% of the world's ministers and give less than 5% of their annual income to missions.

To carry the heart of God is to carry a heart for the nations. Allow Him to enlarge your heart and expand your current focus.

☙❧

Pause for thought:

What specifically is the Holy Spirit asking you to do in regards to extending the Kingdom of God among the nations?

March 6th

THE PRAYING CHURCH

"I will give you the keys of the kingdom of heaven; whatever you bind on earth will be bound in heaven, and whatever you loose on earth will be loosed in heaven"

Matthew 16:19

Paul Billheimer, in his book, "Destined For the Throne," says, "If the church will not pray, God will not act . . . He will never go over the head of the church to enforce His decisions. He will not take things out of her hands. To do so would sabotage His training program . . . If she will not pray, God will not act because this would abort His purpose to bring His church to her full potential as co-sovereign." (Page 50)

It is amazing how easy the purpose and focus of prayer gets distorted. Could the reason we do not see more prayers answered be that God does not recognize them when He hears them? Jesus states it like this: *"You want something, but don't get it. You kill and covet, but you cannot have what you want. You quarrel and fight. You do not have because you don't ask. When you ask, you do not receive because you ask with wrong motives that you may spend what you get on your pleasures."* (James 4:2-3)

We have made prayer something primarily for us. Prayer has become the means by which we get God to give us what we want. This is a far cry from what Paul Billheimer described prayer to be. When Jesus taught the disciples to pray, the praying for personal needs was part of the instruction, but only after they had prayed for the coming of the Kingdom and the doing of God's will. Only in the coming of His Kingdom and the doing of His will are personal needs met in a lasting way.

As we review our commitment to intercession, let us do so upon a foundation that will support us for years to come. Our focus is the Lord and the outpouring of the Holy Spirit on our cities, our churches and our families. In praying for the release of the Holy Spirit, all personal needs will be met beyond expectation. As we seek first the Kingdom through prayer and intercession, everything else will be added to us.

March 7th

HE WORKS ON BEHALF OF THOSE WHO WAIT

"Since ancient times no one has heard, nor ear has perceived, no eye has seen any God besides you, who acts on behalf of those who wait for him"

Isaiah 64:4

Our focus has been the battle we've been commissioned to wage. Our opponent is not flesh and blood, but principalities and powers. The victory is assured, for it has already been won. Our responsibility is to enforce that victory over rebellious spirits who have failed to bow their knee to the Lord of lords and King of kings.

Every inch of ground we win is contested. Every battle won is done so in worship and prayer. We are gaining ground. Though it seems limited in the physical realm, it is much more wide spread in the spirit. Every prayer offered, every confession spoken, assures us the victory. Though the apparent victory may not be immediately realized, wait.

"They that wait upon the Lord shall . . ." The operative words are *wait* and *shall*. When we wait, we shall, for the Lord works on behalf of those who wait.

Those who desire to war must learn to wait. Waiting is of strategic importance because it is here in the season of waiting that we are purged from all that which is displeasing to God. Impatience, ambition, carnality, presumption, pride and the rest, all must go. Waiting is the means by which the Commander-in-Chief squeezes these attributes of the world out of us and conforms us into His image.

Spiritual authority is proportional to humility and dependency on God. Apart from Him, we are and have nothing. The Bible warns us about the sin of presumption, which is the attempt to extend God's Kingdom without His specific direction. After the great victory of Jericho, Joshua was deceived by the Gibeonites, because he did not inquire of the Lord. (Joshua 9:14)

We are destined to win. That victory is assured as we learn to wait on the Lord. Now is the time to increase your posture of waiting and depending on the Lord.

March 8th

BINDING THE STRONGMAN

". . . how can anyone enter a strong man's house and carry off his possessions unless he first ties up the strong man"

Matthew 12:29

The Bible clearly reveals God as the owner and ruler of planet Earth. *"The Earth is the Lord's and the fullness thereof."* (Psalm 24:1) But Satan, as a thief in Father's territory, usurps that which is not his and as a squatter must be evicted by the legal owner.

Long before we arrived, they were here; powers and principalities that rule the air; strongholds of discouragement and failed starts that rob us of faith and perpetuate the snare of unbelief.

These are the strong men we must bind before we can impact our cities as we desire. Jesus gave us the keys of the Kingdom and told us whatsoever we bind on Earth will be bound in Heaven. We have been called to war. You are being called to war specifically over this stronghold of discouragement. Would you battle with me on this?

My suggestion is to begin in repentance. Discouragement robs us of faith, and without faith, it is impossible to please God. So let us begin by repenting from not being pleasing to the One who is most dear. Then let us attack the gates of hell. Not once or every now and then, but repeatedly. As we attack the strongholds of darkness, the walls are being torn down brick by brick, but as soon as we let up we face the risk of the enemy replacing each brick. The only answer for this is to pray without ceasing, so there is no opportunity given to the devil to rebuild the wall.

Calvary assures us the victory. Our God has promised us the land. Let us be faithful warriors and *tie up the strong man* who holds that which belongs to our God.

‿‿

March 9th

A HOUSE OF PRAYER

"Jesus entered the temple area and drove out all who were buying and selling there. He overturned the tables of the money changers and the benches of those selling doves. 'It is written,' he said to them, 'My house will be called a house of prayer'"

Matthew 21:12-13

This proclamation of Jesus was both a prophetic proclamation and a proclamation of desire. As He spoke those words, He was speaking from the perspective of prophetic desire and from the perspective of future reality. He desired His Father's house to be a house of prayer. He knew that as a result of the Holy Spirit's working in the church, His church would indeed become a house of prayer.

Jesus had nothing against free enterprise. There was nothing in His theology that forbade the establishing of a business and the making of a profit. His actions were simply to illustrate the priorities of His Father's house. His Father's house was not to be run as a business; rather it was to be a house of prayer. That is to say, prayer is the foundation upon which all is to be built. Yes, this is simple and even basic, but all too often overlooked.

Those who have ears to hear are hearing the prophetic stirring of a fresh emphasis on prayer. No, this is not the type of prayer that promises us everything we ever longed for. Prayer that is motivated by the selfish desire of the heart is becoming a thing of the past. The prophetic work of the Spirit, in these days, is mustering an army of intercessors who will stand in the gap on behalf of the purposes of God and pray for the outpouring of the Holy Spirit on their family, their church, their city and their nation. This stirring began in the '80s; now it is gaining its momentum and is being unleashed in the '90s and will move us forward into the next millenium.

☙❧

March 10th

SUFFICIENT PRAYER COVER

"Devote yourselves to prayer, being watchful and thankful"
Colossians 4:2

Have you ever gone into a situation with the dreadful realization that you were not adequately prepared and it was too late to do anything about it? If so, you will remember the sense of helplessness and despair. Preparation is the key to success. It is the difference between hitting the mark and missing it altogether.

The body of Christ is currently enjoying the outpouring of the Lord's favor. His presence is manifest as we gather, and His visitation is evident to all. But are we prepared for the next move? Have we laid adequate foundation in order for us to sustain Father's desire? My conviction is that we have not. More specifically, I am afraid we do not have adequate prayer preparation in order for us to receive what the Lord desires to send to us.

Yesterday's prayer base will not carry tomorrow's visitation. If we desire to keep up with what the Holy Spirit is saying, our foundation of prayer will have to increase accordingly. If it does not, the visitation of God will become shallow and short cycled before it accomplishes what it was intended to do.

Prayer that will prepare us adequately is prayer that is waged from two fronts.

1. PERSONAL PRAYER. This is prayer done in your own prayer closet. Just you and the Holy Spirit laboring together, interceding on behalf of those issues He brings to mind. It is daily prayer, hourly prayer, prayer that is done without ceasing.

2. CORPORATE PRAYER. This is prayer done with your spiritual family. It is turbo prayer, for there is a power that is limited to only those times when the corporate body joins together to pray. Without a strong corporate prayer, there will not be sufficient preparation to inherit the next move of God.

I appeal to you to increase your prayer base. Pray every day for the favor and blessing of God. Take every opportunity over everything the enemy would attempt to do in order to hinder God's moving. If you have not already, join with a group of intercessors in order that we might unleash that power that is reserved for when two or three gather together in His name.

March 11th

PLANNED PARENTHOOD

"For those who God foreknew He also predestined to be conformed to the likeness of His Son, that He might be the firstborn among many brethren"
Romans 8:29

Everything God does, He does with strategic purpose and planning. Nothing in the economy of God happens by chance or surprise. His sovereignty destines it and the matter comes to pass. So it is with our adoption into the family of God. In eternity past, Father, Son and Holy Spirit covenanted together so that Father would get what He desired. His desire was for a vast family of sons and daughters. His desire was to prepare a bride for His Son. Jesus covenanted to give His life as a ransom to purchase the family's redemption. The Holy Spirit covenanted to give Himself to walk alongside the sons and daughters and make the eternal purpose of God real in their lives. So, with that plan as their central view, each gave their lives for the fulfillment of God's desire.

"Predestined to be conformed to the likeness of Jesus that He might be the firstborn among many brethren." This is planned parenthood at its best. Father's plan from the foundation of time has been to secure a multitude of sons and daughters and then conform them into the image of Jesus Christ. His plan did not involve leaving us as we were. Father, Son and Holy Spirit covenanted together to purchase our salvation; then they work together to bring about a transformation in our lives that will result in our glorification.

According to Romans 8:30, this is a process that begins with our predestination. We are not the result of some random lottery. We were predestined by God to be part of the family. Not only were we predestined, but we were called, called by name and given a purpose. Those He called, He also justified. He paid the penalty of sin just as if we had never sinned before. Our sin is no longer in the recollection of God. It has been erased by the blood of Christ. Those He justified, He also glorified. The end result of the Trinity's covenant is our glorification. That glorification is the realization of their desire and the transformation in our lives. In becoming like Jesus, do not worry, we will not stay the same. Parenthood works. We are being and will be transformed.

March 12th

INTERPRETING THE TIMES

"When you see a cloud rising in the west, immediately you say, 'It's going to rain,' and it does. And when the south wind blows, you say, 'It's going to be hot,' and it is. Hypocrites! You know how to interpret the appearance of the earth and the sky. How is it that you don't know how to interpret this present time?"

Luke 12:54-56

Though Jesus presented this to the crowd as a rebuke, I believe He would present it to us simply as a challenge. Can you interpret the present time?

The ability to discern what the Holy Spirit is saying, so as to be prepared, is the challenge that is presently before us. Before we can dress ourselves in readiness, we must be able to discern the present time. Then we will know how to dress and what to do.

For some, discernment is a gift while for the rest, it is a result. Some have the ability to discern without any prior action. For most, the ability to discern the present time comes as a result of the individual's intimate relationship with Christ. Interpreting the times is not the result of us gazing into our crystal balls, but rather the result of our gazing into the living Word of God. As a corporate people tune their ears to the Holy Spirit and discipline their lives in the word, the result will be the ability to interpret the times and know what we must do. This will lead us to both a personal and a corporate discovery.

Whether it be personal or corporate, it will require sacrifice. Sacrifice is the heart of the Gospel, but the good news is our God will supply our every need according to His riches in Christ Jesus. (Philippians 4:19) We need not fear the cost, only pray for a heart that is willing.

☙❧

March 13th

EXPECTING HEALTH

"If you diligently heed the voice of the Lord your God and do what is right in His sight, give ear to His commandment and keep all of His statutes, I will put none of the diseases on you"

Exodus 15:26

Here is another one of the great "IF" clauses of the word of God. Divine health is not an automatic covenantal promise. It is a promise of the covenant that is guarded with a condition. If we do what the condition stipulates, we can expect to live with the hope of divine health. But, if we disregard the terms of covenant, the walls of protection are broken down and sickness has free reign in our life and in the life of our family.

Exodus 15:26 gives us four conditions for hope of divine health:

1. HEED THE VOICE OF THE LORD: The hope of divine health begins with hearing. It is the hearing of God's desire to keep us sick-free. Without the hearing, we have no expectation of divine health. Hearing also involves the continual hearing of what God's new Word is to you.

2. DO WHAT IS RIGHT: It is not enough to hear. Upon the hearing, we must do the doing. Hearing and obeying is the pathway to healthy living.

3. GIVING EAR TO HIS COMMANDS: "Giving ear" means to ponder His Word. There is a cleansing and healing factor in the meditating on His Word.

4. KEEP HIS STATUTES: This means to guard and protect what you take. It means guarding the truth from the lies of the enemy. It means protecting yourself from the lies of sickness when the truth says we can expect healing.

I believe the Lord would like to lift our expectation in the area of health and sickness. According to the promise of God's Word, we are to expect divine health and contend for it in our family and congregations.

If sickness has been a problem for you, examine the conditions, align your life to them and expect health.

March 14th

THE IMPORTANCE OF FAITH

"Without faith it is impossible to please God"

Hebrews 11:6

Wow! That makes it pretty clear. It leaves little question as to how important faith is. Faith is so important that without it, it is impossible to please God. In other words, do not even try, because regardless of your efforts, you will not please Him. Works apart from faith will not please. Holiness apart from faith will not please. Anything that is done apart from faith is unpleasing before God.

Why does faith please God? Human nature is to encroach into God's sphere. Many sins including willfulness, pride, and independence, etc., all have blurred the distinction between man and God As a result, we often assume responsibilities that are uniquely God's.

Faith brings into focus God's distinction. When a people walk by faith, they walk in the reality that apart from Christ they can do absolutely nothing. Faith allows God to be God and man to be man. Faith will not devalue God or overvalue man. Faith is pleasing to God, because it sees men in a place of need and allows God to have entrance into their lives.

Faith is the bridge of relationship between God and man. Our faith allows God, with whom all things are possible, to join forces with us and in us as His delegated representatives. Through faith not only are all things possible for God, but *"All things are possible to him who believes."* (Mark 9:23) Consequently, faith partners us together with God as co-laborers and thrusts us into the field of harvest.

Now faith begins to take on a clearer focus. It is not to be selfishly motivated. Faith is not a means for self-indulgence. It is not to get something bigger and better. Faith is the means by which God channels His life through us and impacts the world.

We must cry out for a major release of faith.

◊

March 15th

A CITY WITHOUT WALLS

"Jerusalem will be a city without walls"
Zechariah 2:4

The writer of Hebrews tells us in chapter 11 that God is designing and building a city. Deep within the heart of God has been the desire for a city, a city with a foundation, a city of the redeemed which fully expresses the life and glory of their God.

The prophet Zechariah gives us some insight into a key design characteristic of that city. He says that the city will be erected without walls. He goes on to say, that in exchange of the walls that separate and isolate, God Himself will be a fire around the city. He will protect it, and His glory will be within to transform it.

According to Hebrews 12:22, we are the new Jerusalem, the heavenly Jerusalem, God's building. The design of this heavenly city will be as he described before, *"a city without walls,"* a city with nothing to isolate or separate its people.

Isolation is a demonically inspired strategy designed to prevent the city of God's desire. Isolation is a curse to the body of Christ because it stands diametrically opposed to the joining that God desires. It subtly undermines the coming together of God's people and in so doing prevents the building of the city. What this strategy of isolation produces are attitudes of suspicion and independence. Though these attitudes are contrary to God's way, they are being viewed as virtues in the church today. We have allowed the sociological climate of the world to erect walls of isolation, suspicion and independence in the church.

Praise God these walls are coming down! The church is getting wise to the strategy of the accuser and beginning to search for the city. In the search, we are allowing the Holy Spirit to remove from us the walls of separation in exchange for His fire to protect and His glory to transform.

છ૭

March 16th

THE BLESSED HOPE OF ETERNITY

"If only for this life we have hope in Christ, we are to be pitied more than all men"

I Corinthians 15:19

As humans, we tend to be creatures of extreme. We vacillate from one extreme to the other almost losing sight of the previous extreme we once held so dear. The current emphasis takes on an all-consuming focus and the balance is in threat of being lost.

This is a truth that is clearly illustrated in the tension between eternity and the present. For so long, Christianity focused so intently on eternity that it lost all perspective of the present. Consequently, our influence became irrelevant and many perceived it as death insurance, not a relevant lifestyle. In the attempt to dispel this misconception, the pendulum swung to the extreme of relevancy and in so doing, we lost all perception of eternity.

In Paul's defenses of the resurrection, he once again focuses our thoughts on eternity. Hope for this life is essential. Without it, we exist in a misdirected and continually defeated state. But the resurrection serves as a continual illustration that the present must be continually balanced by the hereafter.

It's the reality of Christ's resurrection that promises us hope in the hereafter. Yes, we can have hope in Christ for the present. He is an ever present, always relevant God. But being bigger than the present, we can also have hope in Him in the future.

Are you worried about your future? Do you fear for provision? Are you concerned for your health? Does the well being of your children and grandchildren after you are gone worry you? Then put your hope in Christ. Just as He has proven Himself faithful in the present, He will prove Himself faithful in the future. No, the thought of eternity need not be accompanied by fear and apprehension, for the Christ we serve is risen and ever lives to offer us a blessed hope and a glorious eternity.

March 17th

PROPHET OR KING

"When Jesus entered Jerusalem, the whole city was stirred and asked, 'Who is this?' The crowds answered, 'This is Jesus, the prophet from Nazareth in Galilee'"

Matthew 21:10-11

Was that all Jesus was? Just a prophet from Nazareth in Galilee? The triumphal entry of Jesus into Jerusalem is a dramatic story of tragic outcome. It builds with the prophetic fulfillment of the donkey ride. Imagine how the disciples felt when they found the donkeys just how Jesus told them they would be. Not just one donkey, but two. Not just any two donkeys, but a donkey and its colt. They entered the city and just as Jesus told them, the donkeys were there. As Jesus entered the city on the donkey, the city erupted into spontaneous praise. The crowds threw their cloaks to the ground and cried out Hosanna, Hosanna! A city wide worship service? Not exactly! How could these same people who cried Hosanna, Hosanna, be crying crucify Him, crucify Him, just a few days later? We read the answer to this question in verse 11, *"This is Jesus, the prophet from Nazareth."* All they saw was a prophet.

Though this event had all the elements of a Holy Ghost worship service, it was not. The people were not worshipping God; they were worshipping a man. Yes, the man was indeed the incarnate God, but they did not know Him as that. The people knew Jesus only as a prophet from Nazareth and it was the prophet they were too stirred up about, not the Son of God. Jerusalem had 1,000 prophets and Jesus was just another one of them to these people. This is why they could cry "crucify" a short time later.

Christianity is the acknowledgment of the sovereignty of Jesus Christ. Have you acknowledged the fullness of His sovereignty or do you relate to Him more as a prophet than as a king. Prophets speak, but kings rule. Is it just the words of Jesus you have received or have you received His sovereign rule? Is He just a prophet from Nazareth or is He your King, at whom every knee shall bow and every tongue confess Jesus Christ as Lord?

○₿○

March 18th

THE FIRST ONE IS FREE

"To comfort all who mourn and provide for those who grieve in Zion . . . to bestow on them . . . a garment of praise instead of a spirit of despair"
Isaiah 61:2-3

It is amazing how quickly that spirit of despair can overtake what was once a fruitful and joyful life. Like a weed left unattended, soon it has taken over the entire garden.

Heaviness and despair are destructive in their outworking. Not only do they reek havoc on our spiritual lives, but also on our emotional and physical lives. Proverbs 17:22 says, *"A cheerful heart is good medicine but a crushed spirit dries up the bones."*

God's remedy for the dryness of bones is the oil of gladness. The secret is the ability to tap into this oil and release its flow, so that the garment of praise may take effect. Praise is the means by which the oil of gladness flows. As we made the choice to put on the garment of praise, there is an exchange that takes place in the spirit. An exchange of despair for gladness, heaviness for joy. The reason it is called the "garment of praise" is because as a garment, it often begins as an outward act. It is the putting on of something over something else. Even as you put on your coat over your upper body, you put on praise over your despondency and despair.

Though it begins outward, it does not remain there. Praise has a way of working itself in. Soon that garment of praise has turned into an oil and that oil is moistening the bones. Those bones that were once dry and brittle are now becoming soft and flexible. The heaviness that was all consuming has now been replaced by gladness. You begin to feel the skip back in your step. The song of the Lord is once again on your lips and the season of restoration is in full bloom.

Make no mistake about it, praise is a wonder drug. As we praise, the Holy Spirit lifts the despair. But be careful; praise is a narcotic. Praise is highly addictive. If you do not watch it, soon you will not be able to get enough. Before long, you will realize you cannot live without it.

So, have a praise on me. Begin a song of praise. The first one is free.

March 19th

HIDDEN FROM SIGHT

"After he said this, he was taken up before their very eyes and a cloud hid him from their sight. They were looking intently up into the sky as he was going, when suddenly two men dressed in white stood beside them. 'Men of Galilee,' they said, 'why do you stand there looking into the sky? This same Jesus who has been taken from you into heaven, will come back in the same way you have seen him go'"

Acts 1:9-11

*A*llow me to take some editorial license and highlight the essence of these three verses:

"A cloud hid Him from their sight. They were looking intently into the sky. Why do you stand there looking intently into the sky? . . . He will come back in the same way you saw him go."

It is amazing to me the energy that is spent on figuring out the time and the season of our Lord's return. Two thousand years later and we are still *"looking intently into the sky."* Books, articles and charts all seem to have it figured out, some even to the day and time, yet the Scriptures make it very plain that His return will be just like His going, i.e., a cloud will hide Him from our sight.

They could not see Him go and we will not be able to recognize His coming. Sure, there will be signs of that coming, but not substantial enough that would warrant everyone to drop what they were doing and begin looking intently into the sky. Star gazing has cost the church its influence of being salt and light. Though we expect His bodily return, it must not come at the cost of abdicating our personal and corporate influence.

In order to occupy until He comes as He instructed us, it will require that we keep both eyes on the task with maybe an occasional glance to the sky.

☙❧

March 20th

THE COST OF PUBLIC EDUCATION

"... which he commanded our forefathers to teach to their children, so the next generation would know them, even the children yet to be born, and they in turn would tell their children"

Psalm 78:5b-6

"I am much afraid that schools will prove to be great gates of hell unless they diligently labor in explaining the Holy Scriptures, engraving them in the hearts of youth. I advise no one to place his child where the Scriptures do not reign paramount. Every institution in which men are not increasingly occupied with the Word of God must become corrupt."

This is quite a powerful quote. Who could have made such a dogmatic statement about the condition of our public schools? Was it some far-right extremist? Perhaps a present-day crusader against liberal infiltration? No, this was a quote of Martin Luther, who, hundreds of years ago saw the prophetic bankruptcy of any educational system that was not built upon the Word of God.

The Word of God is clearly our only standard for belief and practice. Yet, when it comes to the education of our children, some still believe it is not detrimental to school our children under a system that makes no room for the Scriptures and, in some cases, even becomes hostile to them. At best, this confuses our children and at worst, teaches them indifference toward God. No child can learn effectively in an environment of confusion, nor gain wisdom with a heart of indifference, for the fear of God is the beginning of wisdom.

Do the Scriptures reign paramount where your child is educated? Christian school or not, does your school labor diligently in explaining the Holy Scriptures?

If not, are you willing to experiment on your children and take the chance that they will serve their purpose in this generation? As caretakers of their destiny, are you as parents doing all that can be done to lay a foundation built upon the rock that will weather the storms of life?

Perhaps a change is in the wind.

March 21st

FROM GOD'S PERSPECTIVE

"It is better that I go away. Unless I go away, the Counselor will not come, but if I go, I will send him to you"

John 16:7

What a sales job that must have taken. Imagine Jesus trying to convince the disciples that it was better that He go away in order that someone they had never met or would ever be able to see could come. As you could imagine, the disciples struggled with this concept. They said to each other, "What does He mean . . . we do not understand what He is saying."

Very seldom does that which Jesus deems better come wrapped in the packages that we think a better gift should. In our way of thinking, a better gift does not come through death, conflict, loss, suffering or any other perceived negative. But God's ways are not our ways. Though we perceive these gifts as negatives, He perceives them as the initiatory steps that announce that which is better.

David tells us in Psalm 4:1 that he was enlarged in distress. I would prefer that it read, "I was enlarged in success," but it does not. Success often makes us complacent, whereas distress gets us moving. The biblical records repeat a consistent pattern. When the people of God were blessed, they went astray. When they were afflicted, they got back on track. What turned out to be better was not the blessing, but the affliction.

The challenge before us today is to accept God's evaluation of a matter rather than our own. If He considers His way better, can we find the grace to embrace it as such, or will we continue to reject it, opting for that which we have decided is the best?

March 22nd

SOWING AND REAPING

"Do not be deceived, God cannot be mocked. A man reaps what he sows. The one who sows to please his sinful nature, from that nature will reap destruction..."

Galatians 6:7-8

Its from the ground of absolute conviction that the apostle Paul writes, *"Do not be deceived, God **cannot** be mocked."* Notice Paul doesn't say "God will not be mocked or "It's not a good idea to mock God." He says, *"God cannot be mocked."* The sovereignty of God is His place of immunity from man's mockery. Man may do what he is going to do and say whatever he wishes to say, but when all is said and done, God is not the one mocked, man is. God cannot be mocked by man. Though man may try to knock God, His sovereignty shields Him from man's vanity and puts the mockery back onto man.

The law of sowing and reaping is the most basic of all spiritual laws and perhaps the most violated. How many of the situations and circumstances that you currently find yourself in are the result of a violated law? The apostle instructs us that when we sow to please the sinful nature, that very nature will destroy us. When one makes a decision to sow to their selfish nature, selfishness becomes their destruction. If they sow to bitterness, bitterness destroys them. If they sow to discord, that same discord turns on them and becomes their very destruction.

I have observed this law in regard to the sowing of negativity. My observation has been that negative people are quite often sick people. They are those who constantly struggle with some kind of physical ailment. The sickness they struggle with is the result of the sowing of negativity. Those negative seeds that are sown give birth to destruction and that is revealed in physical ailments and emotional struggles.

The answer to this destruction is found in the seed we sow. If we sow to the Spirit we will reap spiritual life. Sow to faith and reap faith. Sow to love and reap love. This is a law that can not be violated for it was established by God Himself and cannot be mocked.

March 23rd

HAVE THEY NOTICED A CHANGE?

"And we, who with unvieled faces all reflect the Lord's glory are all being transformed into his likeness with ever increasing glory"
                                                II Corinthians 3:17-18

In his book, "We've Got a Future," Francis Anfuso makes some very insightful statements. He says, "The church has lost the edge in telling others to change because she refuses to change. Our 180 degree turn at conversion was not meant to be an isolated incident, but the beginning of a new way of life. A life of change. Changing for a Christian should be as familiar as brushing his teeth." (Maybe that is why the church has so many cavities.)

Imagine the change the early believer had to embrace. The disciples had to change from a face to face, day in and day out relationship to Christ to one with the promised Comforter. The profile of the church would change from being 100% Jewish to ultimately 99.9% Gentile. Change was to become a way of life.

How are you with change? Before you answer "just fine," let me ask you a few questions. Do you sit in the same seat every Sunday? Do you fellowship with the same people? Do you sit in the same chair every night at dinner? Do you drive the same route every day to work? Do you shop every week at the same store? Often our response to the question of change is "no problem," but when we take a close examination of our life, we discover we are creatures of habit and often resist change.

Have you changed lately? If you had to convince someone of your change, what would you show them? Would there be enough evidence to convince them? Has change been translated into behavior?

Our responsibility to be salt and light mandates us to lead society into change. In order to do that with integrity, we must become examples of change.

Let us expose our lives to the constant search of the Holy Spirit and allow Him to bring our lives into conformity with Christ. Let us be willing to embrace whatever change is needed in order for that to happen.

֍

March 24th

DESIRE AND PREPARATION

"So then, brothers, stand firm and hold on to the teachings we passed on to you, whether by word of mouth or by letter"

II Thessalonians 2:15

A desire to serve the purposes of the Lord, though noble, is not enough. In order for that desire to be translated into fruitfulness, it must be combined with preparation. The future, we've been told, belongs to those who are prepared for it.

In 1945, Japan surrendered to America and its allies. A few short months after that surrender, General Douglas MacArthur sent an urgent telegram to the executive director of Gideon's International. The telegram reported an incredible hunger for the Gospel and requested 1,000 missionaries and 30 million Bibles.

The Japanese people were open to the Gospel because they perceived the god they worshipped was not powerful enough to defeat the God of America, so they wanted to worship the God of America.

In the weeks that were to follow, the director of Gideon's was grieved with the reality that his organization was not prepared to meet the magnitude of that request. The missionaries and Bibles which eventually were sent, were inadequate to satisfy the spiritual hunger which existed. Because America was unable to teach the Japanese how to worship the true and living God, they began to worship what they perceived to be our god. As a result, the country is now dominated by materialism and secular humanism. This was a window of opportunity which could not be satisfied by desire alone.

What are you being prepared for? What is that "thing" that when Father thought of you, He equipped you to function in that area as no one else can? Now is the season of your preparation. *"Study to show yourself approved, a workman who needeth not to be ashamed."* (II Timothy 2:15)

May it never be said of us that the level of our preparation was inadequate to satisfy the window of opportunity. When the call sounds forth, *"Whom shall I send and who will go for me?"* may the answer be, *"Here I am Lord, send me,"* and may there not be a hesitation due to the lack of our preparation.

March 25th

WHICH FAMILY ARE YOU?

"For this reason I kneel before the Father, from whom His whole family in heaven and on earth derives its name"

Ephesians 3:14-15

In Ephesians 3, the apostle Paul speaks of the families in Heaven and on Earth having a name. Have you ever stopped to ask yourself the question, what is the family name of those in Heaven and on Earth? The Hebrews placed great significance in a name. A name was a representation of a significant event or unique characteristic. Based on that definition, I would like to submit to you a few of the family names that we run into on a regular basis. In fact, these names are so prevalent, they have certainly reached the status of a dynasty or clan.

The first family are those we have all grown to know and appreciate, the Wannabees. You remember the Wannabees. They are the family who is ever wanting, but never getting. Then there are the Needabees. The Needabees are those we meet who are fully aware of what they need, but the problem is they always remain exactly that, in need. Then there are the close cousins of those just mentioned. These are the Couldabeens, the Shouldabeens and the Mightabeens. Fine families these are, but depressing to be around because they always live in the past, dreaming about what could have been and should have been and what might have been.

Though these families are propagating like rabbits and all indications show they may soon outnumber the rest, they are not the names from which the families in Heaven derive their names. The families in Heaven derive their names from the original family that started it all, the Iams. It all began with Father I am, who turned it over to His Son. Since that time, multitudes of Iam families have been born. You can spot this family anywhere. The unique characteristic of this family line is that they do not live in the past dreaming of what used to be or in the future dreaming of what could come. They live in the now, they are the Iams, not the Iwases or the Imightabeens. They seize their destiny, for it is in their blood not to put it off and lose their cutting edge. Theirs is royal blood. They are the Iams.

◈

March 26th

WHAT IS YOUR NAME?

"... I will write on him the name of my God "
Revelation 3:12

In times past, we have spoken of our pursuit of the family name. We have introduced to you the Wannabees and the Gottabees and we contrasted them with the Iams. In the family of God, we find our heritage with the great Iams.

Today, we want to introduce you to two other infamous families, the Whyaskers and the Whataskers.

Surely you have met them both before. The Whyaskers are those who always ask why. To them, everything and everyone is suspect. They know little of trust and even less of the sovereignty of God. Providence is simply a concept, but has little reality in the Whyasker's life. Each trial and every circumstance are greeted with the question, why? Father, why did you let this happen?

In contrast, there are the Whataskers. To this family, the question is not why, but what? To them, motive is not the issue; purpose is. They are not so much interested in why God is allowing trials and circumstances to happen; they want to know what God is trying to produce in them. Sovereignty is a settled issue and providence is a reality. Each trial and every circumstance is greeted with the question, what? Father, what do you want me to learn in this situation?

To which of these two families do you most closely identify? Are you a Whyasker or a Whatasker? I submit to you that, as children of God, we need to be Whataskers. For us the issue is not why, because as children we must trust the motive of our Father and embrace His sovereignty. As children of God, the issue for us is, what? Conformity to the image of Christ is our goal, so the question must be: WHAT?

March 27th

THE PRIORITY OF ONE

"But seek first His kingdom and His righteousness and all these things will be given to you as well"
Matthew 6:33

Everyone talks today about the importance of priorities. From self-help seminars to Sunday sermons, priorities have center stage. But with the new-found interest has also come a multitude of varying opinions as to how that priority list should read. Varying perspectives call for varying priorities. It is what we center our life and philosophy on that will determine the arrangement of these priorities. Those who center their world in the church will say the church is number one. Those who center their lives in career will most certainly defend their jobs as top priority and will have Scripture and verse to defend their case.

To understand the rule and reign of the Kingdom of God is to understand that in setting priorities in this Kingdom, the list begins and stops with one and that is the Kingdom. Jesus instructed us to establish, as our only priority, the Kingdom. He promised that if we would establish the rule and reign of God's Kingdom in our lives as our primary pursuit, He would give us all other things as a result.

Religion breeds confined commitment. Religion always seeks to give God His place. It may give Him a good place. It may give Him His place in the family, His place in the career or even His place in church, but to give God *a* place rather than *the* place is to confine God and miss the mark of the Kingdom's rule. To understand the supremacy of God and His Kingdom is to understand that even giving God first place is to put Him at par with all the others. The Kingdom of God is to transcend all other pursuits in our life and reign as the place. As we exalt the Kingdom of God and unify our lives behind its pursuit, Jesus promised that all the pursuits and things that are necessary to the fulfilling of our destiny would be added to us by His hand.

Whenever we put one of the "things" first, God becomes our servant to fulfill that thing. If family is our first priority, we make God to be the One who serves us in serving our family. If church is number one, God is made to revolve around us as we give our priorities in serving the church. Regardless of how noble these pursuits are, God cannot be reduced to the serving of man or His Kingdom is reduced to a subservient role. God, alone, is almighty and His Kingdom, alone, is first. He is the first and the last, the all in all. Everything we need is found in Him. While the things of this life have their place, God and His Kingdom have been exalted to occupy the place.

❦

Pause for thought:

Where does your list of priorities put the Kingdom of God? God and His Kingdom are a priority of one. Why not simplify the issue by ridding yourself of lesser pursuits and embrace the priority? What will that look like specifically in your life?

March 28th

THE BALANCE OF WEALTH

"After all God can give you everything you need so that you may always have sufficient supply both for yourselves and for giving away to other people"

II Corinthians 9:8-9 (Phillips)

We need to focus on eternal wealth. That is the wealth that we will take with us. Though in the long run, this is the wealth that is most important, be certain that Father is not satisfied with just prospering us with temporal wealth.

Paul makes it quite clear in the above passage that Father's desire is twofold. From the abundant supply of His storehouse, He will give us the power to make wealth for these reasons.

1. FOR OUR ENJOYMENT: Ecclesiastes 5:19 says that God gives man wealth and possessions and enables him to enjoy them and that is a gift from God. It is God's gift to us to enjoy the wealth and possessions He has allowed us to possess.

Money in and of itself is not the root of all evil. It is the love of money that leads to evil. Solomon said, "Whoever loves money never has money enough. Whoever loves wealth is never satisfied with his income." (Ecclesiastes 5:10)

2. TO GIVE AWAY: I Timothy 6:18 says *"Command those who are rich in this present world . . . to be rich in good deeds and to be generous and willing to share."* The abundance of Father's supply is released upon us in order that we might become a channel of His blessing to others. This is a truth that was so clearly illustrated in the early chapter of the book of Acts. As needs arose, the pipeline of Father's blessing and provision began to flow. That pipeline was the fellow members of the body. As God had prospered them, they would sell what they had been blessed with and use their supply for the giving away to other people.

Therein the balance of prosperity is measured. Temporal wealth is not at the expense of eternity, nor is eternal wealth at the expense of the temporal. Both are enjoyed in their proper balance and from the correct perspective which is "enough for yourselves and for giving away to other people."

March 29th

THE FORWARD LOOK

"You ought to live holy and godly lives as you look forward to the day of God and speed its coming"

II Peter 3:12

The Christian walk is a goal-oriented walk. Jesus did not leave us to an aimless journey, but rather He clearly spelled out the goal and then empowered us to reach what He expected.

The forward look is a goal oriented look. It is a look that makes room for time. Though a football team has a touchdown as its goal, it does not expect to make that touchdown in one play. At times, 100-yard touchdowns happen and when they do, all rejoice, but those times are few and far between. Most often the goal is realized after a series of downs that include yards gained and yards lost.

So it is with the Christian life. God has established Christlikeness as the goal. But to become like Christ does not happen overnight. Christlikeness is a life-long process that happens one step at a time. Little by little, with God's means of accomplishment. As long as we are moving, we will reach the goal. The only cause for alarm is when the process stops because we refuse to move.

As the process unfolds, we must remember that our acceptance in God is not based on our performance; it is based on our position. God's love for us is unconditional. He loves us, not because of anything we do. He loves us because our lives are hidden in Christ. When He looks at us, He sees His Son and because He loves His Son, He loves us. The place of our progress does not better our standing or make us more loved. We are loved and have good standing only because of Jesus. We progress, not to be accepted, but to be effective and fulfill His desire for us.

So, as you look forward to the day, do so from a position of confidence and assurance of acceptance.

○○○

March 30th

SONS OF THE KINGDOM

"... The good seed stands for sons of the kingdom..."
Matthew 13:38

*F*ather's answer to the needs of this world was a Son. *"For God so loved the world He gave His one and only Son."* (John 3:16) To act as a son or daughter of God is the highest call a believer can carry.

There are many believers in the Kingdom of God who, by their behavior, would not be identified as sons. Though they would be defined as sons of God by position, they would not be identified as sons by behavior. Paul makes it quite clear in Romans 8 that we are all sons by virtue of our new birth. He goes on to say in Romans 8:14 that those who are led by the Spirit are sons of God. To be led by self-interest means though you are a son by position; you are not acting as a son by virtue of behavior.

"For you did not receive a spirit that makes you a slave again to fear, but you received the Spirit of sonship." (Romans 8:15) Sonship is an aspect of who the Holy Spirit is. Sonship is not just a good teaching; it is an impartation of the Holy Spirit. When you say someone has a spirit of fear, it is because they consistently act fearful. So to have the Spirit of sonship is to continually act as a son. The Spirit of sonship working in us takes who we are by position and makes us the same by behavior.

It is maturity that qualifies us for the full rights of sonship, not position. Paul tells us in Galatians 4 that as long as the one who is a son by position is a child; he is no different than a slave. To receive the full rights of sonship, the child must be taught and trained by his guardians. Then when the child qualifies by maturity, he comes into the full rights of Sonship.

There are many in the Kingdom of God who are sons by new birth, but slaves by behavior. The Holy Spirit comes to the church today in search of sons. He comes as a guardian to train us. He comes to discipline us. He comes to transform us from children into sons. This process of becoming sons is the Holy Spirit's doing. Sonship is a Spirit that works within us. It is not about us mustering up new levels of willpower to become. It is simply about yielding to the Spirit of sonship within and allowing Him to bring us into the presence of a loving Father where we are changed into the likeness of Christ.

Sonship is a place of deep rest and confident trust. Sons trust in their Father's ability to do what He promised He would do. As a son, I can rest in the reality that my Father is able to do abundantly more than anything I could imagine. He is ever able to change me from the child I am and bring me into the full rights of a son.

⚭

Pause for thought:

In what ways are you still behaving as a child or a slave? Being a son or daughter, how do you see your relationship to Father God?

March 31st

FROM CHILD TO SON

"For unto us a child is born and unto us a son is given"

Isaiah 9:6

As children of God, we have been born into the family of God. When we were brought in, God changed more than just our outward environment. He also changed our bloodline. He delivered us from the kingdom of darkness and brought us over in the Kingdom of His Son. He changed everything about us. Though the bloodline has been changed, we are still in need of coming into the maturity of sons.

Although Jesus was the incarnate God, He was still a child in need of becoming a son. The government Jesus was intended to carry could not be placed upon the shoulders of a child. Jesus was required of God to grow even as the Galations 4 child had to grow with his tutors. As He grew in stature He became the son given. To be given, you must become a son.

When Father announced His pleasure of Christ at His baptism, it was more than just a reiteration of identity. When Father declared *"This is my beloved son in whom I am well pleased,"* (Matthew 3:17) He was declaring that Jesus was no longer just a *"child born,"* but that He had qualified as a *"son given."* Jesus had satisfied His Father's requirements of sonship. Jesus had carried His Father's heart. He had selflessly given Himself to fulfill the covenant they had made in eternity past for Father to get what He desired. He is not a son in the biblical sense who has not absorbed His Father's spirit, heart, vision and purpose, desiring to please Him in all things. It is the carrying of our Father's heart that qualifies us to be mature and ready to run the Father's business.

As it was for Jesus, so it is for us. We come in as a *"child born,"* but God's desire is that we would become a *"son given."* As we yield to the work of the Holy Spirit, obeying Him in all things, we can expect the grace of God to work in us to become a son.

April 1st

THE APPOINTED TIME

"For the revelation awaits an appointed time; it speaks of the end and will not prove false. Though it linger, wait for it; it will certainly come and will not delay"

Habakkuk 2:3

Dreams are a gift from God. To each and every man a dream is given. Cursed is the man who has no dream; challenged is the man who does.

Dreams come to us in stages. Conceiving the dream is exciting. Possessing the dream is Heaven. But stewarding the dream is life. It is in the stage of stewardship that most dreams are aborted. Aborted due to a misconception of God's timing. Dreams have a way of lingering. From the moment of conception to the moment of possession is that period called "time." It is during this period of waiting that we must learn to steward the dream and not forsake it for a self-induced religious substitute.

Timing is everything in the Kingdom of God. God always waits for the appointed time. We read in Galatians 4 that at the appointed time, God sent His Son. The Book of Acts tells us that the Heavens contain Christ until the appointed time. God works by appointment only. The revelation awaits an appointed time and God keeps his own appointment book.

Waiting is our family way. God has waited an eternity for His corporate Christ to come forth. While we wait for the appointed time, we are tested by the dream and tested for the dream. While we wait, God works. During the time of waiting, the dream matures and becomes clearer. What we received in part matures and so does our ability to represent it. While we wait for the dream, we are enlarged. Waiting is a necessary step in the process. Waiting is not a negative aspect of the dream; rather, it is quite positive. While we wait, God works. He works in us to process us. So in the process of waiting, we become all that is necessary to faithfully represent the dream we carry. Delays in the Kingdom of God are not determined in terms of timing, but in terms of becoming. Timing is not defined in terms of hours and days. Timing is defined in terms of Christlikeness and transformation. When God sees Christlikeness in us, the appointed time will come forth.

So be assured that as you wait, God is working on your behalf. Though the revelation begins, it will certainly come, so wait patiently.

April 2nd

PROPHET AND LOSS

"But whatsoever was to my profit I now consider loss for the sake of Christ. What is more, I consider everything a loss compared to the surpassing greatness of knowing Christ Jesus my Lord"

Philippians 3:7-8

To be a prophet in the Kingdom of God, you must first be a loss. God is not interested in self-made men. We serve a backward Kingdom. In this Kingdom, the way up is down and profit is defined as loss.

Christlikeness begins with loss. To gain Christ begins with the losing of our own self-determining ways. Man's way is to determine himself through his defined goals. Once his goals are clearly defined, he sets his prescribed course and then through self determination and lots of willpower, he sets out to run his course. God's way is quite the opposite. The Kingdom of God is not received on the basis of self determination, but on the basis of self surrender. In God's Kingdom, the Holy Spirit defines our destiny and sets our course. Once our course is set, He strategically guides us through a lifetime of surrender and loss.

The pathway of our journey is strewn with the discard of self-righteousness, self-interest, self-centeredness and anything else that finds its focus in self. At any place in the journey where God's will crosses our will, that place is marked with loss. To progress beyond that mark, we must lose. We must lose that thing that crosses with God's desire or the progress of our spiritual journey. No, we do not lose our salvation; we just stop our pursuit.

"To gain Christ," as the apostle Paul put it, our whole lives must be unified behind this desire. To simply possess an intellectual intent will not fulfill our desire. To gain Christ, our entire being, spirit, soul and body must unify behind our desire and move in the direction of that desired end. To do that requires loss. It requires the loss of sin. It requires the loss of those subtle things that so easily beset us. It requires the loss of sleep, recreation, pride, reputation, and the list goes on and on. You say, "Well, that's a lot of loss." No, not in comparison to what is gained. In the comparison of gaining Christ, these things are not a loss at all. As the apostle put it, they are garbage in comparison of knowing Christ and becoming one with Him.

Are you willing to face loss in order to become a prophet? The greater the prophet, the greater the loss. It is a backward Kingdom.

April 3rd

KISSERS OR CLEAVERS

"Then Orpah kissed her mother-in-law good-by, but Ruth clung to her"

Ruth 1:14

It is often said that relationships are the most valuable things in life. While this statement holds a measure of truth, it is not entirely true. It is not relationships in general that are of such great value. Everybody has relationships. Some of them are good and some are bad. We have a relationship with our spouse. We have a relationship with our dentist. We have a relationship with our dog and we have a relationship with God. Relationships in and of themselves are just a form. What determines the value of the relationship is its quality, its longevity and its purpose.

History is not a testimony to man's inability to sustain relationships over a long period of time. It is not our ability to enter into relationship that presents the problem, it is our ability to sustain that relationship and keep it focused forward on its eternal purpose. Left to ourselves our tendency is to sabatage what God joins together and become self-destructive.

Loyalty has fast become a lost virtue in the age that we live. Abandonment is the spirit of this age. The philosophical mindset of the day no longer values loyalty and relational committment.

It is this spirit of abandonment and relational disloyalty that the story of Ruth addresses. Orpah abandoned her relationship to Naomi with a kiss. Ruth on the other hand, clung to Naomi and rejected the foundation of mutual benefit as the basis for their relationship. Whether intuitively or by revelation, Ruth saw that destiny and the joining of God was the basis of her relationship to Naomi.

Destiny and relationships are inseperable. It was the destiny of Ruth to become the great Grandmother of King David and for her line to ultimately lead to the Messiah. But that destiny was unseparably tied to her relationship to Naomi. Without Naomi, Ruth would have never met Boaz. It took Ruth and Boaz to produce their son Obed who gave birth to Jesse who gave birth to David.

Kissers are those who forsake their destiny. Cleavers are those who guarantee it. Kissers are those who with the spirit of this age in them, go the way of separation at the point of conflict. Cleavers are those with the Spirit of Christ who inspite of the conflict, embrace the joining of the Lord and cleave to those they have been joined to.

The extent of our destiny will be determined by the depth of our localty to those God has joined us to and by the longevity of that joining. Ruth clung to a person, not to a thing or a concept. Covenant relationships are personal relationships. They are made with real, live, flesh and blood people.

Are you a kisser or a cleaver? Is your tendency to run in the face of relational conflict or work out what might need to be sorted? Your destiny may be predicated upon that relationship that is now being tested. Who knows what that relationship may bring forth? For the sake of God's eternal purpose, cleave to those the sovereignty of God has joined you to. Recognize the tactics of the enemy to divide you.

ଔଓ

April 4th

THE INCOMPARABLY GREAT POWER

"... who through the Spirit of holiness was declared with power to be the Son of God by his resurrection from the dead: Jesus Christ our Lord."

Romans 1:4

How exciting it is to once again celebrate the resurrection of our Lord Jesus. The grave could not contain Him. The power He possesses is a power that cannot be confined nor limited in any fashion. That power serves as a constant reminder that what He has spoken will come to pass regardless of the obstacles that stand before it.

Lest our rejoicing is limited to one Sunday a year, let us remind ourselves of what that power secured for us, His church. Paul stated it this way:

> *"I pray that the eyes of your heart may be enlightened in order that you may know His incomparably great power for us who believe. That power is like the working of His mighty strength which He exerted in Christ when He raised Him from the dead."*
>
> Ephesians 1:18-20

How much power did it take to raise Christ from the dead? We can only speculate. But one thing is certain: However much power it took, that power is ours. Ours, not to consume upon our own lusts, but ours to enable us to live up to all that our Father calls for.

What a deal. What He expects, He gives resurrection power in order for it to be accomplished. There is nothing He requires for which He does not give the power for it to be realized. With a deal like that, there is never a need to reduce the standard, only to tap into more power.

Part of our glorious inheritance is that resurrection power. His victory was so absolute, so complete, that it has passed right through the generations and is applicable to us today.

So whatever our need, let us remember the answer is *"Christ in you the hope of glory."*

April 5th

THE ROCK OF PERSONAL DISCOVERY

"I keep asking that the God of our Lord Jesus Christ, the glorious Father, may give you the Spirit of wisdom and revelation, so that you may know him better"

Ephesians 1:17

The triumphal entry that took place on that first "Palm Sunday" is the tragic story of man's fickleness. One day the people were crazy with praise and adoration for Jesus. With loud voices they cried, *"Blessed is the King who comes in the name of the Lord."* Impulsively, they took off their cloaks and lined the road to Bethany with them. But then, just a few days later, many of those same people who cried *"blessed"* were now crying, *"crucify Him, crucify Him."*

Fickleness comes in the absence of personal discovery. Those who had personal revelation of who Jesus was stood with Him until the end. But those who followed Him because of what others had said were swayed by the direction of public opinion. As long as public opinion was favorable, they cried *"blessed,"* but as soon as the tide of public poll turned, so did they.

What is the level of your personal discovery? Is your knowledge and relationship to Jesus built on the rock of personal discovery or is it built upon the fickle sands of what others say? A good indicator of your true condition is worship. If you are built upon the rock of personal discovery, you will worship Him first for who He is, then secondly for what He does. But if you are built upon the sand of what others say, your worship is limited to what He has done because you have no revelation of who He is.

"The whole crowd of disciples began joyfully to praise God in loud voices for all the miracles they had seen." (Luke 19:37)

Not knowing Him on a relational basis, they could only praise Him for the things He had done.

As we recognize the triumphal entry, why not allow Him to triumphantly enter your heart in a new way. If your relationship to Him or understanding of Him is based on others and not personal discovery, allow Him to enter you anew and put your life on the rock of personal discovery.

April 6th

LET IT RAIN, LET IT POUR

"Ask the Lord for rain in springtime"

Zechariah 10:1

"*You have not because you ask not,*" declares the book of James. Our receiving runs in direct proportion to our asking. If we expect to receive the spring rain, we will have to ask for it.

Everyone has experienced the emotion of spring. We call it spring fever. The sun comes out, the temperature increases and we would like to throw all responsibility to the wind and enjoy life. However, the evidence of spring is more than an emotion. The evidence of spring is not just something felt; it is sun. It is seen in the swelling of the buds, the blooming of the bulbs, the awakening of dormancy. It is a tangible reality, not just a subjective emotion.

Well, the evidence of the spiritual spring is also evident. The dormancy of our winter is past, the swelling of fruitfulness is all among us and the evidence of increase is seen by all. While we rejoice and take great courage in this fact, we stand the risk of short-circuiting the visitation of God if we do not follow His instruction.

The word given in II Kings 12 declares, *"Strike the arrow to the ground."* A complete victory is the goal. Now the Lord says, *"Ask for rain in the springtime."* Rain in the Scriptures is symbolic of spiritual blessing. It is not enough to just enjoy the spring; we must ask God for the outpouring of His blessing in the spring in order that His divine visitation would be sustained for its appointed time.

For some time, the Holy Spirit has been laying a foundation of prayer and intercession. Our churches will be houses of prayer. We need to ask the Lord for rain in our time of spring. Let us ask Father for the blessings that will sustain this current visitation. Our desire is not for the blessing that we would consume upon ourselves, but rather the blessings that would further the work of the Kingdom in our churches, in our cities and in the world.

☙❧

April 7th

THE SON GIVEN

"And a voice from heaven said, "This is my Son whom I love; with him I am well pleased."

Matthew 3:17

This incredible declaration over Jesus was not just a reiteration from Father of Christ's identity. No, this was a declaration to be sounded throughout time and eternity that Jesus was no longer just the child born. Now, through obedience, He had qualified to become the Son given.

Isaiah prophesied in chapter 9 that unto us a child would be born and unto us a Son would be given and He would be called the everlasting Father. Although Jesus was the incarnate God, He was still a child in need of becoming a son. The government that He was expected to carry could in no way be placed upon the shoulders of a child. Jesus was in need of maturing and growing from the place of a child into the full responsibility of being a son.

"When the time had fully come, God sent his Son." (Galatians 4:4) Father is desirous of sending sons. If Sonship was the pattern for Jesus' sending, surely it is the same for us. God is desirous of developing in us the attributes of a son. Childhood is automatic, Sonship is not. Childhood is a guarantee, Sonship is a choice. I am born as a child and if I so choose, I become a son. You can be forty years old and still be a child. So it is in the Spirit. You can be saved for decades and never become a son. In the Spirit, stages of maturity are behavior determined. That is, I am not a son just because I have been saved thirteen years. I am a son only when I believe as a son. This is why the apostle Paul said in Galatians 4 that a son is no different from a slave unless he grows up and matures. What qualified the son for his inheritance is the fact that he puts childish ways aside and behaves himself as a son. Then and only then does he come into the full rights of his Sonship. (Galatians 4:5)

Sonship is not just a position. It is also a behavior. In Romans 8:15, Paul says we have received the Spirit of Sonship. The Spirit of Sonship expresses himself in behavior. As the Spirit of Sonship is released in me, He affects everything I see, everything I say and all that I do. The Spirit of Sonship is like a pair of colored glasses. When they are on me, everything I see is affected by those glasses. Everything I see takes on a different perspective, because the glasses cause change. So it is with the Spirit of Sonship. Once I see Sonship, I see everything differently. I no longer strive to be accepted; I am a son, I am accepted.

I no longer perform; I am a Son, I need not prove anything. I am no longer independent; I am a son. The Spirit of adoption is alive within me.

ം

Pause for thought:

Are you behaving as a Son? How are you co-operating with the Holy Spirit to mature you and call you up to be a son or daughter?

April 8th

RESURRECTION POWER

". . . and his incomparably great power for us who believe. That power is like the working of his mighty strength, which he exerted in Christ when he raised him from the dead . . ."

Ephesians 1:19-20

The early success of the Christian Church is an historic phenomenon that must be explained. We are told that shortly after the death of Jesus, the disciples were hiding in Jerusalem behind locked doors. Fear had taken them off the streets and relegated them to the back room. They were locked out of society, hiding in fear of the Jews.

After three years of intensive ministry, there was not an over abundance of fruit to show for Christ's labor (at least not on the surface). There were 11 disciples who still were adherents to The Way. It seems that the total was only 120. After all the miracles, profound teachings, and people raised from the dead, all that lined up to be counted were 120, and even they were far from being able bodied representatives. They were hurt, disillusioned, torn by the loss of the One in which they had placed all their hope.

However, just a few days later, things took a dramatic twist. The 120 grew to 3,120. Shortly after that, the number of men reached 5,000. The fear was transformed to boldness, the hurt turned to power, and the loss produced a resolve. These simple unlearned fishermen were turning their known world upside down. They were taking Jerusalem by storm and soon the entire world would feel their impact.

But why? Why the transformation? What was the secret to their successes and the key to their power? In a word, it was RESURRECTION. That single event transformed the early church from weak, fearful and disillusioned into the most powerful force this world has ever seen other than Christ himself. The only explanation to the success of the early church is the resurrection. According to Ephesians 1:20, the same power that raised Christ from the dead is also at work in us.

The transformation continues . . .

☙

April 9th

THE SAME POWER

How exciting it is to once again celebrate the resurrection of our Lord Jesus. The grave could not contain Him. The power He possesses is a power that cannot be confined nor limited in any fashion. That power serves as a constant reminder that what He has spoken will come to pass regardless of the obstacles that stand before it.

Lest our rejoicing be limited to one Sunday a year, let us remind ourselves of what that power secured for us, His church. Paul stated it this way:

> *"I pray that the eyes of your heart may be enlightened in order that you may know . . . His incomparably great power for us who believe. That power is like the working of His mighty strength which He exerted in Christ when He raised Him from the dead . . ."* (Ephesians 1:18-20)

How much power did it take to raise Christ from the dead? We can only speculate the answer to that question. But one thing is certain: However much power it took, that power is ours. Ours, not to consume upon our own lusts, but ours to enable us to live up to all for which our Father calls.

What a deal! What He expects, He gives resurrection power in order for it to be accomplished. There is nothing He requires that He does not give the power in order for it to be realized. With a deal like that, there is never a need to reduce the standard, only to tap into more power.

Part of our glorious inheritance is that resurrection power. His victory was so absolute, so complete, that it has passed right through the generations and is applicable to us today.

So, whatever our need, let us remember the answer is *"Christ in you, the hope of glory."*

☙❧

April 10th

WHEN GOD HIDES

"I looked for the one my heart loves; I looked for him but did not find him. I will get up now and go about the city, through its streets and squares; I will search for the one my heart loves. So I looked for him but did not find him"

Song of Songs 3:1-2

Sometimes it seems as if Christ is hiding Himself. The sweetness of fellowship and close communion that you have always experienced, seems to fade into silence and obscurity. You search for Him, but He cannot be found. You pray, but He does not seem to answer. You read, but receive no revelation. You go to the meetings and leave without any apparent impartation. You long for that sense where He is so near to you and you are so dear to Him.

To those who have had a functional relationship, this dilemma of silence is nothing to be alarmed at. But to the one who has known of the relationship of deep intimacy, silence is of grave concern. When the voice of the one you love is silent, your heart begins to die. Your spirit begins to cry out in desire. As Solomon wrote of the lover for the beloved, you begin to search. You search the cities and its squares in hopes of finding that voice of intimacy once again. Your prayer turns to a cry of desire. Desperation begins to work its power in you.

Salvation is God finding us. Intimacy is our finding God. When God seems to be hiding it is time to forsake all in search of Him whom your heart loves. We must never become satisfied with intimate memories. God does not intend to be a past lover, but a present lover. Often He hides Himself to heighten our desire. He hides Himself to deepen our pursuit. He hides Himself to teach us to forsake all else in pursuit of Him.

"Scarcely had I passed them when I found the one my heart loves." (Song of Songs 3:4) Keep searching. You will find Him as you seek Him with all of your heart.

☙❧

April 11th

TWO STRIKES AGAINST ME AND A FAST BALL ON THE WAY

"From the sixth hour until the ninth hour darkness came over all the land"

Matthew 27:45

What a way to end. Not exactly what you would expect from a King trying to establish His Kingdom. Go out in a blaze of glory, rewind this whole thing, save the best for the last, raise Lazarus from the dead, then call for the legion of angels to take you away just as they are about to do you in. (Speilberg style)

On that ground, the disciples had to pick up the pieces and establish what they were commissioned to do.

We live in a world that has trained us to live by virtue of odds. Like spiritual bookies, we evaluate the odds and if the odds seem to be in our favor, we perceive God is giving us the go.

While that may be an acceptable mode of operandi for the world, it is not at all how Kingdom sons and daughters are to make decisions and conduct their lives.

The resurrection serves as a constant reminder that Jehovah God is an odds buster. It teaches us that when we have two strikes against us and a fast ball on the way, God is ready to come to bat. If during the sixth to ninth hour of darkness we wait for Him, we will see the results of resurrection power.

All of this is just a nice Easter message until it is measured against the circumstances of your past and the difficulties of your present. It may still be your sixth or ninth hour, but whatever hour it is, you might be standing on miracle ground and not even know it.

When we are in the tomb of our circumstances, we must never focus on the stone. We must focus on the promise—because somehow, regardless of the darkness of the hour, that stone is going to roll away.

Our God is not limited by the odds. He drives the bookies crazy, for He prefers the decks stacked against Him. Then there is no question as to who deserves the glory and who suffers defeat.

April 12th

THE CROWNING EVENT

"'Don't be alarmed,' he said. "You are looking for Jesus of Nazarene, who was crucified. He has risen! He is not here. See the place where they laid him"

Mark 16:6

Resurrection day is no ordinary event. It represents so much more than a good excuse to buy the children new outfits or one of those few days they can eat all the candy they want. Easter Sunday or better said, Resurrection Sunday, is the single most important event of Christendom. More important than Christmas, for without the resurrection, Christ was just another baby born in controversy. It is more important than His life and teaching, for without the resurrection, His life and teaching were simply that of a great prophet. It is even more pivotal than the crucifixion, for without the resurrection, He is not distinguished from the two thieves who died with Him. The resurrection, which we celebrate, is the single event of all history that distinguishes Jesus Christ from every other prophet who ever claimed deity or revelation and substantiates every word uttered from His mouth.

He stated boldly, *"I am the way, the truth and the life; no one comes to the Father except through me."* (John 14) Without the resurrection, these are the words of a self-deceived egomaniac. But with the resurrection, these are words that every man and every woman must either believe or try to discredit. If they attempt to discredit them, the one thing that looms ever before them and loomed ever before Christ's critics is, where is the body?

Oh, this is no insignificant event that can be masqueraded with chocolate bunnies and speckled eggs. The resurrection of Jesus Christ is the crowning event of history that every individual must reckon with, for by it, all are incriminated. If we embrace it with all of its ramifications, we are brought into relationship with Jesus Christ and eternal fellowship with God. But, if we ignore it or reject it, we will suffer eternal separation where there is *"weeping and gnashing of teeth."*

If you have never considered the words of Christ, allow the resurrection to prove their validity. Valid truth requires a response, so respond to His words by turning from your sin and accepting Jesus Christ as your way to the Father.

છ૪૭

April 13th

UNGODLY BELIEFS

"We demolish arguments and every pretension that sets itself up against the knowledge of God and we take captive every thought to make it obedient to Christ"

II Corinthians 10:5

The mind is our primary arena of battle. We wrestle not against flesh and blood but against principalities and powers. This wrestling is not a physical struggle. The battle is spiritual and most often our mind is the field of conflict.

The center of this conflict focuses on ungodly beliefs that exalt themselves against the knowledge of God. These ungodly beliefs are mindsets that trap us into certain patterns that prevent a sustained growth and perpetual movement deeper into the purposes of God. They work as grids over our minds that reinterpret the truth of God's Word and add a "yeah-but" to everything God says. "Yeah, God's Word is true, but it doesn't work for me." "Yeah, He forgives, but He won't forgive this one." "Yeah, everyone else's marriage may change, but mine won't." Yes, the Word of God is all powerful, but our ungodly beliefs rob us of the faith to appropriate God's Word and renders it ineffective as pertaining to my experience.

Ungodly beliefs also work through the mindsets of fear, unbelief, shame, self pity, hatred and unforgiveness. Generational sin, bad choices, hurts of the past, etc, produce in us these ungodly beliefs. Once they are established they give the devil a foothold to reinterpret God's promise to work in our lives and set us free.

Ungodly beliefs are lies that need to be taken captive. Our freedom is tied to our ability to demolish these arguments and take the ungodly beliefs captive. We take them captive through discernment. We discern that our mindset is contrary to the truth of God's Word. Upon seeing the lie, we confess the sin of unbelief and appropriate God's forgiveness. Forgiven, we stand and declare the truth of God's Word as pertaining to the ungodly belief. In declaring the truth of God's Word, we take back the ground upon which the devil has erected a stronghold.

God's Word alone is true. Examine your beliefs in light of God's Word and let His Word frame your perspective of truth.

April 14th

A TIME FOR PUTTING ASIDE

"When I was a child, I talked like a child, I thought like a child, I reasoned like a child. When I became a man, I put childish ways behind me"

I Corinthians 13:11

To become a man in the Kingdom of God is not automatic. Though we are born children, not all become men. Maturity in the Kingdom is not age determined, but behavior determined. I am mature only when I act mature. I am no longer a child only when I have consistently put childish ways behind me. Maturity comes as the result of purposeful decision. The decision centers on the purposeful action of putting childish ways behind.

Many remain in the place of childhood because they refuse to grow up and put childish ways aside. The "Toys R Us" jingle, "I don't want to grow up; I'm a Toys R Us kid" is quite evident in the Kingdom as well. As long as childish ways are left to remain in our lives, we will never mature into the fullness of God's desire.

Childish ways are not necessarily sinful ways. Childish ways may simply be things that were appropriate in our lives when we were children, but now that maturity is God's focus, they must be put behind us. It is quite obvious that sinful ways are to be put behind us. No one would argue about this. It is the less obvious ways that cause us to stumble. It is those childish ways that are not clearly defined as sinful, but nevertheless are wrongful behaviors for the place God desires to bring us.

We know we are coming into maturity when we no longer determine our behavior on the basis of right and wrong, but rather on the basis of if it is appropriate for the destiny that is mine. Maturity is the ability to regulate our decisions on the basis of expedience instead of legality. As the apostle Paul stated, *"All things are lawful, but not all things are expedient."* (I Corinthians 10:23) To come into full maturity requires the willing yielding over of things that from a legal standpoint are certainly permissible, but from an expedience standpoint are not advisable.

For some, these childish ways are sports. There is certainly nothing spiritually illegal about sports, but if your focus on sports has become all consuming, it will keep you childish and prevent your full maturity. For others, it may be eating habits, television, sleep, entertainment, humor, possessions. These are all things that in and of themselves are permissible, but when placed in the pathway of maturity become stumbling blocks for us. Perhaps they are not for others, but they are for me and if it keeps me stumbling, I must put it behind me.

૮૩৪૦

Pause for thought:

Is it time for you to put some things aside? Has the Holy Spirit been putting His finger on some issues in your life? If so, simply yield, put those things behind you and come into the maturity God so desires.

April 15th

A SENSE OF URGENCY

"For Christ's love compels us . . . those who live should no longer live for themselves but for Him who died for them and was raised up again"

II Corinthians 5:14-15

Religion dulls our sense of urgency and redefines our focus of priority. Religion, which can be defined as an empty form without the presence of Christ, is a thief. It robs us of godly intention and keeps us forever enslaved to issues of no consequence.

Religion exists upon substitutions. Unable to produce the substance of reality, it feeds upon shadows. Religion substitutes love with duty, purpose with performance and urgency with complacency. To be full of the love of Christ is to be filled with a sense of urgency. Where there is agape love, there is no complacency. God's love and our complacency cannot cohabit. When we are touched by the love of Christ, we are filled with a sense of urgency. His love brings with it a compulsion. It produces a sense of urgency that becomes a motivating factor to override fear, indifference and any other excuse that keeps us from stepping out and risking obedience.

What the church lacks today is a sense of urgency. The dullness of religion and the redefining of priorities have left us in a state of complacency and indifference. The compelling love that Paul spoke of is often just a concept. The motivation that comes from that compelling love is absent from our experience and behavior. What the church needs today is to be rectified with that compelling love. That level of love will bring with it an urgency for the unsaved. It will stir the same compassion Jesus was stirred with when He saw the multitudes as sheep without a shepherd.

When that kind of compulsion grips our heart, propriety is cast to the wind. When a sense of urgency has your heart, fears pale in significance. The "I can'ts" that once limited you, do so no longer. The reasoning and rationalizing that once determined your behavior are now replaced by emotion. The emotion of the urgent enables you to do things you've never done before. Fears are overcome with boldness. Excuses are replaced with results. Dreams become realities. We are no longer living for ourselves, but we are living for Him.

Some who live only for themselves will never possess a sense of urgency.

To live for Christ is to live in the urgent. It is to live above our fears. It is to live above our indifferences and our complacencies. To live for Christ is to live in the vital and exciting.

A sense of urgency comes by way of impartation. As we acknowledge our complacency, Christ comes to replace that indifference with His urgency. Hard hearts and cold love are replaced with compassion. Behavior that was once ruled by fear, is no longer. A law that once kept us from godly desire is overruled by a higher law. The law of urgency now becomes our driving force.

Pause for thought:

Ask God today to replace the limitation of human love with the limitless compulsion of Christ's love.

April 16th

A FORCE OF THREE

"And the things you have heard me say in the presence of many witnesses entrust to reliable men who will also be qualified to teach others"

II Timothy 2:2

The nature of the Kingdom of God is to build beyond yourself. Those who carry the heart and nature of God never build for just themselves. God's nature is generational. His focus never begins or ends with one generation. Standing outside of time, God is able to see the beginning from the end, and in so doing, build "what is" from the perspective of "what shall be."

In the Old Testament, God often identified Himself as the God of three generations. He is referred to as the God of Abraham, Isaac and Jacob. God has stored up the generations in the heart of man. With each person comes direct responsibility of three generations. The treasure God gives to one generation must be faithfully passed on to the second, who will impart it to the third. Though we each carry a direct responsibility for three generations in our hearts, our responsibility does not begin or end with three. The three generations simply identify our place in the wall that God is building throughout time. What motivates us to labor on that wall is the fact that our accountability reaches back as far as Abraham, and reaches as far forward as eternity. When we catch a glimpse of the ancient path and the eternal highway, our three generations take on added significance.

The Gospel story can be clearly seen as the story of a father and a son. The pattern by which God builds is the pattern of a family. Fathers formulate the vision. Sons demonstrate the vision. Grandsons authenticate the vision. It takes the fortitude of a father to persevere through the storm of formulation. It takes the zeal of a son to pay the cost of demonstration. It takes the integrity of a grandson to handle the glory of authentication.

Are you building beyond yourself? Can you see the three generations within you, and in seeing them, live your life beyond yourself?

☙❧

April 17th

THE UNPARDONABLE SIN

"Forgive us our debts as we also have forgiven our debtors . . . for if you forgive men when they sin against you, your heavenly father will also forgive you. But if you do not forgive men their sins, your father will not forgive your sins"

Matthew 6:12,14

Much speculation has been given over the years as to exactly what the unpardonable sin that Jesus spoke of is. Some have said suicide because one who commits suicide commits murder and has no opportunity to confess their sin before dying. Others have differing opinions for differing reasons.

Though Jesus never described in obvious detail what the unpardonable sin is, what he describes in the above passage is quite concerning. With simple clarity, Jesus said if we do not forgive, we can not be forgiven. Without being forgiven, we will in no way receive our eternal reward. Consequently, many commentators believe the unpardonable sin to be an unforgiving spirit. If we do not forgive, we can not be forgiven. It is not that Father would not pardon us; He can not pardon us if unforgiveness is harbored in our hearts.

Unforgiveness is a slow death. To harbor unforgiveness is to experience death on the installment plan. Unforgiveness manifests itself in progressive stages of sickness, disease and mental health. Over the years, I have seen the results of unforgiveness and the lives of those who refuse to let go. Slowly they turn into negative people who begin to face a continual stream of misfortune. This misfortune may reveal itself in chronic sickness from headaches to panic disorders to back problems. Soon the person becomes a slave to his unforgiveness.

To withhold forgiveness from someone is to become enslaved to them. To not forgive the one who wronged us is to give that person control over our lives. They control us in that our focus is always on them. Our decisions are determined by whether or not it will involve them. Our devotion to Christ is robbed because our focus is directed to the person who did the wrong. Unforgiveness becomes an all-consuming focus. Consequently, the person who wronged us wins twice, once in the wrongdoing, twice in the controlling of our focus. Do not give anybody control over your life, especially someone who has wronged you. Forgive them, and in so doing you will open the way for forgiveness to flow to you and give God an opportunity to deal with the wrongdoing and execute vengeance.

April 18th

THE HOLY SPIRIT

"How be it when he, the Spirit of truth, is come, he will guide you into all truth, for he will not speak for himself"

John 16:13

This has been called the age of the Holy Spirit. With Jesus at the right hand of God, the Holy Spirit has been sent to guide us into all truth and reveal the heart of God to His children.

But, oh how misunderstood the work and the person of the Holy Spirit is. Some see Him as an "it." For some He is just a manifestation. For others He is just a gift. But the Holy Spirit is not an "it," or just a manifestation, or a gift. The Holy Spirit is a person, who in His coming, brings manifestation and gifts, but He is a person. He is God. The Holy Spirit is the third member of the Trinity who plays center stage in the work of the church. His focus is to reveal the mystery of God and empower the saints to do the work of ministry.

The Holy Spirit is the most neglected member of the Godhead. Many interpreted the verse *"He will not speak of Himself"* (John 16:13) to mean that the Holy Spirit wants no personal attention. Consequently, we focus our attention on Father and Jesus and have many times remained ignorant or ill-informed concerning the work of the Holy Spirit. *"He will not speak of Himself"* does not mean he will never speak about Himself, for the Holy Spirit speaks of Himself over 200 times in the Scriptures. The more accurate understanding of this phrase is that the Holy Spirit does not speak out of His own resources, but speaks what He hears the Father say. A misinterpretation of this verse has led to a de-emphasizing of the Holy Spirit's work. As a result, we have suffered from a lack of knowledge of the very one who has been sent to reveal the Father and guide us into all truth.

Do you know the Holy Spirit as a person? Have you ever developed a personal relationship with Him? He is your guide. He is your teacher. Why not start one today?

April 19th

PLAYING GOD

"Don't be afraid. Am I in the place of God?"
Genesis 50:19

In all the Christian plays I have been to over my lifetime, I have never yet met someone who played a good Jesus. The character of Jesus has got to be the most difficult role to play. Everybody has an opinion as to how Jesus should be portrayed, and no matter how one plays the part, they never meet everyone's expectation. For some the actor's hair is too long, for others his face is too short. To some the character is too weak, for others it is too strong. To be cast as Jesus could very well be a career-ending part because the fact is, nobody plays God well, except Himself.

Joseph clearly understood that no man is capable of playing God. Implied by Joseph's question to his brothers is the reality that anytime we withhold forgiveness or entertain resentment, we step into a realm that God reserves only for Himself. It is in forgiveness that we are reminded that we are mere men who have been forgiven, and he who has been forgiven much should forgive much.

Unforgiveness can become like a god to us. Whenever we choose to hold onto unforgiveness, that unforgiveness begins to control us and give our life direction. Decisions begin to be made on the basis of the unforgiven issues. The issue begins to consume our focus and captivate our passion. Soon our devotion is misdirected because we can not keep our mind focused on the Lord. Unforgiveness is a taskmaster that enslaves those who fall to its enticing control.

The driving force behind unforgiveness is vengeance. Vengeance is an attitude that says, "If I forgive, the person who wronged me will go free." Vengeance is an attitude that puts us in the role of God by saying, "I must get back at this person and even the score." Whenever we act vengefully, we play the part of God and put the government back upon our shoulders. This is why unforgiveness can be a sin leading to death; our bodies and souls cannot handle the weight and responsibilities of playing God.

You say, "But I was clearly wronged." I am sure you were, but being wronged is not your focus. Your focus should be *your* not doing wrong. Joseph was clearly wronged, and for thirteen years he paid the price of being wrongfully accused, but in spite of that wrongdoing he was able to stay free and restore his brothers by saying, *"You intended to harm me, but God intended it for good to accomplish what is now being done, the saving of many lives."* (Genesis 50:20)

To play God is a career-ending decision. If you are trying to do it, get out and let God alone do what only He can do.

CR&O

Pause for thought:

In what relationships are you playing God in? What issues of forgiveness still need to be issued?

April 20th

A CALL FOR JUSTICE

"No one calls for justice, no one pleads his case with integrity . . . So justice is far from us . . . justice is driven back . . . truth has stumbled in the streets, honesty cannot enter . . . The Lord looked and was displeased that there was no justice"

Isaiah 59:4, 9, 14-15

Whatever God creates, He creates with design. Whatever He makes, He fashions and forms it with distinctives. When someone looks upon something God created, there is a certain signature to it, certain distinctives that make it uniquely God's.

So it is with the family of God. There are certain distinctives about God's family that distinguishes it from all else. Distinctives like righteousness, humility and mercy. But there is a distinctive that, for the most part, has been abandoned by the evangelical church, and once again God is calling us into account. The distinctive I refer to is the mandate to uphold and maintain justice.

As we search through the Old and New Testament alike, we find the heart of God unquestionably wrapped up in the cause of justice:

> *"Follow justice and justice alone so that you may live and possess the land."* (Deuteronomy 16:20)
> *"To do what is right and just is more acceptable to the Lord than sacrifice."* (Proverbs 21:3)
> *"Who through faith conquered kingdoms and administered justice."* (Hebrews 11:33)

With the heresy of dualism, which is the separating of the sacred and the secular, the spiritual and the natural, the evangelical church abandoned the physical world to focus only on those things that could be qualified as uniquely spiritual. So our focus became only those things that deal with man's spirit and his soul. Anything that focused on man's body and his welfare was labeled "the social gospel" and looked upon critically. The void left by the evangelicals was filled by the liberals and in a perversion of truth, anything that dealt with justice and help for the oppressed was considered anti-spiritual.

"The Lord looked and was displeased that there was no justice."

The heart of God cannot be divided into spiritual and natural. God is a Father, and His heart for His children extends over all. Hunger is not irrelevant to His cause. Mistreatment of the oppressed is not outside His concern. God created the whole man, and the cause of justice is just as important as is the cause for prayer. His Kingdom is not divided, and His rule extends over all.

To bring pleasure to the heart of God should be the cry of every son and daughter. Justice pleases the heart of God. Justice for the oppressed is not a social concern; it is a family concern. God is a Father, and when any of His children suffer, He suffers. It is in the face of the suffering that He enlists us into the cause. The family is in need.

"Is not this the kind of fasting I have chosen: to loose the chains of injustice and untie the cords of the yoke, to set the oppressed free and break every yoke?" (Isaiah 58:6)

ଔଡ଼

Pause for thought:

Justice requires action. How are you prepared to take action?

April 21st

HE DID IT HIS WAY

"I tell you the truth, the Son can do nothing by himself; he can do only what he sees his Father doing, because whatever the Father does the Son also does"

John 5:19

Jesus was the least original man who ever walked the Earth. He never had an independent thought, he never had an independent action. There was nothing in Jesus that saw independence as virtue. The pattern the Son demonstrated to us is a lifestyle of emulation and representation.

We live in a day and age that has defied the concept of individuality. I say concept because, though everyone claims to be passionately individualistic, they all dress like their peers, talk like their peers and act like their peers. Individuality is nothing but a myth. It is something we have all pretended to be, but the reality is we are all a composite of our parents, friends and the source we look to in life.

Years ago, as a young minister, I conducted my first funeral service. The man was the father of a young lady in our church. He had died of liver disease brought on by an alcoholic lifestyle he had decided upon years earlier. Prior to his death, the man had requested as his special song, Frank Sinatra's "I Did It My Way." Imagine it; the man died from his alcohol problem and he requested a song that glorifies self-achievement, even when the fruit of his achievement killed him.

To hold on to the rights of individuality and independence is to miss the Kingdom. For some, the result of originality and independence is death. If not physical death, it will certainly result in spiritual death. Jesus clearly demonstrated that life is found on being a Father pleaser. Originality is a myth. Individuality is overrated. What brings eternal purpose and satisfies the inner cry is to bring pleasure to the heart of God by thinking His thoughts and doing His will, His way.

If you were to rate your level of independence from God, what would your score be? Do you seek Him first before all else? Do you lead a sacrificial lifestyle and yield your daily decisions over to Him? Does the rule of His government extend over every aspect of your life or is it just the "spiritual" ones?

Jesus could do nothing of His own. He only did what He saw His Father doing. He did it Father's way, and He calls us to do the same.

April 22nd

BREAKING THE TYRANNY OF UNFORGIVENESS

"You intended to harm me, but God intended it for good to accomplish what is now being done, the saving of many lives"

Genesis 50:20

Perhaps the single most important quality operating in Joseph's life was the quality of forgiveness. Though an incredible injustice was done to Joseph by his brothers, he did not see vengeance as something he had to execute. His trust in God's sovereignty was deep enough that he was able to release his brothers and trust the misfortune of his circumstances to the providential hand of God.

Unforgiveness is a trap that renders many ineffective and robs them of their God-given identity. How do we get out of this trap, if we find ourselves in it?

1. RELEASE VENGEANCE. (Romans 12:17-19) Vengeance is anything we do to even the score. Vengeance is motivated by a root of bitterness, so Paul instructs us to release vengeance and give God room to avenge. Vengeance manifests itself on two levels. Active vengeance is seen in the act of slander, gossip and the purposeful exposing of those who do us wrong. Many of the books written today, exposing churches that abuse or people who have done wrong, have been motivated by a need to even the score.

Passive vengeance is an attitude that refuses to release the wrongdoer. Bitterness is passive vengeance. Though it may never be translated to action, the attitude is left to fester and entrap the person to the circumstance. Vengeance is God's doing. Release those who have done you wrong and let God even the score.

2. RECOGNIZE THE REDEMPTIVE PURPOSE OF THE WRONGDOING. (Genesis 50:20) Often the providential hand of God allows situations to come into our lives in order to accomplish His purpose of Christlikeness and the saving of many lives.

Are you willing to become a Joseph in order to see the saving of many lives? The saving of many lives begins with the saving of ourselves from the tyranny of unforgiveness. God is always able to turn bad situations around for the good as we are willing to look for the redemptive purpose in the misfortune.

3. DEMONSTRATE FORGIVENESS WITH ACTION. (Genesis 50:21) Not only did Joseph forgive, he then acted upon his forgiveness by caring for his brothers. When forgiveness is demonstrated by a tangible act, we close off the devil's access and overcome evil with good. Action is what seals the word of forgiveness. The word of forgiveness triggers the choice, then the action seals the process. Jesus acted upon His forgiveness of Judas by washing his feet and serving him communion. It was this action that sealed His resolve to walk in the freedom of forgiveness and not give the devil a place to erect a stronghold.

Has someone done you wrong? Has some misfortune touched you that has enslaved you to the tyranny of unforgiveness? You can break the stronghold of unforgiveness by releasing these circumstances into the providential hand of God. In so doing, not only will you free yourself, but in so doing, you will also see the saving of many lives.

ೞ∞

Pause for thought:

If "action is what seals the word of forgiveness," what action do you feel the Holy Spirit prompting you to do?

April 23rd

SHOWN BY GOD

"You are well aware that it is against our law for a Jew to associate with a Gentile or visit him. But God has shown me that I should not call any man impure or unclean"

Acts 10:28

When the Kingdom of God invades our life, not only is our religious perspective changed, but everything is turned upside down. The coming of the Kingdom is a blessed invasion that radically changes all previous perspectives and mind-sets that are contrary to God's way of thinking.

Perhaps one of the most difficult mind-sets to be invaded is a cultural one that discriminates against a particular people or group. Such was the case between Jews and Gentiles in the first century. Not only was it contrary to Jewish culture to associate with a Gentile, it was against their law. The Jews were so entrenched in their superior mentality that laws were written to enforce their separation from Gentiles.

When it came time for God to invade this mind set, even God faced a major ordeal. Knowing that it would take more than a simple word, God put Peter in a trance. While in the trance, Peter saw a vision of a large sheet, coming down from Heaven, containing all kinds of animals, clean and unclean. Then he heard a voice saying, *"Get up, Peter. Kill and eat."* Peter's response was, *"Surely not, Lord."* The words "surely not" do not go together with the word "Lord." To say "surely not, Lord" is to show that you do not understand the meaning of the word "Lord." To understand Lordship is to say, "Surely, yes, Lord!" But sometimes our culture takes such a predominate place in our mind-sets that even Jesus has a difficult time getting us to obey. So difficult was the change for Peter that three times he had to be shown the same vision. Even after the third time, Peter was still wondering what the meaning of the vision meant.

In times of mind-set redefinitions, we must be willing to be shown by God the right way. Peter's vision was a racial redefinition. His cultural mind-set excluded all Gentiles from relationship and association with God. But God the Father had a different plan. As a Father, His will was inclusive, not exclusive. His desire was for all His children, regardless of the skin color or cultural definitions, to be included in His family. In seeing the vision, Peter saw that *"God does not show favoritism, but accepts men from every nation who fear Him and do what is right."* (Acts 10:34-35)

What mind-set do you hold? Does your mind-set discriminate against people of other skin colors, or anyone who is different from you? Do you show favoritism? If so, ask the Holy Spirit to come in that blessed invasion and show you, as He did Peter, Father's heart for all of His kids, red, yellow, black and white. They are all precious in His sight.

☙❧

April 24th

A TIME FOR EVALUATION

"Examine yourselves to see whether you are in the faith; test yourselves"

II Corinthians 13:5

*M*aturity involves the ability to ask ourselves the tough questions. Self-government under Christ and taking personal responsibility are foundational cornerstones of living in the Kingdom of God. As the Holy Spirit does His work of transforming us into the likeness of Christ, we must give Him continual access of examination to determine whether we are building according to the pattern He has shown us.

It is in asking the tough questions that we are forced to evaluate our pursuits to determine whether we are pacifying ourselves with movement instead of experiencing real progress. Movement can work as a spiritual narcotic that pacifies the cry for accomplishment. God deserves results. His goal for us is fruit, not just activity. We must all face our tendency to be so busy in our lives that we never have the time to evaluate our progress. Our activity can mask the limitations of our accomplishment. Without a time of evaluation, all of our work can be much ado about nothing. This evaluation comes by the Spirit of God within and through the help of trusted people God has placed in our lives. These trusted people keep us from unnecessary levels of subjectivity.

The Kingdom of God is a forceful advance. Our evaluation is to determine if we are advancing with it. Ultimately, we measure ourselves against Christ in regard to character and life formation. But in our time of evaluation, we must also measure our progress against the place we received the baton of the Kingdom. Our responsibility in the work of God is to advance the revelation and further whatever it is that we have been given in God to steward. We measure ourselves against Christ in regard to character and personal transformation, but in regard to finishing the race given us to run, we measure ourselves against where we received the baton and where the finish line marked out for us is. In that evaluation, we must be courageous enough and honest enough to make mid-course adjustments when necessary. We need the courage to examine what is in the light of what should be.

If it is working, do not fix it. If it is not working, that is, if your present pursuits and stewarding of your life are not producing the fruit of God's desire, then stop and make the necessary changes.

April 25th

SUCCESS IS SUCCESSION

"And if you have not been trustworthy with someone else's property, who will give you property of your own?"

Luke 16:12

In these days of commercial gain, success has many different faces and many different definitions. For some, success is simply getting to the top. How you get there matters little; just get there. The drive to succeed is a God-given desire, but when that drive is jaded by sin and ambition, success becomes an idol of distraction.

By what standard will you define success? In the Kingdom of God, success is wrapped up in Sonship. In God's Kingdom, success is found in succession. To succeed is to replicate the life of Christ in our lives and then train others to replicate it in theirs. I succeed only as the succession of Christ's life and purpose is reproduced in me and in those I lead.

In God's eyes, success is defined in terms of family. Jesus was a success, for He came to do the will of Father. What validated Jesus was the fact that He did not come to serve His own vision, but to fulfill the vision of His Father. According to Luke 16:12, being trustworthy with what belongs to someone else is what qualifies us to receive our own. The process of succession is found in serving God's vision as it is expressed in your pastor, parents, ect. As that vision is passed on to you and you give yourself to serve it, you are being trained in the quality of trustworthiness and being prepared to receive vision of your own.

The world defines success in terms of origination, but God defines it in terms of succession. Jesus was the least original man who ever lived. He only did what He saw His Father doing. We do not have to be so original; just learn how to be a son. In I Kings 8:20, Solomon defined his success as succeeding his father David. As we receive from our Heavenly Father and the spiritual fathers He has placed in our lives, the Spirit of Sonship will bring us into the true meaning of success. This success may not be accompanied by plaques or medals, but it will bring with it a *"well done good and faithful servant, enter into the joy of the Lord."*

April 26th

SWALLOWED INTO HELL, ALIVE

"As soon as he finished saying all of this, the ground under them split apart and the earth opened its mouth and swallowed them, with their households and all Korah's men and all their possessions"
Numbers 16:31-32

Father has a way of getting our attention. To see the Earth open up and swallow Korah and all of his followers must have been a sight that Israel would not soon forget. It is not every day that the Earth opens up and swallows someone into hell, alive. Korah and all of his followers certainly got the point, but it was too late for them. God took these extreme measures in order to validate the authority of His leadership in Moses and remind the people that to bring accusations against His appointed ones was to bring accusations against Him. Korah's sin was not a sin against man; it was a sin against God.

You would think after such a demonstrative display of force, the people would have got the point. But verse 41 tells us, *"The next day the whole Israelite community grumbled against Moses and Aaron."* Carnally inspired human sympathy is a trap that blinds us from seeing the way of the Lord and recognize the authority He has ordained.

The accusation against Moses was also an accusation against God. Moses was in the position he was by God's authority, not his own. If Moses would have been a self-appointed or self-commissioned leader, it would have been a case of man against man. But Moses was in his position by divine commission, so any challenge of the position was also a challenge against the One who ordained the position.

Korah's rebellion was not a sin against man, but one against God. The punishment Korah and his followers received is a reflection of God's attitude toward dishonoring those in divinely ordained positions. When leaders fail as they sometimes do, Galations 6:1 gives us our direction. We are to restore such in a spirit of gentleness. In so doing, we address the issue of leadership sin and honor the position God ordained.

Let us take a lesson from Korah and let it serve as a remembrance that to sin against God is a terrible thing.

April 27th

BEFORE I DIE

"Why spend money on what is not bread, and your labor on what does not satisfy? Listen, listen to me, and eat what is good, and your soul will delight in the richest of fare"

Isaiah 55:2

What must you get done before you die? What is the one thing or the many things that you must finish before your number of days come to an end?

It is questions like these that cause us to stop and evaluate the fruit of our pursuits from an eternal perspective. Everyone will build something. Everyone will produce fruit. The question is, will we build on the eternal and produce a product in keeping with the Kingdom of God? Can what we are building stand the fire of God's evaluation?

What we are currently pursuing and giving ourselves to are the tracks that take us into the future. With this being the case, will the tracks you are currently traveling on take you to your destination of desire? Do those tracks run in line with those things you must accomplish before you die?

Where you start your journey determines where you will end. You ca not start heading south and finish in the north. Your beginning point sets your direction. To finish on those things that satisfy, we must begin there as well. We ca not expect to labor on the temporal and then receive an eternal reward. To finish on the eternal, we must begin in the eternal.

Before you die, allow me to encourage you to build your life on the eternal. Some people set goals of making their fortunes before they die. Others want to travel the world. While these are fine and good, they do not answer the cry of the eternal. The cry of the eternal centers you on those issues of an eternal nature, such as your relationship with Christ, your spouse and your children. The cry of the eternal says before I die, I must establish a foundation so that those who follow me with faith can take the purpose of God further than I.

April 28th

HEARERS AND THINKERS

"Now the Bereans were of more noble character than the Thessalonians, for they received the message with great eagerness and examined the Scriptures every day to see if what Paul said was true"

Acts 17:11

It is not enough to know what you believe. You must also know *why* you believe it. Far too many Christians have satisfied themselves with just knowing what to believe. "Tell me what to believe," they say. "I don't have the time to figure out *why* I should believe it."

If our sphere of responsibility stopped with ourselves, knowing just what to believe would be enough. But our sphere of responsibility goes beyond ourselves into others. Often the others we have responsibility for are unbelievers. As we interact with unbelievers, they are more interested in the *why* we believe than in the *what* we believe. If we are unable to give a solid explanation to the *why*, the *what* loses its power of persuasion.

In order to present a solid explanation of what we believe and why we believe it, we must train ourselves to become thinkers. A thinker is not satisfied with just hearing a body of information. Once the information is heard, a thinker will examine the content and put it up against the grid of Scripture. Once the content is put up against the grid of Scripture, truth can be found. It is only those statements that line up with Scripture that qualify as truth. Without the responsibility of thinking and Scripture comparison, all information would be taken in and the possibility of it becoming misinformation is extremely high.

This type of critical thinking must always be balanced with noble character. The Bereans were not negative people who did not believe a word anyone said. They were thinkers of noble character, so with great integrity, they measured what they heard against the absolute standard of God's Word.

Next time you hear something, take it in, think about it and measure it against the Scripture. In so doing, you will both confirm the truth and make it your own.

෴

April 29th

COMING OUT

"Depart, depart, go out from there. Touch no unclean thing. Come out from it and be pure"

Isaiah 52:11

God is a God of distinction. In His holiness, He seeks for a people of separation from all that which is contrary to His way. From the foundation of time, His desire has been to have a people who are uniquely His. His word to His people has been a word of separation, a word of no mingling with foreign gods and foreign people. It has been a word to come out and be separate from the world He has sent us into.

The tactics of the enemy are insidious and subtle. Slowly and consistently he works to breakdown the believer's resistance and slowly leads them into a lifestyle of compromise and accommodation. Rarely does the real sin happen overnight. Rather, it is a series of subtle compromises designed to lure the victim into the snare without the person being aware of what is coming down upon them.

The young person may say "I will just go to the party and not get drunk." The business man may say "I will just avoid the truth but I won't lie." With good intentions these subtle compromises begin to become larger and larger until the victim is lured into blatant sin. The tragedy is, by then they do not even seem to care.

The strategy is consistent. Isolate the victim from fellowship. Cut them off from their life in the word. Reduce their prayer life to a form and ritual. Neutralize them through compromise. Destroy them through sin. Soon their hunger for God is being replaced by that which does not satisfy.

Has the subtlety of compromise put its strangle hold on you? Depart before it is too late. Come out while you still can.

April 30th

FROM ONE MAN

"From one man he made every nation of men and he determined the times set for them and the exact places where they should live"
Acts 17:26

From one man. The heart of God began with one and interestingly enough it has always remained with one. From one man we were made and though we now number many, we remain one. Biologically speaking, man is one species. Physiologically speaking, man is one in anatomical structure and blood. Sociologically speaking, man is one in characteristic and need.

Where man has strayed is in his psychology. We have allowed another Gospel to shape our thinking; consequently, we no longer see ourselves as one race, but multiple races. Origin determines outcome. So if you begin with one race, it does not matter how many people you add to that race, you always have just one.

"From one man He made every nation." Paul uses the word "nation" here, not race. Race is not used in the Bible, except in regard to a contest of speed. Nation is the word used to acknowledge our distinctives, for in the eyes of God, there is only one race. To use the word race as a physical or psychological designation is not biblical. Nation is a political designation, whereas race has come to mean a physical one. But God recognizes no essential physical or psychological differences in people, nor does science. When you go to the blood bank, you do not ask for white blood or black blood or yellow blood. You just get blood. Yes, there is a difference in their color, but in the eyes of God, the difference is not essential or cause for division.

"From one man He made every nation of men." We must recognize the oneness of our origin and put aside the elitist attitudes that separate and divide. God is our Father and we are His kids. Consequently, we are all family, and in family there are no grounds for racism.

May 1st

A CALL FOR PIONEERS

"Therefore go and make disciples of all nations..."
Matthew 28:19

*T*here are those who go, and there are those who go, "where no man has gone before." All are commanded to go, but some receive a call that is quite unique. Theirs is a call to go into uncharted waters. Theirs is a call to blaze a trail for the generations to come. It is a call of the pioneer.

America was built on the spirit of the pioneer. Legends have been built around the pioneering spirits of Daniel Boone and Davey Crocket. They were the trailblazers. Their courage and determination led them into new lands and virgin frontiers.

Plowing virgin soil is hard work. To go, where few have ever gone, is like building on the frontier. To build, you must first secure the land, clear the trees, cut the wood. You do not just move into a beautifully decorated home. To be a trailblazer requires a person of adventure, someone with a stick-to-it passion that keeps going when the going gets tough.

Once that cabin is built, it becomes easier for those who are to follow. A generational ministry calls for pioneers. Pioneers who, with tremendous courage, plow virgin soil and conquer uncharted frontiers. Pioneers, in whose hearts are the generations to come. When pioneers build beyond themselves, their sons become farmers and their sons become storekeepers, carpenters, and road builders. Cities are built upon the spirit and call of the pioneer.

The church today is in tremendous need of the pioneers. Many Christians are simply bored and apathetic because the spirit of the pioneer has been replaced with safe programs that promise security at the cost of adventure.

Is the pioneering spirit in you? Maybe it is time to get out of the boat and walk on the water!

May 2nd

FAITH AS A FOUNDATION

"Now faith is the substance of things hoped for..."
Hebrews 12:1

There are many things in life that we can choose to build upon. Each person chooses for himself what he will use as his foundation. Some choose those things which turn to sand, and others choose that thing which becomes the everlasting rock.

Faith is not any ordinary substance. The Greek meaning of this word "substance" is "a thing to put under." Faith is a foundation. Faith is that thing we put under our walk with God and our life in the Kingdom. This is one of the reasons why it is impossible to please God without faith. He knows without it, there is no foundation to lay for that which he does in our life.

The faulty foundations of this life will never meet with God's approval. Though we have been taught to build our lives upon the foundation of reason and reality, they stand in direct contrast to faith. Reason says, if you can not pay your bills on 100% of your income, how can you tithe and expect to pay them on 90%? Faith says the 90% given in obedience to God will cover far more than 100% given apart from faith. This principle of faith is proven day in and day out in those who honor God with their tithe.

Apart from faith, we can do nothing to find the approval of God. Faith is both our beginning and it is our end. Every step we take is to be a step taken in faith and by faith.

Let us begin to ask God for an increased measure of faith. Let us look for opportunities to embrace, wherein our faith will be challenged and increased as a result.

May 3rd

PEOPLE OF HIS PRESENCE

"'My Presence will go with you, and I will give you rest.' Then Moses said to him, 'If your Presence does not go with us, do not send us up from here.'"

Exodus 33:14-15

How important is the Presence of God? Is it "a" thing or is it "the" thing? Is it limited to Sunday, or is it daily? Does it come only by God's initiative or have you learned to take the initiative to find it?

For Moses, the Presence of God was everything. He was so unimpressed with himself and his own abilities, he said, in effect, "Unless You go with us, it will not happen."

God has always sought a people who possess a passion for His Presence. He looks for those who seek Him for who He is, not because of religious duty, manipulative pressure or any other external force. The cry for His Presence begins from within, like the pangs of hunger that never go away unless you satisfy them.

This level of passion begins with the revelation of need. It begins as we ask God to show us both the futility of self-effort and the importance of His Presence. As our eyes are open to this reality, we find a holy desperation developing from within, where we begin to cry out as Moses did, "Give me Your Presence."

The Presence of God is not a past memory or a religious event; it is a moment by moment reality reserved for a people of desire. As people of desire, we must learn how to wait in His Presence. You can not rush the Presence of God. You can not come and say, "Okay, God, I have five minutes . . . speak." You must learn to come into His Presence and just be there. We come only by the shed blood of Jesus Christ. We come through thanksgiving and praise. Once there, we learn to honor His Presence. Once there we begin, as Moses, to cry out to experience that Presence moment by moment in an ever increasingly intimate manner.

May 4th

THE SEPARATION TACTIC

"He who separates himself seeks his own desire. He quarrels against all sound wisdom. A fool does not delight in understanding but only in revealing his own mind"

Proverbs 18:1-2

Without a doubt, our enemy's number one tactic of attack is relational conflict. Knowing the strategic importance of relational unity, he seeks to divide relationships so as to undermine the desire of Christ. Time and time again, we have seen his evil schemes put to work. Someone comes into the church and raves about the life they sense and the excitement they carry for the vision. In the course of time the inevitable offenses come, and the enemy's strategy of division begins to work its evil desire. Soon the excitement for the vision turns into criticism, and the shortcomings of the church become the focus rather than the life of God that was once felt. As the people's eyes are opened to the negative side, they begin the decision-making process of separation. Other activities begin to crowd out those planned by the church. Sunday morning remains a must, but all other congregational gatherings become optional. Soon the accusation of too many meetings arise. The people begin to seek their own desire, and God's desired harmony of purpose is broken.

Offenses are in no way excusable, but they are inevitable. We must strive for Christlikeness, so we will not offend; but, if offenses arise, we must never allow the enemy to use them to cause our separation from those Christ has joined to us. (Ephesians 2:21)

Are you being separated from those you have been joined to? Has the tactic of cynicism already separated you? If so, recognize the source of your separation and side with the one who stands for unity. Go to those you have become separated from and seek to restore the unity Christ has given.

May 5th

THE TASTE OF AUTHENTICITY

"So he said to the man who took care of the vineyard, 'For three years now I've been coming to look for fruit on this fig tree and haven't found any. Cut it down! Why should it use up the soil?'"

Luke 13:7

The parable of the barren fig tree of Luke 13 is enough to put the fear of God in you. The parable makes it very clear, the issue with God is fruit. He planted a tree and expected it to produce. When it did not, the answer was very clear: cut it down because its purpose is to produce fruit, and if it is not going to fulfill its purpose there is no reason to "use the soil."

The test of the fruit is its authenticity. It must not only look authentic, it must taste authentic. Looks can be deceiving, but taste is sure proof.

To be authentic in the Kingdom of God is to be like Jesus. In this Kingdom, there is one standard and one standard only: *Jesus*. To be like Him is to be like Him! To be like Him, we must ask ourselves a few pointed questions:

1. What would Jesus do? As we face each circumstance in life, as we evaluate every decision we make, as we determine appropriate behavior, all must be done from the perspective of, what would Jesus do in this situation? To determine the correct answer, we must ask ourselves a second question.

2. What did Jesus do? He faced the same temptations and difficulties we do, and faced them without sin. To learn how he did it, we must commit ourselves to a serious study of the gospels and be prepared to walk in that which we discover.

The answers to questions 1 and 2 lead us to our final question; and that answer will determine the quality of our fruit.

3. What would Jesus have me do? The first two questions may be nothing more than a nice study. Question three will determine the level of your sincerity and willingness.

Let us ask these questions of ourselves and each other, daily, in order that Father might find in us the fruit He desires.

May 6th

THE TWO SIDES OF FAITH

"To each has been given a measure of faith"
Romans 12:3

The Scriptures refer to faith, both as a noun and as a verb. Some verses refer to faith as a thing we possess and other verses refer to faith as an action that possesses us. Faith that we possess has been given to us as a gift. *"To each has been given a measure of faith."* (Romans 12:3) But, the faith that possesses us is learned faith. It is faith that comes to us as we embrace the One who is faithful.

Faith that possesses us is a faith of action. It is a faith that demands demonstration and an area to prove the power of God. The amplified Bible describes the action in words like "prompted by faith, actuated by faith, urged on by faith, aroused by faith and motivated by faith." It is faith that comes to us and forces a response from us. There is nothing complacent or passive about faith.

Because of faith, Sarah received physical power to conceive a child. This was a faith beyond her original measure. It was an action faith given in proportion to the calling she was given. Sarah's original measure of faith was not enough for her to overcome the natural laws of childbirth. She needed a supernatural supply. In the face of need, the Scriptures say, *"By faith, Sarah received..."* She did not earn it, she did not do anything to qualify herself for it, she simply received it. The impartation of faith was God's doing. The calling to conceive a child was God's doing and the enablement to give birth was God's doing. All Sarah had to do was posture herself before God to receive the miracle and then act in obedience.

Entering into the faith realm is entering into the faith that possesses us and then thrusts us into action and demonstration. It is not of our doing, but entirely of His.

May 7th

THE BLOOD IS EVERYTHING

"His divine power has given us everything we need for life and godliness through our knowledge of him who called us by his own glory and goodness"

II Peter 1:3

The apostle Peter stated quite boldly that everything we need pertaining to life and godliness is ours through Jesus Christ, our Lord. (II Peter 1:3) What a promise and what a provision. We serve a God who has provided for our every need.

One of the ways God has ordained for this provision to come is through the blood of Jesus Christ. Little did Satan know that as the blood of Jesus fell to the ground, it was purchasing for those to follow everything they would ever need to live a life of victory over sin and death.

The writer of Hebrews lists for us just a few of the purchased benefits of the blood.

> - Destroyed Satan (Hebrews 2:14)
> - Destroyed the fear of death (Hebrews 2:15)
> - Cleansed our conscience (Hebrews 9:14)
> - Cleansed Heaven (Hebrews 9:23)
> - Given boldness (Hebrews 10:19)
> - Promised perfection (Hebrews 13:20)

How many times have we struggled to possess in our own strength what the blood has already given us? Somehow, we think we must add something. "It's far too simple," we reason. Yet, who made us God's counselor? If He ordained everything we need to live a life of victory, having been given through the blood, then our response is to accept it, not second guess it.

The blood plus nothing is God's acceptable payment. Nothing you or I could ever add would enhance our standing before God. The payment was paid by Christ, so trust the blood.

❀

May 8th

THE LIVING WORD

"For the Word of God is living and active. Sharper than any double-edged sword, it penetrates even to dividing soul and spirit, joints and marrow; it judges the thoughts and attitudes of the heart"
Hebrews 4:12

The greatest evidence we have of our Father's love is the power of His Word. He did not leave us alone; He did not leave us in a state of weakness to struggle through life's problems. He gave us His Word. The power of God and the keys to our release are contained in His Word. He sent His Word and the people were healed. Our cleansing is through the Word. His Word will not return void. His Word is truth, and the truth sets us free. God's answer and avenue of release is the Word.

Perhaps the greatest revelation man will ever know is the realization that our very life is predicated on the Word God declared to Israel in the wilderness and reiterated by Christ in His temptation, *"Man shall not live by bread alone, but by every word that proceeds from the mouth of God."* (Matthew 4:4)

One of the great needs we face is to build our life on the objective truth of God's Word. That is, truth that is not based on our feelings or the confirmation of emotional sharing, but truth that is embraced purely on the fact that God said it and that settles it. The emotional sharing is a needed ingredient of our walk, but it cannot be the foundation that our experience is built on. It is the difference between candy and food of substance. Life would be boring without it, but it does not have that which is needed to sustain and nurture.

Paul exhorted his son, Timothy, to *"study to show yourself approved, a workman who needeth not to be ashamed."* (II Timothy 2:15) Let us build our lives on the foundation of God's written Word. As we face areas of needed release, we need to look to the Word for truth and confess that Word in the face of the present difficulty.

ଔଷ୍ଠ

May 9th

RENEWAL OF COMMITMENT

"Remember this, fix it in mind..."

Isaiah 46:8

"How soon we forget," the saying goes. The mind often has a predisposed condition of forgetfulness. We forget birthdays, anniversaries and other important dates. We forget appointments, commitments and other things we have given our word to.

Forgetfulness has always been a problem to the children of God. The issue of forgetfulness was one the children of Israel encountered on a continual basis. As the Lord brought them into the promised land, He did so with a reminder, *"remember that you were slaves in Egypt and the Lord, your God, brought you out of there with a mighty hand."* (Deuteronomy 5:15)

Israel was prone to forgetfulness, so we see the Lord instituting a precaution to ensure success. That precaution was simply the renewal of covenant and commitment. Once the initial commitment was received, the Lord would return some time later for a recommitment of their desire and a renewal of His intention as well.

Genesis 12 records the initial call of Abraham to leave his country and people and become the father of many nations. Three chapters later in Genesis 15, the Lord renews His covenant with Abraham, then 24 years later in chapter 17, He renews it again with the act of circumcision.

Renewal came to combat the problem of forgetfulness and the resulting dissipation. Could the Lord be calling you today to a time of renewal and recommitment? Maybe it is the renewal of your marriage vow. Maybe it is the renewal of your calling or vocation. Maybe it is a renewal of your commitment to lead an intercession group. Maybe it is a renewal of a personal commitment you made before to the Lord.

Renewal may be as simple as a private word between you and the Lord, or it may mean the public declaration of intention. Whichever it requires, do not forget to do it.

☙❧

May 10th

A MOTHER'S HONOR

"The angel went to Mary and said, 'Greetings, you are highly favored. The Lord is with you . . . Do not be afraid, Mary, you have found favor with God. You will be with child and give birth to a son and you are to give him the name Jesus.' . . . 'I am the Lord's servant,' Mary answered. 'May it be to me as you have said.'"

Luke 1:28-38

Herein lies the heart of motherhood, *"I am the Lord's servant, may it be to me as you have said."* Abandonment to another is the spirit of motherhood. The willful laying down of one's life in order to see the successful nurturing of another. This selfless attitude of Mary expressed to the angel is the same selfless heart that is daily expressed in a mother giving her life for her children and family.

Just how important is the office of a mother? In a day when the battle for identity rages, just how important is the role and responsibility of a mother and for that matter, a woman? The fact that Christ's birth came through a woman speaks volumes about a woman's significance and the importance of motherhood. Almighty God could have brought Christ into the world any way He chose, but He chose to do it through a woman. Herein lies the wonder of God's plan. He chose a teenage girl in the obscure village of Nazareth to reveal the mystery of the incarnation. He chose a teenage virgin to become the mother of the Son of God. God chose to share the greatest secret of all creation with a woman. This speaks clearly of the value and worth of women and motherhood in the sight of God.

In a day when the identity and worth of a woman is up for re-definition, we must never forget that it was through them that God chose to inaugurate His plan of redemption. It was through the abandoned heart of Mary that the redeemer came.

We honor our mothers for their selfless courage and the willing abandonment to their family and to their calling in God!

May 11th

POWER OF THE HOLY SPIRIT

"Jesus full of the Holy Spirit returned from the Jordan and was led by the Spirit in the desert . . . Jesus returned from Galilee in the power of the Spirit"

Luke 4:1, 14

To walk in the fullness of the Holy Spirit is a state that most would be satisfied with. Compared to what we currently have, the fullness of the Spirit would be a nice promotion. But Jesus was not satisfied with the Spirit's fullness. He would not quit until He had received the Spirit's power.

Where does your level of satisfaction lie today? Will the fullness of the Spirit satisfy you, or are you going to press on for the power of the Spirit?

To be like Jesus means we will not be satisfied until we walk in the power of the Holy Spirit. To walk in the power means we walk above the level of natural ability. Above the level of our own understanding. Above the level of our own giftedness. Above the level of natural effectiveness.

The world is longing to see Kingdom power released through normal people. No side shows, no religious gimmicks, just pure unadulterated Holy Spirit power being released in a simple way.

How? How is it to be done? Well, I have asked myself that same question for some time. The closest I have come to an answer is that we will get it the same way Jesus got it. We face and press through temptation through the power of the Holy Spirit. The sovereignty of God uses temptation in our lives to empower us.

ೞ

May 12th

REWARDED FULLY

"Watch out that you do not lose what you have worked for, but that you may be rewarded fully"

II John 1:8

A full reward is God's portion for His own. He is not satisfied with us walking away with only a partial reward. He wants us to experience the fullness of His blessing and desire.

We have been placed in this world as stewards of revelation. There are certain revelations of truth that God reveals to either an individual, a congregation, or to a generation. In order to receive a full reward, that person, congregation, or generation must steward that truth to the end without forsaking it in the heat of battle. Spiritual warfare is designed to cause us to forget. We forget who we are, and we forget the truth the Holy Spirit has revealed for our stewardship.

All truth is guarded by controversy. Truth is a razor's sharp edge with deception on either side. Through the power of the Holy Spirit, we are able to steward that truth through the mine fields of deception. Sometimes in the midst of the battle, mistakes are made. Through misapplications of the truth or through partial understanding, people are hurt. It is when people have been hurt by the misapplication of truth that stewardship becomes so important.

Can we steward truth into the fullness of understanding without forsaking it during the process of revelation? The spiritual landscape of the church is strewn with half-built buildings of truth. These are the result of those who ran with partial revelation, only to stop short of the full reward. In the process, they were hurt, and most likely those around them were hurt as well. In the hurt, the temptation is to forsake the truth in exchange for safer ground.

To walk in revelation is to walk on new ground. Whenever a people pioneer new ground, they stand the risk of hurt. To minimize the risk, we must learn to keep the revelation to ourselves until it comes into the fullness of understanding. People are hurt with truth, because it has been applied before its time. Hurt comes as the result of someone trying to run with partial understanding. As God instructed Daniel to wait upon giving the revelation, we must learn to keep the matter to ourselves until the Holy Spirit has had ample time to test us and purify what we see. You have been entrusted with a treasure. Steward it into its fullness, so that you may receive its full reward.

May 13th

IF

"If you fully obey the Lord your God"
Deuteronomy 28:1

Like water, the nature of man is to seek the path of least resistance. Hardship and difficulty tend to be repulsive to our flesh, so we often spend twice as much time in our attempt to find an easier way than it would have taken to simply do what was necessary. Because of this tendency toward least resistance, it is easy to fall into a self-deception that enables us to redefine godly expectation. What the Word of God makes conditional, we would like to think as unconditional. Below are a number of promises that are conditional upon our fulfilling the preceding requirement. Take a look at them and see whether your natural man has the expectation of possession without the determination of obedience.

- Galatians 5:9 — We will reap a harvest *if* we faint not.
- Revelation 2:7 — We will eat from the tree of life *if* we overcome.
- Revelation 2:11 — We will not be hurt by the second death *if* we overcome.
- Revelation 2:17 — We will be given the hidden manna *if* we overcome.
- Revelation 2:17 — We will be given a new name *if* we overcome.
- Revelation 2:26 — We will be given authority over the nations *if* we overcome.
- Revelation 3:12 — We will become a pillar in the temple of God *if* we overcome.
- Revelation 3:21 — We will sit with Him on the throne *if* we overcome.
- Matthew 6:33 — We will be given all things *if* we seek first the Kingdom of God.
- Romans 10:9 — We will be saved *if* we confess Jesus as Lord.
- Matthew 2:21 — We can move mountains *if* we have faith and do not doubt.
- Romans 6:5 — We will be united with Him in resurrection *if* we are united with Him in death.

The reason God makes these promises not only conditional, but also impossible, is because He seeks to bring us to the end of natural strength and align us with His supplied strength. The good news of godly expectation is we can fully expect His strength if we have admitted our weakness. (II Corinthians 12:10)

May 14th

FROM POTENTIAL TO PROGRESS

"They go from strength to strength until each appears before God"
Psalm 84:7

The Bible describes the spiritual life as a walk of progress, not potential. How we rejoice when we discover a person of great potential! But, the fact of the matter is, everyone is a person of tremendous potential. Potential is worth something, but it will not "pay the bills" or fulfill God's intended desire.

Moving from potential to progress does not just happen. Progress requires a plan, a plan that leads one from passion, to a person, to a purpose.

➤ PASSION. All spiritual progress must begin with and center itself in the person of Jesus Christ. Without passion for Jesus being in the center of progress, motive, supply and destination, it all goes astray. It is our passion for Him, worked out in daily replenishing, that stays the course and brings us to the proper destination.

➤ PERSON. It is a known fact that you will take yourself only so far. Without someone in your life to push you and encourage you to go further when everything else says "stop," you will stop short. It is for this reason athletes look for a coach—someone they can become accountable to, someone who will expect more of them than they expect of themselves.

➤ PURPOSE. Without a purpose, passion and person are aimless. It is purpose that directs potential toward destination. There is no need for a coach if there is no game. There is no need for passion or a person if there is no divine purpose that you are pursuing. Pursuit is what defines progress. Without proper pursuit, there is no progress, though there may be activity.

Thank God for potential, but separate from the rest and add to that potential, passion and to your passion, a person, and to the person, purpose.

May 15th

OVERCOMING TEMPTATION

"Jesus, full of the Holy Spirit, returned from the Jordan and was led by the Spirit in the desert..."

Luke 4:1

Jesus was led into the wilderness full of the Holy Spirit, and after 40 days, He returned in the power of the Spirit. Our focus during times of fasting and prayer is, how do we walk in the power of the Holy Spirit?

So far, our conclusion has been, we walk in the power of the Spirit the same way Jesus did. It took 40 days of fasting for Him. As important as fasting is to the process, there is more.

Between the fullness and the power, Jesus had to overcome satanic temptation. The overcoming of temptation is another key to the release of God's power. The softness of our culture has produced a weakness in most that makes overcoming a difficult task. But on these occasions, Jesus faced satanic temptation and overcame it by the power of God's Word. This was not just a brief random attack. Jesus faced the temptation for 40 days and overcame.

1. TEMPTATION OF BASE DESIRES. *"If you are the son of God, tell this stone to become bread."* Base desires, whether they be the desire of the eyes, the ears or the mouth, if they are not brought under the rule of the Holy Spirit, they will prevent the pure release of God's power.

2. TEMPTATION OF FALSE WORSHIP. *"The devil led Him to a high place and in an instant showed Him all the kingdoms of the world . . . if you worship me, it will all be yours."* Satanic strategy is to divert Kingdom pursuit by giving us what is already ours outside of God's provision and timing. Success is only success if it comes from God's hand. While success that is provided for by the devil has a look of promise, it always destroys before it runs its course.

3. TEMPTATION OF TEST AND BLAME. *"Do not put the Lord your God to the test."* When walking in the will of God, testing is a moot point, for the will of God becomes a clear and defined issue. But, when we miss the Lord and take matters into our own hands, life becomes a test of trial and error. Mostly error, I might add. It is usually at this point of error that we blame God for the predicament we are in, forgetting that it was we who strayed from His will, not God. Power is waiting for those who, armed with the Word, shall overcome in the face of temptation.

May 16th

LOVE FOR THE LOST

"But many who heard the message believed, and the number of men grew to about five thousand"

Acts 4:4

Madison Avenue was not even yet a thought. No advertising budget was ever approved. Even if it were, there would have been no agency to hire. "Megatrends 300" had not been written, and there were no ecclesiastic consultants to contact in order to get the message out. Yet, in a very short period of time, the disciples experienced one of the greatest periods of church growth this world has ever seen. Without TV, without billboards, mass mailing, telephone sales or any other 20th century convenience, they evangelized their known world.

How? Listen to these words of the apostle Paul as he reveals the Kingdom strategy that revolutionized the world and continues to do so today:

"How can they believe in the one of whom they have not heard? And how can they hear without someone preaching to them. . .How beautiful are the feet of those who bring good news" (Romans 10:14-15)

Without fanfare and campaign, they accomplished the task by word of mouth and beautiful feet. They did it because they took the time to get involved in people's lives and in the process tell them of the good news. They knew nothing of a "personal" faith. Their religion was not a "private" matter. Without it going public, it was not a valid faith.

How are your feet? Ugly feet or beautiful feet? Sad feet or happy feet? Though we have at our disposal the convenience of modern day advertising, it does not satisfy the mandate for us to tell others of the good news and introduce them to Christ's body.

Our focus has been the family; it must now be balanced with the lost. If you do not already have unbelievers in your life, work to do so. If you have not already done so, invite them to church. Be sensitive, yet be persistent. Remember, few wars are won with one shot.

Let us work to beautify our feet.

⊗

May 17th

DELAYED BLESSINGS

"For the revelation awaits an appointed time, it speaks of an end and will not prove false. Though it lingers, wait for it. It will certainly come and will not delay"

Habakkuk 2:3

A day to the Lord is like a thousand years and a thousand years is like a day." God is not bound to or directed by our perception of time. His decisions are not pressured by the immediate, for He decides from an eternal perspective.

Trust begins by submitting to God's timetable, not holding Him to ours. Often we make the end our focus, where God's focus is the process. He could just answer our prayer, but His desires for us run deeper than just answers. Through the process of waiting, God's desire is to develop in us a maturity of trust. This maturity is seen in the ability to trust Him in His timing and find no fault in His process.

Trust is a major issue when it comes to delayed blessings. Delayed blessings are only delayed according to our perception of time. From God's timetable these blessings are not delayed, but only awaiting their appointed time. Delayed blessings are not denied blessings, they are simply those issues of life awaiting the sovereignty of God's faithful timing. Moses waited 40 years; Abraham waited 25. It was 30 years before Father released Jesus to minister. Every revelation has an appointed time. Until that time comes to its fullness, God keeps every prayer, every tear, and every hidden desire bottled up in remembrance and they are never forgotten.

Are you laboring through the process of delayed blessings? Father is mindful of your desire. He has heard your every cry and knows of your appointed time. He knows no delay, only rightful timing. Though your answer may linger, wait for it. It will certainly come and not delay.

෴

May 18th

A NEW CREATION

"Therefore if anyone is in Christ, he is a new creation. The old has gone and the new has come."

II Corinthians 5:17

The grace of God is that which enables us to satisfy the demands of a new governmental order. To be a Christian means the death of everything that was former and the embracing of everything that is new. It means to forsake our former standards of governmental conduct and come under the governing way of the Kingdom of God.

Jesus Christ is not simply a new reference point in the believer's life. He is our life. When we are born again, everything associated with the old passes away, and Jesus' way becomes our new way. His culture becomes our new culture. His will becomes our new will.

Departmental salvation is the perspective that allows Jesus to save certain departments of our life, but not recreate our whole being. Departmental salvation allows Him to save our prayer life and our moral life, but our work life and our emotional life stays the same. Consequently, we can pray well and no longer have bad thoughts, but on the job we still lie, cheat, steal and at home lose our temper with the kids.

To become a new creation means that every department of my old life has been declared dead and passed away. Now the focus of the Holy Spirit is to bring my thoughts and actions into harmony with God's new intention for my life. As a new creation, I put away those things that are associated with the old: pride, independence, gossip, anger, negativity, etc. All of those are buried with the old and I begin to renew my mind by putting on humility, submission, kindness, and compassion.

Your old way is dead. Bury it before it stinks you to death.

May 19th

YOU HAVE GONE TOO FAR

"They came as a group to oppose Moses and Aaron ... you have gone to far ... why do you set yourselves above the Lord's assembly?"
Numbers 16:3

*I*t was not one of Moses' better days. With Korah and 250 appointed leaders against him, Moses faced an enemy that still runs rampant through the local church. That is the enemy of insolence and the undermining of leadership.

With a determined vengeance, they sought to remove Moses from his God-appointed position. Their accusation? He had gone too far. His behavior in question? He had obeyed God by putting a Sabbath breaker to death. (Numbers 15:36)

From the perspective of Korah and the 250, Moses had gone too far. But Korah and the 250 saw only from a limited perspective. From their vantage point, it looked as if the action of Moses was arbitrary and harsh. But they saw only a limited piece of the whole picture. Moses was the one anointed of God to see the entire plan for the community, and it was Moses whom God had spoken to and given the directive.

This tactic of division is still prevalent in the church today. Congregational members with limited perspective and vantage rise up in rebellion because they perceive a certain injustice. Though what they see may be correct from their vantage, they have not been gifted of God to see the whole picture.

Romans 12:3 tells us that we have all been given a measure of faith. The word *"measure"* in Greek is the word "metron" and it means a sphere. As long as we stay within our sphere of faith, we have grace to see clearly and make correct judgments. But when we move outside our God-defined sphere, our perspective is carnally motivated. Moses carried the "metron" for the whole assembly. Korah and the 250 carried the "metron" for their appointed task. It was when they tried to extend their "metron" beyond the "metron" of Moses that God stepped in and had the Earth swallow them up.

The undermining of leadership is perhaps the greatest problem the church faces today. Usually it is motivated by self-appointed individuals who see perceived or real problems, but move outside their God-given sphere to deal with them. In seeing a gnat-sized error, they force the people to swallow a camel-sized error of loveless correction.

With the God-given ability to see the whole, Moses warned those influenced by Korah to separate themselves from him, for he knew that the Earth was about to swallow Korah, his family and all those who had been swayed to his position.

For the sake of unity and the awaited return of Jesus, separate yourselves from self-appointed critics who, with limited perspective, seek to bring correction to that which God never graced them to address.

ෆ800

Pause for thought:

How is your attitude and actions honoring your God-ordained leaders?

May 20th

A CHANGE OF FOCUS

"With this in mind, we constantly pray for you"
II Thessalonians 1:11

With what in mind? It was the coming of the Lord. Though the coming of the Lord was Paul's focus in his letter to the Thessalonians, when it came to his prayers of intercession, his focus changed. When Paul begins to pray, he makes the condition of the church his focus, not the coming of the Lord.

The Scriptures reveal two aspects of Christ's coming. First, there is that which Christ must do as the head. Second, there is that which we must become as a church body. For years, the church has focused on what Jesus must do and has left unattended that which we must become. Jesus himself told us *"It is not for us to know the times or dates the Father has set . . ."* (Acts 1:7) Yes, scores of books have been written and sold on the times and seasons of His coming. Though we are not supposed to know it, we have made its discovery a major focus, while books on our becoming, sit idle collecting dust on the bookseller's shelves.

Father is quite capable of determining the time of Christ's return without our books. It is high time the church leaves that which belongs to God, to Him, and begin to focus on that which belongs to itself. Our focus must become one of maturity, unity, holiness, and perseverance. These are the things the Scriptures say God is waiting for. (John 17; Ephesians 5; II Thessalonians) Though the prophecy of end time events is important, it is Christ's concern and becomes a diversionary tactic of the enemy when we attempt to fix dates and times.

Let the church return to a focus of holy living. Let the church return to a focus of unity. Let the church return to a focus of maturity. Jesus is doing quite well on His own. Let the church return to a single eye focus on Jesus.

May 21st

IN THE KING'S PRESENCE

"Therefore, since we have been justified through faith, we have peace with God through our Lord Jesus Christ, through whom we have gained access by faith into this grace in which we now stand"
Romans 5:1-2

While on a recent trip to England, I was awed as we toured many of the palaces and castles. I was amazed with the heritage and history that spanned the hundreds of years that were represented in each place of residence. As we toured, I took note how difficult it was to reach the chambers of the king. It was only after going through long corridors, dining halls, galleries, studies and various chambers of other dignitaries, that we finally reached the chamber of the king. As I reflected on the protocol, I was impacted by the access we have to the King of kings. Through faith in Christ, we can boldly come right into the very presence of the King without any protocol or need of anything, except the blood of Jesus Christ. Through faith in Christ, we have gained access to the presence of God.

It is interesting to note that other than the finished work of Christ, nothing else is needed to come in. Man often has a difficult time accepting the simplicity of this truth. How we try in vain to add to Christ's work with our feeble attempts at righteousness. We think that we must add our sacrifice and religious duties. But, none of this adds to our access. Jesus alone made provision for us. We will never or need ever to improve on what Jesus has already done for us.

Do you struggle with accepting your placement with your Heavenly Father? Jesus has already satisfied Father's just demands. You need not try to add to what He has already done. Come on into the King's chambers. He is waiting.

⊗

May 22nd

A CALL TO OBEDIENCE

"This is love for God: to obey his commands"

I John 5:3

One of the greatest discoveries a person will ever make is the discovery of personal purpose. Without a sense of divine purpose, it is difficult to become useful in the Kingdom of God. Usefulness in the Kingdom is simply laying hold of that for which we have been apprehended, then giving our whole being to the fullness of its realization.

But standing between us and the fullness of our purpose is a law. A law in that we can attempt to alter it, redefine it or even outright deny it, but it still remains absolute. To be used and productive in the Kingdom of God, one must pass through progressive doors of purity. Purity is a law. The writer of Hebrews tells us to *"make every effort to be holy, for without holiness no one will see the Lord."* (Hebrews 12:14)

"This is love for God: to obey His commands." One of the great controversies facing the church today is the balance between grace and obedience, the balance between justification and holiness. One side would teach that Jesus paid it all and His sacrifice was so complete, so satisfying to God that there is nothing else we can do. The other side would teach that obedience is central to the teaching of Christ and holiness is essential to Kingdom life. The answer to this argument is not a balance of the two, for they are both correct providing you are using them for the proper application.

Justification has to do with my relational standing before God; nothing can be added to that. Holiness has to do with my personal usefulness in the Kingdom of God and that must progressively increase as I grow in maturity. Obedience does not make me more righteous before God, but it does express my love for Him in a more complete way and opens the door for a deeper level of intimacy.

So rather than try to balance the two, why not enlarge your perspective of both and embrace them in their fullness rather than in their reduced state.

⋘⋙

May 23rd

A HEART OF THANKFULNESS

"Were not all ten cleansed? Where are the other nine? Was no one found to return and give praise to God except this foreigner?"
Luke 17:17-19

Just how important is a heart of thankfulness? It could be easily said that unthankfulness is one of the most prevalent, yet unexcusable, sins of humanity. So much is taken for granted. So much is assumed. So much is done for others without even a word of thankfulness.

Upon seeing this attitude and the nine, Jesus addressed it head on. He said, *"Were not all ten cleansed? Where are the nine?"* Their lack of gratitude did not surprise Him, but it did disappoint Him. To deal with the problem, He did not revoke the healing of the nine. Rather than taking from the nine, He chose to give to the one. Upon the returning of the one Jesus said, *"Rise and go; your faith has made you well."* This word "well" means to be saved and made whole. Implied in this passage is the fact that the nine were just healed. Only the one, who returned to give thanks, was saved and made whole. No one ever thanks God without receiving even more to thank Him for. What we favor, we receive more of. When we favor God for what He has done, we receive more of Him.

Cultivating a heart of thankfulness is what keeps God and His works from becoming commonplace. To allow God and His works to become common is to profane the worth of God. To profane something is to make it unhallowed and public. There is nothing unhallowed about God or His works. Thankfulness is both an attitude and an act that keeps the works of God holy in our lives. As we offer up the sacrifice of thankfulness, we draw a line that says, "We hallow you for what you have done and do not treat it as common or profane."

Let us never take for granted or call common the holy works and person of God.

May 24th

A NARROW MINDED BIGOT

"I am the way and the truth and the life. No one comes to the father except through me"

John 14:6

If Jesus were alive today, they would still crucify Him. The accusation would be that He is a narrow minded bigot. Well, we would have to agree; He was exactly that. On the account of being narrow minded, He was indeed. Jesus stated, with unquestionable clarity, that the way to eternal life was narrow and few there are who find it. In regards to being called a bigot. Webster defines a bigot as "one who is obstinately or wholeheartedly devoted to their own belief or opinion." Jesus was indeed that. In fact, He was so narrowly bigoted about His opinion that He had the nerve to say He was the only way and no one could get to God except they go through Him.

Now Jesus was either correct in His bigotry or He was stark raving mad. America has become a melting pot of syncretistic thought. Our philosophical direction is taking us into the fusing together of different forms and beliefs into a melting pot of lawlessness and nothingness. Absolutes have been abandoned for the new cultural norm of tolerance. Tolerance has become more important than justice. Truth has become all inclusive and is now redefined as a mixture of whatever you want it to be. Those unwilling to accept the new syncretistic values are labeled as discriminating bigots. Anyone left standing on biblical absolutes is branded as narrow and archaic. Well, be of good cheer. We are in good company.

Jesus need not defend the accusations because they are true. I have quit trying to defend Him from the scoffers. When they accuse Him of narrow minded thinking, I agree. Jesus Christ was the most narrow minded man who ever lived. But when you are God, you can afford to be narrow.

The church stands the risk of completely giving in to syncretism. The subtlety of syncretism is that it dilutes the distinguishing factors of Christianity and removes the Kingdom. In order to mix Christianity with anything else, you must remove the Kingdom of God for the Kingdom is a government that mixes with none other. Syncretism does not deny Jesus; it simply dethrones Him.

Has Jesus been dethroned in your thinking and mixed with various religious formulas and traditions? If so, it is time to repent. Jesus can not be given a bold place. He already holds the bold place. Acknowledge His bold place in your life.

May 25th

A NEW OPINION OF EACH OTHER

"I have given them the glory that you gave me, that they may be one as we are one"

John 17:22

The cross of Jesus Christ is both vertical and horizontal. That is, it rightly relates us to God and to one another. As we enter into the act of worship, we are telling God, in our own words, who we see Him to be. After hearing these words of adoration, He responds back by allowing us to experience glory.

Glory in the Greek is the word "doxa." Doxa is interpreted as opinion, judgment and view. As I give God glory, I am giving Him my opinion of who I see Him to be. But worship is a dialogue. It is two-sided. It does not stop with just my opinion. Jesus also gives us His glory. Jesus responds to our worship with the release of His glory. An aspect of that glory is to impart to us the opinion He has of ourselves and each other. He gives us His glory that we may be one, as He is one with the Father.

Worship, though directed to God alone, is explicitly tied to one another. If I come into the worship service upset with my brother, Jesus desires to change my opinion of my brother. As I begin to worship, my heart is turned toward God. As my focus is turned to Him, He imparts His glory or His opinion of my brother. At that point, I have a choice. I can accept the opinion of Jesus and change mine, or I can rebel and hold on to my criticism of my brother. God's heart is that my opinion would change and come into conformity to His own.

As the glory of the Lord transforms us, we begin to see one another with the eyes of Christ. We no longer see each other after the flesh, but we see one another in the spirit. At this point, the walls of separation are pulled down, and Christ's desired level of unity is released.

Does your opinion of someone need to change? If so, receive the glory and exchange your opinion of them for God's.

May 26th

A PRECEDING WORD

"Forget the former things; do not dwell on the past. See, I am doing a new thing! Now it springs up; do you not perceive it?"

Isaiah 43:18,19

The possibility remains of the purposes of God passing us by without us ever perceiving their arrival. Could it be that we could be so dull of hearing, so limited in our vision, so self-related, that we do not perceive the hour of God's visitation?

From time to time, the Holy Spirit brings to a people a word from God that is a preceding word of direction. This word is far deeper than just a word of encouragement and comfort. It is a word of announcement. It is a word intended to stop a people and cause them to evaluate and adjust, if necessary. It is a word that requires a change of direction.

When a word like this comes, we have the possibility of two responses. The fear of the unknown can promote anxiety, apprehension and for some, even unwillingness. Or the challenge of the unknown can promote excitement, adventure and dependency on the Lord. The choice is really up to us and it is all dependent on what we are going to allow to frame our perspective. Fear will force us to save ourselves and hold on to our personal sense of security, whereas faith will cause us to thrust ourselves into the purposes of God and enjoy the freedom of a spirit-led walk.

The spirit-led walk is a walk in adventure because, as the apostle puts it, *"we see in part."* (I Corinthians 13:8) Sure, Father has been faithful to give us the road map, but a road map does not give a detailed reordering of every sharp turn, hill or valley. It gives us some general expectations, but it only shows us in part. So it is with this walk of faith. As people of faith, we go out as Abraham went *"not knowing where he was going."* (Hebrews 11:8) All he knew was God was leading and his heart was willing to follow wherever He should go, even if it meant the sacrifice of Isaac which represented everything Abraham ever labored for.

As Father re-routes us, whatever that re-routing will mean, may He find the spirit of Abraham in us.

૭૩⬥ை

May 27th

A WINDOW AND A MIRROR

"He is the image of the invisible God"
Colossians 1:15

"*Who do men say that I am?*" When Jesus asked Peter this probing question, He was asking perhaps the most important question ever asked. Nothing is more important than developing a correct Christology. It is our understanding of who and what Jesus Christ is that properly relates us to God, ourselves, life, truth . . . to everything.

In Jesus Christ, God was incarnated. He was God made flesh, the image of the invisible God. Jesus was both fully God and fully man. If He were only man, He would be irrelevant to our thought and perception of God. If He were only God, He would be irrelevant to any experience of man. In order for Christ to represent God to man and man to God, He had to be both fully God and fully man.

In Christ we see both a window and a mirror. He is the window through which we see the very nature of God. He is indeed the likeness of God, but He is so much more. Jesus is the exact representation. More than a portrait, more than a reproduction. He was the incarnate God who became flesh and dwelt among us. By looking at Jesus, we can see into the very likeness and being of God. When we see Jesus, we see God in all of His fullness and bodily form. But, not only is He a window into the likeness of God, He is a mirror revealing our human possibility. Jesus, the man, mirrors to us the possibility of what we can become. He reflects the standard and establishes the goal of who we are created to be. He is the exact representation of what man was destined to become before the fall. Jesus Christ was a representation of God perfect enough to become a manifestation of God. He was also a representation of man perfect enough to become the standard for man. The window of God and the mirror of man.

"*And we . . . are being transformed into His likeness.*" (II Corinthians 3:18) Man's created destiny is to become like Christ. As we behold the image of Christ, we are transformed into His likeness. The likeness we see in the mirror becomes us. The old ways fall off as our gaze is continually turned to Him.

Mirror, mirror on the wall, make me like Jesus most of all.

May 28th

A WINNING ATTITUDE

"iIf you pay attention to the commands of the Lord your God that I give you this day and carefully follow them, you will always be on top, and never at the bottom"

Deuteronomy 28:13

We are a covenant people. The covenant promises *winning* to those who obey and curses to those who disobey. Obedience brings with it promised victory. When we obey, the power of the covenant assures us that we will always be on top and never on the bottom.

Though the victory is promised, sometimes the difficulty is allowing ourselves to win. For some, winning is an unbearable responsibility. The promise of being an example and the focus of attention is too much to carry.

Winning begins in the mind. It comes first in our attitude, then in our actions. This is why the Scriptures exhort, *"Let the weak say I am strong."* (Joel 3:10) Our attitude must be influenced before our actions will change. So the aim is to develop a winning attitude by beginning to think like a winner regardless of our outward reality.

The apostle Paul is an excellent example of this. It seems that the outward reality of Paul's life had little to do with the inner attitude that controlled his life. Whether Paul was facing hunger, shipwrecks or beatings, he was still a winner. Whatever the circumstances that Paul faced, he always remained the head and was never the tail.

They say, behavioral psychologists tell us we become what we think about the most. "If we think *winning* enough, we will become a winner." But this is not just a positive thinking mind game; it is the truth of God's Word. *"As a man thinketh on his heart so he be."* The primary root meaning of the word "thinketh" is to split open and act as a doorway. In other words, our thinking becomes the doorway to our becoming. A winning thought is the doorway to success.

Perhaps it is time for you to renew your thinking by putting away negative thought and begin thinking positively.

May 29th

AT PEACE WITH GOD

"... giving thanks to the Father who has qualified you to share in the inheritance of the saints ... and through Him (Jesus) to reconcile to Himself all things ... by making peace through His blood, shed on the cross"

Colossians 1:12,20

Man, by nature, is separated from God. By his deeds, he is at war with God. The sinner is dead in his trespasses and in his sin. Apart from Jesus Christ, man is deserving of nothing but judgment and death. Though man might argue for his own self righteousness, the cosmic court of Father, Son and Holy Spirit has already ruled. The penalty of sin is death.

But Jesus Christ cancelled that penalty. Through the blood shed on the cross, the penalty of sin and death was cancelled, and those who repent are legally declared forgiven and at peace with God.

It is hard for the human mind to grasp this depth of forgiveness. To accept that one would freely give their life in ransom for ours is an act too costly to understand. As a result, we often think we must add something to the work of the cross. It is for this reason that mankind constantly struggles with guilt and condemnation. Somehow, we think if we sin without feeling a sense of self-induced guilt, we have become reprobate. Though man needs to feel the conviction and godly sorrow for his sin, guilt is a lie from the enemy of our soul and an attempt to add something to the completed work of Jesus Christ. But when something is completed, it cannot be added to. In His parting words on the cross, Jesus declared, *"It is finished."* In that declaration He was sounding a truth to every principality and power, to every nation and tribe, to things past and things to come. God is satisfied. Nothing more need be done. Nothing need be added. The blood satisfied God and in so doing we were legally declared to be at peace with Him.

Not only are we at peace, but we also have been qualified to share in the inheritance of the saints. (Colossians 1:12) This qualification is past tense. Long before we thought of adding to it or were afraid we took away from it, God said, "You are qualified." We could never work enough to receive what we already have. So stop striving and trying to add to what Jesus already did. You are legally declared to be at peace. Accept it. Believe it. Enjoy it.

May 30th

ANOTHER CHANCE, YES; SAME OPPORTUNITY, NO

"... because you did not recognize the time of God's coming to you"
Luke 19:44

One of the great challenges throughout the ages has been the ability to discern what the Holy Spirit is saying to the church. History reveals the church erring at both extremes of either missing the Holy Spirit when He comes or manufacturing Him when He does not. It was this very thing that Jesus faced in His coming. Though He came to His own, His own did not receive Him. The natural man is bent on missing God. The tendency to miss our visitation brought Jesus to tears. As a father who sees his children missing their opportunity, Jesus wept over the reality that people did not recognize His coming to them.

It is critical that we recognize the Holy Spirit's visitation because it does not last forever. The "time of God's coming" means a "fixed and designated time." Because it is a fixed opportunity of time, we must respond while we have opportunity. Though God is faithful to give us a second chance, we are never given the same opportunity. If we respond to God in His first coming, there is always an extra measure of grace to respond. If that opportunity is missed, another chance is usually given, but it never comes as easy as it would have on the Holy Spirit's first coming. There is no opportunity to respond to the Holy Spirit's leading as today's. This is why the writer of Hebrews says, *"Today if you hear His voice, do not harden your hearts."* (Hebrews 3:7)

To recognize the Holy Spirit's coming, we must keep our hearts soft, humble and willing. Pride is a visitation stopper. Pride is a death sentence on the Holy Spirit's visitation. According to Leviticus 26:19, pride turns the Heavens to iron and the Earth to brass. It dries up the visitation and aborts the harvest.

The Holy Spirit desires to come to you. Keep your heart humble and willing, for in your humility, God will grace you with a visitation of His manifest presence.

May 31st

BOASTING IN OUR WEAKNESS

"My grace is sufficient for you, for my power is made perfect in weakness"

II Corinthians 12:9

Man is always looking to build his strengths in order to succeed. "Expand your mind, enlarge your experiene, capitalize your strengths," they tell us. Survival of the fittest is the way of the world, and only the strong survive.

But not so in the Kingdom of God. The Kingdom of God is not built upon the strength of man, but rather it is built upon his weakness. In the Kingdom of God, what one cannot achieve in one's strength, they will be able to achieve in their weakness. Acknowledging our weakness is not an admission of failure, but an acknowledgement of source of supply. God has ordained that He alone will be the supply of His Kingdom. He does not desire or need our help.

Consequently, the enemy does not attack us at our point of weakness, but at our point of strength. We are most vulnerable and open to attack where we are the strongest. It is at our point we often let our defense down, thinking the enemy will attack us at our weakness. Knowing this, our enemy often attacks our strengths and there gains the victory. Perhaps prayer is our strength. The enemy will attack our prayer life through diversion and cause the focus of our prayer to turn to self. Perhaps faith is our strength. The enemy will turn faith inward to be consumed upon possessions and in so doing divert faith's focus.

May our boast not be in our strengths, but may we boast in more things that show weakness. Apart from Christ, we can do nothing. In His Kingdom, the weak are strong and the strong are weak.

છ૪૦

June 1st

BY MY SPIRIT

"Be still and know that I am God"

Psalm 46:10

Often we face times in the Lord when everything we do seems to turn out right. Our dreams come to pass, our desires are fulfilled and our pursuits are successful. Suddenly everything seems to come to a grinding halt. The times we have of victory and release are turned to times of struggle and process. What once came with tremendous ease and definite joy, now comes by constant effort and repeated choices. Our most often uttered prayers become "Why?" "Father, what are you trying to say in all of this? Where have I missed the turn?"

The processing of the Lord is part of the price of completion. The capstone of completion is the desire of everyone's work, but between the foundation stone and the capstone is the processing hand of God. It is during this time that He is able to humble us and prove to us that the glory of the work belongs to Him and to Him alone. Having begun in the spirit, we are not made perfect in the flesh, so the Lord's encouragement to us is to be still and know that He is God.

This word "still" in the Hebrew means to cease from action. To forsake and let alone. So often when the time of processing comes, God lifts His hand of blessing voluntarily to prove us. It is during this time that the flesh jumps in to take over where God left off. So it is this action that the Holy Spirit says, "Be still," cease from your own initiative, forsake any self-induced effort to do the work of God. If we are obedient, the processing of God will work its course and we will once again see the mighty hand of God working on our behalf.

The word *"still"* is followed by the word *"know."* This word *"know"* means to ascertain by seeing. Whenever God is able to find a people who are willing to cease from their own efforts and wait for the moving of God, those saved people will know by seeing with their own eyes that God is faithful and will bring to pass the work He has begun.

"Though the vision lingers, wait for it; it will certainly come and will not delay." (Habakkuk 2:3)

June 2nd

CONSEQUENCES

"Do not be deceived: God cannot be mocked. A man reaps what he sows"

Galatians 6:7

Life is ordered by law. The covenant Word of God is the invisible law structure of life. When God spoke, He set into motion an irrevocable way. When that way is obeyed, we are blessed. When that way is violated, we suffer the consequences.

God maintains His sovereignty even when allowing man's choices. Though we choose for ourselves, we can not choose the results of our choices. God does allow us to exercise our will, but His irrevocable way is always in effect. If our free will has chosen God's way, then we are blessed. But, if our will has chosen a way contrary to God's will, we suffer the consequence.

God always has the last word. Man is in constant pursuit of "kicks." But, for every "kick" found outside of God, there is a "kick back." The "kick" lasts for a while, long enough that some might think they got away with the wrong doing. But, sooner or later the "kick back" comes because God always has the last word. Every action, every decision contrary to God's covenantal Word carries with it a consequence. The consequence may be immediate or it may take time for it to manifest, but as sure as God's Word is true, the consequence will come.

Wrongful decisions are often like writing bad checks. At the point of purchase, you get away with the wrongdoing, but once that bad check hits the bank, the consequences begin to fall. If restitution is not made, then an arrest is imminent.

Are the consequences of life's choices taking their toll on you? Surrender to the will of God and let the consequences be His instruction to you.

June 3rd

EMBRACING THE SEASON

"There is a time for everything, and a season for every activity under heaven"

Ecclesiastes 3:1

In the early '60s, a group called The Birds put this passage of Scripture to song. They entitled the song, "Turn, Turn, Turn." The turning of life is a law. Seasons turn. No season remains. Every year we move through winter, spring, summer and fall. You might say, "Why can't it always be spring; why not a perpetual summer?" It is because God has ordained the seasons. Each season carries with it a specific and strategic purpose.

Spiritual life has its seasons as well. Spiritual life is not always the freshness of spring. Often we face the barrenness of a spiritual winter, only to be followed by the fruitfulness of spiritual harvest.

Seasons are designed of God to deepen us. Seasons help us grow stronger. Roots grow deeper when the winds blow strong. Deeper roots make for stronger lives. Winds produce character, strength and uniqueness of style. Seasons reinforce the sovereignty of God. There is nothing like a sudden spiritual storm to remind man who is in charge. Seasons help to produce humility. There is nothing like the barrenness of a spiritual winter to bring us back into reality after a fruitful summer.

Seasons are a law; there is nothing you can do to stop them. To fight them is to fight the Lord. Everything has its season under Heaven. Everything has its divine season. Spring is a time of planting and release. Summer is a time of great growth and maturity. Fall is a time of reflection and evaluation. It is a time of great change. Winter is a time of dormancy and repair and preparation of planting and harvest.

Do not fight your season. Recognize it for what it is and yield to its activity.

June 4th

NO CLUB MED

"Be self controlled and alert. Your enemy the devil prowls around like a roaring lion looking for someone to devour"

I Peter 5:8

The devil takes no vacation. He has no down time and no mandatory rest breaks. The seasons of the year mean nothing to him, so spring fever is of no consequence and the summer let up is nonexistent. The devil will just as soon devour you in July as he would in January. Evening is just as good of a time for him as is morning. The weekends are the same to him as the week day. The devil is an opportunist, so whatever the time or the season, as long as the opportunity is right, he will devour.

Problem is, we take vacations. We have down time and recognize mandatory rest breaks. The seasons are very real to us. Spring fever is distracting and the summer let up is quite real. Many think weekends are for fun and after a long day at work, the evenings are to relax. Mix this mindset with that of the devil's and the devil's victory is sure.

This is why Peter admonishes us to, *"be self controlled and alert."* Life is a war zone not "Club Med." We must continually gird our minds for action and resist the temptation to take a spiritual vacation by letting up for just the summer months. Such a mentality is appropriate in a "Club Med" vacation setting, but not in a war zone. In war, there is no letting up.

While you are vacationing this summer, may I encourage you not to take a vacation from Jesus. He is our immunity from Satan's attack. The more we press into Him, the greater is our power to resist and withstand anything the devil may launch against us. Find your rest in Jesus not away from Him, and by the way, *"do not forsake the assembly together of yourselves."* Resist the temptation to let up and instead press in.

☙❧

June 5th

FATHER'S GIFT

"Do not leave Jerusalem, but wait for the gift my Father promised, which you have heard me speak about. For John baptized with water, but in a few days you will be baptized with the Holy Spirit"

Acts 1:4-5

We live in the age of the Holy Spirit. The Holy Spirit is the promised gift from the Father who has been commissioned of God to reveal Kingdom truth which is unable to be perceived by the natural mind. Without the Holy Spirit guiding, teaching, revealing and enabling, there is no progression or growth in the Kingdom of God.

Therefore, it is no wonder the Holy Spirit is the most neglected and misunderstood member of the Trinity. It has been the strategy of our enemy to relegate the Holy Spirit to the realm of controversy and negate His work through misunderstanding and fear. The enemy has used the fear of emotionalism, speaking in tongues, abuses of the past and others to shroud the Holy Spirit in skepticism and doubt, consequently, preventing the work He has been commissioned to do. Without the present ministry of the Holy Spirit, there is no one to ensure Kingdom entrance, real Kingdom membership, implement Kingdom obedience, build Kingdom character, furnish Kingdom gifts, empower Kingdom outreach, produce Kingdom growth or secure Kingdom victory. In the absence of the Holy Spirit's work, man has sought to fill the void with personality, skillful management, creative imagination, personal charisma, talents, financial strength, political action and educational prowess. None of these, without the impartation of the Holy Spirit's life, will produce fruit in keeping with the Kingdom of God.

The current focus on self-help is a wrongful focus. It was self that produced the sin; a further focus on that same self is not going to solve the problem that was created. The Holy Spirit is God's answer to man's problem. He must learn to cultivate a relationship with Him, for He will reveal the Father. He is not an "it" used of the Father and Son to do their bidding. The Holy Spirit is God. The third member of the Trinity commissioned to be our comforter and guide.

As you seek the Kingdom, seek and know the Holy Spirit better. Seek to cultivate a deeper relationship with Him. As you do, you will gain a greater understanding of Father, Jesus and the Kingdom of God.

June 6th

THE CERTAINTY OF GOD'S PROMISE

"By faith Abraham, even though he was past age—and Sarah herself was barren—was enabled to become a father because he considered him faithful who made the promise"

Hebrews 11:11

The writer of Hebrews gives us a perspective of encouragement in regard to waiting for God's promise. He directs our attention to Abraham, who waited twenty-five years from the time God promised him he would be the father of many nations and the time he bore the promised son. All throughout those twenty-five years, he never lost hope. Paul tells us in Romans 4:18, *"Against all hope, Abraham in hope believed and so became the father of many nations."* The odds were against him, but he believed because he knew our God is an odds buster.

We are in a walk of hope. Hope speaks of a confident expectation. A sure anticipation. Faith is the evidence of what is hoped for. Paul tells us in Colossians 1:5 that faith and love *"spring from hope."* That confident expectation and sure anticipation is the well from which the purposes of God are realized. Hebrews 6:18-19 tells us, *"We who have fled take hold of the hope offered to us, so that we may be greatly encouraged."* We have this hope as an anchor for the soul, firm and secure.

As we identify the strong man of discouragement and despair over a city, prayer is a crucial means of defeat but only a partial means. The other means of defeat is to counteract these spirits with their positive counterparts, i.e., hope and encouragement.

God is calling us to "take hold of hope," for in hope is our encouragement. We must hold on to that "confident expectation" in God's promise and encourage one another to do the same. Let us look for any opportunity to encourage each other and encourage the work of God, for therein will we see the strong man of discouragement defeated.

"Hope that is seen is not hope at all. Who hopes for what he already has? But if we hope for what we do not yet have, we wait for it patiently." (Romans 8:24-25) *"Those who hope in the Lord will renew their strength. They will soar on wings like eagles, they will run and not grow weary, they will walk and not faint."* (Isaiah 40:31)

June 7th

EXPECT VICTORY

"As a man thinketh in his heart so is he"
Proverbs 23:7

*W*inning is an attitude that begins in the mind before it is realized in the arena. The mind of man plays a paramount role in what he is able to accomplish. Because it plays such an important part, what we put into our minds has strategic importance.

Self-help prophets are making millions of dollars telling us something the Word of God has told us years ago. The Word tells us what goes into our minds will determine, to a large extent, what we become. What goes in will come out. What we sow into our minds, we will reap in our actions. Actions begin in our mind. So in order to become all that God intends, we must feed our minds with God's thoughts.

Jesus understood this principle of first the mind, then the actions, so the thrust of His teaching focused on arresting the mind. He made the inner man His focus, not the outer man. While people of His day struggled with external law and ritual, they failed to see where issues of life truly originated. They spoke of murder while Jesus spoke of hatred. They spoke of adultery while Jesus spoke of lust. They spoke of an earthly kingdom while Jesus spoke of the Kingdom being within to rule over our minds and our hearts.

The battle over our mind is won through the choice of our wills. We win because we make the choice to win. Jesus has already purchased our victory. Whether that victory becomes ours is determined by what we choose to believe. Adversity is never a sentence of defeat. The sovereignty of God makes it our training ground of victory.

Expectations determine outcome. If you expect to lose, you probably will. Whereas, if you expect to win, the victory of Christ becomes our reality. God has made provision for our victory through the cross of Christ. Let us expect victory over defeat.

June 8th

FREE FROM ACCUSATION

"But now he has reconciled you by Christ's physical body through death to present you holy in his sight, without blemish and free from accusation"
                                                            Colossians 1:22

Free from accusation. Not only are we fully reconciled to God through Christ, but we stand before God without blemish and entirely free from accusation. This does not mean the accusations do not come; it simply means that when they do come, they have no credibility or anyone to listen to them.

The power of accusation is the lie. The reason accusations have so much effect on us, once we have been freed from them, is we believe the lie. Satan is the father of all lies and the accuser of the brethren. The fuel of his accusation is lies. Though we have been declared legally free from the effect of those lies, many still believe them rather than believing the truth of God's words. What we choose to believe is what determines the outcome of our lives. The truth says we are holy, free, with purpose, identity and destiny. The accusations say we are unholy, bound up, without purpose, identity and going nowhere. What we choose to believe determines who we will become and what we will accomplish. The accusation is indeed powerful but the truth is more powerful yet. The truth sets us free from the power of accusation.

Gossip and slander among the believers is one of the enemy's sources of information to propagate his lies. Whenever we speak unkind words against each other, we provide the enemy further information to propagate his accusations. Gossip and slander are like an all-you-can eat buffet for the accuser. We must stop the gossip and slander in order that we might dry up the accuser's source.

The truth of God's word is our defense against the accuser of the brethren. We overcome evil with good. We overcome the lie with the truth. The word of God washes us from the power of accusation. Positionally, we are free from the accusations. Christ's blood washes us from every accusation of our experience. Jesus has made every provision for us to be free. All that is left to do is believe it.

                                                                              ଓଷ୦

June 9th

GRACE GIVEN

"Set your heart fully on the grace to be given you when Jesus Christ is revealed"

I Peter 1:13

Whenever Jesus is revealed, a fresh supply of grace is given. Grace is a communicable attribute of Jesus Christ. It is not something apart from Him; grace *is* Him. Grace is the very life of Jesus indwelling in us to fulfill the just requirements of the law.

The Scriptures define righteousness in terms of relationships, not requirements. What makes us righteous is not the fulfilling of prescribed requirements, but the embracing of a desired relationship. Father God desires relationship with His people. Relationship to Christ releases trust in God's ability. The more we know Him, the more we trust Him. The more we trust Him, the more free we become. Sin is a violation of a trust relationship. We trust God by fixing our eyes on the grace He supplies. With every temptation, God provides a way of escape. So, before we sin, we first must refuse the supplied grace provided to overcome that temptation. That refusal of grace is a violation of trust and akin to spiritual adultery. Breaking the law is a violation of rules. Refusing grace breaks the heart. Breaking a law does not have the same effect as breaking God's heart. His heart is for relationship. His heart is to supply grace.

Grace is the consciousness that Christ's performance satisfied our requirement. A consciousness of His bold performance is much more liberating than the self-consciousness of our lack. The awareness of our lack keeps our focus set upon ourselves, not upon the grace to be given when Jesus is revealed. Grace can be illustrated in the difference between water skiing and parasailing. Both involve a boat, water and a person. To ski, one must have strength and the ability to get up and maneuver the ski. To parasail, all one must do is get strapped to the harness, and the power of the boat and the ability of the sail do the rest. Grace is to strap our lives to the harness of Jesus Christ and fix our hearts on the grace to be given when He is revealed.

ଙ୍କ

June 10th

GRIEVING THE HOLY SPIRIT

"Do not let any unwholesome talk come out of your mouths . . . and do not grieve the Holy Spirit . . . get rid of all bitterness, rage and anger, brawling and slander, along with every form of malice"
Ephesians 4:29-31

Isn't it interesting how sandwiched in between the exhortations of our relationships to one another is the command not to grieve the Holy Spirit? Though the apostle does not say it directly, the implication is clear. We grieve the Holy Spirit when we are hurtful to each other. How can this be so? It is because we are the temple of the Holy Spirit. (I Corinthians 3:16) The Holy Spirit has chosen to take up His residence within the housing of our earthen vessel. When that vessel is hurt or maligned, the contents are grieved. When we grieve others, we grieve Him. When we attack the temple, we attack the Spirit.

For far too long man has separated Jesus, the head, from His body. Consequently, we can confess allegiance to the head while we are abusing the body and we think we are doing God a favor. But Jesus did not see a separation. He said, *"As you have done it unto the least of these my brethren, you have done it unto me."* (Matthew 25:40) Jesus saw no separation from Himself and His people. Yes, we worship Him only, but we must remain clear and unified with our brothers as far as it concerns us.

According to the apostle Paul, God's eternal purpose was to destroy the dividing wall of hostility that had separated His children and create in Himself one new man. Jesus accomplished that on Calvary but it cost Him His all. Our unity was purchased by the precious blood of Jesus. It is for this reason the apostle tells us to *"make every effort to preserve the unity of the Spirit in the bond of peace."* (Ephesians 4:3)

Our unity is essential to the eternal purpose of God. Let us carry God's heart and keep our relationships clear.

⚜

June 11th

HE OVERCAME BY BEING OVERCOME

"In the world you will have trouble. But take heart! I have overcome the world"

John 16:33

Jesus Christ was an overcomer. There was nothing easy about what He came to do and what He was able to accomplish. He chose the way of greatest difficulty and overcame with an abundance of grace.

That Jesus overcame, considering the circumstances He faced, is amazing. But how He overcame those circumstances is more amazing yet. Jesus Christ overcame by being overcome. He did not overcome by winning, rather, He overcame by losing. In the willful laying down of His life to be overcome by the sin of the world, Jesus overcame the power of sin and broke its stranglehold forever.

Jesus overcame the need for getting by giving. He was overcome by hate that He might overcome in love. He was overcome by the religious rulers that He might overcome in the spirit of a servant. Jesus modeled for us that we overcome as we are willing to be overcome. When we seek to save our lives, we lose the power to overcome. But as we willfully lay our lives down as a sacrifice unto the Lord, we overcome. We serve a backward Kingdom. Those who overcome in this Kingdom are those who are willing to lose what they cannot keep in order to gain what they cannot lose.

As we are overcome, Jesus turns our captivity and we become overcomers. If we take things to ourselves without Jesus just giving them to us, those things will ruin us. We cannot be truly prosperous until we have been overcome by the need to give. As we are overcome by giving, then Jesus can give to us the riches of the Kingdom.

Do not fear losing. You serve a backward Kingdom. Jesus first takes away before He gives back. As we lose our lives for His sake, we will find them.

☙❧

June 12th

IN AND AT

"To the holy and faithful brothers in Christ at Colosse"
Colossians 1:2

The apostle Paul opens his letter to the Colossians by clearly identifying the two spheres Christians move in. He wrote to the holy and faithful who are *in* Christ *at* Colosse. A Christian always lives in two spheres. He is in a certain place in the world and he is also in Christ. As believers, we live in two dimensions. We live in this world and are responsible as ambassadors to represent the Kingdom of God.

But above and beyond this world, we are always *in* Christ. Being *in* Christ is not circumstantial. Being *in* Christ is an absolute that does not change from day to day. Though the locational sphere we find ourselves in may change daily, the relational sphere we have *in* Christ is constant. That is why circumstances make little difference to the Christian. Our peace and our joy are not dependent on where we are *at* but who we are *in*. We may be *at* a painful place. We may be *at* a confused place. We may be *at* a place of training or *at* a place of discipline. Wherever we find ourselves *at* we find ourselves *in* Christ. Consequently, we can find ourselves *in* righteousness, peace and joy.

Because we are always *in* Christ, we can do any task with all of our hearts. It matters not how menial, painful or unpleasant the task may be. It may be far less dignified than we would expect, its reward far less substantial. It may carry no recognition of man. Nevertheless, those who are *in* Christ do it diligently and wholeheartedly, without murmuring, for they do their work as unto the Lord. What we do must always flow out of who we are "in," not where we are *at*. We must build our lives on the foundation of absolutes, not situations.

We are all *in* our own Colosse, but we are all *in* Christ. The providential hand of God has permitted whatever our outward circumstance may be. Wherever you find yourself *at*, draw from who you are *in*. In Christ you can do all things. *In* Christ you can find the strength, the wisdom and the resources needed to overcome. Christ is your life, and *in* Him you live and move and have your being.

June 13th

INERRANCY OF SCRIPTURE

"For the prophecy never had its origin in the will of man, but men spoke from God as they were carried along by the Holy Spirit"
II Peter 1:21

The Bible is, in fact, the inspired Word of God and is without error. One of the greatest challenges facing the church today is the issue of the inerrancy of Scripture. Is the Bible the all-inspired Word of God, without error, or does it just contain passages of inspiration that must be mined out as one would mine for gold? The very foundation of orthodox thought throughout the church age has been the inerrancy of Scripture. Church creeds declared boldly and church fathers were willing to give their lives in order to preserve this sacred truth. Recently a deception of neo-orthodoxy has subtly crept into the church. This deception is an attempt to build an evangelical house on a liberal foundation. It adheres to the basic tenets of evangelical thought, but rejects the very foundation of that thought in the inerrancy of the Holy Scriptures.

Orthodox theology concerning Jesus Christ states that Jesus was fully God and fully man. Not only has He always been fully God; in His incarnation He became fully man as well. He was and is God and He became and is man. In the same manner, the Bible is fully of God and fully by human authors. It is fully inspired by God, and it was fully written by men as they were carried along by the Holy Spirit. The fact that men were the divinely inspired agents to write does in no way take away from the inerrant inspiration. *"All Scripture is God breathed."* (II Timothy 3:16) The Word of God speaking of itself states it is fully inspired, not partially. Once one settles for partial inspiration, then man becomes the god that decides which part is inspired. One man believes these verses and another believes those, and everyone is left to their own private interpretation. Paul puts an end to that speculation and boldly states, *"All Scripture is God breathed."*

We must guard ourselves against the deception of neo-orthodoxy. Two provisions were made to bring God and man together. The first is Jesus Christ whose shed blood satisfied God's just demands. The second is the Bible which is God's fully inspired word that reveals the nature and way of His Kingdom. If we lose the Bible, we have lost our pathway.

❧

June 14th

FAMILY

"He decreed statutes for Jacob and established the law in Israel, which he commanded our forefathers to teach their children"

Psalm 78:5

As fathers, we are preparing the way for our children who will follow. Though it was Solomon who was given the privilege to build the temple, he was greatly inspired and assisted by his father, David, who prepared the way.

Children tend to mirror their father's values or adopt the exact opposite, depending on whether the Father has won the children's respect. If a father has won his children's respect, they will willingly adopt his values. But, on the other hand, if the father has neglected the children in his pursuit of temporal gain, they will most likely embrace the opposite of that which their father endorses.

God is a generational builder. The Scriptures are full of examples where the father was entrusted with the vision, but the son was given the task to build. This is why it is so vital that we build our lives so as to win our children's respect. If they feel neglected or replaced by the vision we hold dear, they will go in search of an alternate vision.

Time and attention are the biggest contributors to respect. Words are important, but mere words of affection and affirmation will only frustrate. But, when words are mixed with time and attention, you have a sure winner in gaining your children's respect.

Today, we honor your position as fathers. Have you won your children's respect? Do they know themselves to be more important to you than your job and your pursuit of temporal gain? Have you been able to instill into them values that will perpetuate the vision you embrace?

I encourage you today to examine the condition of your house and see if your children are prepared to build after you are gone.

ଔଡ଼ଠ

June 15th

THE CURSE OF FAMILIARITY

"They are to teach my people the difference between the holy and the common and show them how to distinguish between the unclean and the clean"

Ezekiel 44:23

Familiarity is a thief—the sliest of all thieves, for it robs you without ever lifting a hand. The subtlety of familiarity is the fact that familiarity causes you to rob yourself. "It takes nothing from you; it only causes you to take everything for granted and in so doing, you lose it all."

The aim of familiarity is deadly. Its goal is to take what is most priceless to us and make it appear as if it were common. Familiarity breeds more than contempt. It is also the father of broken hearts, missed opportunities and the insatiable desire for more. With a single stroke, familiarity turns the sparkle into the drab, the exciting into the mundane and the holy into the common.

Familiarity does not rob you of your salvation; it just causes you to forget what it was like to be lost. You treat prayer as common and therefore do not pray. Worship becomes routine and devotional time is regarded as religious. With the passing of time, it infiltrates your heart with boredom and covers the cross with dust so that you are safely out of the reach of change.

Familiarity will not steal your home; it simply paints it with a coat of drabness. The evening gown is replaced with the bathrobe. Nights on the town become evenings in the recliner and romance is replaced with routine. Your children are not taken; you just become too busy to notice them. The seduction of procrastination becomes full grown. There is always next summer to coach the team and next week you can teach them to pray. The poison of the ordinary has deadened your senses to the magic of the moment.

No, there is nothing common about the Christian life and nothing subtle about the curse of familiarity.

(rewritten from an article of unknown origin.)

June 16th

LOSTOLOGY

"For the Son of man came to seek and to save what was lost"
Luke 19:10

Lostology is the study of being lost. According to Jesus, man is lost. Regardless of how man feels about his own condition, according to Jesus, He is lost.

Believe it or not, being lost is not necessarily bad. Staying lost can be eternally terminal, but being lost makes you a candidate for being found. A person who is unwilling to acknowledge being lost is incapable of being found. Being found is predicated upon acknowledgment of being previously lost.

When people are willing to admit they are lost, they in the same confession acknowledge that they are people of purpose. By confessing they are lost, they acknowledge that there is a particular place they need to be and are not there. People who have no directional purpose may admit they lack direction, but they do not acknowledge that they are lost.

When Jesus said He came to seek and to save what was lost, He was saying He came for those who have spiritual purpose. From God's perspective, there is a place we need to be. Father created us to serve His purpose and become His inheritance. He sought us out and saved us in order that we might fully serve His purpose and become part of His vast family.

When people are willing to admit they are lost, they, in the same confession, acknowledge that they are of value. By describing us as lost, Jesus places upon us spiritual value. Father God cares that we are not where we are supposed to be and he values us enough to search us out, redeem us and place us back on the right track. We are not disposable to God.

In this Kingdom, being lost is good news. Staying lost is not so good, but being found begins with acknowledging our "lostness" and fully embracing God's plan to recovery.

૱

June 17th

SUPPORTING LIGAMENTS

"From him the whole body, joined and held together by every supporting ligament, grows and builds itself up in love, as each part does its work"

Ephesians 4:16

Father has taken every precaution for His children to be one. Not only has He built us together into a dwelling in which He lives by His spirit, He has also held us together, bone to bone, with every supporting ligament. A ligament is a connecting or unifying bond. It is the tough bond of tissue connecting the bones or supporting organs in their place.

A doctor friend of mine once said, "When it comes to medicine, the issue is the tissue." According to the apostle Paul, when it comes to relationship in the body of Christ, the issue is also the tissue. Without the forming of spiritual ligaments, there is no joining together of the individual bones. Individual bones piled together do not make the body. The body of Christ is not a pile of isolated bones. It is a creation of strategically placed bones that are held and cemented together by supporting ligaments.

Ligaments are simply the relationships between the bones. As I, an individual bone, open my life up to another bone, a relationship is formed. It is the recognition and nurturing of that relationship that keeps me joined together with that other bone. Neglect of the relationship will result in the separation of the bones. Attention to the relationship will guarantee the future joining of the two bones.

The joining of the bones is God's doing. The nurturing of the ligaments is ours. Paul concludes this verse with the phrase, *"as each part does its work."* Ligaments are not automatic. People do not just naturally come together and stay together. Connecting bones takes purposeful work. It requires each part doing this work. Ligaments will mean each part doing its work of forgiveness. The joining of bones will come with certain offense. Though not purposeful, offense will come. In the face of offense, each part must do its work of forgiveness. Ligaments will mean each part doing its work of laying down personal agenda. Two bones going in opposite directions cannot be joined. Each bone must do its work of recognizing God's agenda and yielding to the direction of the whole.

Relationships in the body of Christ should come naturally, but most often they do not. Most often they work like Paul expressed. Work simply reveals the reality that we've been brought into a war. The focus of that war is to separate what God has joined together. This is why we see so many divided relationships, church splits, racial hostility and broken marriages. Division is a strategy of demonic warfare, because Satan hates what God has joined together.

It is for this reason Paul exhorts us in Ephesians 4:3, *"Make every effort to preserve the unity of the Spirit through the bond of peace."* Ligaments are work, but the result is well worth the effort required.

※

Pause for thought:

Who are you working with to do your part? Is there division that you need to work out so that God can effectively join you?

June 18th

A NOBLE DESIRE

"If anyone sets his heart on being an overseer, he desires a noble task"
1 Timothy 3:1

Leadership does not just happen. It comes as the result of a purposeful and deliberate decision. It comes as one sets his heart to embrace the responsibilities and character of his calling. Though leadership is birthed by a call, it is realized by a choice—the call we have nothing to do with. The call is a result of God's sovereign choice, but the setting of the heart is entirely up to us. Leadership is produced as a result of divine initiative embracing human responsibility.

To set our hearts on being overseers literally means "to crave" being an overseer. It has to do with a burning desire or an inner compulsion to lead and care for the people of God. It is the same word that, when used negatively, is translated lust. Lust is a powerful force. It is a negative drive that controls. But on the positive side, that same drive and force is to be channeled into seeking after the things of God.

Many have developed a false humility in their concept of leadership. As the Holy Spirit awakens the desire within them to lead, they perceive that desire as ambition or grasping for position. Consequently, they resist the desire and never embrace the training necessary to fulfill the call. Though ambition and grasping for position are wrong, God is quite capable of sorting out our motives if we allow Him.

If God has placed a desire in your heart to lead, then pursue that desire. To deny the desire because of a fear of ambition would be to deny the call of God. If the desire is there, then place yourself on the altar for the Holy Spirit's inspection and go for it. You are desiring a noble task.

The world is in dire need of those whose hearts are set. Do not fear your desire; only be strong and courageous.

☙❧

June 19th

YESTERDAY'S TOMORROW

"Consecrate yourselves, for tomorrow the Lord will do amazing things among you"

Joshua 3:5

Today is the tomorrow that was spoken of yesterday. Yesterday we said God was going to do amazing things tomorrow, and that tomorrow is today. The Lord is indeed doing amazing things. What we have labored and interceded for is beginning to unfold among us.

Celebration life, faithful service, victory in trial, lives saved are all signs of the fact that Father is doing amazing things. But, oh how easy it is to take it all for granted! Familiarity is robbing us of a greater blessing and release of resurrection life. A grateful spirit will prompt greater blessing from God and also will prompt church growth, for people want to be around places where life is flowing. If the enemy can not stop the life, he will seek to cause us to become familiar with it and in so doing, will limit the experience of that life to the limited few who are enjoying it. The end result is God's purposes are hindered, not because of anything direct, only that which is indirect.

An aspect of consecration is separating ourselves from that familiar spirit. Often we discount what God is doing in our lives because of familiarity. Whereas, if we saw in others what He is doing in us, we would be amazed.

Let us seek the Lord for a new appreciation of the work He has done in us and then allow that appreciation to flow out and draw the prodigals back into Father's house. Our enthusiasm over the Lord's work is one of the best evangelistic tools we possess. As we witness the amazing things, let us begin to shout them from the roof tops.

∞

June 20th

IT'S NEVER TOO LATE!

"Therefore, since the promise of entering His rest still stands, let us be careful that none of you be found to have fallen short of it"
Hebrews 4:1

William Barclay, the great Scottish theologian, said in his commentary on Hebrews that this verse could be translated, "Beware lest you think that you have arrived too late in history to enjoy the rest of God."

We look at the accomplishments of men like Luther, Calvin, Edwards, Finney and think that the great days of spiritual accomplishment are over. How easy it is to look back at the past and think that we will never experience or do the exploits which they did. Somehow we think that God was more powerful and much more exciting then. To think that is to conclude that somehow His power has diminished over the years, and His willingness to display His glory is waning.

To this attitude, the writer of Hebrews says, in effect, "Never!" He writes a warning to the people of God exhorting them to believe that it is still God's day. Jesus is the same yesterday, today and forever. If He was capable of doing it in the past, He is capable of doing it today. Never think you have arrived too late in history to be used. Never think, "If only I were alive in the Bible days." You are alive in the Bible days! These are just as much God's days as those days were when Jesus walked the Earth. God is just as sovereign now as He was then. He is just as powerful today as He ever was. The only difference is, us.

What keeps us from the exploits of a Luther, Calvin or Finney is not God, but us. We serve the same God with the same power who carried the same desire to touch us (as His people) and impact a world. That desire wants to be joined with a person who is available enough and courageous enough to step out and believe that God will do what He said He would do. God's desire is for His people to believe that it is never too late! History has not passed them by.

Perhaps that person is you. Perhaps 100 years from now, history will record your name as one who believed that this was your hour and accomplished historical things for the Kingdom of God. Why not you? It is never too late.

June 21st

BACKSLIDING

"Therefore, we must the more eagerly anchor our lives to the things that we have been taught lest the ship of life drift past the harbor and be wrecked"

Hebrews 2:1 (Barclay)

Very few people ever fall into sin. The real threat for believers is not turning their backs on God, but rather drifting away from Him. In our terminology, we speak of falling away from God, but the real issue is "slipping slowly away." This is why we have used the term backsliding. It is not "back falling" or "back plunging," but backsliding. Slowly, consistently, over time, we make certain decisions; we allow certain disciplines to lapse and almost without notice, we find the fire that once burned so hot to be but a flicker.

Backsliding happens as the result of conditioning. To fall away would be too obvious and too abrupt, the contrast stark enough to catch our attention and shock us into change. So, slowly over time, our spiritual senses become conditioned to compromise. Our ability to discern right and wrong becomes dull. Our desire to please our Heavenly Father becomes clouded. Little things begin to drift away. Daily devotions are robbed by the distractions—spiritual intimacy robbed by urgency. Our focus on Jesus is blurred by the multitude of life's responsibilities that compete for our attention. Soon we find our ship drifting off course. No, the ship is not in danger of sinking. Everything appears to be in order.

The subtlety of backsliding is long before the ship is affected, the course is lost. The aim of backsliding is our course in life. Its aim is our destiny. So while we are examining our ship, making sure all is right, we are slowly drifting off the predetermined course the sovereignty of God has planned. The ship still looks good. We still go to church. We still call ourselves Christians, pray, read the Bible and do all the things Christians do. Where we have been affected is in the fulfilling of our destiny.

Conditioning comes as a result of many things. Friendship with the world is a conditioner. Close relationships with unbelievers can slowly condition us away from righteous character. Television is a major conditioner. As we watch TV, the sins of carnal living can become a way of life. Each immoral act is like a seed planted in our field. As each seed comes to life, our ship is taken off course.

Beware of the slide. Keep an ear turned to the Holy Spirit. As He turns you away from the things that would alter your course, be sure to turn with Him.

June 22nd

GOD IS SO BIG

"Now to him who is able to do immeasurably more than all we ask or imagine, according to his power that is at work within us"
Ephesians 3:20

How big is God? What is the level of your limitation upon God? All of us limit God to one degree or another. God is without measure, yet in our human limitation, we cannot relate to something without measure. So into our relationship with the immeasurable God, we bring our need to keep things within measure. So we are always placing God within the box of our comforts and concepts. Because He is without measure, He is always moving outside the box of our limitations.

Whatever the level of our limitation upon God, He is able to do immeasurably more. Just how much is immeasurably more? To ask that question is to reveal our need to place a measure upon God. Whatever the measure we come up with, "God is bigger!" He is able to do immeasurably more than we decide He can do. The limit of God's ability is not defined by us, but by Himself.

In order for us to experience that ability, God must become BIG in our thinking. How much can you imagine God to do? Whatever the level of your imagination, He is able and willing to do immeasurably more. How much have you asked Him to do? Whatever the level of your desire, He is able and willing to do immeasurably more.

Our concept of God does not limit Him; it just limits our experience of Him. God desires to become BIG in our thinking in order that we might know Him as He really is. The God we currently know is only a portion of who He really is. As we allow Him to get bigger, we begin to know Him in the fullness that He intends to reveal Himself.

If God is able to do immeasurably more, then it is time to dispense with small plans. Our vision and plans must be to commensurate with the bigness of God. He is a BIG God, so let us make big plans. A small God means a small vision. A small God means small expectation. A small God means small results. A BIG God means all these things without measure.

God becomes BIG as we begin to confess Him as so. Begin to confess and remind yourself God is so BIG. As you do, you will be given opportunity to test your confession. God will prove Himself in the test and as a result, your concept of His size will increase.

❧

Pause for thought:

How much can you imagine God to do? Whatever the level of your imagination, He is able and willing to do immeasurably more. How much have you asked Him to do? Begin to confess it.

June 23rd

AN EMPTY CUP

"But we do see him who was for a little while made lower than the angels, Jesus himself, crowned with glory and honor because of the suffering of his death, a suffering which came to him in order that by the grace of God, he might drain the cup of death for every man"

Hebrews 2:9 (RSV)

*M*an faces a constant battle between what he is and what he was meant to be. Man is clearly not what he was intended to be. Hebrews 2:7 says, *"We were made a little lower than the angels."* In Hebrew, the word for angels is *Elohim*, which is the normal word for God. We were created to be a little lower than God, but because of our sinful choices, we find ourselves as creatures frustrated by our circumstances. We were created to have dominion over all things, but we do not. Instead, we are defeated by our temptations and subject to our sinful nature. Though we should be kings, we often act as though we are slaves.

It is into this conflict the writer of Hebrews declares Jesus Christ drained the cup of death for every man. The writer makes clear that man is not what he was created to be, but into that misfortune Jesus Christ came in order that by His life and death and glory, He might make man what he was intended to be. Jesus Christ died to rid man of his frustration. By His death, He exchanged our frustration for His mastery, our shame for His glory, our failure for His victory. Jesus died to recreate man until he becomes what he was originally created to be.

Make no mistake about the condition of man. Outside of Christ, man is sinful and only worthy of death. Man is not a little god. Outside of Christ, our cups are full of death. But by the grace of God, Jesus died in order that He might drain that cup of death for every man. Now, in Christ stands the possibility of becoming all God intended us to be.

The only way this is possible is through an exchanged life. Our life for His. Our will for His. Our plans for His. Through the exchanged life, Jesus takes everything we are not and gives us all that He is. As we pour our lives into Him through prayer, study, availability, willingness, etc., Jesus communes with us and in that communion exchanges our life for His.

June 24th

GRACE LOVE

"Who shall separate us from the love of Christ? Shall trouble or hardship or persecution or famine . . . for I am convinced that neither death nor life, neither angels nor demons, neither the present nor the future . . . nor anything else, in all creation, will be able to separate us from the love of God that is in Christ Jesus our Lord"
Romans 8:35-39

How could Paul have been so convinced of God's love? What did he know about God's love that so persuaded him that nothing in all of creation could ever separate him from it? Perhaps it was due to the perspective of love that Paul possessed. Nothing can separate us from God's love only when that love is predicated upon nothing but God Himself.

There are three stages of love in our love for God and each other. The first stage is love based on gratitude. Gratitude love is the love of merit. It is love that acknowledges what God has done for us and gives love in return. Gratitude love says, "I love because . . ."

The second stage of love is relational love. Relational love says, I love because of who He is. It is love based on the holiness of God's character and moral perfection. Relational love does not need things; it has Him.

The third stage of love is grace love. Grace love simply says, I love. Grace love loves for no reason. It is a love of complete surrender, even if God does not meet our expectations. God loves us with grace love. His love for us is unconditional; therefore, nothing can separate Him from us. In order for our love for Him to be inseparable, we must love with the same grace love. Grace love says my love is not based on anything other than my will to love; therefore, nothing can separate me from that love. Grace love says even if circumstances try to change my perspective of God, my love for Him is not predicated on my perspective of Him. Therefore, I continue to love Him.

Are you persuaded that nothing will separate you from the love of God? Allow the Holy Spirit to take you into the realms of grace love in order that the conviction Paul possessed will be yours as well.

○③❀○

June 25th

EVEN WHEN WE CAN'T SEE IT

"We live by faith, not by sight"

II Corinthians 5:7

It was with great expectation we planned our trip to the Grand Canyon. Even though we did not feel like making the long drive, we felt to behold one of the seven wonders of the world was worth the trip. The drive began early in the morning with the heat reaching 100 degrees. As the small rental car labored to keep us cool, we kept reminding ourselves the result would be worth the trip. As we neared the canyon, our expectations began to heighten. Carload after carload was there to witness the same wonder we came to see.

As we entered the canyon, signs led us to one of the first viewing points. What we had only seen in picture, we would now be able to capture with our own eye: Red Rock Canyon, one mile deep. I was awed as I imagined standing above a canyon and being able to look down over 5,000 feet. With racing hearts, we approached the lookout rail, only to find the canyon completely fogged in. With towels over our heads to shelter us from the torrential rains, we stood at the edge of one of the seven wonders of the world unable to see anything but a blanket of fog covering the entire canyon.

It was then that the Holy Spirit quieted my heart with a simple, but profound truth. Though I could not see the canyon, it was still there. Though I could not see it with my eyes, nevertheless, I stood at its very edge and it was just as real in the fog as it was on the clearest days. I was in the Grand Canyon. Beneath my feet was a wonder of God's creation.

How often do we stand at the edge of God's provision, only to walk away because the fog of circumstances keeps us from seeing the wonder of His provision? Sooner or later the fog will lift, and when it does, the wonder will be there. The fog comes and goes, but the canyon of God's wonder always remains. His promise is stronger than the fog; His word more enduring than the circumstance.

What has God promised? Does the vision tarry? If so, wait. You stand at the edge of provision. Once the fog lifts, the wonder is yours.

June 26th

COST OR INVESTMENT

"Store up for yourselves treasures in heaven, where moth and rust do not destroy and where thieves do not break in and steal. For where your treasure is, there your heart will be also"

Matthew 6:20-21

It has been said that salvation is free, but the Kingdom of God will cost you everything. Is the Kingdom of God a cost, or is it an investment? Recently, while going over the schedule of a leader, the man commented on the price his ministry was costing his family. My reply was, "If you are doing what you are doing in obedience to the Lord, it is not a cost, but an eternal investment."

When one decides to set up an IRA account for their future retirement, they set aside a specified amount each year to put into that account. As they are making payments into the account, they should not view those payments as a cost, but rather an investment because they will receive a future reward for their sacrifice.

So it is with our labor for the Kingdom. A strictly temporal look would see the cost of time and resources. The temporal would see the cost as further complicating an already complicated life. We might see the cost of risk, rejection, and possible persecution, but the closer we look, the more we see the eternal reward of spending our life for the purposes of God's Kingdom. As we see the rewards, we realize that the return is high and the costs are relatively low, especially when we recognize that ultimately they are not costs at all; they are investments that pay eternal dividends.

I cannot imagine a safer investment than to invest in the work of the Kingdom. How better could we spend our lives than to spend them on the One who will reward us for eternity?

◊

June 27th

A PAST IN OUR FUTURE

"Look to the rock from which you were cut and the quarry from which you were hewn"

Isaiah 51:1

Everything about God speaks of roots and foundations. God is generational, both in His thinking and in His behavior. What has happened before is preparation for what is yet to come. The past generation sets the pace for the generation to follow. Each generation inherits a responsibility to be faithful to the generations that have gone before, lest they lose what has been imparted.

A people cut off from their past have an altered future. It is not that they do not have a future, for God is eternal. As long as there is an eternal God, there will be a future for His people. The question we must face is: Will we walk in the fullness of that future? A people cut off from their past are unable to walk in their future's fullness, for the very root that produces the fruit of their future has been severed. Once the root of our past has been severed, the fruit that root was intended to produce is lost.

It is for this reason that the Bible continually urges us to remember. *"Remember my covenant, remember the wonders, remember you were slaves."* Forgetfulness is a tactic of spiritual warfare. A people, prone to forgetfulness, are cut off from their past. God went to extreme measures to assure His children's remembrances. He instructed them to build memorials. He made sure that every covenant was sealed with a symbol. He kept His covenant in a book to be preserved throughout the ages. All of those served to refresh their memory and keep them linked to their past.

Remember, there is a past in your future. Never forsake your foundations or forget the rock from which you were cut.

June 28th

BECOMING OFFENSIVE WITH OFFENSES

"An offended brother is more unyielding than a fortified city and disputes are like the barred gates of a citadel"

Proverbs 18:19

Offenses are as much a part of everyday life as blessings. Though blessings are more easily welcomed, offenses are an essential aspect of our maturity process. As long as we are housed in this temple called "flesh," offenses will be inevitable. We must never excuse them or become familiar with them, but we must be willing to overlook them if they come, for in overlooking an offense, we promote love. (Proverbs 17:9) This being the case, whenever we do not overlook an offense, we degrade love.

Jesus said in Matthew 18:7 that it is inevitable that stumbling blocks come. In other words, there is not a whole lot you can do to prevent them from coming, but you can do everything to keep them from having a negative impact on your life. God has given us control over the response we choose when offenses come. We can either choose to embrace them as the inevitable process of Kingdom life, or we can take matters into our own hands and react to the offense by developing a hard, unyielding heart.

An offended heart is the first step toward relational breakdown and broken covenant. Once someone's heart has been offended, it is very difficult for them to yield to the process of reconciliation. An offended heart causes one to view words and actions through the eyes of offense. If offense is your starting point, then further offense will be your destination. If you start with a problem and focus on a problem, you become a problem. Offenses have a way of making captives out of people. Once people become offended, they soon become passive in their ability to do anything about the offense. What makes offended people so unyielding is their lack of desire to do anything about their condition. Becoming offensive with your offenses is taking the initiative to bring your offense to the cross and leave it there.

The cross is the answer for an offended heart. More counseling will not fix it; more understanding will not change it. What heals an offended heart is the realization that the sovereignty of God permitted that stumbling block to come to fix something in you. As you embrace that perspective and yield to its processing, you become free, and the offense becomes your servant, rather than your taskmaster.

June 29th

FROM SHADOW TO SUBSTANCE

"In the past, God spoke to our forefathers through the prophets at many times and in various ways, but in these days He has spoken to us by His Son"

Hebrews 1:1-2

Christianity is the journey out of shadow into substance. Outside of Christ Jesus, everything is mere shadow. Only in Christ do we find true substance. The prophets were a shadow used of God to prepare the way for Christ. Now that Christ has come, we have substance. What man needed was a perfect priest with a perfect sacrifice and Jesus was both. In His manhood, He can take man to God and in His diety, He can bring God to man.

The sacrifice Jesus brings is the sacrifice of Himself. The prophets of old used many methods to convey truth. But Jesus revealed truth by being Himself. He was the embodiment of His message. It was not so much what He did that shows what God is like; it was who He was. The prophets were the friends of God, but Jesus was the Son of God. The prophets grasped a piece of God's purpose, but Jesus was the purpose. In the prophets, there was the continuity of God's plan, but in Christ was the consummation of that eternal plan.

Jesus is the embodiment of God's heart to His people. In Christ, we discover the depth of God's love for those whom He creates. Jesus reveals that God's heart does not consist in crushing men and reducing them to abject servitude, but in serving them and demonstrating the power of suffering love. Jesus Christ lives not as our judge, but rather as our intercessor who intercedes for us, so that we might enter into the presence of God. We come into His presence not to hear His justice condemn us, but to hear His love plead for us.

The prophets saw His love only through the shadows. They saw only a part and could only speak from the revelation they knew. Jesus Christ is the fullness of God. As we behold Him, we move from the shadows of partial reality into the substance of eternal truth.

Are you still lurking in the shadows? It is Christ's desire to continually reveal the depth of God's heart for us that He might unify us with the heart of God and build us into a people of substance.

June 30th

TRUST AND OBEY

"Today if you hear his voice do not harden your hearts"
Hebrews 4:7-8

Though God's love is unconditional, His promises are not. As it was for the children of Israel, God makes a promise. In order for us to appropriate that promise, we must fulfill certain conditions. Unless those conditions are fulfilled, we remain outside the provisions of promise. To obtain the conditional blessing of God, two things are essential, trust and obedience.

Trust is rooted in a revelation of the character of God. To know God is to trust Him. To know His character is to know that God is trustworthy. What He has said, He will do. He will do what He said, but for us to experience that work, our trust must give Him opportunity.

Trust is also rooted in God's sovereignty. Trust is the acknowledgment that God is omnipotent, omniscient and omnipresent. God rules the affairs of His children when our trust in Him allows it.

Trust is also rooted in God's providence. Trust is the acknowledgment that God is directing my life to fulfill the desires of His will. Nothing comes into my life that His providence did not allow. Adversity, suffering and pain are all servants of the providential hand of God. Trust is not just believing what God says is true. Trust is the willingness to stake our lives on those promises.

Obedience is also essential to obtain the blessing of God. In any realm of life, success depends on obedience to the word of the expert. A doctor says, "You can be cured if you obey my instructions." A trainer says, "I can make you a champion if you embrace my discipline." Likewise, God says, "I am the expert on life; I can make you a winner if you obey my word."

Obedience has always been the weakness of God's people. Like a ship prone to wandering, we have wandered away in favor of our own way. Obedience is the daily dying to our own way in favor of God's way. It is the continual saying of *"NO"* to our own desires in order that we might fulfill His.

Today, if you hear His voice, trust and obey. The saying goes, there will always be a tomorrow, but for every man there comes a day of no more tomorrows. Today is our opportunity to trust and to obey. By doing so, we will enter into the fullness of God's promised land.

July 1st

A MUCH NEEDED REST

"By the seventh day, God had finished the work he had been doing, so on the seventh day he rested from all his work. And God blessed the seventh day and made it holy because on it he rested from all of his work of creating that he had done"

Genesis 2:2-3

It is interesting to note that day seven of creation never came to a conclusion. Days one through six all had a morning and an evening; that is, they had both a clear beginning and a definite end. But on the seventh day, the day of God's rest, there is no mention of evening. From this, rabbis have concluded that while the other days came to an end, the day of God's rest had no ending; the rest of God was forever. Though Israel never entered that promised rest, the promise still remains today.

"There remains then a Sabbath rest for the people of God." (Hebrews 4:9) Just as God's rest was forever, there is a rest available for us today. The writer of Hebrews goes on to explain what that rest is. *"Anyone who enters God's rest from his own work just as God did from His."* (Hebrews 4:10)

To enter the rest of God is to cease from your own labor in exchange for the life that comes from God. This exchange of labor has to do with both the focus of our labor and the strength of that labor.

Focus is simply whom we are doing it for. To rest from our own work is to stop laboring for things that serve ourselves and not the purposes of God. The first secret to entering the promised rest is to die to personal ambition and self-centered desire. Anyone alive to himself will never enter into the rest of God. The first step into God's rest is to so desire His will over our own that we wholeheartedly offer our lives over to Him.

The exchange of labor also had to do with the supply of strength to do what God expects. Our greatest strength is our weakness. From the beginning, God has expected us to quit trying on our own to do His will and allow His strength to be expressed through us. Our only effort is the effort to enter into the rest. Once we are there, we can expect a continual supply of His strength. The hardest aspect of getting in is the admission of weakness. From our perspective, "I can't" is a negative confession, but from God's, it is quite positive. God waits for that admission of weakness, for then and only then can He release the Holy Spirit who will usher us into that Sabbath rest.

July 2nd

THE CANCER OF NEGATIVITY

"Whatever is true, whatever is noble, whatever is right, whatever is pure, whatever is lovely, whatever is admirable, if anything is excellent or praiseworthy, think about such things"

Philippians 4:8

Throughout time, negative thought patterns and speech have been a stronghold of God's people. Ten times in the wilderness, Israel grumbled against God and accused Him of mistreatment. Over time, this negative attitude became a stronghold that ultimately prevented them from entering the promised land.

Negativity is like a cancer. It spreads through the body of Christ affecting everyone it touches. Like any communicable disease, it has a means of transmission. Negativity travels through the body of Christ through three primary agents of transmission: self pity, sarcasm and envy.

Self pity is negativity *internalized.* Self pity can be discribed as pride having a bad day. Pride is the root of self pity, which is an attitude that says, "I deserve better, God was wrong with this one." But I Corinthians 10:13 tells us that the temptations we all go through are common to man. Self pity tells us we are the only one who has to endure such temptation. God tells us we all face similar temptations. The answer to self pity is a revelation of God's sovereignty and the corresponding trust that sovereignty brings.

Sarcasm is negativity *vocalized.* Every sarcastic word is like a knife that cuts. Sarcasm is a thief that robs people of their faith and their joy. Sarcasm comes from the Greek word "sarkasmos" which means to tear flesh or bite the lip in rage. Sarcasm is caustic language that whether it is meant to or not, tears people's self esteem and leaves them void of faith and joy. The answer to sarcasm is abstinence.

Envy is negativity *externalized.* It is negativity projected on to someone else due to the resentment of a perceived advantage they have. Envy is a resentful desire to possess what is not yours. Envy is a big league problem. The answer to envy is love. I Corinthians 13:4 tells us love does not envy. Where there is love you will find a void of envy.

July 3rd

THE TAKING OF OFFENSE

"And they took offense"

Matthew 13:57

Offenses are always taken, never given. No one can give you an offended heart. You alone are the guardian of your heart and you alone determine whether or not your heart will be protected. Others may give cause for offenses, but whether or not the offense is taken is purely up to you. In the face of cause, you alone are the ruler of your heart. What you do with the offense will determine whether your heart remains soft and yielding or whether it becomes hard and unyielding.

There is a progression of offense. An offended heart begins with a cause. Someone says something, does something or does not do something that creates a cause for offense. At this point, you have a choice to either take offense or take the cross. A choice to take the cross is a choice to yield your perceived right for offenses to Jesus in order to maintain an unoffended heart. A choice to take offense is a choice that will harden your heart and hinder your ability to hear God and remain one with, His body. Following the choice of offense is separation. Separation from those you took offense with begins in the heart. It begins with attitudes and feelings.

Once the heart separation has taken place, excuses begin to flow. "He who separates himself, looks for an excuse." The excuse that is presented is usually not the real issue; it is only a diversion to take the focus off the offended heart. Once the excuse is offered, it must be justified. Since the mind will justify what the heart desires, the person makes further choices to convince themselves that their excuses are justified. Once the excuse for heart separation is justified, physical separation follows. By the time physical separation happens, the person is usually unwilling to acknowledge that it can all be traced back to a personal offense.

The cross of Jesus Christ is God's answer to an offended heart. Taking up our cross daily involves the choice to yield our perceived right to be offended over to Christ. Instead of taking offense, we must take the cross and allow the cross to turn our hearts in the direction of Christlikeness. Consequently, our hearts remain soft and yielding. As long as our hearts are soft, faith is fresh. Once our hearts become hard, faith is held captive.

Have you taken offense? It is not yours, so give it back. Give it to God. Yield your perceived right to be offended to Him. In so doing, you will remain yielded and God will be free to pour blessing upon you.

※

Pause for thought:

Has offense spoiled the freshness of your faith? Is your perceived right to be offended worth the separation between you and a covenant brother or sister?

July 4th

THE HOPE OF WITHHELD DESIRE

"For I know the plans I have for you," declares the Lord ... "plans to give you hope and a future"

Jeremiah 29:11

In a consumer society, hope does not sell well. Faith will sell and so will love, because both promise an immediate reward. But the very nature of hope promises nothing immediate, except a deep rooted confidence founded in the faithful power of God. To the spiritually minded, that is a lot, but to the carnally minded who look for immediate gratification, hope is less desirable.

God's plan for His people is to give us hope. How can He give us hope without first withholding desire? *"But if we hope for what we do not yet have, we wait for it patiently."* (Romans 8:24-25) By withholding the evidence of godly desire, God teaches us to hope. Faith teaches us thankfulness, because it carries with it the evidence of what is hoped for. (Hebrews 12:1) Hope teaches us trust, because it carries with it no immediate reward, except the gift of eager expectation.

Hope turns our focus and pursuit solely upon Jesus. In the void of immediate reward, our focus is taken off things and placed upon the giver of promise. In the process of this fixing, we are learning to continually yield our desires over to Jesus. It is the yielding of our desires that keeps us from the sickness of deferred hope. Deferred hope is simply expectation that did not meet our time table. The sickness of deferred hope comes when we do not yield our desires in the face of unfulfilled expectation. Real hope says, hope that is seen is not hope at all. So in the light of unfulfilled expectation, we must continue to trust God and keep our eyes fixed on Him.

Could Jeremiah 29:11 read, *"For I know the plans I have for you," declares the Lord, "plans to withhold your desires, for in the hope of withheld desire is your future?"* Our future is found in the hope of yielded desire. Our future is found in the hope of godly trust. Our future is found in the hope of eager expectation of God fulfilling His promise. We have been eager to learn faith and love, for they both promise immediate reward. God's desire is that we would be equally willing to embrace hope, for all three, faith, hope and love are remaining attributes we are to possess.

"For the creation was subjected to frustration . . . in hope that the

creation itself will be liberated . . ." (Romans 8:20-21) The frustration you are experiencing is the frustration of that which is not seen doing its work. Though it may seem contrary to godliness, it is part of the very process wherein your Heavenly Father is securing your future.

☙❧

Pause for thought:

What desires do you need to yield to the Lord?

July 5th

ENGAGEMENT

"If you confess with your mouth Jesus is Lord and believe in your heart that God raised him from the dead, you will be saved"

Romans 10:9

Paul's word to us in Romans is not just a formula for salvation; it is a spiritual principle for life. The spiritual life is a life of engagement. Spiritually speaking, life does not just happen to us; we must engage it. We do not just make mental assent and become saved. To be saved, we must engage our mouths and hearts. As a result of that engagement process, we are saved.

Every day we face the choice of engagement. Many born again believers go through their everyday lives and only engage God on Sundays. The thought of engaging God in their work places or in their recreation is foreign. Some attend church regularly and still never engage God. The fact that we are present in church does not guarantee an engagement. Engagement is a choice of the will. Any engagement with God is preceded by a choice to give yourself over to Him. Without giving yourself over, we may observe, but we will never participate in spiritual life. Participation comes as a result of engagement. When we make a choice to engage God in worship, we become a participator of worship. Without the choice to engage, we become passive observers whose hearts become hardened and whose ears become dull.

There are many attitudes that keep us from engaging God. Certainly stubbornness is one. Perhaps the songs being sung are not to our liking, so in stubbornness we refuse to give ourselves over. Those who make it a practice to engage God, will find a way of engagement regardless of the song selection.

Pride is another attitude that keeps us from engagement. Pride will keep us from seeing the worth of God, and in so doing, stunt the freedom of our expression. The humble have little difficulty with engagement. The depth of their gratitude enables them to engage immediately in order that they might express the depth of their appreciation.

Whatever the attitude is that keeps us from engagement, it is our loss. To engage God does Him no favor. God has made Himself accessible for our benefit. When we engage Him, we become like Him. The longer our engagement, the clearer our transformation.

Are you an engager or an observer? To engage God is to give yourself fully to Him regardless of how strange the process may seem to your natural mind.

∞

Pause for thought:

What is keeping you from engaging? Are you willing to give yourself to Him?

July 6th

OBSERVER OR PERCEIVER

"Now these things occurred as examples, to keep us from setting our hearts on evil things as they did"

I Corinthians 10:6

There is a major difference between one who observes and one who perceives. Observing is simply seeing what takes place, but not having any understanding as to why it took place. Perceiving is the ability to see beyond what you see and understand why and how it took place, so as to either prevent it from happening again or repeat it, depending on the nature of its outcome.

Most will go through life only observing. They will see their mistakes; they will see others' mistakes, but they will be helpless to make the necessary changes, for they are only observing those mistakes, not perceiving why and how they took place.

Perceivers ask questions. They ask the Holy Spirit what and how. They examine every situation, asking for discernment, taking notes and then making necessary changes so they don not repeat past failures.

Failure is a servant if we view it with perspective. If perspective is added to failure, then failure becomes a learning experience, but without perspective, failure is failure. Fail once, call it learning. Fail twice, call it advanced learning. Fail three times, call it stupidity. By the third time, the power of the Holy Spirit is certainly able to reveal what needs to be done in order to turn the cycle of failure and change.

"My people are destroyed from the lack of knowledge." (Hosea 4:6) This verse is not speaking of a knowledge of the facts. Fact of the matter is we know more than we ever have. The knowledge the Lord speaks of has to do with perception. The people of God are destroyed due to a lack of spiritually perceiving the facts they know.

Pray: Ask God to make you a perceiver. Study the Word; seek to find its wisdom in relation to the situations in which you find yourself.

July 7th

CALL TO OBEDIENCE

"This is love for God: to obey his commands"

I John 5:3

One of the greatest discoveries a person will ever make is the discovery of personal purpose. Without a sense of divine purpose, it is very difficult to become useful in the Kingdom of God. Usefulness in the Kingdom is simply laying hold of that for which we have been apprehended, then giving our whole being to the fullness of its realization.

But standing between us and the fullness of our purpose is a law. A law that we may attempt to alter, redefine, or even outright deny, but it still remains absolute. To be useful and productive in the Kingdom of God, one must pass through progressive doors of purity. Purity is a law. The writer of Hebrews tells us to make every effort to be holy, for without holiness, no one will see the Lord. (Hebrews 12:14)

"This is love for God: to obey His commands." (I John 5:3) One of the great controversies facing the church today is the balance between grace and obedience, or between justification and holiness. One side would teach that Jesus paid it all and His sacrifice was so complete, so satisfying to God that there is nothing else we can do. The other side would teach that obedience is central to the teaching of Christ, and holiness is essential to Kingdom life. The answer to arguments is not a balance of the two, for they are both correct providing you are using them for the proper application. Justification has to do with my relational standing before God, and nothing can be added to that. Holiness has to do with being used in the Kingdom of God and that must progressively increase as I grow in maturity. Obedience does not make me more righteous before God, but it does express my love for Him in a more complete way and opens the door for a deeper level of intimacy.

So instead of trying to balance the two, why not enlarge your perspective of both and embrace them in their fullness, rather than in their reduced condition.

○൭൱○

July 8th

INSPIRATION OR TRANSFORMATION

"And we, who with unveiled faces all reflect the Lord's glory, are being transformed into his likeness with ever increasing glory, which comes from the Lord, who is the Spirit"

II Corinthians 3:18

How easy it is to settle for shadow and miss the substance. How easy it is to become enamored with the vehicle and forget the destination. As creatures, we are continually satisfying ourselves with the secondary when the primary awaits our pursuit. The good is good, but the best is the best. God never intends for His children to settle for the good. His will is for us to press for the best.

Jesus Christ gave His life to become the firstborn of many brethren. The Holy Spirit comes in the church today in search of the corporate Christ. To become that corporate Christ, we must be transformed into His likeness. Redressing our current state will not do. Transformation is not a remodel; it is a complete destruction and total reconstruction.

Sons of the Kingdom do not settle for second best. Sons will not settle for inspiration, but will press for transformation. Inspiration is shadow; transformation is substance. Inspiration is the vehicle, transformation is the destination. Inspiration is the secondary, transformation is the primary. Inspiration is good, transformation is best. Sons of the Kingdom recognize that inspiration is necessary to bring transformation about, but will not abort the process until the fruit of Christlikeness is seen.

Inspiration is temporary, transformation is eternal. How many times have you been inspired by good preaching only to go home in the same condition you came? Inspiration is good, but in and of itself, it will leave us short of transformation.

Transformation comes as a result of continually placing ourselves in the presence of a transforming God. As we sit in His presence and allow Him to search us by the Spirit and examine us by the Word, the process of transformation takes place. Transformation is not our doing, it is His. We come into His presence; He transforms. What God expects of us is desire and placement. That is, we desire change and place ourselves in a position to be transformed. To do so we do not just listen to a message preached, we take notes on that message and then place ourselves before the Holy Spirit and allow Him to search us with it. That Word then penetrates us and the truth contained therein transforms us. Inspiration is what makes the process fun; transformation is what makes the process complete.

※

Pause for thought:

Have you been settling for the good and missing the best? Inspired, but not transformed? Present yourself before God anew as a candidate for transformation. Come before Him daily and ask Him to change you into the likeness of Christ.

July 9th

WHEN CLAY IS GOOD AS GOLD

"In a large house there are articles not only of gold and silver, but also of wood and clay, some are for noble purposes and some for ignoble. If a man cleanses himself from the latter, he will be an instrument for noble purposes"

II Timothy 2:20-21

The Scriptures reveal Satan as the father of all lies. It has been with tremendous effect that he has used those lies to rob us of our God-given potential. Often his strategy is to twist Scripture and even use it to substantiate his lies. The subtlety of his lies sounds something like this: "The Scriptures say some are gold and some are silver, some are wood and some are clay. Some are used for noble purposes and some for ignoble. You are most definitely clay; therefore, you will never be used." Buying into this lie causes us to sell ourselves short and either settle for some menial task or give ourselves to temporal issues, since we have no real purpose in the spiritual.

But if you take a close look at this verse, it is saying something completely different. The verse never says only the gold or silver qualify for noble use. It simply says there are gold articles and there are clay articles. Gold does not make you honorable or clay dishonorable. It is not the pot that qualifies you as noble or ignoble. What qualifies us as noble is our practice and our behavior. "If a man cleanses himself from the latter, he will be an instrument for noble purposes." He may still be a clay pot, but he will be a clay pot used for noble purposes. What qualifies us as noble is giving ourselves wholly to the purpose we were created for. A gold pot given to taking out the garbage is not a noble purpose. A clay pot given wholly to serving the King makes that clay pot a noble article of honor.

The subtlety of this lie keeps many in a continual state of comparing "pots." We must quit comparing "pots" and believe the truth of who we are in Christ. We must cease comparisons and give ourselves wholly to fulfilling our created purpose. You may be a clay pot or you may be a gold pot, but you, the pot, are not the focus. The focus of God is the treasure held within. A clay pot given wholly to the purposes of God will make a gold pot out of anyone.

July 10th

TO KEEP IT, YOU MUST GIVE IT AWAY

"Give and it will be given to you. A good measure, pressed down and shaken together and running over, will be poured into your lap. For with the measure you use, it will be measured to you"

Luke 6:38

We serve a backward Kingdom. To receive what we need, we must often do the exact opposite of what we think. To live, we must die. To receive, we must give.

God's desire for us is to have fruit that remains. It is not enough to just have an experience with God and not come away with lasting fruit. Lasting fruit is the result of giving away what God has already given. The principle of the Kingdom of God is simply this: To keep it, you must give it away. Giving it away opens the channels for a greater supply. Only in giving it, can we keep it.

The blessing and favor of God is never meant to be consumed solely upon ourselves. We are channels through which the Holy Spirit pours His blessing to others. As we freely give what has been poured into us, a blessing beyond measure is received. If we keep what has been poured in, soon it spoils and becomes stagnant. Life soon becomes stale and listless. Vitality is drained, adventure is gone; it is time for a transfusion.

Giving reopens the channel. As we give in evangelism, the flow of adventure is released. As we give to the Holy Spirit, the flow of power is released. As we give financially, the flow of prosperity is released. According to the measure we give, it will be measured back to us.

How is your measure these days? Is it time to prime the pump? Give and it will be given to you. Give sparingly and you will receive sparingly. Give abundantly and you will receive in like manner.

○‍○

July 11th

A PHOTOGRAPH OF GOD

"Jesus Christ is the radiance of God's glory and the exact representation of his being"

Hebrews 1:3

The Scriptures say no man has ever seen God and lived. Even Moses was only permitted to see the backside of God as He passed by. Moses was not allowed to look upon God face to face lest he die. Though we have never looked upon God, face to face, we have seen a good photograph of Him. Jesus Christ is the exact photograph of the likeness of God. When you have seen Jesus, you have seen God. He is a speaking image of everything God is. Anything we would ever want to know about the character and likeness of almighty God is found in the person of Jesus Christ. Without Jesus, God is unknowable.

High power electrical voltage is unusable in its raw state. In fact, unless the voltage passes through a transformer, it is quite deadly. If you were to plug your toaster into a power plant, you would become toast. It is the transformer that breaks the power down and regulates it into usable power. The detrimental becomes the friendly, and the deadly becomes useable.

Jesus Christ is God's transformer. Through the life of Christ, the deadly power of God is transformed into usable power. The very power that would kill us in a direct dose is regulated into transforming doses that charge us slowly rather than killing us immediately. The Holy Spirit regulates the proper amount of power at the proper time in order to accomplish the proper result.

Jesus Christ is all we need in our quest to find God. When we are not permitted to look upon God lest we die, the photograph found in Christ is the next best thing to being there.

July 12th

WHEN HEAVEN PARTIES

"In the same way, I tell you, there is rejoicing in the presence of the angels of God over one sinner who repents"

Luke 15:10

What were the events that surrounded your conversion? Did it seem rather uneventful to you? Perhaps it was a prayer of repentance, a tear of sorrow, followed by a deep assurance of your acceptance by God. Though that might be the extent of what you saw, it most definitely sells short what took place in the Heavenly realms.

The Bible tells us when a sinner repents, in effect, Heaven parties. When sinners turn from their rebellious way and return to their redeemer, all of Heaven erupts into a celestial celebration of joy and thanksgiving. Father's desire for the prodigals to return home runs so deep that when one does, He calls for the angels to prepare a feast and for the cosmic celebration to begin. At the rate of conversions taking place today, Heaven never stops partying.

By reading the parables of the lost sheep, the lost coin and the prodigal son, we catch a glimpse into the heart of God for His children who are lost. In all three parables, there are a few threads of consistency. First, something of great value was lost. People are of tremendous value to God. He extends His mercy and does what He does for us simply because He loves people so much. Second, that which was missing warranted an all out search until it was found. Jesus demonstrated this truth in willingly laying down His position in order to redeem mankind. He gave His all in order to find us who were lost. Even as the Father sent Him, He is now sending us to do likewise.

Lastly, all three parables reveal that when that which was lost was found, there was great rejoicing. God rejoices over the repentance of one of His lost children and He gives us a part in that process; one of life's greatest adventures is the adventure of leading someone to Christ.

Let us join the party and enter into the celebration!

☙❧

July 13th

SELF-PROMOTION

"Now Adonijah, put himself forward and said, 'I will be king'"
I Kings 1:5

From the fall of man, self-promotion has been the temptation of every man. It's the temptation of the "I wills." *"I will ascend, I will sit enthroned, I will make myself . . . ."* (Isaiah 14:13-14) Self promotion finds its very root in the likeness of Lucifer. Its motivation is rebellion and its aim is to be like God rather than being an instrument of God.

David's son, Adonijah, faced this very temptation and lost. Stronger than his love for his father, stronger than his devotion for God, this drive for self-promotion caused him to undermine his father's authority and usurp the loyalty of David's men away to follow himself.

"Adonijah then sacrificed sheep, cattle and fatted calves . . ." (I Kings 1:9) Self-promotion always seeks for some kind of religious justification. Adonijah was not a priest nor was he authorized to carry out the functions of a priest. Even as a self-appointed king, the king was not to offer sacrifices. (I Samuel 13:19) Those who are self-appointed will search for any religious expression to give external confirmation of their appointment. It may be a person of position; it may be the favor of a group of power. Whoever it may be, their motivation is to find what only God can give.

Promotion comes only from the Lord. Man may confirm God's promotion and is certainly to acknowledge it, but man is never authorized to either promote himself or see himself as God's committee of promotion.

"No one from the east or the west or from the desert can exalt a man. But it is God who judges, He brings one down and exalts another." (Psalm 75:6-7) Adonijah would have done well to acknowledge the promotion of the Lord, for the Lord had already appointed Solomon to reign as king. Solomon's appointment was confirmed by the anointing of God, not the committees of man. Self-appointments always seek for committees, for that is all they have. God's appointments rest in the anointing, for the anointing is always the issue that separates those who have been self-appointed and those who have been chosen. Resist any temptation toward self-promotion. Wait for God's appointment, then you can rest in the anointing.

July 14th

THE DECADE OF HARVEST

"The harvest is plentiful, but the workers are few. Pray the Lord of the harvest to send forth workers into this harvest field"
Matthew 9:37

The '70s brought us the charismatic renewal and the infiltration of the Holy Spirit across denominational lines. The '80s will be remembered for the structuring of the body of Christ and the much needed return to prayer and intercession. Now, well into the '90s, the question looms before us: What will the next several years be remembered for?

I would like to make a prediction. I believe this period will be remembered for the decade of harvest. The question has never been the willingness of God, but the availability of man. These past years have afforded much needed equipping. That equipping has not been for us to consume upon ourselves. It came in order to prepare us for the coming harvest. The fields are ripe and ready. It is time to thrust in the sickle and reap.

Perhaps history will remember the harvest of the '90s along with the great revivals of Finney, Wesley and the rest. Could this be the great revival of the 20th century that America has yet to experience? Perhaps the biggest question is: Will we participate in this harvest or simply watch it? Will you be a worker or merely an observer?

Being a Christian does not automatically mean we are a work. If that were the case, Jesus would have never exhorted us to pray that the Lord of the harvest would send us more workers. They would have already been there. No, the apostle Paul described to his son, Timothy, what qualified one as a worker when he wrote, *"Study to show yourself approved as a worker . . ."* (II Timothy 2:15) Workers are defined by preparation and then action.

To participate in this expected harvest is reserved for those who are prepared and act. The rest will witness it from the grandstands, not the arena.

As for me and my house, we will take the arena. Give me the arena or give me death.

July 15th

ORIGINATORS OR IMITATORS

"For there is one God and one mediator between God and men, the man Jesus Christ"

I Timothy 2:5

God does not hold an original expectation for each of His creation. That is, every expectation God has for man is already found in the person of Christ. Consequently, man need not strive to be original. He simply needs to pattern himself after Jesus, the pattern Son.

Man was never intended of God to be an originator. His purpose for us is to be imitators. As imitators we do not originate, we represent. To represent something is to re-present it. As representatives, we do not present something new or different. We re-present what Jesus has already presented. Through the act of representing, we are imitating not originating. Heaven presents it; we represent it.

Pride drives us into the curse of originality. Rather than imitating, we are sucked into the compelling need to originate. As with Lucifer, rather than being a representation of God, we seek to make ourselves equal to God.

Originators must win the victory. Imitators simply enforce it. Originators must defeat the devil. Imitators walk in the reality that he is already defeated. Originators must pray to gain the promise. Imitators pray to release the promise. Originators seek to become the factory. Imitators are the distribution center. Originators are originals. Imitators are copies.

We were created in the image of God, created not to be originals, but imitators of that which is perfect. Being in the image of God, we are as copies of the original. We have a striking resemblance of our maker. Any attitudes or actions in our lives that are contrary to the way of God, are contrary to our created order. We were created to be like Him, to act like Him, talk like Him, think like Him. Everything about us is to be like Him, for we are meant to be His imitators.

Man has lost all understanding of being imitators. Rather than seeking to imitate God, we have come to believe He is here to make us more original. We have elevated originality and independence to the level equal to spiritual gifts, when in reality they are in direct opposition to the pattern established by Jesus, who clearly stated He only did what He saw His Father doing. We are to relate to

Jesus exactly the same way He relates to Father. He is our pattern and His pattern is one of imitation, not origination. Though He is the King of kings and the Lord of lords, He is also the least original man who ever walked the Earth. He was perfectly content and fulfilled in being an imitator of He who is life and truth. If it was good enough for Jesus, it is good enough for me.

଒ଌ

Pause for thought:

How are you re-presenting Christ?

July 16th

FROM CONSUMER TO PRODUCER

"Simon, Simon, Satan has asked to sift you as wheat. But I have prayed for you, Simon, that your faith may not fail. And when you have turned back, strengthen your brothers"

Luke 22:31-32

Peter's turning back was not an end in itself. He was turned back in order that he might become a turner. He was healed in order that he might become a healer. He was ministered to, in order that he might do the work of the ministry.

The Father's goal for every believer is to move from consumer to producer. We all come in as consumers. In our infancy stage we consume. That is the nature of our development in Christ. But Father intends to move us past spiritual infancy into maturity. Maturity is measured by our ability to produce more than we consume. As long as we are alive we will consume a certain level. Consumption is a basic principle of life. In light of that consumption we must look for opportunities of production to offset the levels we consume.

Leaders are producers. The nature of leadership requires increased levels of consumption, but a leader will always press beyond self-centered consumption and press to be a producer. A vision to produce turns a sheep into a shepherd. A vision to produce turns a child into a Father. A vision to produce turns one who has been led, into one who is a leader. The very nature of our calling in Christ requires we become producers. We are a Kingdom of priests. As priests our focus is ministry. Our focus is to minister both to the needs of our God and to the people He has called us to serve. This focus on ministry requires the continual turning over of everything we take in. It is the process of taking in and turning over that keeps us alive in our spiritual walk. Without the turnover, lethargy and apathy set in. Without the turnover we fall prey to spiritual obesity. Spiritual obesity is the result of consuming more than we produce. The excess knowledge, blessing and spiritual gifts, turn into a self-related focus. It is only as the knowledge we take in is turned over into teaching others that we fulfill our call. As the blessings we received are used to bless others, we touch one of the main reasons for which we were blessed. As the spiritual gifts we possess are used to strengthen others, we complete the cycle as Jesus told Peter to do.

From consumer to producer. From sheep to shepherd. As we are given to, let us give to others.

July 17th

SUMMERTIME BLUES

"Whatever you do, work at it with all your heart, as working for the Lord, not for men"

Colossians 3:23

Summertime. Our long awaited time of fun and relaxation. For most, summer affords the opportunity of family vacations and outdoor involvement. These activities are vital for personal renewal and family bonding, provided they do not become a distraction to the whole.

What and who are we vacationing from? At times, our souls cry out, "I must get away." What are we trying to get away from?

Summertime often affords the devil an opportunity. Recognizing it as a time for fun and relaxation, he takes full advantage of our change of focus. A focus of fun and relaxation often neutralizes spiritual pursuit. Momentum is stopped due to improper focus.

Perhaps the area of greatest impact is corporate momentum. Vacations, weekends away, day picnics often neutralize the corporate gathering due to the lack of attendance. Though our focus should not be numbers, reality is when a good percentage of the people are gone, morale is affected. When the morale of the people is low, it is very difficult to enter into a spirit of praise and receptivity to the Word of God. A consensus of understanding is vital if a people are going to move together. When a good percentage of the people are gone, it is impossible to reach consensus.

Rest is as much of a spiritual principle as is pursuit. But in our time of rest, let us be discerning that we do not give the devil an opportunity. As we make our plans for vacations and such, let us do so with consideration of the corporate momentum. As we plan our summer, let us be careful that we do not communicate to our children that fun is more important than our personal and corporate relationship to Christ.

❦

July 18th

CHRISTOCENTRIC

"When Christ who is your life appears, then you will also appear with him in glory"

Colossians 3:4

*I*t was Pete Rose who said, "I was born to play baseball." Pete Rose was "baseballocentric." With baseball as his center, all Pete thought and acted upon centered itself upon how it related to baseball.

The apostle Paul was Christocentric. As you read Paul's writings, you soon discern that he was totally captivated by the person of Jesus Christ. Some are satisfied with Christ being the most important part of their life. For Him just to hold a preeminent place is sufficient to fulfill their Christian obligation. Paul's christocentric philosophy took Christ's place beyond preeminence. Jesus Christ was not just the most important part of Paul's life, Christ was his life.

"For me to live is Christ." (Philippians 1:21) *"It is no longer I who live but Christ who lives in me."* (Galatians 2:20) Christ-centeredness was not just a concept or a teaching of Paul's, it was a reality. Paul had counted everything else in life as a loss in order that he might gain Christ. With everything else counted as gone, Christ became his life.

To be Christocentric means everything in life is measured by and interpreted through the framework of Jesus Christ. His life and way become a filter that our every thought and action must pass through. As our way passes through the filter of Christ, everything changes. The things we once valued, we no longer value. With Christ as our filter, we set giving above getting, serving above ruling and forgiving above avenging. Ambitions that once dominated our practice are now powerless to touch us. Our centers have been changed and our values have been redefined and now Christ is our captivation.

The story is told of a young school boy who was Christocentric in his thinking. His teacher had asked the class what kind of animal is brave and fury and has a bushy tail? The young boy raised his hand and answered, Jesus. Thinking the boy had misunderstood the question, the teacher asked it again. The second time the boy blurted out, Jesus. When the boy's father was told of the situation, the father said to his son, "Now son, you knew the teacher was talking about a squirrel." To which the son replied, "Yes, I knew she was talking about a squirrel, but she should have been talking about Jesus."

Pause for thought:

To the one who is Christocentric, everything should center in and find its meaning in Christ. What is the center of your life? Is Christ just a part of your life or can you say like Paul, Christ is my life?

July 19th

IF YOU BUILD IT, HE WILL COME

"So she said to her husband, I know that this man who often comes our way is a holy man of God. Let's make a small room on the roof and put on it a bed and a table and a chair and a lamp for him. Then he can stay there whenever he comes to us"

II Kings 4:9-10

As the man of God passed by the Shunammite woman, so the presence of God passes by us. In His passing He desires to stay. For Him to stay He needs a place. As the Shunammite woman made a place for the man of God, we must make a place for the presence of God.

The place God desires is not a room with a table, lamps and chairs. He seeks a room in our heart. He seeks that secret place in our heart, emotions and will that is uniquely His. It is that secret place that is given to no one but Him. It is to this secret place that He desires to come and rest, not just pass us by. He is not content with passing by. He desires to come and live.

How easy it is for that secret place to get cluttered. Unless careful attention is given, that secret place soon becomes quite cluttered. Hurts of the past can take up a tremendous amount of room. Besetting sins consume a lot of livable space. Unforgiveness creates a major mess in our secret place. With these and other issues clouding our focus, it is quite difficult to keep our secret place clean. If left to clutter our peace, these unresolved issues will be the seeds of our future failure.

The secret places in our lives are in need of being cleaned out and prepared. The manifest presence of God is seeking a place where it can dwell, a place that has been properly prepared. A cluttered heart cannot move into the realm of faith. As we mature in our desire for intimacy, we discover that there are issues that must be cleared away if we are to consistently maintain that secret place. Sin separates. The broken fellowship of sin robs the intimacy that is reserved for that secret place. To prepare Him a room is to put these besetting sins behind us so as to nurture the presence of God.

If you build Him that secret place, He will come. In coming He will reveal His heart and His way. God's glory is to conceal a matter. Our wisdom is to search it out. Let the search begin in that secret place where our hearts are laid bare before an all-loving Father.

July 20th

THE PRIDE OF ORIGINALITY

"What has been will be again, what has been done will be done again. There is nothing new under the sun"

Ecclesiastes 1:9

Originality is a myth. Under divinely inspired wisdom Solomon declared, *"There is nothing new under the sun."* Though what is being done has already been done before, we deceived ourselves into believing that we are the first ones to have ever thought it or put it into practice. A thought comes to mind and we perceive it to be an original thought. We find ourselves emulating others we respect, and we think, "I must be myself," believing, being ourselves is to be original.

Fallen man is consumed by a drive to be original. He is on a quest to think original, act original and be original. The problem is there is no such thing as original. Man's search is in vain. Though he searches in vain, pride creates an illusion of accomplishment. Pride creates a false reality of originality. Soon we are acting like we are original. We denounce anything that would be an emulation of the emulator, then we act like the others who perceive themselves to be originators. The issue is not will we emulate or originate. There simply is nothing to originate. So the issue is one of who will we emulate. Will we emulate the emulators or emulate those who in vain perceive themselves to be originators?

Jesus Christ was the least original man who ever walked this Earth. Not only was He not original, He had absolutely no desire whatsoever to be original. With tremendous confidence He stated, *"I only do what I see my Father doing."* (John 5:19) Jesus never sought to originate. His goal was to abide. He understood and boldly declared that apart from His abiding relationship to Father, He could do nothing. Consequently, He replicated the life of the Father, not His own.

The world defines success in terms of origination. God defines it in terms of succession. To succeed in life is not to originate something unique to ourselves. To succeed is to replicate the life of Jesus Christ and follow His example of emulating the life and work of Father. The drive to be original comes at the loss of the original. Our goal in the Kingdom of God is not originality, but conformity to Christ. *"Those God foreknew He also predestined to be conformed to the likeness of His Son."* (Romans 8:29) From the beginning, Father's intent for man was to be image bearers. We were not to originate, but to emulate the image of God. When sin entered the picture so did the drive to be original.

Originality is not the way of the Kingdom of God. We do not have to be original, for there is nothing new under the sun. If there are no originators, only emulators, then let us emulate Jesus Christ, the pattern One.

☙

Pause for thought:

Are you ready to have your level of success measured by your Father and not by those around you? In what areas of your life might that measurement need to be changed?

July 21st

THE SILENCE OF THE LAMBS

"When the woman saw that the fruit of the tree was good for food and pleasing to the eye and also desireable for gaining wisdom, she took some and ate it. She also gave some to her husband who was with her and he ate"

Genesis 3:6

The fall of man is a vivid example that silence is not golden; it is deadly. Most of us have pictured Adam absent from the temptation of Eve. Surely, we have thought if he were present he would have said something. We have wanted Adam absent, for then we could blame the fall solely on the woman. The problem is, Adam was not absent. Fact is, he was quite present. Adam was with Eve when she was tempted and according to the scriptural record, he did not say a word to cover his wife, warn her, or do anything to prevent her seduction.

Perhaps the real tragedy of the fall was not the fact that Eve ate the forbidden fruit, but that Adam did not say anything to prevent it. Adam's sin did not begin with his eating, it began with his silence. It was not what went into Adam's mouth that caused him to sin, it was what did not come out. As the serpent came and engaged Eve in her seduction, Adam did not say a word. As the serpent twisted the words God had spoken, Adam said nothing to expose the serpents lies. What might have happened if Adam spoke up? What might have happened if Adam covered his wife and spoke to the issue of the serpents deception? Though Adam was present, he was absent. His silence removed him from being the least bit effective.

Silence is not something that was unique to Adam. Almost every man struggles to one degree or another with silence. To bear the image of God is to have our tongues loosed. The Bible says, God *spoke* the worlds into existence. To remain silent would have meant to withold creation. The spoken Word of God not only creates, it sparks faith. *"Faith comes by hearing and hearing the Word of God."* (Romans 10:17) This is hearing the spoken Word of God. Silence can be deadly to man. Silence is a faith thief.

As a lamb, Jesus was silent before His accusers. Jesus died a lamb, but rose a lion. Lambs may be silent, but lions roar. There is nothing silent, passive or apathetic about a lion. Lions are not silent in the presence of a foe. A lion is awakened by pending danger. He comes alive in the face of battle. Silence is given to a lamb, but to a lion is given the roar.

The silence of the lamb purchased our salvation, but it is the roar of the Lion that secures our conquest. The time of silence is past. Now it is time to roar. It is time to loose our tongues and warn, admonish, instruct, affirm, rebuke, testify and declare the goodness of God in the land of the living.

※

Pause for thought:

What specific situations can you speak into today? How does the Holy Spirit want to use your words to comfort, encourage, affirm, rebuke and testify?

July 22nd

THE PATTERN SON

"In those God foreknew he also predestined to be conformed to the likeness of his Son, that he might be the first born among many brothers"

Romans 8:29

Jesus Christ is the pattern Son. He is the exact representation of everything Father intends for us to be. As a builder, Father builds according to the blueprint. The blueprint is the exact representation of how the building is to look. Jesus Christ is the builder's blueprint. He is the pattern we hold our lives against and seek to conform ourselves to. Everything He is, we are to be. Everything He did, we are to do likewise. What He pursued, we pursue. He is our focus, our goal, our means, our everything. He is Father's total answer for man's total need. Whatever is the question, Jesus is the answer. We search in vain if we search outside of Christ.

Our church forefathers have fought throughout the ages to preserve the truth that being the pattern Son, Jesus Christ was fully God and fully man. To give us a pattern that is impossible to copy would be cruelty. In establishing Jesus as the pattern, Father had to make Him fully man in order to place Him within our reach. He had to be acquainted with the things we are acquainted with. He had to face temptation as do we. He had to be tempted as man is tempted, without sin, in order to establish the pattern for us to follow. Being the firstborn among many brothers, He had to establish the way.

If Jesus were just fully man, it would not have been possible for Him to save us. The just demands of God required a spotless sacrifice, one without sin. The man Jesus could not save man. The salvation of man required a sacrifice that was fully God. One without sin needed to come and become the sin of mankind in order to satisfy the righteous requirement. Jesus Christ was exactly that; being fully God, He was without sin. Being fully man, He was acquainted with our grief. Jesus Christ satisfied the righteous demands of God and the spiritual need of man. Being fully man, He became someone we can follow. Being fully God, He is someone we can worship. Jesus Christ is in the same person, a man we can follow and a God we can worship. He is our total and complete answer. Nothing is lacking in Him and in Him there is no need. He is the complete and consummate example for us to follow and the sovereign supreme for us to worship.

In Christ, the search is over. Jesus Christ is everything we need.

Whatever our lack might be, Jesus is our supply. Whatever might need to be added, Jesus is the pattern to follow.

ଓଡ଼ିଆ

Pause for thought:

What things we have added to your life because you have failed to fully see how Christ fills every need in our life?

July 23rd

MOVING FROM JESSE'S HOUSE

"Then Saul sent word to Jesse saying, 'Allow David to remain in my service, for I am pleased with him"

I Samuel 16:22

King David was a rejected son. Though he was a rejected son he still fathered a nation. When Samuel came in search of Jesse's son, David was left in the field to tend the sheep. Jesse left David to tend the sheep knowing Samuel would choose one of his own to be king. David never used his rejection by his father as an excuse. In spite of his past, David moved forward to possess that which was his.

There came a time in David's journey when he had to leave Jesse's house. David's house of destiny was the house of the king. To live in the king's house, David had to leave the house of his past. Past rejection, past ridicule from his brothers, were all part of his coming to the king's house. But now he was in the house of the king. Having left the past, he was able to step into the future.

To become the people of destiny Father intends us to be, we will have to leave the house of our past. Past failures, past limitations, past ways of viewing ourselves all need to be forsaken in order that we might step into the King's service. In the King's service there is freedom. In the King's service is the reward of His pleasure. To find that pleasure, David no longer lived in the house of his past. He lived in the house of his destiny.

So it was with Moses. Moses reached a place in his journey where he refused to be called the son of Pharaoh's daughter. (Hebrews 11:24) To become the deliverer of Israel, Moses could no longer allow his past to define him. He had to be defined and directed by his future. The past had too many hindrances. The past had too many opportunities of diversion. To deliver a people, Moses had to refuse the encumbrances of his past and press on into his future. Moses could not afford to live in his past.

God's plan for us is a future and a hope. To possess the future we must not remain bound to the past. The past house of limitation must be forsaken for the house of the King. In the King's house is our future and the reason for which we were born. The house of our past has no hold on us. Even as Moses, even as David, left the house of their past, we can leave ours in exchange for the service of the King. Perhaps it is time for you to move from Jesse's house.

July 24th

NO HALF WAY COVENANTS

"All the people that came out had been circumcised but all the people born in the desert during the journey from Egypt had not"

Joshua 5:5

*I*t is hard to imagine something as primary to the covenant as circumcision would have been neglected while in the desert. The very symbol ordained of God to be the sign of the covenantal status was neglected for an entire generation. Since the second generation had never been circumcised on the way, Joshua had to stop the journey and make sure this symbolic act of the covenant was taken care of.

Circumcision was more than just an outward sign. Circumcision, like any of the symbols of covenant was an outward demonstration of what had taken place within the heart. The generation that came out of Egypt understood the symbolism and carried the heart. But somewhere in the process of the journey, they failed in their ability to hold on to what they knew and impart it to the generation to come. Maybe after 400 years of captivity they began to think it was too hard to be the covenant people. Maybe it was that seed thought that opened the door to compromise and made allowances in their thinking for themselves and for their children.

Without a generational focus of the Kingdom of God, it is easy to make allowances for those who will come after us. Like the Puritans of years ago, half way covenants are formed in fear that our children will not be able to pay the depth of the price we did. Human reasoning tells us that half a covenant is better than no covenant at all, so we humanize the sacred and filter the difficult. Any decision based in fear is a decision doomed to fail. Our way is the way of faith, not the way of fear. We need to appropriate faith for the covenant and faith for the generation to come. The way of the Kingdom is not a way of decreased expectation, but one of increase. As our children see us embracing the covenant with great joy, it will stir in them a desire to do likewise. They will come into the Kingdom the same way every generation has and will continue on the way in like manner. They will come in with a full understanding of the covenant and a full willingness to embrace its demands. Let us never underestimate the zeal of the generation which follows. The zeal of youth is such that they will rise to the level of expectation. If so challenged, they will push themselves to do exploits and to enjoy the process of it.

The allowances one generation makes for the next are often more to accommodate their over-indulgences, not their children's.

God's grace is sufficient for every demand He would make upon us and the generation to come. Knowing Him to be a God of grace, let us believe Him for full and complete obedience, both for this generation and for the generations to come.

⊗

July 25th

SET INTO FAMILY

"Near the cross of Jesus stood his mother . . . When Jesus saw his mother there and the disciple whom he loved standing nearby, he said to his mother, 'Dear woman, here is your son,' and to the disciple, 'Here is your mother'"

John 19:25-27

The Kingdom of God is rooted in and finds its full expression in family. To discover the Kingdom is to discover family. Without a clear understanding of the nature of family, you will never understand the fullness of the Kingdom.

As Jesus hung on the cross dying, He looked down and saw Mary and John. Inspite of the pain He was currently experiencing and the incredible magnitude of that moment, family was so deep into His being that He was able to see through everything else and take a moment to assure the recognition and joining of family. *"Woman, here is your son. Son, here is your mother."*

Family is central to the purposes of God on this Earth and in the age to come. There is nothing peripheral or insignificant about family. Father is a family man and family is the very context that He chose for His purposes to unfold.

Heaven is arranged as a family. The Godhead is defined as a family. The church is the family of God. It is in family we are born. It is in family that we worship. It is in family that we battle. A famous Israeli leader was once asked the secret to the success of Israel's military might. The leader's answer was clear and concise. He said, "the secret to our success is we go to war as a family." To battle for your father, mother, sister and brother is to battle at your height of passion and effectiveness. Family awakens internal instincts that are otherwise left dormant.

"God set the solitude in families" (Psalm 68:6). Have you recognized and accepted your setting into family? God set you into your physical family and according to I Corinthians 12, He sets you into spiritual family as well.

☙❧

July 26th

SETTLING THE ISSUE OF TIME

"There is a time for everything"
Ecclesiastes 3:1

You do not walk long with God before you must face the issue of time. It takes time to do the things God calls us to do. It takes time to mature. The more useful one is to the purposes of God, the more time it requires. As each day passes and we see the business of our schedules, we keep encouraging ourselves that it is going to get better. If we can just get past this month, we say, next month will be clear sailing. Problem is, next month has the tendency to fill up as well. So does the next and the next. Month after month of deferred hope can give the devil a foothold. Our hope must be in God's enablement to manage our time, not in the hope that we will get more of it.

To each is given the same 24 hours. No one receives more and no one receives less. Learning to manage the 24 we have been given is the secret to effectiveness in the Kingdom of God. The management of our time begins with having the proper value system. If we value time in the presence of God, training in His word and the fellowship of the saints, we will never view church or meetings as taking up too much time. The issue becomes tapping into something that we value more than the perceived loss of time. Few people ever resent the time it takes to spend money, take exotic vacations or even eat chocolate! The reason is, they value these events more than the time it takes to do them. The reason many resent the time it takes to learn the Kingdom way is because they have not placed a high enough value on the Kingdom way. They value time more than they value the Kingdom. As we get to the place where the Kingdom is valued more than time, we will discover that there is indeed a time for everything.

A generational philosophy of the Kingdom means time. To build for the generations to come means we must take the time to do it right. If the Abraham generation takes the time to do it right, the Isaac generation will have sufficient time to do it right for the Jacob's to follow. If the Abraham's compromise in hope of saving time, the Isaac's who follow will have to do double duty. They will have to take the time to rebuild Abraham's foundations and build their part as well.

God promises sufficient time. There is time to build according to the pattern of God's design. Settle the issue that to seek the Kingdom first will take time and the better we are at managing that time, the more responsibility Father will give us to carry. For the sake of generations to come let us embrace the necessity of time.

July 27th

OBEDIENCE IS BETTER THAN SACRIFICE

"Sacrifice and offering you did not desire, but my ears you have pierced. Burnt offerings and sin offerings you did not require. Then I said, here I am . . . I desire to do your will, O my God."

Psalm 40:6,7

The challenge of God's people throughout the ages has been the ability to keep in step with Him. The fact that His ways are higher than our ways means we often seek after and desire those things that are contrary to His way. Religion causes us to place our focus on sacrifice, whereas God's desire is for us to focus on obedience.

To obey is better than sacrifice. The psalmist declares quite clearly that God's primary desire for us is not sacrifice, but obedience. Much of our sacrifice and offerings toward God are nothing more than guilt sacrifices subconsciously designed to cover the cry of disobedience. Due to the guilt of not obeying the voice of the Lord, we fall into a religious mode of trying to do things for Him in an attempt to cover over the sin of disobedience. How easy it is for our labor in God to be built upon the altar of working for God rather than simply obeying what God has already said.

"Sacrifice and offering you did not desire but my ears you have pierced." The true desire of God is for us to have listening ears. Obedience to the will of God begins with hearing ears to listen to the voice of God. A listening ear is the result of a surrendered heart. An unsurrendered heart will cause us to do twice the amount of work in not obeying than what it would have taken to obey. Often that work is full of sacrifice and noble behavior that is motivated by carnal desire rather than simple obedience.

Father's heart for us is quite simple. His desire for us is to do His will. In simple obedience, we discover freedom from the religious performance that seeks to silence the cry of guilt by busying ourselves with sacrifice, rather than obedience to the will of God.

July 28th

HOLDING OTHERS' SIN

"Then he fell on his knees and cried out, Lord do not hold this sin against them"

Acts 7:60

To live like Christ is expected, to die like Him is heroic. Little is spoken of Stephen's life, but in a few small words, volumes are said of His death. Not only did Stephen live like Christ, but in forgiving his attackers and not holding their sin against them, He died like Christ as well.

Unforgiveness is the decision to hold someone else's sin. Though we may not be aware of it, when we refuse to forgive those who wronged us, we make the decision to hold the sin of their wrong doing. To hold sin against others is to hold sin. Stephen died free, for he refused to hold the sin of his attackers.

It is the holding of others' sin that imprisons us. In Christ, our sin has been removed. It is the holding of others' sin that often condemns us. Jesus instructed us in Mark 11:25, *"When you stand praying, if you hold another's sin against them, forgive."* Forgiveness is not optional, for unforgiveness is the purposeful decision to hold sin. Jesus Christ died to free us from our sin, so He certainly does not intend for us to hold someone else's sin.

The Christian life is a life of reciprocal obligation. Never was our walk intended to be one-sided, especially in the area of forgiveness. Reciprocal obligation demands that we return in like manner, as we have received. Tradition has made forgiveness unconditional, when in reality, Jesus placed a major condition on it. In no uncertain terms Jesus stated that to receive forgiveness we must extend it. *"If you do not forgive men their sins, your Father will not forgive your sin."* (Matthew 6:15) Our willingness to forgive those who have hurt us is a condition that qualifies us to be forgiven. To hold others' sin against them is to take their sin upon ourselves.

The parable of the unmerciful servant shows us that to hold sin against others is quite hypocritical. Having received the maximum of mercy, who are we to demand justice from others? To hold sin against others is to ignore the fact that Jesus did not hold sin against us. To have received mercy from God, but demand justice from others, is nothing less than hypocritical. Forgiveness motivated in mercy and grace is our family way. For the sake of freedom and obedience to Christ's command, we must forgive those who have wronged us. We must extend mercy to those who have hurt us; for as we measure it out, it will be measured back to us.

○○○

Pause for thought:

Is there any person the Spirit has brought to your mind that you have become enslaved to because of your decision to "hold their sin?" If so, what are you willing to do in order to remove yourself from a curse of disobedience and to gain your freedom in Christ?

July 29th

EMPOWERMENT

"But as many who received him, he gave power to become the sons of God"

John 1:12 (KJV)

To give power you must first have received power. We have been given power to become the sons of God. This is not just a power of strength and might. This is a judicial power of rule and government.

To the sons, Jesus gives the judicial authority to manage our domestic affairs. When in the process of doing so, we will discover the disfranchised and deprived. Power is given to us in order that the sons have something to give away. To those whose rights have been deprived, sons carry the regal authority under God to restore every right, and legal standing as ordained by God. Empowerment is not doing peoples' work for them; that is welfare. The essence of empowerment is putting people in touch with the fullness of their riches in Christ and then placing ourselves in a position to receive from them. Jesus demonstrated this both with John the Baptist and the Samaritan woman. Though He was God, He placed Himself in a position to receive from both of them. When John refused to baptize Him because of who He was, Jesus said *"this must be so in order to fulfill all righteousness."* Though Jesus was God, He said to the woman, *"Will you give me a drink."* He put the woman in touch of what she had and then placed Himself in a position to receive. As sons, we must follow Christ's example. We must seek to enable people to see who they are in Christ and the gifts Christ has given them. Then we must place ourselves in a position to receive from them.

Whether it be disenfranchisement of race, class, or agenda, there are scores of people who have been deprived of the right power and privilege of God's family. Father is coming to His family and empowering His sons with judicial authority to refranchise the disfranchised and return every right, power and privilege regardless of color, class or gender. Power received is to be power given.

July 30th

TREASURES OR STUFF

"Do not store up for yourselves treasures on earth where moth and rust destroy, and thieves break in and steal. But store up treasures in Heaven"

Matthew 6:20

On more than one occasion I have had the unfortunate responsibility to sort through all the remaining possessions of one who had passed away. As I sorted through and valued each piece as a keeper or not, I thought, how tragic it is for someone else to be placing a value on everything that another person gave their life to accumulate. In just a matter of a few minutes the results of a person's entire life can seemingly be reduced to a "keep it or toss it away."

One should never build their lives in such a way that the fruit of their pursuits is left behind for someone else to determine its value. A wise man builds on the eternal. When one builds on issues that are eternal, they do not have to leave them behind. We can take issues of an eternal nature with us. Consequently, no one will go through these issues and determine them to be of no apparent value. A wise man will guard his pursuits to guarantee their eternal focus.

Everyone will leave something behind. Stuff is always left behind. Those who build their lives on stuff will leave this life empty handed. The accumulation of their life pursuit will be placed in a box and sorted among loved ones with much being tossed out for being of no perceived value. The value of stuff is in the one who owned it, not in those who will receive it.

Treasures stored up in Heaven will be sorted by no one. Those who seek first the Kingdom of God are those who find their true accumulation taking place in Heaven. Consequently, what is left behind is only stuff. The true treasures of relationship to Christ, friendships, love, wisdom, a good name—these things and others are qualities of an eternal nature that no one can sort.

July 31st

A HEART FOR THE NATIONS

"Ask of me, and I will make the nations your inheritance, the ends of the earth your possession."

Psalm 2:8

The heart of God is inseparably wrapped up in the nations. To carry His heart or represent Him in anyway is to have a heart that is open for His desire as it pertains to the nations.

As it was with Abraham, so it is with us today. The purposes of God begin with the individual, but always lead to the nations. Abraham's call was an individual call, but his destiny was to be a father of many nations. King David's call was an individual call, but his purpose was to rule a nation. The call of God reaches out to us as individuals, but He equips us for and sends us to the nations.

God's desire is to give His people the nations as their inheritance. To receive those nations, we must first carry God's heart for them. To carry God's heart for the nations can be quite different than having a heart for them ourselves. Many times we discount our involvement in the nations saying we just do not have a heart for them. The fact that we may not feel a particular emotion about the nations does not mean we are not still responsible to carry God's heart for them. Carrying God's heart for a nation is a decision of the will before it is a feeling of the emotion. Knowing God created and loves a particular people is reason enough for me to love them and care for them. If a particular feeling of emotion follows that decision of the will, I will rejoice. But if it does not, I must still carry God's heart for them.

Only in the nations do we find the full expression of God's family. Let us open our wills to the nations and let our hearts follow after.

August 1st

BY WHAT STANDARD

"If you love me then keep my commandments"
John 14:15

The pursuit of the American dream . . . Climbing the ladder of success . . . Many have climbed the ladder only to discover it was leaning against the wrong wall. Success is the American dream. Seminar after seminar, books, tapes and volumes of literature, all promise success. But, by what standard do we measure success? How easy it is to be swept into the American dream only to find out its end result looks more like a nightmare than a dream. Greed, materialism, meism . . . are the fuel of the American dream.

The American dream has measured success by the result, not the process. "Whoever finishes with the most toys wins." Do they? If the result is the measurement of success, then, however you get there is justified. Consequently, the process is often ignored with an ends justified the means rationale.

If result is the standard of success, then Jesus was an absolute failure. Thirty three years of Christ's ministry ended in fragmentation, betrayal and even death. Failure, or the wrong standard of success?

The Word of God sets the process, not the result, as our standard of success. Success is not measured by what we have accumulated at the end, but by our level of obedience through the process. "What shall it profit a man if he gain the whole world but lose his own soul?" The obvious answer is nothing, because gain is not the measurement of success. Jesus said in John 15 that those who were fruitful would be pruned (taken away) in order for them to be more fruitful. Loss was a sign of success and God's blessing, not failure. The apostle Paul told us it is the kindness of God (His giving to) that leads us to repentance. Here gain is a sign of judgment, not reward.

The seeking of God's Kingdom first promises success. (Matthew 6:33) A Kingdom perspective of life will properly frame our standard of success and assure our ladder to be leaning against the correct wall. Let us find ourselves seeking after Kingdom reality, not the American dream.

August 2nd

THE STANDARD OF REVELATION

"When Jesus came to the region of Caesarea Philippi, he asked his disciples, "Who do people say the Son of Man is?""

Matthew 16:13

Though He asked them the question, it really was not what concerned Him. The disciples were being set for a monumental evaluation that every believer must face. One day, as Jesus was conversing with His disciples, He asked, *"Who do the people say the Son of Man is?"* After responding to His question, He seems to disregard their answer and goes right for the jugular. *"But what about you? Who do you say I am?"* In the final assessment, it matters very little what other people say. The only thing which really matters is what you and I, as individuals before God, say and believe.

The progressive revelation of God seems to be such that His providence leads us into a family in which we are to be nurtured and trained in the ways of the Kingdom. But it is not long before the work of the Holy Spirit is to cause us to solidify what we believe regardless of what other people say. Therein lies an incredible fine line of balance. We must be open for adjustment and correction, but once truth is bought, we must be unwilling to sell it or compromise that which we believe regardless of what others do.

The nature of the battle we are in will mean, at times, those we admire most may abandon the way. At times, they might even be the ones who trained us in the way, but for one reason or another, have forsaken it for an easier path. At that point, the question looms ever before us, "What about you?" Did you follow this way and embrace a particular truth because of what others said, or did you see its truth in the word and embrace it as your own? If you made it your own, then it should matter little what others do. But if your ownership of truth was dependent on others, then you will be tossed to and fro depending on what others say.

As it was for Peter, the spirit of revelation must be our standard of truth. As we search the Scriptures and the Holy Spirit reveals truth, let us own it on that basis, not on the basis of what others say or do not say. Let us be ready, so when the penetrating question of, *"Who do you say I am?"* comes, we will have an acceptable answer.

August 3rd

COUNTING THE COST

"If any man come after Me, let him first deny himself and take up his cross"

Matthew 16:24

So you want to follow in His footsteps? That is certainly something to which we all aspire. But, are we willing to pay that kind of price?

While visiting Disneyland a number of years ago, we found it to be quite convenient. One price at the gate got us into the park and once inside, all attractions were free. We could ride to our heart's content at no additional charge.

Though it may be like that in the "magical kingdom," it most certainly is not in the "ultimate Kingdom." In this Kingdom, the Kingdom of God, it is no charge at the gate, but once inside, it costs us all we have.

The Scriptures are very clear that salvation is free. No one can earn it, for it is offered as a free gift. But the bargains end there. Though meeting Him might be free, to follow after Him will require installment payments of everything we own. The further we go with Him, more is required. What was acceptable last year may be required of us this year.

Paul stated it this way, *"When I was a child, I talked like a child. I talked like a child and I thought like a child. When I became a man, I put childish ways behind me."* (I Corinthians 13:11) The childish ways were acceptable while he was a child, but, in order to behave himself as a man, those ways needed to be pushed aside.

Maturing in the purposes of God comes at a tremendous cost. For some, it is through many trials and tribulations. For others, it is through the death of dreams and personal pursuits. Our Father knows exactly what "our cross" needs to be and that will be the payment of our progression in this Kingdom.

Do you still want it? Are you willing to pay for it? The truth of the matter is, it is too late, for once you have seen the "pearl of great price," " there is no going back. Your only sensible option is to "sell it all and buy the field." To stagnate is death on the installment plan.

સ૩૯૦

August 4th

THE PRICE OF PROGRESS

"King David replied, 'No, I insist on paying full price. I will not take for the Lord what is yours or sacrifice a burnt offering that costs me nothing"

I Chronicles 21:24

No wonder it was said of David that he was a man after God's own heart. His devotion was so pure, his commitment so deep, that he was unwilling to offer to God that which was of little value to himself.

The pathway to maturity and usefulness is paved with the stones of personal sacrifice. The journey is full of voices offering an easier way. Satan offered Jesus the kingdoms of the world without the cross. It sounded so good. The crown, without the conflict. The prize, without the price. But ultimately, it would have cost Him everything. The fact of the matter is this: we will pay. We will either pay up front and do it God's way or we will pay as we go, the price of doing it our own way. God's way is difficult at first, then easier as it goes. Man's way is easy in the beginning, but the end thereof is death.

What has the Kingdom cost us thus far? What will it cost us in the future? Are we willing to offer to God a sacrifice that costs us something? Everything? What if it costs us our dreams? What if it costs us more time? What if it requires more of our money? What if it comes at the price of our personal goals? In all these things, can we see the hand of God and embrace the spirit of David by saying, "I will not sacrifice that which costs me nothing" nor will I, "Take for the Lord what is yours," but rather I will own it myself by making it my own and offer to God what is of personal value to me.

Be it certain that Father is up to something and it will cost us. But, be of good cheer, for His way is the way of life and what He requires, He also supplies.

August 5th

TURNING OFF THE BLUE LIGHTS

"No one else dared join them, even though they were highly regarded by the people"

Acts 5:13

What a contrast from your typical church scenario today. The strategy of the Holy Spirit was to lift the standard high enough that the people respected the commitment, but feared the cost of involvement. This is a strategy that is proven day in and day out. The things that we desire are the things that cost the most. What we want the most are those things that are not easily had.

So why have we tried to make Christianity so easy?

In our attempt to increase, we have tried to do God a favor and put Him on sale. The theology is, if it costs less, more people will buy. But, in this market, just the opposite is true. The Holy Spirit purposefully set the non-negotiable price. He determined it would cost everything, knowing that the magnitude of the price would highlight the value of the relationship. "Blue Light Specials" were not a part of His plan.

In our attempts to make church "user friendly," I am afraid we have created our own alternative. Low cost, low involvement and low value. In order for us to experience the results of the early church, we will have to return to the expectation of the early church. Repentance, water baptism, Holy Spirit baptism, selling all, daily involvement—these and much more were all part of the expected standard. There was nothing easy about it. There was such a level of expectation that it created a legend that people feared, yet nevertheless, many believed because of the discerned value.

Though recent marketing skills have attempted to reduce its value, the gospel is not, nor at any time will be, on sale. The greatest "selling" point of the gospel is its high expectation—for that determines its value.

Let us return to New Testament expectation in order that we might experience New Testament results.

August 6th

AT WHAT PRICE SUCCESS?

"Unless the Lord builds the house, they labor in vain who built it"
Psalm 127:1

Life was passing him by and he had not yet realized his financial goals. With four kids and a dog, he had no home, but a rental to house them. All of his friends owned homes, some owned two, but in spite of his efforts, he still couldn't afford the down payment. How it angered him to think that month after month his payment was going to someone else's financial investment, not his. His wife never pressured him, but how she longed for a place she could call home.

So with the conquering instinct, he plotted his course. Hard work, overtime, possible job change and even relocation. If everything went according to plan, in three years he would have enough for a down payment.

Soon the work began to come. It began with a late night here and a few there. Soon it involved Saturdays and an occasional Sunday. It was not long before work was the total focus. Early mornings, late nights and every Sunday. The plan was working according to design. The extra money was coming in and the totals were tracking just as expected.

So what was the problem? Why was it not filling the void? Why were they not both happy? At what price success?

This story or ones similar to it could be told over and over. With good intentions, we set out to accomplish noble goals, but we do not always secure the Lord's blessings and discern His leading. Unless the Lord builds the house, our labor accounts to nothing. In other words, unless we do it His way, all of our work will be in vain. Oh, we might accomplish the goal, but the issue is, "What did we lose in order to meet it?" Maybe our spouse? Maybe our children? Perhaps it came at the expense of our intimacy with Jesus.

"There is a way that seems right to a man, but the end thereof is a way of death." Our plans apart from Him will only produce death. Late night hours at the cost of family, working Sundays at the cost of relationship to Jesus and the body is not worth whatever financial goal it might achieve. The only way to success is to give it all to Him and allow Him to guide your path.

And guess what—He will do it and you will succeed. If you are building your house, stop now and give it to Him while there is still time to rebuild.

August 7th

KNOWING MORE THAN GOD

> "Who has understood the Spirit of the Lord, or instructed him as his counselor? Whom did the Lord consult to enlighten him and who taught him knowledge or showed him the path of understanding"
>
> Isaiah 40:13-14

With almost a hint of sarcasm, the prophet penned these questions. Obviously, the answer was "no one," and the prophet knew that, yet he asked the questions anyway. He asked them, for he was trying to make a point. He was stressing how man, in spite of his limitations and finite understanding, often thinks he has a better way than God. A plan more thoughtfully executed. A strategy with more desirable results.

It is in the face of this attitude that Isaiah asks, "When did you become the Spirit's counselor? When did the Lord consult you in order to see the way more clearly?" How does an attitude like this emerge? Is it as blatant as someone rising up in pride and saying, "I know more than God?" No, I do not think so. It is far more subtle than that. No one would boldly declare, "I know more than God." Yet, in our stubbornness, we will often adopt philosophies contrary to Scripture and in essence say, "God, that was a good idea, but I have a better one."

Cultural influence is perhaps the greatest offender. Often, we allow the cultural architects of the day to become the Lord's counselor. "Spanking is a form of child abuse," they tell us, so many accept their word on it rather than God's. Though corporal punishment has been abused, we must seek to change the abuse, not redefine the truth. Yes, we are empathetic to those who have been damaged from the misapplication of discipline and we are equally empathetic for those who never received any discipline at all. But before we change our beliefs, let us be sure that God has been our instructor, not the reactions of man.

☙❧

August 8th

WHO SEARCHES FOR WHOM?

"Ask the Lord of the harvest, therefore, to send out workers into his harvest field. Go! I am sending you out like lambs among wolves"
Luke 10:2-3

If no one comes to Jesus unless the Father draws them, then why must we go and try to lead them to the Lord? Does the truth of predestination preclude our involvement in evangelism, or do we play a strategic role in the salvation process?

Coming to Jesus Christ is not something we initiate or control. The saving knowledge of Christ is something we respond to, not initiate. The Scriptures make it quite clear that we did not choose Christ; He chose us. He was the One who took the initiative. We simply responded to His invitation. Fortunately for us, His invitation is extended to all. Though it is extended to all, not all respond favorably. So, according to Luke 10, our sending is *"to every city,"* but our focus is to be to only those who are being drawn. Yet, how do we know who those are? How do we know who will respond favorably and who is being drawn?

The answer is quite clear; we do not. There is no way for us to know, so God does not place the burden of responsibility on the Christian. The burden of responsibility is on those who are lost. We serve a backward Kingdom. In the Kingdom of God, we are not sent out as the searchers; we are sent out as the searched. We are not sent as the hunters; we are sent as the hunted. Jesus put it this way, *"I am sending you as lambs among wolves."* What is that supposed to mean? In the natural who is the hunted, the lamb or the wolf? If a lamb was sent into a pack of wolves, who would be the hunted? The lamb is sent not to be the hunter, but to be the hunted. The lamb is not sent to be the searcher, but to be the searched.

A lamb sent into a pack of wolves is sent in for one reason, to become bait. The lamb is sent to get the wolf's attention. So here is how the process works. It is Father's will that all would be saved. He initiates the drawing process to every wolf. Those who respond, find a lamb at their door. The lamb is sent as bait to lead the wolf to Jesus. The bait is sent so that those who perceive their need and respond to Father's drawing love, will have someone to surrender to.

So our part in the process is not to force their conversion, but to be a surrender point. Too often we have gone in as wolves and tried to force conversion. We have taken God's responsibility and have tried to become the one who draws rather than the bait. Consequently, people get a bad taste of Christianity because they feel handled. We get a bad taste of evangelism because we feel rejected and Jesus is reduced to something you can choose or reject.

To go as lambs among wolves is to go in an attitude of vulnerability. It is to go in humility, gentleness, and meekness. It is to go where the wolves are and to get involved by serving as Jesus did.

☙❧

Pause for thought:

Do those who know you, know you as a lamb? Are you where the wolves are, or have you become satisfied with being a lamb among lambs?

August 9th

A SERVANT NAMED REJECTION

"Though the world was made through him, the world did not recognize him. He came to that which was his own, but his own did not receive him"

John 1:10-11

Rejection is a certain reality of being a servant of God. Some things in life just happen, and rejection is one of them. You need not go in search of it, for it will find you. Regardless of your desire to avoid it or your ability to hide from it, sooner or later rejection will find you.

Jesus was a man marked by rejection, and His was not a mild case. Those who were His by creation and soon would be His by redemption, rejected Him. He came to His own, and His own rejected Him, and He never sought inner healing for it. Rejection was a reality of being the Son of God. Regardless of His desire to avoid it, the sovereignty of God designed it, and in God's sovereign design, rejection served to conform Jesus into the fullness of Father's desire.

Could it be that the church is spending all of its energy to be healed from the very things that conform us into the likeness of Christ? Could it be that we see rejection as an enemy, when in reality it is a servant? The issue for us today is not being healed from rejection, but learning how to persevere in the face of rejection.

Rejection by its very nature is designed to cause us to withdraw. The enemy uses it to undermine our security and confidence so as to force us from the front lines of Kingdom pursuit. Defeated and rejected, we withdraw as a servant, we defeat the enemy at his own game. Rejection as a servant causes us to withdraw into our relationship to Jesus, and in that abiding place, we die to our need to be accepted. From that place of identification we become dead men who have nothing more to lose, so with boldness and Christ-confidence, we can be sent where those who fear rejection would never go.

To be like Jesus is to identify with Him in His rejection. Rejection is not something to run from. Our healing comes from seeing that rejection is a servant that forces us into a deeper identification with Christ and the confidence of godly acceptance.

August 10th

ZEAL FOR YOUR HOUSE CONSUMES ME

"His disciples remembered that it is written: "Zeal for your house will consume me"

John 2:17

If there was ever anyone who had a right to become familiar with and take for granted attending church, it was Jesus. Think about it. He was and is in church 24 hours a day. From eternity past until eternity future, He has been in church and ever will be in church. That is, if we see church not as a meeting, but as a place in which we corporately come into the presence of God.

No, there was nothing presumptuous about His devotion to the house of God. He guarded His commitment for God's house with a cloak of zeal. It was not a commitment of convenience or a devotion of duty. It was a holy zeal, for He was driven by the presence of God, and when He saw those who took that presence for granted, He was overcome with righteous indignation and cleared God's house with a whip.

His zeal for God's house was so strong that at the age of twelve, Mary and Joseph could not find Him for three days. When they finally located Him and scolded Him for His behavior, His response was, *"Why were you searching for me? Didn't you know I had to be in my Father's house?"* (Luke 2:49) The Scripture goes on to say, *"But they didn't understand what He was saying to them."* (Luke 2:50)

Could it be that we do not understand either? Could it be that we have grown familiar with "church" and now take it for granted? Could it be that we have forgotten the power of the corporate dynamic and have allowed, at times, obstacles to keep us home? The issue is not meetings. The issue is a zeal for the presence of God that would motivate us in such a way as to press through whatever obstacle is placed before us to prevent our coming into that corporate presence.

If an individual presence was enough, Jesus would have been satisfied, for He experienced that in perfection. But His zeal was for the house of God. For us to be Christlike, we must be motivated by nothing less. Let us never allow the enemy to keep us from God's house.

August 11th

ENCUMBERED EXPENSE

"For where your treasure is, there your heart will be also"
Matthew 6:21

Our focus should be building on eternal principles with an eye for an eternal reward. The promise is if we do so we can take our wealth with us, for the true wealth which will have accumulated will be eternal wealth. (i.e., wealth that is transferable)

In the world of finance is a term called, "encumbered expense." Encumbered expense is that which has been spent, but is not yet due. The money has been committed, but it has not yet been collected. In order to get an accurate accounting of your financial state, you must compare your available funds against your encumbered funds. The balance is the measure of your true wealth.

As we examine the subject of biblical prosperity, we must do so from the perspective of encumbered expense. Many evaluate the value of their spiritual life with factoring in that which has been committed, but has not yet been collected.

For example:
A father neglects his wife and children in order to establish and build his career. As the paychecks begin to grow, his perception is he is prospering, but in reality his encumbered expenses are simply outstanding. Soon they will come due and when they do, the true wealth of his estate will be measured. Paychecks will be measured against loss of his wife's loyalty and affection. Stocks and bonds will pale compared to the alienation and rebellion of his children.

A couple decides, since they can not take it with them, they will do their best to enjoy life to its fullest now. They forsake principles and give themselves to the building of their estate. Whatever it takes is their motto. But in the process, they encumber some expenses. At the day of judgment, their work is tested by fire and it suffers loss. Since it was built on temporal values, it is burnt. Encumbered expense renders their estate worthless.

If riches were valued before we paid the bills, we would all be richer, but unfortunately they are not. So, let us build with the least amount of encumbered expenses.

August 12th

A WORSHIP CENTER

"For in Him we live and move and have our being"
Acts 17:28

Worship means little to a center that has not been turned. If you and the purposes that surround your existence are the center of your life, then worship will pale in its importance. On the other hand, if your center has been turned and the person of Jesus Christ takes center stage, then worship holds the permanent place.

How easy it is for our centers to revert back to us. With just a little neglect and a few bad choices, we begin that backward fall that changes our center and silences our worship.

When worship becomes dry and laborious, the first place to look is at you. Has your center changed? Worship has everything to do with focus. If your focus is diverted away from the Lord onto self, then you become the object of worship and the ability to worship Jesus freely is hindered. The turning of our center frees our focus, enabling us to turn our eyes completely upon Him.

Where the Holy Spirit is desirous of taking us will require that Kingdom center. We have just begun to taste what His intent is for us in praise and worship. Imagine the joy that will come in a people who are free from inhibitions and free to fully express their hearts in love and adoration to their King. This is the type of worship Father is seeking.

Let us allow Him to lift our expectation. Maybe the limitation you have placed on yourself is in need of a lift. Maybe it is time for you to lift your hands in worship without inhibition. Maybe it is time for you to dance. Maybe it is time to kneel. The issue for all these expressions is not having to do any of them, but being free to do all of them.

ೋ

August 13th

TRANSFERABLE WEALTH

"Do not store up for yourselves treasures on earth, where moth and rust destroy, and where thieves break in and steal. But store up for yourselves treasures in heaven"

Matthew 6:19-20

So how are your eternal investments doing? If you were to check the balance of your eternal accounts, what would you find: a negative balance or an account growing well beyond the current rate of interest because it is receiving consistent deposits?

In the above passage, Jesus gives us a hint what we can expect in our eternal behavior. He gave us clear instruction to store up treasures in heaven. The instruction cuts right through the lie we've been taught all of our lives that, "we can't take it with us." Matthew 6 tells us we will take it with us provided we have built on eternal principles with an eye toward an eternal reward.

Somehow most have developed the mentality that Heaven will be the great equalizer. Once we pass through those pearly gates, everything will be wiped clean and we will all be issued a new and equal supply. But, this is contrary to biblical teaching. When Jesus told us to, *"store up treasures in heaven,"* it was not so He could amass a huge supply, then redistribute it all equally. He told us to store it up for we will all have an individual level of wealth that will be determined by our steps of obedience and investment while here on Earth.

This has nothing to do with salvation. Our salvation is purely by grace. What I am addressing is our level of wealth once we get there. The fact we were to store up treasures indicates there will be some form of economic trade in heaven. The currency of eternity will not be dollars and cents, but it will be the currency of a good name (Proverbs 22:1), the currency of relationship (Philippians 3:7-8), the currency of faith (John 2:5), the currency of wisdom (Proverbs 8:18), and the currency of the Holy Spirit (Ephesians 1:13-14). Those who will be "rich" in eternity will be those who have sown to eternal principles.

So, as an eternal investment advisor, I counsel you to invest in currency that is transferable. Do not give yourself to the food that spoils, but for the food that endures to eternal life.

August 14th

BEING LED BY THE SPIRIT

"Those who are led by the Spirit of God are the sons of God"
Romans 8:14

All true freedom begins with the mastery of self. The Holy Spirit comes to take control of our lives and set us free from the mastery of sin. Through the power of His indwelling presence, He enables us to live above the laws of carnality and self rule.

Man is made up of a three part expression. The human, the carnal and the spiritual. As the Holy Spirit comes to His people, He comes to deal with all three. He comes to deliver the human, to displace the carnal and to enthrone the spiritual.

Jesus Christ came to set the human free. His deliverance was so complete that those who find themselves hidden in Christ are free from condemnation because they have been delivered from the law of sin. The law of the Spirit of life lifts us to a higher reality. Deliverance is not found in the mastery of methods, it is found in relationship. As we learn of the person and work of the Holy Spirit, our deliverance is realized. Deliverance from human limitations is found in the Holy Spirit. It is not bad to be human, it is just limiting. God's desire is to free us from human limitations by hiding us in Christ and empowering us with the Spirit of life.

The indwelling presence of God also displaces our carnal nature. Through relationship with the Holy Spirit our cravings, impulses and unrestrained desires are displaced until our deepest craving becomes that of pleasing God. As we learn to hear and be led by the voice of the Holy Spirit, we find the carnal being displaced by the spiritual.

The work of the Holy Spirit is a process As we enthrone the Spirit of Christ, we become His sons and daughters. Sons of God are those who are not just saved, but have willingly embraced the continual leadership of the Spirit by saying no to self and yes to God!

August 15th

IN IT OR OF IT

"They are not of the world anymore than I am of the world"
John 17:14

How we stand in relationship to the world determines whether or not we will fulfill our destiny. Knowing this to be true, Jesus made our relationship to the world a focus of His prayer to the Father.

As one traces the history of the church, we see that one of its greatest challenges has been its relationship to the world. We see it moving in and out of three differing postures.

1. ISOLATION. There is a fine line between being set apart (sanctified) and being removed. The tactic of our enemy has been to lure the church into isolation so as to remove any possibility of influence and leadership. Isolation removes all opportunity for us to be salt and light

2. ACCOMMODATION. Being set apart means the church marches to a different standard. The tactic of the enemy has been to criticize that standard and, over time, reduce it. This criticism produces an insecurity that leads to accommodation. Accommodation is the failure to see the new order of the Kingdom of God. It is the failure to see that we have been called to be a contrasting culture. *"You shall have no other gods before me."* (Exodus 20:3) In Hebrew, the word "before" could be translated "beside." Accommodation is the attitude that allows the gods of compromise, career, pleasure, greed, etc., to come alongside us and force us to become "in the world and of it."

3. OBEDIENT INVOLVEMENT. Obedience must precede any involvement in the world. *"In the world, but not of it."* Obedience in our involvement is what sets us apart, but keeps us involved. Without involvement there is no opportunity for the salt to salt or the light to light. Obedient involvement leads us to become the friend of sinners so as to rescue them from the fire.

How do you stand in relationship to the world?

> ➢ Of it, but not in it.
> ➢ In it and of it.
> ➢ In it, but not of it.

August 16th

OVER-TAUGHT AND UNDER-PRACTICED

"Do not merely listen to the word and so deceive yourselves. Do what it says."

James 1:22

No generation has ever experienced the depth of spiritual information that is available today. Daily we are exposed to the television, radio, newspaper, books, cassette tapes, and sermons. Information is in abundance, but practice is easily neglected. In a sea of information it is quite easy to miss it all. Sometimes, we are so eager to take things in, but we do not have the time to work them out. Our notebooks fill up with notes, but our behavior remains unchanged.

Becoming doers of the Word is indeed a challenge. Without a purposeful strategy, very little will ever be translated into behavioral change. Once we receive the Word, we become responsible to work the Word through to change. The process of change begins with being responsible to write the Word down in order that you might remember what was said. Without a record of what was said, most will forget the Word within 24 hours. After writing the Word down, you must review what was said. Reviewing is the stage where the Holy Spirit is able to interpret the Word to your personal set of circumstances and make it applicable. It is in the review state that you pray the Word through, taking key points of the message and praying them into our life and situation. It is in the review stage that you look for other verses that support the point and develop the message into something broader and deeper.

Next comes the state of action. It is here that you do what was said. A message on prayer without praying is just Word. A message on leadership without leading is ineffective. You hold the keys to action. No one can do it for you. Do you feel over-taught? Perhaps you are just under-practiced. Apply what you have and you will indeed desire more.

August 17th

THE IMPACT OF ONE

"Let us throw off everything that hinders and the sin that so easily entangles and let us run with perseverance the race marked out for us."

Hebrews 12:1

Have you ever struggled with the sense of your own self worth and ability to effect change in a world that is lost and heading nowhere fast? "Lord, what can I possibly do; can I really make a difference?" One of the most important battles you will ever win is the battle over your personal mission and strategic placement in the purposes of God. You are not a product of random choice, but one of strategic selection. Father God chose you for a specific purpose. Effectiveness in the Kingdom of God begins with discovering what that purpose is.

God is in the business of building upon one-talent heroes. Those God selects are not necessarily the gifted, but the faithful. He looks for those with the talent of humility, availability and dependability. I am convinced that behind every multi-talented giant is a one-talent hero used of God and responsible for the hero's success. No, they are not celebrated. In fact, you probably never hear anything about them, but without their contribution the hero never would have been.

Who can estimate the value of the apostle Paul's talent and contribution to the Kingdom of God? He is responsible for 14 of the 21 New Testament epistles. Through his writings we have possessed our understanding of law versus grace, the gifts of the Spirit, the cross and resurrection. It is because of Paul the gospel came to the Gentiles. Next to Jesus, Paul plays the most strategic role in all of Christendom. But without the one talent of a man named Ananias, Paul might have died blind. We read in Acts 9 that God blinded Paul and for three days he was unable to see. God appeared to Ananias in a vision and told him to go and pray for the apostle Paul. Some would say if Ananias would not have gone, God could have sent someone else. But Paul, too, had a vision. In his vision, he saw a man named Ananias come and place his hand upon him to restore his sight. (Acts 9:12) If someone named Fred would have come, it would not have been true to the vision Paul received. It had to be Ananias. This is the first and last time we hear of Ananias, but that simple act of obedience changed the life of Paul and 2,000 years later continues to write history. Never underestimate the impact of one. Never say I have only this one talent, for that talent given by God, can change the world.

August 18th

GENERATION NEXT

"Even when I am old and gray, do not forsake me, O God, till I declare your power to the next generation, your might to all who are to come."

Psalm 71:18

Why is it that children are often so bored with church? I think the answer to that question is quite plain. Ninety-nine percent of the local churches' focus misses our children entirely. Consequently, they perceive it to be irrelevant until they become "grown-ups." All too often we force feed what appeals to us rather than adopting the methods so as to appeal to them. Francis Anfuso put it this way, "We fail our children by forcing them into spiritual rituals that have nostalgic relevance for us, but mean little to them." As a result, they perceive the church to be their parents' church rather than theirs.

To capture the next generation, we must appeal to that generation by being relevant to their desires and needs. Ken Davis, in his book, *How To Speak to Youth*, writes, "Our audience will change. If we don't change with them, our message will not be heard. Our message will never change, but our methods must be updated constantly." What appeals to adults most probably will not appeal to their children. This is a fact beautifully illustrated in the battle of the beverage wars. In spite of the fact that coffee is this nation's number one selling beverage, the industry has ignored the youth market for over two decades. So now we have an entire generation of young adults who have grown up preferring Pepsi to coffee because Pepsi captured them in their marketing to the "Pepsi Generation." People are drawn to what appeals to them. In order to capture them, our appeal must be directed to them.

If we fail to capture the next generation and equip them to take the purposes of the Kingdom further than we are, we fail. If that goal is not indelibly written into our vision, we have only half a vision. Half a vision will not carry us into the future. Statistics show that the majority of those professing to be born again received Jesus before the age of 25. Yet, those same statistics tell us the average age of church members is 55. Why the discrepancy? It is because, though they were born again, they perceived the church to be irrelevant. Consequently, they never joined the church.

Francis Anfuso, in his book, *We've Got a Future*, gives us some helpful strategies on how to bring our children along in the purposes of God.

- ➤ Challenge them with a positive message.
- ➤ Use their music, humor, clothing, art, literature.
- ➤ Provide leadership for them to emulate.
- ➤ Have a unique name and logo.
- ➤ Use dynamic visual images.
- ➤ Be daring and different.
- ➤ Make serving God fun.

Christianity is only one generation away from extinction. Let us pray and be open to the ministry of the Holy Spirit in whatever creative container that may come in.

August 19th

SUBTLE WANDERINGS

"Return to me with all your heart, with fasting and weeping and mourning"

Joel 2:12

How easy it is at times to wander. Radical departures are quickly detected, but subtle wanderings are often unnoticed until the realization comes that you have wandered from your course and are now lost.

To wander is to sway from the course a small degree at a time. Never is it blatant. It is a missed prayer here, an opportunity to read the Word there. Small issues of disobedience have a tendency to become large issues of disobedience. What begins as a small degree over time becomes a major chasm. Days become weeks; weeks become months. Soon we have forgotten who we are and have wandered from our course. Once you have tasted life on the edge and have wandered away, it is hard to return. But, what is impossible with man is possible with God.

The return back to the cutting edge requires our whole heart. Ninety percent may have carried you before, but to return to something once you've left it requires one hundred percent. Only God can give you that level of desire and determination. Desperation has a way of producing godly desire. It is only when we are desperate to see a certain matter accomplished are we willing to pay the price to possess what is desired.

Fasting is quite often Father's vehicle of return. Through the discipline of fasting, God is able to sharpen our focus which most probably caused the initial departure. Focus is what keeps us on the straight and narrow. Fasting provides us opportunity to push aside natural desires and focus completely upon Jesus. As we focus on Him, we become like Him. As we become like Him, we find that actions, contrary to His way, are altered. Attitudes are adjusted and behavior is changed.

Have you wandered from the way? Have you lost your intensity of purpose? Perhaps it's time you return to Him with all your heart. Perhaps it's time to call a fast and refocus your desires.

August 20th

THE EXPECTATION OF ANTICIPATION

"Behold the former things have come to pass, now I declare new things. Before they spring forth I proclaim them to you"

Isaiah 42:9

Spirit led anticipation brings with it an inherent power. Anticipation has the power to stir faith, risk and courage. Throughout Scripture we see God continually using anticipation to stir His people to desire and possession. *"For I know the plans I have for you saith the Lord, plans to prosper you and give you a future."* (Jeremiah 29:11) A verse like that builds our anticipation and releases expectation.

Anticipation means to foresee and deal with in advance. God uses anticipation to announce His pending intent. Anticipation is the engagement of divine initiative and human responsibility. Since man is God's chosen vessel of labor, He must draw us into His intention in order for His desire to come to pass. Through anticipation, responsibility is engaged and action is realized.

Why doesn't God just do it and catch us all by surprise? God has purposely restrained Himself to our participation. Through anticipation, vision and purpose are established. Without anticipation, we could either limit God or get so far ahead that we would miss Him. Through anticipation, God is able to develop His intention and frame for us how something will come to pass and how it will affect our lives.

Anticipation is a gift from God. It comes through His initiative. There is not a lot we can do to get it, but there is a lot we can do to lose it. It comes through prayer and listening to His announcement and is lost through unforgiveness, cynicism and negativity.

Ready your heart for His coming, by putting away attitudes that rob you of anticipation.

൪෩෨

August 21st

THE WAY OF FAITH

"For my thoughts are not your thoughts" saith the Lord. "As the heavens are high above the earth so are my ways higher than your ways"
Isaiah 55:8-9

The fact that God's ways are higher is a truth that is hard realized. It is quite easy to acknowledge it in principle, but quite another story when it affects our practice. Like so many things in the purposes of God, it is easy to acknowledge in theory, but when it begins to make demands on our behavior, that is a different story.

An area that clearly illustrates this truth is the area of knowledge. To most American minds, knowledge is supreme. We all spend a minimum of twelve years pursuing it and most go on to graduate work to expand what they already have. Those who have completed their post-graduate studies and now have initials after their names are highly revered; especially if those initials are Ph.D. or Th.D.

Though knowledge is admirable and those who have graduated are to be respected, the just do not live by knowledge. Americans live by knowledge, but the just "live by faith." It is precisely at this point that God's ways begin to rub many. For most of our natural lives, we have been trained to trust in and live by knowledge. But, as we move deeper into the purposes of God, the more we see knowledge taking a back seat to faith. Faith has the preeminent place in the purposes of God.

Many have shrunk back when faced with the expectations of the Kingdom way, because they tried to walk in this way according to knowledge rather than faith. Through the eyes of knowledge, God's ways are impossible, but through the eyes of faith, all things are possible.

If you find yourself overwhelmed with the difficulty of the task, perhaps your problem is knowledge. God's ways are beyond figuring out. Your only answer is to let go and begin the adventure of faith. God's ways are higher than our ways, and His way is the way of faith.

ଷ୫୦

August 22nd

FIT FOR THE GLORY

"On the day he comes to be glorified in his saints and to be admired in all them that believe"

II Thessalonians 1:10

No wonder we have waited for 2,000 years! When Jesus comes, He will come to be glorified in His saints and to be admired in all who believe. I am afraid that if He came now or any other time in the last 2,000 years, it would have been viewed as a rescue job, not a crowing glory.

Expectation determines outcome. Because the church has expected rescue, there has been nothing to call her out of complacency into responsibility. Seeing the church's condition, Christ is waiting for the bride to make herself ready. (Revelation 19:7) Perhaps this readiness will be defined by responsibility, wherein she can handle the glory and the world can, with integrity, hold her in a place of admiration.

This will require a change of focus. As long as our focus remains on our own rescue, prosperity, blessing, etc., we will not come into the required level of maturity. Father's cry of the ages has been for a people He can share His glory with. (John 17:22) This is the ultimate in co-laboring with Him; an expectation of maturity in order that we might be containers of His glory, rightly representing Jesus Christ to a dying world.

Imagine what that day will be like. As a mature bride, we will stand in His coming, sharing His glory with Him. His desire is to share it with us. Our desire is to give it right back.

To partake in that type of glory will require a major working of the Holy Spirit. This is why Paul prays in II Thessalonians 1:11 for us to be counted worthy. For the sake of Christ's coming, make this prayer your daily cry, "Father, make us worthy of our calling."

August 23rd

PROVING OUR SPIRITUALITY

"Brothers, if someone is caught in a sin, you who are spiritual should restore him gently. But watch yourself or you also may be tempted"
Galatians 6:1

The Kingdom of God is contrary to man's natural way. Casualties are a certain reality as we try to navigate the way of the Kingdom. The question is not so much will someone sin, but if they do sin, how will that sin be handled?

Confrontation is a privileged action in the body of Christ. Christians are not to be those who avoid each other in conflict or ignore relational problems. We are to confront those doing wrong. Since restoration is always the goal of our confrontation, the apostle Paul defines a few clear guidelines.

1. The restoring should only be done by the spiritual. *"You who are spiritual should restore him gently."* If one is not led and controlled by the Holy Spirit, they are not to be trusted with the privilege of confrontation. Confrontation is an entrustment given only to the spiritual.

2. The goal of the confrontation is always restoration and reinstatement. If the goal of the confrontation is anything other than restoration, it is carnally motivated and self-appointed. The spiritual confront in order to restore.

Wrongdoing does not take us out of the way of grace. Yes, in extreme cases the wrongdoer may not be restored to a particular position, but they must always be restored to the spiritual family and reinstated back into the family way of grace. Often our attitude toward the wrongdoer is, "You are forgiven, but now you will have to perform up to my level of expectation in order to win my acceptance." In doing so, we place them back under the law.

3. Confrontation should be done gently without any sense of superiority. It's nothing short of pride that would expect justice from others when we have been given the fullness of mercy. Humility is our place of immunity before God and each other.

Our spirituality is proven as we seek to restore those caught in sin.

August 24th

WHEN THE SILENCE GETS LOUDER

"A time to be silent..."

Ecclesiastes 3:7

Have you ever faced those times in your walk with the Lord that it seemed as if He was not there? The cries that were once met with quick replies were now left unanswered. The God that seemed to be at your beckoned call now seems to be distant and unresponsive.

There are many reasons why God might remain silent. Certainly, repetitive sin left unconfessed would cause God to distance Himself. The hardness of heart would be another reason why God would not speak into your life situation. The unwillingness to walk in the truth of what God has already said might cause Him to refrain from speaking more.

On and on the list could go, but perhaps the most critical to our current state is the consumption of God's activity solely upon ourselves. When the people of God become consumers only, the involvement of God begins to slowly taper off. In other words, if God's voice is silent, maybe you need to look at your level of consumption as compared to your level of giving.

The prophet Isaiah seems to give credibility to this thought in chapter 58 and verse 9, where we are told that after we loose the chains of injustice, set the oppressed free, feed the hungry and provide the poor wanderer with shelter, *"Then,"* he says, *"you will call and the Lord will answer; you will cry for help and He will say: 'Here am I.'"*

Oh, for the clarity of answer. To have that speedy reply. To know that God is attentive to our voice and desirous of answering our call. Isaiah links that attentiveness directly to our ability to reach out beyond ourselves and give to those in need.

If your silence is getting louder, maybe it is time you begin to give.

※

August 25th

WORK

"I have not stopped giving thanks for you, remembering you in my prayers"

Ephesians 1:16

As we read the prayers of Paul recorded in most of his Epistles, we are reminded of the incredible relationship God has called us to enter into with Him. Ours is not just a relationship of rescue, nor it is just a relationship of blessing. God, in His marvelous grace, has called us into a relationship of co-laboring and co-operating together with Him. He has called us into the family business "Almighty and Sons" and one of our primary portfolios of responsibility is intercession. Twice in Ephesians, once in Philippians and Colossians, twice in Thessalonians, Paul enters into this co-laboring relationship and intercedes on behalf of the church.

Intercession is not a gift reserved for the few. It is a ministry given to us all. Sure, there are those who will carry a deeper burden for prayer, but nowhere in Scripture is intercession described as a gift that only a chosen few possess.

Many Christians will never make the transition into a working relationship with Christ. The reason is our flesh detests work. Our western philosophy has viewed work as a punishment or necessary evil. But God does not view work as such. Like children, we need to be trained in labor. Trained to work hard. Trained to do a good job. Trained to work until the job is done.

Jesus said to them, *"My Father is always at His work to this very day, and I, too, am working."* (John 5:17) To be like Him will mean learning how to work like He does, seeing where He is working and joining with Him in the labor of intercession to see the matter accomplished.

August 26th

THE SPIRIT OF DISQUALIFICATION

"His divine power has granted us everything pertaining to life and godliness"

II Peter 1:3

Herein lies a pretty bold promise. Peter states quite clearly that we have already been given everything we need pertaining to life and godliness. Well, if this is true, and I most certainly believe it is, then why do so many struggle in their Christian walk?

The answer to that question could be as varied as we are. But, in one way or another, all the answers could be traced back to the same common root. The root is the spirit of disqualification. Disqualification is that spirit that causes us to remove ourselves from the race before God has had opportunity to bring us into His victory. Children face disqualification in parents who say, "You'll never amount to anything." or "You are no good." As Christians, we face it in self talk that says, "I'm not qualified." "I'll never measure up." or "I'll never be able to pray like so and so." It is accusatory self talk that contradicts the Bible's evaluation of who we are and disqualifies us from pursuit of the prize.

We are in a war: Christlikeness and our preparation as the Bride is the objective. Our mind or thoughts are the arena of battle, and words are the chosen weapon of attack. Which words we choose determines how we fare in the battle. If we choose words of truth, we receive the prize. If we choose words of disqualification, we receive defeat. The Word of God declares our victory as a concluded fact. If we will simply stay in the race, we will win. The only way we are ever defeated is when we quit and take ourselves out of the race.

If you are facing a difficult time or struggling to overcome, do not quit! Be persistent because your victory is assured, provided that you do not quit.

CBEO

August 27th

THE CALEB COMPANY

"Then Caleb silenced the people before Moses and said, "We should go and take possession of the land, for we can certainly do it."

Numbers 13:30

With odds worse than a million to one, you would have thought it much safer for him to remain silent and go with the flow. But, not this man. He was a man of tremendous courage and what he saw would not let him go. It had captivated him and in that captivation, he had also discovered his motivation. So swimming against the tide of the millions who said it was not possible, Caleb stood and said, *"Surely we can do it."* (Numbers 13:30)

The spies had all seen the same obstacles: powerful people, fortified cities and giants. But Caleb had discovered the secret of his motivation and power. The others saw the people and their great strength, but Caleb saw that the giants protection was gone and the Lord was with Israel. (Numbers 14:9)

Perspective kept an entire nation out of the promised land and perspective allowed two others to enter. The expectation of the Gospel is total and it is consummate. Anything less would miss the mark of the divine. Though the expectation of the Gospel calls us up to ultimate sacrifice, it does not expect us to pay that price in our own strength. The source of the Gospel has always been and will always be the power and enablement of the Holy Spirit.

Last year's payment will not satisfy this year's requirement. As the destiny of God requires we go beyond commitment, we must embrace that expectation with the confidence, "Surely we can do it." As we discover by revelation that the power of the Holy Spirit is our source, we can adopt this kind of attitude. Once we have adopted a "surely we can" perspective, it does not matter how difficult the expectations are because God is our source, whether He is asking little or whether He is asking much. Whether He is asking something as simple as getting out of bed or something as difficult as dying to our dream, He is the supply for both.

Extraordinary times call for extraordinary people. Leading the way of this extraordinary group will be the "Caleb Company." These are those who refuse to focus on the difficulty, but rather focus on the reality that the Lord is with us, so surely we can do it.

August 28th

PRESENTING OURSELVES

"Be ready in the morning, and then come up on Mount Sinai. Present yourself to me"

Exodus 34:2

Intimacy begins with presenting ourselves to the Lord. How easy it is to present our needs, our personal agendas, and never present ourselves. Intimacy begins with vulnerability. It begins as we are honest before God and share with Him our true condition and desire. How easy it is to hide behind our many requests thinking that we've hidden our condition. But, God is the One who searches the heart. All things are laid bare before Him whether we share them with Him or not. Sharing our condition does not inform God, it simply opens up the channels of communication and builds a direct link of relational provision.

Israel had no problem in presenting themselves to Moses. How content they were with Moses hearing God for them. How about you? Does having someone tell you what to do satisfy you, or is there the spiritual desire to present yourself before God and hear directly from His voice the needed direction in your life? God's desire is to relate to us as a Father. This relationship is dependent upon us presenting ourselves before Him. He is always there, waiting in eager expectation.

So, get ready. Tomorrow morning, go up into the presence of God and present yourself to Him.

August 29th

PRISON OR PRISONER

"As a prisoner for the Lord, I urge you to live a life worthy of the calling you have received"

Ephesians 4:1

Whose prisoner are you? What are you a prisoner to? Self deception would say to most, "I am a prisoner of no one. I am free."

Reality tells us we are all prisoners to someone or to something. Some are prisoners to self, thinking only of themselves and basing their decisions solely on the factors of how they serve themselves. Others are prisoners to careers. Life's decisions are determined solely on the basis of how they would either further their career aspirations or hinder them. Still, others are prisoners to fear, indulgence, urgency, pleasure . . . on and on the list could go. The fact is, everybody is a prisoner. What separates one from the other is the type of prison they are in.

There is a prison that leads to freedom. Yes, prison and freedom seem to be a contradiction of terms, but only in the light of man's natural thinking. Humanistic thinking would establish freedom as a goal. Biblical thinking recognizes there is no such thing as "freedom" and exchanges the bondage of self-centered living for the freedom of becoming a prisoner of the Lord Jesus Christ.

To be a prisoner of the Lord, Jesus Christ acknowledges the fact that we are captivated by His presence. Our lives have become subject to Him, our purpose for life is found in Him, our coming and our going are centered in Him. He is our life and our focus.

Whose prisoner are you? What are you a prisoner to? Perhaps it is time to exchange your prison and become a prisoner of Jesus Christ.

August 30th

READY YOUR HEART

"Prepare the way of the Lord"

Isaiah 40:3

Have you ever had someone show up at your home unexpectedly? There you sat relaxing with the house looking like a hurricane just passed through. The children's toys littered the floor, dishes were still in the sink as you sat in your pajamas. Then you heard it! The door bell rang and panic struck in your heart. Immediately, you went into warp drive trying to pick the place up while your guest stood outside wondering why it was taking so long for you to answer and why there was so much noise coming from inside.

Readiness is both a spiritual and physical principle. Babies do not just arrive. For nine months their coming is announced, allowing you to ready the house for their arrival. So it is in the spiritual realm. Jesus did not just come. First, John the Baptist was sent to prepare His coming. John's ministry was a ministry of readiness . . . sent by God to ready the attitudes and practices of the people so they would be prepared to receive the Lord.

Preparing for someone's visit only requires a surface preparation . . . a quick vacuum, dusting and general cleaning. But, if someone is coming to move in, it requires permanent preparation. Preparing for the arrival of God's glory requires a permanent preparation. It requires that we ready our hearts to allow God the freedom to do whatever He desires to do. This means that we must enlarge our expectations because God desires to move outside the box of limitations we place on Him. He may come in people you did not expect. He may come in a way you did not expect. Israel missed His coming, for he came in the unexpected.

Ready your heart in prayer and study of the Word so He may come to you in His fullness.

August 31st

THE IMPORTANCE OF INTIMACY

"He called his twelve disciples to himself and gave them authority"
Matthew 10:1

Long before there is authority, there is intimacy. Spiritual authority and effectiveness begin with spending time with Jesus. Before Jesus gave the disciples authority to go, He called them to Himself. It was there, out of their intimacy and time spent with Him, that they were able to drive out evil spirits and heal every disease and sickness.

How easy it is to fall into a relationship without fellowship . . . to know Him, but never spend meaningful time with Him. In so doing, we develop a utilitarian relationship with Christ. A relationship that uses the Lord for what we need, but never relates to Him on the basis of intimacy. To love Jesus is to spend time with Him. Those we love the most we spend the most time with, because love leads us to the desire of fellowship.

Much of the church of Jesus Christ has become weak and anemic, because we have lost the desire of intimacy. Jesus has been relegated to just another one of the things in a busy schedule. When Jesus becomes just another one of our many things, He is given His token place. Somehow we manage to carve out an hour on Sundays to give Him. Giving Jesus His token place may qualify you for relationship, but it most certainly will not qualify you for fellowship. Fellowship requires time. It requires a daily coming to Him. To be with Him in the fellowship of prayer, the fellowship of worship, the fellowship of study in His word. Out of this time of fellowship, we discover the power of intimacy and the ability to be effective in a world in desperate need.

You have given the Lord your life; now give Him your time and discover the joy of intimacy.

September 1st

A KINGDOM WORK ETHIC

"Whatever you do, work at it with all your heart as working for the Lord, not for men"

Colossians 3:23

America was established on the foundation of a Kingdom work ethic. The men and women who came to this country came with a determination and drive to work hard and do whatever it takes to fulfill the vision that had been born in their hearts. For some it meant death, for others it meant long toilsome hours of hard work. But as the years have passed, this Kingdom work ethic has been eroded away. Workers' rights, more pay and many other motivations prompted by greed have become more important than the satisfaction of "putting in" a hard day's work.

What was the secret of this work ethic our forefathers possessed? The Apostle Paul points out two key characteristics of a Kingdom work ethic in the above verse.

1. WORK WITH ALL YOUR HEART — Workers' rights have taught us all we need to give is eight hours a day with a break in the morning and one for lunch. A Kingdom work ethic teaches that you work at it until the job is done or at least the portion set for the day. When you work at something with all of your heart, you look for opportunities to work harder and smarter, not opportunities to work less. When we understand the truth of Christ in us, it enables us to work at a level far above natural ability. Christ in us causes us to work with heart and soul.

2. AS WORKING FOR THE LORD — How easy it is to forget for whom we are working. Our eyes are taken off the Lord and we begin working for the paycheck, the promotion, the company, or the boss. To work for anyone other than the Lord is to sell yourself short. When our perspective is clearly the Lord, we are energized with an eternal motivation. The temporal is not enough to generate a Kingdom work ethic, but when we have an eye on our eternal inheritance, even our work habits are altered.

So let us see ourselves at our work place as emissaries of the Kingdom of God.

September 2nd

SEED SOWN AMONG THE THORNS

"Other seeds fell among thorns, which grew up and choked the plant"
Matthew 13:7

Our response to the word "sown" determines the effect of that word in our hearts. Jesus said the seed sown among the thorns were those ensnared by the worries of life and the deceitfulness of riches. In other words, the life of God's Word had been choked out because of distractions.

To hear the Word of God involves more than just listening. In the Greek language the word "hear" means "to attend to." So, in order to hear the Word, it must generate some type of action or response to what was said. Distractions are those things in our lives that keep us from attending to the Word. We listen to the Word preached, but the time needed to "attend to" the Word, making its personal application and discerning its needed action, is robbed. Therefore, the benefit that would have come from the Word is never realized.

Please note that the thorns grew anyway. The picture we see in this parable is the sown seed sat for so long, the thorns had plenty of time to grow and choke the Word out. My question is, why did not the seed grow first, choking out the thorns? Whatever grows fastest will choke out the competitors. Distractions keep us from responding quickly to the Word. Without a quick response, the thorns will steal the intended fruit of the sown Word.

Are there distractions in your life aborting the fruitfulness of God's Word? Are you quick to respond to the spoken Word? Perhaps it is time, through the Holy Spirit's power, to lay the axe to any spiritual distraction in your life.

September 3rd

SEASONS AND THE WORD

"There is a time for everything, and a season for every activity under the heaven"
Ecclesiastes 3:1

People, like nature, go through various seasons. As in the natural, we all experience the differing seasons of life. There are the seasons of sowing and there are the seasons of reaping. There are the seasons of waiting and there are the seasons of growing. All of these are seasons ordained of God and part of His providential intent.

But, there are other types of seasons we go through. These are self-inflicted seasons that come as a result of spiritual neglect, not natural cycle.

In a providential season of God, you embrace His sovereignty and wait the season out. But, if it is a self-inflicted season you are in, you must cry out for understanding and make the necessary adjustments.

In the parable of the sower, Jesus describes four responses to the Word of God. Three of these responses lead us into self-inflicted seasons of spiritual strain and conflict. Our response to the Word of God, whether that be the written Word, spoken Word, sermon or book, it is critical. The way we process that Word determines our level of spiritual understanding and usefulness. Neglect will lead to spiritual death. Familiarity will harden our hearts and dry up the soil of receptivity.

Knowing this, Jesus points out the various responses and corresponding conditions of the heart. The first was the seed sown on the path. These are those who hear the Word, but do not understand. Hearing only is not the goal; understanding is our objective. The second was the seed sown on the rocks. These are those who have no root, so the seed springs forth, but dies due to the lack of stability. The third was the seed sown among the thorns. These are those who receive the Word, but it is choked out by the worries of this life and the deceitfulness of riches.

Are you in the midst of a self-inflicted season? Perhaps it is time you examine your response to the Word.

September 4th

SEED SOWN ON THE ROCKS

"What was sown on the rocky places is the man who hears the word and at once receives it with joy, but since he has no root he lasts only a short time"

Matthew 13:20-21

According to the parable, the seed sown on the rocks were those that have no root. Take note that it is not the seed that has no root and lasts only a short time, but it is the person who has no root and, consequently, he lasts only a short time.

One of the many benefits of covenant relationships is the root of stability they provide. In praying for the Body of Christ in Ephesians 3:27, the apostle Paul prays that we would become rooted people. When a person has no root, he becomes like the ship of the sea tossed to and fro. Whatever the latest wind of teaching, they receive it with joy. The problem is, because of poor "rootage," the joy lasts only a few weeks, then it is on to some other new thing before it has been able to produce lasting fruit.

The goal of teaching is not just the process of receiving; it is the doing of the teaching's intent. Without proper roots, everything remains a teaching or a concept and is never translated into fruit. Without fruit, the teaching remains in the head and never reaches the heart or practice.

If the issue of fruitfulness is of concern in your life, perhaps it is time to look at the condition of your root. Is your life rooted firmly in Christ? Is it rooted firmly in the Word? Is it rooted firmly in the church? Is it rooted firmly in the relationships God has joined you to?

September 5th

THE SEED ON THE PATH

"When anyone hears the message about the kingdom and does not understand it, the evil one comes and snatches away what was sown in his heart. This is the seed sown along the path"

Matthew 13:19

According to the parable, the seed sown on the path are those who hear the Word, but do not understand it. How many times have you heard a message or read a book that left you void of understanding? It was not that you could not intellectually grasp the meaning of the message, but there was no spiritual impartation that comes from the spirit of wisdom and revelation.

Earlier in the chapter, Jesus explained the problem of understanding. He explained that it was not mental understanding that was aborting the seed, but rather an understanding of the heart. It was an understanding that comes from working the Word heard, beyond a mental ascent into a spiritual perception. This working is done by taking notes of what was said, then bringing those notes before the Holy Spirit, praying them through, asking the Holy Spirit to amplify them, clarify them and most importantly, apply them.

Jesus explained in verse 14, that due to a callused heart, it is possible to see spiritual things and not perceive them or hear spiritual things and not understand them. This word, "callused" translated means: "to make fat." Fatness due to inactivity. Every time we hear a Word spoken and do not put the Word to practice, another layer of callous is formed over our heart. Soon the layers of callous make us dull of hearing and lethargic in practice because spiritual hearing takes place in the heart.

The good soil is found when the spoken Word is met with an eagerness to responsibly take notes, then bring the Word before the Holy Spirit for Him to lead you to application.

September 6th

A PASSION FOR HIS PRESENCE

"Do not cast me from your presence"
Psalms 51:11

It was said of David that he was a man after God's heart. The burning passion of his life was the presence of God. His passion for His presence was compared to that of a deer panting for water after a long run. This was not a surface desire motivated by selfish gain. No, this was a deep longing generated by David's intimate love and his pure devotion. Now, as he is facing the consequence of his sin, his prayer turns to protect that which is dearest to his heart. In the passion of the moment, David cries out not to save his kingdom or to spare his reputation. The paramount concern of David's heart was the presence of God. He prayed as if to say, "Lord, take it all, but whatever you do, do not cast me from your presence, for I can bear the loss of all things, but I cannot bear the loss of your presence."

To know Him is one thing; to practice His presence is quite another. To know Him as a historical figure is an impacting experience, but to know the fellowship of His presence is a life changing ordeal.

The gentle voice of the Holy Spirit would call those of us who "know" Him into the regular practice of His presence . . . a presence that far supercedes church and formal gatherings . . . but one that is dependent upon nothing other than His love for us and our love for Him.

His presence is one of the few things that will remain. Brother Lawrence, in his classic, *"The Practice of the Presence of God,"* says, "I am doing now what I will do for eternity. I am blessing God, praising Him, adoring Him and loving Him with all my heart." By practicing His presence, we are fellowshipping eternity. Imagine it, doing now what we will do then.

His presence is our consuming passion. Why wait until then, when we have been given life's ultimate privilege, to enjoy His presence now?

September 7th

A WITNESS OF THE WONDER

"Do the work of an evangelist"
II Timothy 4:5

Oh, how "spiritual" the accuser can get, once you begin to talk about evangelism. "You sure can't pressure people." or "It's Jesus that adds to the church, not you." or "If growth becomes your focus, you will surely compromise." On and on the accusations go as he swims frantically in hope of preventing us from fulfilling our commission. For the most part, he has done a pretty good job. While emphasizing equipping and a message of no compromise, many have gone a little too far and have taken it to the point of no witnessing.

"Do the work of an evangelist," Paul instructed his son, Timothy. Paul was not suggesting that Timothy's office was that of an evangelist, but that part of his duty or ministry was to evangelize. Timothy was clearly called of God to be a pastor. Though he was a pastor, he was still commissioned with the task of evangelizing.

Anyone who has been born again has experienced the wonder of wonders! To be born again means that you have passed from the judgment of death into the newness of life. You have been transplanted from the kingdom of darkness into the Kingdom of light. Because the wonder is as personal as our relationship to Christ is, we are all witnesses. This is why the Great Commission was given to all, not just to leaders or a choice few. The commission to go into all the world and make disciples is a universal commission given to young and old alike. We have all been commissioned to be a witness of the wonder that we all have experienced.

Sometimes the freshness of that wonder grows dim as we move further into Christ. As our focus moves to maturity and effectiveness we tend to forget the first principles. Doing the work of an evangelist is God's answer to forgetfulness. To do the work of an evangelist means we continually rehearse the wonder with others, so we constantly remind ourselves.

When was the last time you did the work of an evangelist? Remember, it is not an option; both Jesus and Paul presented it as a command.

Let us take this as an encouragement to be a witness of the wonder!

September 8th

FREEDOM NOT LICENSE

"It is for freedom that Christ has set us free. Stand firm then and do not let yourselves be burdened again by a yoke of slavery"
                                                                            Galatians 5:1

Slavery is indiscriminate. It does not care what you are a slave to as long as you are a slave. Whether you are a slave to sin or whether you are enslaved to "freedom," matters little as long as you are a slave.

Freedom is indeed our inheritance in Christ. But freedom without a foundation of passion for the purposes of God and pure devotion to the person of Christ, can lead to license. Time and again I have seen those without this firm foundation, take their new found knowledge of freedom and use it as an occasion for the flesh. All in the name of freedom, their language becomes mixed with course words, then consuming of alcohol becomes excessive, an occasional smoke of a cigar is thrown in, all in the name of freedom.

While neither course words, drinking or smoking will keep you from Heaven, they can become a new form of bondage that keeps us from walking in the fullness of the freedom Jesus intends for us. Without a foundation of pure devotion to Jesus, the freedom from religion can quite easily become a new religion of its own. It's our devotion for the Lord that keeps us from having to prove to ourselves and to others the limits of our new found freedom. Devotion produces maturity. Maturity is necessary to properly handle the freedom we are given in Christ without that freedom being used as an occasion for the flesh.

Any theology formed in reaction produces questionable fruit. Without a doubt, theology and direction often need reforming. But to attempt its reformation in a period of reaction is quite dangerous, for it will usually swing to far to one side in order to emphasize its point. Freedom will swing to the point of license and license will lead us right back into a new form of slavery.

Our freedom in Christ must always be perceived in the light of our devotion to Christ. One generation's freedom becomes the next generation's license, if along with that freedom, the first generation doesn't also pass on its devotion.

September 9th

REDEFINING JESUS

"Who do people say the Son of Man is?"
Matthew 16:13

Jesus was not asking His disciples this question out of a sense of insecurity. He was not taking a popularity poll to determine His level of acceptance among the people. Jesus asked the disciples this question to assess where the people were in their presuppositions of who He was.

Presuppositions are the grid work through which all of life is filtered. As truth is presented to us, it passes through this grid of our presuppositions. Whether that truth is altered or remains pure depends on the accuracy of our presuppositions.

Throughout time man has struggled with the tendency to redefine God and in that redefinition, reduce Him to just an aspect of His whole being. Rather than being the sum total of all He is, we reduce Him to just being love or just mercy.

Jesus remains who He is regardless of how are presuppositions define Him. But it is our presupposition of Him that determines what we will sell in order to follow Him. Like the pearl of great price, if we perceive it to be of little value, we will not sell much to buy the field. To sell all we have, our presupposition of that pearl must be of immeasurable value.

Faulty presuppostions have caused us to redefine Jesus. Some of our redefinitions are as follows:

- ➢ HISTORICAL JESUS — This is the Jesus who walked the Earth, 2000 years ago but has no apparent relevance or meaning today.

- ➢ RELIGIOUS JESUS — This is the Sunday only Jesus or perhaps the Christmas or Easter Jesus.

- ➢ CRISIS JESUS — This is the Jesus who only becomes real in the midst of great crisis and need.

- ➢ FRATERNAL JESUS — This is the Jesus who comes out only when all the believers are around.

- ➢ ALPHA AND OMEGA JESUS — This is the Jesus we served in the beginning of our life and we hope to serve Him in the end, but in between time He is put on hold.

All of these are mere redefinitions of Jesus that focus on an aspect of His character, but do not capture His entirety.

"Who do you say I am?" (Matthew 16:15) To sell all we have to purchase the field will require us seeing Jesus as He truly is, not just a part, not a redefinition, but the full revelator as revealed in His Word.

○§⃝○

Pause for thought:

How have you redefined Jesus to lessen your personal cost of following Him? Who do you say that He is?

September 10th

DESTINY'S NAME

"To him who overcomes... I will give a new name"
Revelation 2:17

Father expresses His love and intimacy with us in many ways. Though He is transcendent in nature, He is eminent in expression. Everywhere you look, you see the fullness of God's expression to us. Creation, redemption, the Bible, the church, all of these and more are Father's expressions of His love and His eminent concern.

Perhaps, one of the most personal ways that love is expressed is by the individual naming of those who overcome. Father is so personal in His love and awareness, that He will take the time to rename those who overcome.

A person's name is no insignificant matter. In Hebrew, the word name means "position and designation from God." When a Hebrew family named their child, they did not choose the name because of its popularity, but because of its designation and description. Having a God-given sense of what the coming child was to become, they would choose a name descriptive of that purpose. Christ: the anointed one, Peter: the rock, Daniel: God is my judge, Abraham: father of many.

God is a destiny writer. He takes us in our aimlessness; He apprehends us and then writes a destiny for us to fulfill. With that destiny comes a name. A name that simply positions us and describes, in a word, the intent of His call. We see this in God changing Abram to Abraham, Simon to Peter, Saul to Paul. With each name came a position and designation.

What is Father's name for you? I am not suggesting you change your birth name. I am simply saying, as you overcome, God will give you a new name that will describe the position and designation He intends you to fulfill. Witness, Faithful, Trainer, Guide. Names of position, names of designation, names *"known only to him who receives it,"* that we hide in our heart and allow to posture us for the fulfilling of our eternal purpose and position. (Revelation 2:17)

September 11th

FIXING AND SETTING

"Let us fix our eyes on Jesus, the author and perfecter of our faith, who for the joy set before him endured the cross..."

Hebrews 12:2

Success can be defined as the ability to make wise and purposeful decisions. Few people mistake their way into success. Few people drift into success. Those who succeed in life do so because they learned the secret of fixing and setting.

Jesus understood this principle. His ability to endure the cross was not due to some random inspiration, but because He set His course and fixed His will to do the will of His Father. The overwhelming joy of anticipating our salvation enabled Him to set His will regardless of the temptation to take an easier course. His travail in the garden reveals His desire to escape the pain that was before Him, but because His heart was set, He was able to resist the temptation with the resignation of *"Nevertheless, not my will, but your will be done."*

The "carefree," "take it as it comes," "one day at a time" philosophy of the day will never bring us into the fullness of God's desire. To walk in the fullness of God's desire will require the purposeful fixing of our eyes on Jesus and the setting of our wills to the will of our heavenly Father.

Fixing and setting are purposeful and deliberate decisions. They are predetermined choices that have been made before the crossroad of decision. Fixing involves the mind and setting involves the will. Fixing is the act of defining our course, determining our goals and discerning God's purpose for our lives. Setting is the establishing of our wills in unity with our course, then following that course regardless of the temptation to wander. Many have come to believe that the fixing of goals is giving in to carnal living. They think to fix goals is to factor out the leading and spontaneity of the Holy Spirit. Though the possibility of this exists, the fact is the fixing of goals can and should be a Holy Spirit function. Goal fixing is not something we do apart from the Holy Spirit, but rather a very integral part of the Holy Spirit's ministry in our lives. Once the Holy Spirit establishes the goal, our wills must be set behind them in order for them to be realized.

Let us fix our eyes on Jesus and set our wills to follow the course that He determines for our lives.

September 12th

INTERRUPTED BY NEED

"Silver and gold I do not have, but what I have I give you"
Acts 3:6

Have you ever been interrupted by need? In Acts 3, we read that Peter and John were on their way to church. It was just another day and time to go up to the temple and pray. But, on their way to church they were interrupted by a need. Perhaps it was the parable of the good Samaritan that caused Peter to stop. Maybe it was the words of Jesus still ringing in Peter's ear that predisposed him to this interruption. Whatever it was, Peter was interruptable. As focused as he was on prayer, Peter was interruptable.

How interruptable are you? Has your focus on doing the works of God blinded you to the needs that surround you daily? Are you open to the Holy Spirit's interruption?

Fortunately for the crippled beggar, Peter and John had no silver or gold. How easy it is to throw a little money at a need and never get personally involved. Money often prevents us from giving of our spiritual giftings. Peter and John did not have money, but they knew what they did have. They knew they had the manifest power of the Holy Spirit in their lives, so they gave only what they had. When we offer the "only" we have to the Lord in faith, it can heal, enlighten and alter someone's eternal destiny, but to do so we must be interruptable.

The Holy Spirit's desire is to open our eyes to the need that surrounds us. We are the Holy Spirit's agents of change. As we see the need and become His hand extended, lives will be changed and destinies born.

September 13th

MATURITY OF CHARACTER

"Even if I caused you sorrow by my letter, I do not regret it. I see that my letter hurt you, but only for a little while . . . you became sorrowful as God intended"

II Corinthians 7:8-9

How easy it is to focus on the one being used rather than on the One who orchestrated the event. When offenses come, who do you focus on first, God, or the one He used to bring about the sorrow? Paul tells us he was used of the Lord to produce the sorrow, but the offense was not sin on his part, but a divine appointment of the Lord for the purpose of producing repentance in the offended party.

"Godly sorrow brings repentance that leads to salvation and leaves no regret." (II Corinthians 7:10)

Godly sorrow is simply sorrow allowed to come by the will of God. It is sorrow with purpose. Sorrow with divine intention. The result of identifying it as such is *"earnestness, eagerness, longing, concern and readiness to see justice done."* (II Corinthians 7:11)

How often we miss these virtues because our focus has been on the offense. We focus on ourselves, our personal hurt, the perceived injustice and as a result, we miss the virtue God intended to deposit in us through the event.

Paul spoke to the Corinthians as adults. He said, *"if I caused you sorrow, I do not regret it."* In essence, he was saying, "You think I need to apologize when in truth you need to grow up and focus on the things of Christ, not of yourself."

The body of Christ stands in the transitional years from adolescence to adulthood. When we were children, we thought like children, but now it is time to think as adults. Let us begin to think character, purpose, holiness, purity.

God will often risk our being sorrowful in order to produce maturity of character.

❦

September 14th

DECISION COMMITTERS

"In all your ways acknowledge him and he will direct your paths"
Proverbs 3:5

Do you ever feel like you are heading nowhere and getting there fast? Direction is often a complicated issue. All dressed up and nowhere to go . . . In a hurry to get nowhere . . . Don't know if you are coming or going . . . Don't know up from down . . . Can I get there from here?

Charting the course of one's life is a serious issue. This one counts for real. It is not a practice run; we are only issued one life to live, so we best do it right the first time.

Proverbs 14:12 tells us *"there is a way that seems right to a man but the end thereof is the way of death."* How often have we made decisions that seemed so right when they were made, only to discover the outcome to be disastrous? From the limitations of our perspective it seemed like a good decision, but those limitations often prove to be deadly.

It is because of these limitations that we are often bad decision makers. God never intended us to be decision makers. We were meant to be decision committers. To commit our decision process to the Lord and let Him take control of the process and the outcome. It is only in acknowledging His will in our decision making process that we make good decisions. Otherwise, each decision made apart from His will and His involvement is a piece of death that ultimately, if left unchecked, will lead to separation from God.

To acknowledge Him in the decision making process begins first in a heart that is turned toward Him in passionate desire. That is, to want His way more than we want our own. It then leads to diligently seeking Him in prayer and the study of His Word.

To be pro-life is to be pro-active in our acknowledgment of Father's will for our decisions. Commit your way to Him and live.

September 15th

FREE FROM ADDICTION

"It is for freedom that Christ has set us free"
Galatians 5:1

The redefining and culturalizing of sin has wreaked havoc on the freedom of the individual. Once the social architects took sin out of the realm of misbehavior and put it in the realm of medical science, there was no longer a biblical cure for it. The blood of Jesus cleanses us from all sin, but it was never ordained to be a cleansing agent for Medicare.

Dr. William Playfair, in his book, *The Useful Life* describes the difference between the moral model of addictions as contrasted by the medical model.

MORAL MODEL	MEDICAL MODEL
The addict became addicted primarily as a result of immoral behavior.	The addict became addicted primarily as the result of amoral biology.
The addict is first and foremost guilty of sin.	The addict is first the victim of sickness.
The addict is spiritually and morally depraved.	The addict is psychologically and physically diseased.

Dr. Playfair proceeds to expose how the recovery industry has used the medical model of addiction to entrap millions. He goes on to offer clean biblical answers to those bound by the bondage of addictions.

From drunkenness to drugs to overeating and anger, all are described in the Word of God as sin and will be judged accordingly. As with any sin, we have been given a remedy that satisfied God's just demands. That remedy is the blood of Jesus Christ that is freely given to all who are willing to acknowledge their sin and turn in the act of repentance.

If you are bound to addictions, do not trust in man's appeasement that shifts blame. Trust in God's redemption that assumes your blame and sets you free.

September 16th

UNDER THE CONTROL OF THE EVIL ONE

"Love not the world neither those things in the world so if anyone love the world, the love of the Father is not in them"

1 John 2:15

One of history's greatest challenges has been the ability for the church to discern her proper relationship to the world. A strategic description has led us to see "the world" as a neutral zone. Many have visualized life in three categories. We have recognized the Kingdom of Light and have categorized everything good into this Kingdom. We recognize the kingdom of darkness and have categorized everything evil into this kingdom. Standing between these two, we have placed the world and have relegated it to a neutral zone. It is our relationship to the Kingdom of Light and the kingdom of darkness that frames our perspective on the world. If we are in the light, then the world is light. Whereas, if we are in darkness, the world is dark. The world is not neutral. *"The world and everything in it is under the control of the evil one."* (I John 5:19)

To be under the control of the evil one does not make something neutral. To be under the evil one's control makes that thing evil. The Bible tells us not to love the world because the world is evil. Medicine, business, politics, pleasure all find themselves under the control of the prince and the power of the air. It is into this evil system we have been commissioned by God to proclaim the Kingdom of God and demolish those strongholds that exalt themselves against the knowledge of God.

The evil one sets himself up as an evil overseer that seeks to control and influence the thoughts, philosophies and systems that network together and formulate that which is called the world. Satanic strategy has been to lure us into a mind set that sees the world system as neutral. If we see the world neutral, we will have no problem befriending it. But friendship with the world is hatred toward God. (James 4:4)

How are you standing in relationship to the world? Have you become a friend of pride, materialism or greed? Have you made room in your thinking for things that are neutral? *"The world is under the control of the evil one."* (I John 5:19)

September 17th

THE LORD HAS GONE BEFORE YOU

"You are about to go in and dispossess nations greater and stronger than you"

Deuteronomy 9:1

One of the greatest struggles we will ever face is the struggle over self worth and ability. Who am I to dispossess nations? Why are those I am called to dispossess always so much bigger and stronger than I?

These questions of inadequacy and self doubt are ones that everyone of us must face and conquer. It is here in the questions of our mind that the ultimate victory is won. The power of our adequacy has never been the focus of God's concern. He has known from the beginning that our victory was not dependent upon us, but upon Him. Our inadequacy is a known and settled issue without Him. Yes, the nations are greater and stronger than us. Yes, the enemies we go up against are bigger than I. This is why God has promised that He will go before us to destroy them.

"The Lord your God is the One who goes across ahead of you like a devouring fire. He will destroy them; He will subdue them before you. You will drive them out and annihilate them." (Deuteronomy 9:3)

The only time we encounter those greater and stronger than us is after they have already been destroyed by the devouring fire. It is after they have been defeated by Almighty God that they encounter us. Consequently, our ability is of no concern. All God expects of us is to drive out that which He has already defeated.

Never give in to the sense of your inadequacy. Do not listen to the enemy's whispers of doubt, because the Lord has gone before you. He can use you and will use you. In Christ you can do all things.

September 18th

THE QUIET PLACE

"Be still and know that I am God"
Psalm 46:10

In this day of drive-up convenience, how easy it is to force God into our instant expectation. With a drive-through mentality, we often expect God to give us what we need as we run by. But the psalmist declares that the knowledge of God is tied directly to our ability to quiet ourselves before Him.

So much of what we surround ourselves with is designed to keep us hyper. From the moment we wake in the morning till the time we go down at night, we are bombarded with external stimuli. Television, radio, books, newspapers and advertising all scream for our attention 24 hours a day.

Somehow in the midst of the roar, we must find our quiet place. Communion with the Holy Spirit begins in the quiet place. The goal is to know of communion with Him even in the center of the roar, but that discipline is learned first in the quiet places where we are able to still our mind, still our being and know that He is God. This is a place that is free from external distraction and circumstance. It is a place where all other voices that call for our attention are silenced in order that we may center in on the voice of our beloved.

Being still is a discipline. Like any other discipline, it must be learned and is perfected over time. So when you begin to commune with the Holy Spirit, take the first few minutes to quiet yourself before Him. Discipline your mind to align with your spirit, then focus your entire being on Him and Him alone. In the stillness, you will begin to hear Him speak and impart His life. In the stillness, you will find your "drive-through expectation" being replaced with a longing desire to spend more time with Him.

ॐ

September 19th

UNCOMMON PEOPLE

"You will receive power when the Holy Spirit comes on you"
Acts 1:8

The Gospel message is a message of empowerment. With the coming of the Holy Spirit came power. Power to become . . . power to be . . . power to do the work of the Kingdom of God. When we allow the Holy Spirit to come in His fullness, He puts an end to all defeatist talk. Talk like: "I'll never amount to anything." "I couldn't ever do that." "I'm just this or I'm just that." Talk of limitation and disqualification falls away when one understands the power of the Holy Spirit's coming.

When the Holy Spirit comes in power, we are never just anything. When the Holy Spirit comes in power, we are whatever He came to empower us to be. When the Holy Spirit comes, we are not just a witness; we are witnesses. When the Holy Spirit comes we are not just worshipers, we are worshipers. The power of the Holy Spirit's coming takes the just away and empowers us to be what He has called us to be and do what He called us to do.

The coming of the Holy Spirit makes heroes out of common folk. The pattern of God's choosing is consistent throughout Scripture. He consistently chose common people, empowered them with the Holy Spirit and accomplished through them uncommon things. A common man like Ananias empowered by the Holy Spirit became an uncommon man in the eyes of the apostle Paul. A common fisherman like Peter became quite uncommon once the Holy Spirit came upon him.

Heroes are made from common people. It is the power of the Holy Spirit that makes us uncommon heroes. So rather than focusing on your inability's, focus on the power of the Holy Spirit. A change of focus could take you from the common to the supernatural. Someone has to do it, why not you?

September 20th

THE PASSION OF HIS PRESENCE

"How lovely is your dwelling place O Lord Almighty. Thy soul yearns, even faints for the courts of the Lord. My heart and my flesh cry out for the living God"

Psalms 84:1-2

Do you carry this type of passion for the presence of the Lord? David possessed an intensity of desire for the presence of God. To him, it was not something he took for granted. He perceived the presence of God as a privilege and a passion that needed to be cultivated. So deep was his desire for God that it became a cry.

Is there anything in your life that you desire so deep that it has become a cry? Is there anything you yearn for? This cry and yearning simply underscores the depth of desire.

This kind of desire comes as a gift from the Lord. To the one who delights himself in the Lord, God gives him desires. Desire to live righteously, desire to live effectively, desire to live in the presence of God.

If that depth of desire is not yours yet, why not ask Him today to deepen your desire for His presence? Give yourself to the practice of worship and daily communication with Him. Pray that the Lord will deepen your devotion and give you a hunger for Himself.

September 21st

POSTPONED DEFEAT

"When the devil had finished, he left him until an opportune time"

Luke 4:13

Victory that is followed by complacency in reality is not victory, but rather postponed defeat. Our enemy is strategic enough in his thinking to know if temporary victory will lead to greater defeat, the partial victory was well worth the loss.

Our enemy always has an *"opportune time."* He has nothing but time, so he is willing to wait in hope that he might catch us unaware. But if we are wise to his tactics, then the *"opportune time"* he awaits will never transpire.

This awareness that is needed to counteract the enemy's attack is gained only through the proper use of the Word of God. It was through the Word that Jesus overcame and it will be the Word that defeats the enemies coming into our lives as well.

This means that we must become students of the Word. *"Study to show yourselves approved."* (II Timothy 2:15) This is one area where being self taught is a virtue. We have all been given the Holy Spirit to teach us and train us in the proper use of God's Word. But, as in any learning situation, it is our choice as to when we show up for class.

May I encourage you today to not just read the Word, but learn to study it. Learn how to use your concordance, cross reference, word studies, character studies, and historical studies. There are many tools available to help us in our ability to handle the Word; let us take full advantage of them.

Then when that *"opportune time"* comes once again, we will find ourselves defeating our enemies with the Word, even as Jesus did His.

September 22nd

STEADFASTLY DEVOTED

"They devoted themselves to the apostles' teaching and to fellowship, to the breaking of bread and to prayer... Every day they broke bread in their homes and ate together with glad and sincere hearts"

Acts 2:42,46

No, there was nothing casual about their pursuit of God and relationships. These early believers were devoted. One translation says, *"They constantly applied themselves to the apostles' teaching."* Another one says, *"they gave themselves to living out what was taught."* The King James says, *"they continued steadfastly in the apostles' doctrine."*

Steadfastly means to be earnest toward, to be constantly diligent, to attend assiduously all the exercises. These guys were intense. Nothing familiar about their pursuit. They were fully committed and had fully given themselves over to the exercises required to become that visible community of the redeemed.

The same devotion and diligence of the early believer should be the cry of our hearts as well. The road, to becoming all God desires His people to be, is paved with that intense desire and devotion of pursuit. Though many would have us believe it is an easy, laid back, nonconfrontive road, the scriptural record would say otherwise. Though they did it with ultimate joy, they did it at personal cost. To do anything daily, diligently, steadfastly, will require an intensity of action and a passion of pursuit. Oh yes, there is a rest from our own labors, but only so that we might work in the power of His might. To work under His power will require we do twice as much, twice as easily.

"Every one was filled with awe." (Acts 2:43)

This level of devotion guarantees an awesome return.

September 23rd

TESTED BY FIRE

"Each one should be careful how he builds . . . his work shall be shown for what it is . . . the fire will test the quality of each man's work . . . if it is burned up, he will suffer loss"
I Corinthians 3:10-15

What a tragedy to think, after giving yourself to something for such a long period of time, it could be burned up because of its inadequate foundation. Could you imagine the sense of loss if you had to watch everything you lived for and labored for burn because it was not of eternal value.

Most people are savvy to this problem in the physical realm. Years are spent in school to prepare them for their future. A trade is learned and a career is sought out. But the same people pursue the spiritual realm with little or no preparation. The tragedy of it all is the physical realm will be put to the fire regardless of the preparation, for it belongs to the temporal. The only realm which will remain, as we know it today, is the spiritual realm and it often gets the least of our attention.

Here are some questions that must be asked as we pursue our goals in order for us to wind up in the proper place:

1. When you get to where you are going, where will you be?
2. When you get to where you are going, will you want to be there?
3. When you get what you want, what will you have?
4. Is what you want worth Christ dying for?

The fire will test the answer to these questions and more. Our earnest prayer must be, "Father, keep me pursuing and desiring that which is of Kingdom value and pleasing to you, and if for any reason I should stray, let me know in enough time to be able to rebuild, so that I will not lose what I have labored for."

~

September 24th

THE ARENA OF BATTLE

"The weapons we fight with are not the weapons of the world. On the contrary, they have divine power to demolish strongholds."

II Corinthians 10:4

It began in the heavenlies. A cosmic rebellion of astronomical proportion. One-third of the angelic host was snared by an insidious deception. It was a rebellion that pitted itself against the Kingdom of God. It is into this rebellion we were born and commissioned to battle together with Christ in order to bring that rebellion to an end.

But, how do we fight this battle? Where is this war fought? What are the weapons at our disposal and where are we trained in their use? Psalms 149 gives us insight into these questions:

"May the praise of God be in their mouths and a double-edged sword in their hands. To inflict vengeance on the nations and punishment on the peoples, to bind their kings with fetters, their nobles with shackles of iron, to carry out the sentence written against them. This is the glory of all his saints."

Who would have ever imagined that in singing, "Jesus loves me; this I know for the Bible tells me so," we are actually engaging in war and binding spiritual principalities and powers?

This war began in the heavenlies and it is in the heavenlies that it continues. Our commander in chief has ordained that this war is not fought with guns and bullets, but through praise and worship. As we come before the throne of God in worship and praise, not only are we glorifying the majesty of His wonder, but we are pulling down demonic strongholds and binding satanic princes and kings. This is war, and praise is our arena of battle.

So let me encourage you to prepare for battle. Let us get aggressive as we enter into worship and praise. If praise is our opportunity to inflict vengeance, let us do as much damage as is possible. We have been created to labor together with Christ in conquering this cosmic rebellion. Let us war faithfully.

September 25th

THE CALL OF THE HIGHLANDER

"Who shall ascend the mountain of the Lord?"
Psalm 24:3

The mountain of the Lord is not for the ill-prepared. Not just anybody can ascend this mountain. It's not for the faint of heart. It is not for the weak of sight. The mountain of the Lord is reserved for the prepared.

For years, people will prepare to climb the mountain. First, there is the physical preparation, the conditioning of the body and the discipline of the mind. Nothing is taken for granted, for the mountain is cruel and has no sympathy for those who climb.

Perhaps the greatest preparation of all is the selection and relationship to the guide. Those who climb place their lives in the hands of the guide.

A good guide will force you to do certain things that will save your life in the event of danger. A good guide will . . .

➢ Never climb without a plan. Successful climbers file detailed plans, routes that have been studied and carefully mapped out. What is your plan? Have you developed a close enough relationship to our spiritual guide to develop a detailed plan? Have you written that plan out and discussed it with those you walk with, to keep yourself accountable to the way?

➢ Never climb alone. Safe climbers understand the dangers of the mountain. Recognizing the limitations of their abilities, they climb with those who can provide support and protection. Who are you climbing with? Does your personality keep others from wanting to climb with you? Covenant climbing is the way of the "Highlanders."

The Holy Spirit is the guide on the mountain of the Lord. His desire is to call us into deeper relationship with Himself that He might take us up to the high places.

૭૪૦

September 26th

IN PURSUIT OF THE PART

"Watch out that you do not lose what you have worked for, but that you may be rewarded fully. Anyone who runs ahead and does not continue in the teaching of Christ does not have God; whoever continues in the teaching has both the Father and the Son"
II John 1:8-9

Truth is not easily won. Though it may have come easily to you, at some point in time, someone gave blood, sweat, and 'years' to purchase that truth. Truth that grips our heart by revelation comes at a great cost. Usually we realize that to own that truth, something must be forsaken. Like the pearl of great price, we realize that we must sell all to purchase the field.

Truth is guarded with cost so that we will not sell that truth in the heat of battle. It is in the face of compromise that the Holy Spirit reminds us of the price we purchased that truth for.

To protect truth, we must remain on constant guard. We are in a battle, and the focus of that battle is truth. Once truth is obtained, we must watch out that we do not lose what we have worked so hard for. The enemy that we fight is a strategist. If he ca not prevent the purchasing of truth, he will tempt us from another angle. Often his tactic is to highlight a single facet of truth, but cut it off from the balance of the whole. With that single facet of truth, as a consuming focus, he encourages us to run ahead in pursuit of "truth." The problem is when the facet is cut off from the whole; it does not produce the fruit of righteousness.

Those who run ahead, but do not continue in the teaching of Christ, usually get self-righteous. Self-righteousness produces independence and soon they isolate themselves from the rest of Christ's body. The decision to isolate is justified with an attitude that everyone else has sold out, except for them. They become the only ones who are really doing the work of God; everyone else is just playing the game. In order to protect their position, they become critical of the church and judgmental of the saints.

The challenge we face is the challenge of being *"rewarded fully."* Not the reward of a facet of truth, but the full reward of complete truth. The teaching of Christ is the full counsel of God—not just a facet of focus, but the full spectrum. Watch out that you purchase the whole and not just a part.

September 27th

STANDING FIRM

"If you do not stand firm in your faith you will not stand at all"
Isaiah 7:9

Those who stand firm are a vanishing breed. As a people lose their adherence to absolutes, they also lose their ability to stand firm. It is one's belief in absolutes that enables them to stand firm in the storm of controversy and disagreement. Our culture is rapidly becoming spineless and convictionless. The convictions we once possessed, enabling us to risk safety and well being for the sake of the cause, are all but gone.

Out of this mass of apathy, God is raising up a prophetic community capable of standing firm in a sea of compromise. He is calling forth those who have built their lives on the absolute foundation of God's Word and are willing to stand on His Word regardless of the rejection, criticism or misunderstanding it might bring. This prophetic community are a people of resolve. They are those who have resolved to stand firm for truth whatever it takes. What are the "whatever it takes" issues in your life? Are there certain issues you stand on that you have resolved to stand firm, whatever it requires of you? It takes a "whatever it takes" attitude to produce in you the depth of foundation required to keep you standing in the storm?

Our wholehearted pursuit and devotion to Jesus Christ is a "whatever it takes" issue. We must resolve to stand firm in our pursuit of Christ, regardless of the pressures formed against us to divert us. Family is a "whatever it takes" issue. All the powers of hell are currently unleashed against the family in hopes of destroying continuity through the ages. We must resolve to stand firm in our commitment to our family in order to see the baton passed on to the generation to come. The church is a "whatever it takes" issue. Satan's desire is to divide and conquer, keeping God's people in a perpetual state of infancy. Let us stand firm as one, in order that we might see God's desire fulfilled.

September 28th

PLAY THE SQUEEZE

"Don't let this world squeeze you into its mold..."
Romans 12:2

How easy it is to be squeezed into the mold of compromise when issues have not been settled with God. The effects of compromise are like that of an insidious disease. Often its symptoms go undetected until it is too late to treat. It begins all too innocently. It may begin in the blessing of a new job or a personal freedom which must be exercised. It usually begins being a little degree off, but as it grows, it multiplies in cancerous proportions. Soon the entire life is infested with the infection. The tragedy of the situation is the carriers usually defend their "healthy" position right to their dying breaths. The ravages of compromise are a slow, methodical, spiritual death. Finally, the values that were once held, the standards that were once embraced, and the Lord who was once obeyed, are only a memory of who the persons were in their "youthful, zealous" days. Now they are much too sophisticated to embrace such "narrow" viewpoints.

Webster defines compromise as the "blending of the qualities of two different things." In the context of this perspective, compromise is the blending or the attempt to blend the qualities of this world with the qualities of the Kingdom of God. But the attempt is in vain. Try as we may, the Kingdom of God stands alone. It will not compromise with anything. It alone is absolute and needs nothing with which to blend. When we try, we subject ourselves to the wages of sin. Let us not forget the stern reminder of the apostle James, *"Friendship with this world is hatred toward God. Anyone who chooses to be a friend of the world becomes an enemy of God."* (James 4:4)

What begins as a seemingly innocent blending of two differing qualities results in the hatred of God. The individual who compromised may not claim to hate God, but God's evaluation of the compromise is, "You hate Me, and now I am your enemy."

Oh, sure, you have been called to freedom, but do not use your freedom as an occasion of the flesh, but rather walk the straight and narrow way you have been called to walk.

September 29th

HOWDY PILGRIM

"Blessed are those whose strength is in you, who have set their hearts on pilgrimage... They go from strength to strength till each appears before God in Zion"

Psalm 84:5-7

It has been said before and bears repeating, the Christian walk is not a destination, but an ongoing journey or as the psalmist put it "a pilgrimage." We have not been given the luxury of arrival, only departure and travel. The tendency of man is to think that at the crest of the next ridge, the journey will be complete, only to discover the waiting of another valley and beyond that, the challenge of another ridge.

Notice that this pilgrimage requires the purposeful setting of one's heart and will. Without the purposeful setting of one's heart on pilgrimage, we will be overcome by the sickness of deferred hope. If our mind set is the journey will be over as soon as we conquer the next ridge, we will be defeated by the hopelessness that sets in when we discover the valley that lies beyond. But those who have set their heart's in the challenge of the journey, discover the strength that is supplied at designated points.

The psalmist says, *"They go from strength to strength."* This strength is reserved only for those who have set their hearts on pilgrimage. If you are unwilling to make the journey, you will be prevented from receiving the strength. As difficult as the journey might be, it is much easier than remaining idle because the journey promises the strength of God and idleness promises nothing. Perhaps it is time for you to leave that place of idleness and set your heart for the adventure of the pilgrimage.

September 30th

INTIMACY

"I looked for the One my heart loves. I looked for him but did not find him . . . Scarcely had I passed them when I found the One my heart loves"

Song of Solomon 3:1,4

Salvation is God finding us. Intimacy is us finding God. One can be fully saved, yet never discover what it means to have an intimate relationship with Jesus Christ. In the passage above, you can sense the cry of passion the beloved has for her lover. The beloved longed to be in the presence of her lover. She searched for Him but could not find Him. She longed to be in His presence.

Sometimes it is as if God is hiding from us. The presence that we once so readily knew seems to be gone. The clarity of His voice seems to be clouded with various concerns. It is at those times that we must go on the "all night searches" to find Him. When He seems to be gone, we must "pay more careful attention" to find Him.

Intimacy with Jesus Christ requires time. It takes time to connect with God. It may only take a few hours a week to go to church, but to maintain a vital connection with Christ that will take us deeper into spiritual reality, takes an ever increasing measure of time. Not just the quantity of time but also the quality of time. Exodus 33:7-11 tells us Moses would purposely go outside the camp to meet with God. He would forsake normal routine and daily activity in order to be wholly set apart for God. There are times and seasons in our lives that require desperate measures . . . times when we must leave that which is familiar and go outside normal practices in order that we might meet God face to face. We must get away to that solitary place and find the one our heart loves.

Perhaps it is such a time for you. Maybe it is time to forsake TV, newspapers or any other distractions that would compete for your focus and rob you of your intimate pursuit of Jesus.

○✤○

October 1st

JESUS, THE WAY

"You must not do as they do in Egypt, where you used to live, and you must not do as they do in the land of Canaan, where I am bringing you. Do not follow their practices"
Leviticus 18:3

Jesus Christ is the originator of truth. We need not borrow from the world to discover a new idea. We have the creator of all, living within us, waiting to release a flood of creativity to those who ask.

The apostle Paul described the people of God as a peculiar people. Peculiarity often breeds insecurity because we have believed a lie that says, it is better to be like the world than it is to be God's peculiar people. The word of God explicitly forbids the imitation of the world. God's desire has always been for His people to be different, to stand out and be separate from the world. God's people were not allowed to dress, eat or behave like those with whom they lived.

Recently, much of the church world has bought into a lie, saying to win the world, we must become like them. "Relatability" has become the hallmark of evangelism. Jesus attracted sinners because He was vastly different. Sinners drew near to Him because they sensed in Him a quality of life and behavior that they had never sensed before. Oh, they had seen religious leaders and would-be saviors come and go, but Jesus was different and it was that very difference that awakened their desire. The idea that you are going to win people for Christ by becoming more like them is theologically and practically untrue. It is our distinctions that awaken people and draw them to the Lord. Yes, some do reject us because of our distinctions, but we cannot apologize for that because the distinctions are God's doing.

Jesus both taught the way and demonstrated the way. His way was to remain distinct and to allow those distinctions to be the very thing that awakened desire. Let us follow Jesus. He is the only way.

○≬○

October 2nd

LED BY ANOTHER'S DESTINY

"It was revealed to them that they were not serving themselves but you"

I Peter 1:12

To serve beyond ourselves is to carry a heart for the generations to come. Within the heart of every man and woman should be a vision for at least three generations. God chose to reveal Himself as the God of Abraham, Isaac and Jacob. He was not just the God of one generation, but the God of three.

The work of the Holy Spirit is not designed to stop with ourselves. The Holy Spirit equips us in order that we would be able to disciple the generations who are to follow. As we train our sons and daughters, we must do so with the mentality that they must not only grasp it for themselves, but be able to understand it so clearly that they are able to impart it to their children to follow.

There will come a time in our spiritual pilgrimage that we will be led by our children's destiny. As they grow and we train them, the focus will shift from us onto them. No longer will we hold the primary lead, but it will be shifted onto them. At this point, their destiny begins to direct us. So it was with the parents of Moses. Imagine how the mother of Moses must have felt as she pushed that wicker basket out into the deep, not knowing what would become of her son. We have the privilege of knowing the outcome, but as far as she knew, this would be the last she would ever see her son. She did not know that her act of obedience was a necessary step in her son becoming the deliverer of God's chosen people. As her son grew, soon his destiny began to direct hers and the entire nation. Joseph and Mary faced this same reality. The destiny upon the life of Christ soon began to direct them.

Who is it God has placed in your care? What might their destiny be? Equip them now with an eye toward the future, for soon they may be directing you.

꽁뺭

October 3rd

LED POISONING

"Obey your leaders and submit to their authority. They keep watch over you as men who must give an account. Obey them so that their work will be a joy, not a burden, for that would be of no advantage to you"

Hebrews 13:17

An unwillingness to be led is of no personal advantage to you. In fact, an unwillingness to be led can be quite detrimental to your spiritual journey, for God often reveals His will and direction through those leaders He has placed over us.

Many in the church today suffer from a condition of "led poisoning." Led poisoning is a diseased attitude that predisposes one to independence and an unwillingness to follow the direction of leadership. Feeling that their personal relationship with Jesus is all they need, those with led poisoning reserve the right to pick and choose the direction they will submit to. When a particular direction agrees with their agenda, they will follow, but if leadership ever introduces a direction contrary to their way, they rationalize their unwillingness with a "you can not follow man" justification. This is nothing more than religious double talk and a rationalization for their unwillingness to be led.

God has ordained the way of leadership. From Moses to David to Paul to Five-Fold Gift Ministries, God has used and continues to use the avenue of delegated leadership. These are leaders who do not lead of their own will, but lead under divine mandate. It is the mandate that the leader subscribes to, that God expects us to obey and willingly embrace.

Are you traveling with "leaded" or "unleaded" gas? Are you willing to be led by those who have been divinely commissioned to watch over you? It would be of no advantage to you not to do so.

☙❧

October 4th

MEMORIZATION AND MEDITATION

"How can a young man keep his way pure? By living according to your word... I have hidden your word in my heart that I might not sin against you"

Psalm 119: 9, 11

The temptation that faces God's people is no longer subtle. No longer does it lurk in the shadows waiting to deceive. Now it is right out "in your face, without apology," temptation. To remain pure, in a day of open sensuality and sin, requires an aggressive strategy of offensive warfare.

The psalmist faced this temptation in Psalm 119. His strategy was a strategy of memorization and meditation. Memorization and meditation are the means by which we hide the truth in our hearts. It is through these two disciplines that we are able to take the Word of God beyond a superficial understanding down to the depths of its meaning and application. It is at this level we are changed by the Word and kept from sin.

The words of Scripture are living words. They are divine wisdom contained in the shell of written words. God's desire is to break that shell open so that His Word can come forth. As we memorize and meditate on the written word, the outer shell is broken open and the revelation of application issues forth. As we say the verse over and over, the words wash us and begin to expose the lies that have snared us into wrongful theology and sinful behavior. As the lies are exposed, truth begins to redefine thoughts and behavior. As behavior is changed, freedom is experienced and influence is realized. People begin coming and asking why we seem to be victorious and where they can find that same hope.

There is power and promised success in the meditation of God's Word. Has your way become dark and full of snares? Is your ability to say "no" weakening as you go? Hide the word in your heart through memorization and meditation. You will most certainly experience the success promised in so doing.

October 5th

OUR ENGAGEMENT RING

"Having believed, you were marked in Him with a seal, the promised Holy Spirit, who is a deposit guaranteeing our inheritance until the redemption of those who are God's possession"

Ephesians 1:13-14

If the Holy Spirit is just the earnest, can you imagine what the complete inheritance will be like? The word earnest refers to the first down payment that guarantees the recipient of the final payment to come. The earnest of the Holy Spirit can be seen as Christ's engagement ring to His bride guaranteeing His intention of a future marriage. Though the church is not mature enough yet to assume the responsibilities of marriage, Father God has given us the Holy Spirit as a sample of what life will be like when we are fully redeemed.

As a little child, how I loved licking the bowl of cookie dough. With dough covering my hands and fully evident from ear to ear, I would ask, "Mom, when will the cookies be done?" Though I enjoyed the dough immensely, the dough was not the finished product. The dough was just the foretaste of what was to come.

I can not imagine how the Holy Spirit can be just a foretaste, but that is what the apostle Paul explains Him to be. The Holy Spirit is a foretaste of our future redemption. He is God's guarantee that He will make good His promise to bring us into the fullness of maturity and cause us to be ready for the forthcoming marriage.

When the Holy Spirit seals a people, they are no longer the same. The earnest of the Holy Spirit changes ordinary people into extraordinary people. A people who have experienced the foretaste of God's promise become people of valor and might. They become a people hungry for the presence of God. They become a people of promise and pursuit.

You are such as them. You have been sealed with a promise. You are a person of earnest.

☙❧

October 6th

PEOPLE OF DISTINCTION

"Dear friends, I urge you, as aliens and strangers in the world, to abstain from sinful desires, which war against your soul. Live such good lives among the pagans that, though they accuse you of doing wrong, they may see your good deeds and glorify God on the day he visits us"

I Peter 2:11-12

The apostle Peter is not calling us up to some outward flash of conduct but rather to an inner quality of character. The Kingdom of God does not place the emphasis on outward demonstration. The Kingdom of God transforms our character into the likeness of Christ. As our character is transformed, our conduct wins the respect of those we touch.

Religion places the focus on the external. Our enemies will give us the external if they can keep us from the internal. External conformities produce little in the long run. When all is said and done, it is the character of a person that has the strongest say. We can be the most gifted, charismatic leader around, but if we have never opened ourselves up to the character transforming work of the Holy Spirit, our popularity will be short lived. History is full of plenty of examples. We can all remember those who came in charisma and rallied people around themselves long enough until those who came saw the void of character and left in disillusionment. What people build with their charisma, they often destroy with their character.

Our character is critical because we are not here just representing ourselves. Like ambassadors, we are on this earth representing God. When we are representing another it is our character that speaks the loudest. Without the righteousness of character, the ministry of Christ is discredited. Many times our conduct speaks so loud that those around us cannot hear our words. The character qualities that bring glory to God are the qualities of humility, honesty, devotion, sincerity, discipline. Qualities like these and others cannot be ignored. As darkness intensifies, these qualities shine like the noonday sun. These are the qualities that bring us distinction. They separate us from the pagan and bring glory to God.

Continue to expose yourself to the character building work of the Holy Spirit. Eagerly desire humility, integrity and devotion. Let God make you a person of character and in so doing, a person of distinction.

October 7th

POINTS OF LIGHT

"You are the light of the world"
Matthew 5:14

Dull bulbs attract few bugs. It is the attitude a people carry that determines the brightness of their light and the range of their coverage. There is creative power in attitudes, both for ourselves and for those who come in contact with our lives. People come alive when they are around those of positive attitudes. The life inherent in the positive attitude awakens the life within them. The opposite is true as well. Negativism has a way of creating a sense of gloom and complacency.

Negative attitudes put out the light of God. Whatever brightness one carries is dulled when they allow attitudes of a negative nature to rule their lives. It is for this reason that the apostle Paul tells us that in the putting off of the old man, we must also put off negative attitudes. (Ephesians 4:22-24) Negative attitudes are like dirty clothes; they impact our disposition and the disposition of those we touch. To put on the new man involves the putting on of new attitudes. It is *"to be made new in attitude."* (Ephesians 4:23)

Did your salvation affect your attitudes? Is it still affecting your attitudes or have you reverted back to your former ways? How easy it is to come into Christ and never expose our attitudes to the work and way of the cross. To be born again means we experience the new birth of attitudes. Though being born again is a one time experience, to be made new in attitudes is an ongoing moment by moment experience.

In Philippians 2, Paul makes it very clear what these attitudes should be. He says in verse 5 your attitudes should be this . . . humility, brokenness, service and obedience. As a result of these attitudes, Christ was exalted and given the name above every name.

Though we should not expect the same level of reward, we can expect God to honor rightful attitudes. Rightful attitudes make for bright lights and bright lights lead to incredible influence.

October 8th

PART TIME OR FULL TIME

"When Christ, who is your life..."

Colossians 3:4

Religion breeds confined commitment. It is designed to give Jesus His part. He has given His part of our life, His part in society, His part in our thinking and His part of our emotions. But Jesus Christ is not a part time lord. His desire for us is definitely a full time desire. The focus of His work is to bring us out of any part time mentality we may be laboring under and take us into a full time focus.

There is a vast difference between Jesus Christ having a part of our lives and Jesus being our life. The apostle Paul states it quite clearly; Jesus doesn't have just a part, even the prominent part; Jesus Christ IS our life. We are dead and our lives are hid in Christ. When we are born again, God's desire is for Christ to become our life. The old, where we governed our own lives, is passed away and the new, where Christ is our source and supply, is come.

Though Christ being our life is a positional reality, it is often not the case by experience. For Christ to become our life by experience, requires a purposeful decision. It requires that purposeful yielding of our life over to His infilling and control. This purposeful yielding is the setting of our hearts and the setting of our minds on the things above. To set means to be mentally predisposed toward. Our hearts must be predisposed toward Christ. Our minds must be predisposed toward Christ—predisposed before we come to the crossroad of decision. If our hearts and minds are predisposed toward Christ, then when we face the contrary temptations, we are assured of making the proper decisions.

A heart and mind set toward those things that are above, moves us past a part time Jesus into a full time Christ, who becomes our life. He gives us the daily supply of grace to be all that we are designed to become.

October 9th

PARADIGM SHIFTS

"Get up, Peter. Kill and eat." "Surely not, Lord!"
Acts 10:13-14

The words "Surely not, Lord" are a contradiction. To say "No, Lord" is to admit that Jesus is not Lord. "Yes, Lord . . . I am willing, Lord" . . . or . . "Could you clarify that, Lord?" . . . are all within the parameters of honoring the lordship. But to say "No, Lord" contradicts the very reality of what lordship means.

Lordship is a continual paradigm shift. The lordship of Jesus Christ is continually altering our perspective and showing us how small we have made God. Can you imagine the paradigm shift Peter had to go through? In his vision, he sees a sheet come down from heaven full of clean and unclean animals. Then a voice tells him to kill the animals and eat them. The problem was Peter was kosher. His religious tradition did not permit him to eat unclean animals. So it did not matter that God told him to get up, kill and eat; he was not permitted to do so.

Often our religious traditions presuppose for us what God's will is. Over time they formulate conclusions and box God in. The bigger the traditions get, the smaller God becomes. Soon God's word is filtered through the grid of our traditions and the lordship of Christ is conditional upon what our traditions have presupposed.

God is desirous of tearing down the strongholds of our imposed limitations. He is so much bigger than the box we have put Him in. We must continually wash our minds with the Word and allow the Word of God to renew the paradigm that we are viewing God's will through. This does not mean God changes. It simply means that our ability to perceive God's will must be ever enlarging in the light of His written Word, and never restricted to our own self-imposed limitations that God has never subscribed to.

October 10th

RECEIVING THE PROMISE BY GRACE

"Therefore, the promise comes by faith, so that it may be by grace and may be guaranteed to all Abraham's offspring"
Romans 4:16

The test of keeping is a test that every believer must face. This is the test where we discover that God is faithful to keep for us what He has promised and we need not keep it through natural strength. How often have we received the promise of God by faith, only to resort to natural strength during the time of testing and waiting. It is during these times of waiting that God desires to prove to us that He is faithful to keep for us what He has promised to do in us or through us.

Abraham faced this test a couple of times. Once was after he had received the land that was promised as an inheritance. After a dispute with Lot, he had to divide half that promised land and give it to Lot, only to see God give it back to him. Shortly thereafter Abraham faced the ultimate test of God's keeping power. He was called of God to sacrifice his long awaited promise. He was asked of God to sacrifice Isaac. The very thing that God had promised and he had waited years and years for was now being required of him. Abraham had to face the question of God's keeping power. Was God able to keep for Abraham what He had promised? If he were to let go, what would become of the promise?

Why does God make us face such tests? It is to break the possessive bond we have on the promise and turn our focus solely on Him. Often the promise becomes more important than God. The desire to see the promise come to pass becomes so important that we lose sight of God and the promise becomes ours. In order to break that possessive bond and show us that the promise is received by grace, not human effort. God requires the promise of us. He requires that we offer it up in sacrifice to Him. As Abraham did with Isaac, we lay the promise on the altar of sacrifice and die to the possibility of its fulfillment. In this willingness we prove to ourselves that we love the giver more than the gift. We prove that God is more important to us than the promise. Then God resurrects the promise and in resurrection form we know the promise to be so dependent upon God that we never again take it possessively to ourselves. Resurrection puts the promise out of the reach of human effort and possession.

Are you facing the test of keeping? Let go. Faithful is He who promised. He will also do it.

October 11th

FROM SEARCH TO WORSHIP

"Where is the one who has been born king of the Jews? We saw his star in the east and have come to worship him"
Matthew 2:3

Searching can often become an end in itself. Like a narcotic, the search for truth pacifies the need to discover truth. So even though the truth is never possessed, the mind is pacified by the endless pursuit. Paul spoke of a godlessness in the last days and said it would be characterized by those who are *"ever searching, but never coming to the knowledge of the truth."* (II Timothy 3:7)

The wise men were men in search of truth. Their lives had been spent in search of the One born King, but the search was not an end for the wisemen. The Scriptures tell us they were searching in order that they might come and worship.

Our search for truth must always result in our worship of Him who is truth. Truth always leads to Jesus. If it is true, it will lead us to Jesus, because Jesus is truth. Once we are led to Him, we must bow in reverence and worship the One who is true.

Worship is an expression of surrender. We surrender to truth by worshipping the truthful One. To search for truth and never discover it may be an indication of an unwillingness to surrender. As long as the search continues, we never have to draw a conclusion and make a commitment. The apprehension lies in the fear of commitment, because commitment requires the surrender of our personal agendas in order to embrace the truth.

The wise men came in anticipation of surrender. Herod, on the other hand, was also in search of the One born King, but was certainly not predisposed to surrender.

As you search for truth, keep surrender as your goal and once you find it, worship Him who is true.

October 12th

WHEN GOD COMES DOWN

"'How will this be?' Mary asked... The angel answered, 'The Holy Spirit will come upon you, and the power of the Most High will overshadow you.'"

Luke 1:34-35

Man will never work his way up to God. In Gabriel's response to Mary, we find the very essence of God's involvement with mankind and the very thing that distinguishes Christianity from every man-made religion: *"The Holy Spirit will come upon you."* The principle is that theology supersedes biology. In fact, theology supersedes every other "ology" because theology begins with God and comes down.

Christianity is a relationship that comes down. It does not start with man and work up, but it starts with God and comes down. The very essence of Christianity is the Holy Spirit coming upon God's people to accomplish God's will. God asks the impossible, then He "comes down" to do it. Because He "comes down" to do His will, His coming involves mysteries and wonders. Virgin births, old age pregnancies, angelic appearances, visions, priests unable to speak, all of these and more were some of the mysteries that surrounded the coming down of our Lord.

We all too often find ourselves struggling to go up to God when God is pleading with us to die to ourselves so He can "come down." Unfortunately dispensational theology has taught us that God came down once and will some day come down again. But in the mean time, we are on our own to work our way up. Gabriel's response to Mary is also God's response to us. The way of the Kingdom is for the Holy Spirit to come upon God's people and the power of the Most High to overshadow them.

The struggle is over. You can not get up until He comes down.

૱

October 13th

THE PROPER TIME

"Let us not become weary in doing good for at the proper time we will reap a harvest if we do not give up"

Galatians 6:9

"Timing is everything," as the saying goes. As we read the Scriptures, we discover everything we need pertaining to life and godliness is ours. (II Peter 1:3) The posture of the Scriptures is one of absolute victory to those whose lives are hid in Jesus Christ. It is not a matter of getting the victory, but one of aligning our expectation to God's time frame so that we don't become weary in the midst of the wait.

God does not operate on our time frame. God stands outside of time so He is able to see the beginning from the end. In one glance He is able to see the beginning of a matter through to the end of a matter. What we see as linear, He sees as panoramic. What we see as a process of many years, He sees at one glance. Consequently, He only has to act at the 'proper time.' Timing is never a problem for God. When one is able to stand outside of time and see the whole matter, He is able to act at the exact time necessary to fulfill the intention.

"For the revelation waits an appointed time, it speaks of an end and will not prove false. Though it linger, wait for it, it will certainly come and not delay." (Habbakuk 2:3) The Scriptures do not say, "if it lingers." They say, *"though it lingers."* The lingering of the revelation is promised. It lingers for the proper time. It lingers because God is standing outside of time waiting for the proper time to act. Our challenge is to align our expectation to God's time frame so we won't cast away our confidence and opt for a self reduced substitute of God's promise.

Be encouraged in your waiting. As you wait your strength is being renewed. As you wait, the Lord is acting on your behalf. Do not become weary in your waiting; you will reap if you do not give up.

October 14th

THE CURSE OF COMPLACENCY

"Woe to you who are complacent in Zion and in you who feel secure"
Amos 6:1

Security has become the focus of the American dream. In the face of consistent uncertainty, people clamor for whatever level of security they can find. Safety and ease have become their norm.

Though security has become a component of the American dream, it stands in direct opposition of the way of the Kingdom. God calls us to a walk of faith. He calls us to a walk of risk. As He did with Abraham, He calls us to a walk of uncertainty. He calls us to never become complacent with sin.

Complacency in the Kingdom of God is a curse. In the face of complacency and ease, the Holy Spirit is working on two fronts.

1. Revealing a holy dissatisfaction.

2. Restoring a fire of spiritual passion.

Complacency begins when people become satisfied with their current level of spiritual progress. The perception develops that they have prayed enough, witnessed enough, given enough, etc., so they can relax and enjoy their new found security. The cycle of complacency begins with distress that leads to a cry, which opens the door to visitation, prompting satisfaction, resulting in complacency. The Scriptures command contentment, but never satisfaction. Spiritual hunger is what keeps people alive.

With the visitation of the Holy Spirit, comes the restoring of the spiritual passion that was lost to the attitude of complacency. Passion comes as the result of our cry for more. In response to that cry, the Holy Spirit releases a passion that manifests itself in spiritual hunger, intimacy with Christ and the discipline to navigate the way.

Have you become complacent? It is time to cry for more!

October 15th

OWNER OCCUPANCY ONLY

"The kingdom of heaven is like treasure hidden in a field. When a man found it, he hid it again, and then in his joy went and sold all he had and bought that field"

Matthew 13:44

We can thank the Lord that this man knew nothing of contemporary creative finance. If this parable were written from the perspective of present trends, it would have the man financing the field, then renting it out to another in order to maximize his return on investment. But the Kingdom of God is a field that cannot be bought as a rental. This is a field that requires "owner occupancy." You cannot purchase this field with zero-down financing and then let someone else live there in order to make the payments. No, this field requires that you joyfully sell all you have, then come back and purchase the field.

My encouragement is for us to conduct a "title search" of our field and see whether or not there is anything yet owing or some other kind of lien held against it. In order for us to buy the field, Jesus said we must sell all we have. So in order for us to own the title deed of this property, we must first sell all of our fears. Fear has no place in the Kingdom of God. The treasure requires that we sell all of our securities and find our security only in Him and that which He directs us to do. To buy this field, we must sell the control of our own future and trust in Him with all of our heart by seeking His Kingdom first. To *"joyfully sell all"* means we sell every desire for any other field and maintain a single eye for the field that contains the Kingdom of God.

The Kingdom of God and this Kingdom alone is the only thing that will satisfy and give life ultimate meaning and purpose. But certainly, this is a Kingdom that will require all.

October 16th

THE SPIRIT OF ADOPTION

"For you did not receive the spirit of bondage again to fear, but you have received the spirit of adoption, whereby we cry, Abba, Father. The spirit itself beareth witness with our spirit, that we are the children of God"

Romans 8:15-16

Spiritual adoption is much more than just taking someone by choice into relationship. In our culture, adoption is the taking of children, usually at birth, and giving them your name and legally making them your own. We change their environment, but we can never change their heredity. The traits they are born with by heredity are theirs and will remain theirs regardless of the environmental change.

Spiritual adoption is not so. In biblical culture, the Romans, Greeks and Hebrews had a different adoption practice. They adopted sons, but sons who had already been born to them. Finally, when a son had grown to maturity and had proven himself responsibly, he was declared to be a "son" and adopted as a legal heir of the family estate. Adoption did not take place at birth. It was the father's recognition of maturity and ability to handle responsibility in bearing the family name.

"What I am saying is that as long as the heir is a child, he is no different from a slave, although he owns the whole estate." (Galatians 4:1) The Holy Spirit has been given as the Spirit of Adoption, bringing us into *"full rights as sons."* As our teacher, He equips us to maturity, preparing us for heirship, throneship, rulership and joint-ownership in running the family business.

Adoption has nothing to do with babyhood. The Spirit of Adoption is the work of the Holy Spirit within us to take us from slave to heir. There are no princes in the Kingdom who are handed the throne. The Kingdom of God is a Kingdom of heirs made up of mature sons who have been adopted as legal heirs of the family estate.

October 17th

THE SECRET OF CONTENTMENT

"I have learned to be content whatever the circumstances. I know what it is to be in need and I know what it is to have plenty. I have learned the secret of being content in any and every situation"
                                                      Philippians 4:11-12

I have learned the secret of being content. Contentment is a learned response. Both by our sin nature and environment, man is conditioned to want more. Enough is always just a little bit more. So life becomes a quest for more. More wealth, more possessions, more blessings, more, more, more . . .

Desire is a fickle emotion. To desire more of the right things is needful and righteous. But to crucify the desire for that which leads to our ruin is the challenge. The spirit of discernment must be an operative gift in our lives to guide us into the truth of what is a righteous desire and what is selfish greed.

The secret of contentment is found in our perspective. When perspective is out of divine alignment, greed takes over. Once greed is operative in our lives, there will never be enough. It is during these times of greed and self pity that the Holy Spirit brings us into divine alignment. That alignment adjusts our perspective and we are able to see things as they really are.

Recently, while at a meeting, I was standing in the ministry time crying out for more of Jesus. I had been in a relatively dry time and was praying for a deeper sense of the presence and anointing working through me. After several days of God not seemingly answering my prayers, I began to feel sorry for myself. As I stood to pray, I noticed a young lady in her late teens in a wheelchair laying hands on a man in front of me. I was broken by what I saw, for in that picture I learned the secret of contentment. As she gave out of her need, my perspective of what I truly needed was radically adjusted. Self pity was replaced by compassion. Impatience was replaced by heartfelt gratitude and the secret of contentment.

October 18th

THE SERVANT OF ALL

"The Son of Man came to serve"

Mark 10:45

Without a doubt, Jesus Christ was unique. Never before or since has there been someone like Him. But what was it that made Him so distinct? Was it miracles? His teachings? His authority? Yes, all of these most definitely set Him apart. But perhaps even more so was the fact that though He came as a king who performed miracles and revealed the truth, He came to serve. Imagine that, a king who served! Never before had a king done such a thing, nor since has another done the same. Serving is what made Jesus Christ distinct. He came to serve and give, not to be served and receive.

To be conformed into the image of Christ is to become a servant. While on earth the focus of Jesus was to serve. His heavenly focus is to reign, but His earthly focus was to serve. Many want the heavenly focus without first paying the price of the earthly. It was Christ's earthly focus of serving that qualified Him to reign. *"Whoever wants to become great among you must be your servant."* (Matthew 20:26) Serving is not just a stepping stone to greatness, serving is greatness. Service does not lead you to greatness, it makes you great. Those who serve are great because those who serve have become like Jesus Christ.

Service is an attitude before it is an action. Without the attitude of a servant, the actions become legalism. It is the attitude of a servant that seasons the actions in such a way that both giver and receiver see Christ and not each other. The attitudes of a servant are the attitudes of humility, vulnerability, honesty, willingness and generosity. As these attitudes work their way into our lives, they affect our actions and turn our focus away from ourselves and onto others.

Do you want to be like Christ? Before you can become like His heavenly focus, you must first embrace His earthly focus. To become like Christ is to become a servant. Look for opportunities to serve. Serve your family. Serve your church. Serve your employer. Serve your community. In so doing you will distinguish yourself and mirror the image of Jesus Christ.

October 19th

THE POWER TO BECOME

"But you will receive power when the Holy Spirit comes on you"
Acts 1:8

God's eternal purpose is not just to take us to heaven, but to empower us to live victoriously and Christlike here on earth. The ministry of the Holy Spirit is to infuse us with the dynamic power of God in order that we might become the glorious church without spot or wrinkle that Jesus is coming for.

The power to become is in the Holy Spirit. As we learn to yield to the indwelling presence of the Holy Spirit and come into right relationship with Him, we discover the life changing power He offers. It is a power that transforms us from the fallen image of Adam into the glorious image of Jesus Christ. As we learn to know the Holy Spirit, He forms in us the very character and likeness of God.

This power to become is often void in our lives due to the lack of relationship with the Holy Spirit. The Father we have known and the Son we have known because we can most relate to a father and a son, but how do we relate to a spirit? How do we relate to a Holy Ghost? The answer to that question is quite simple. We just do it! We press past our rational limitations and take the time and effort to know the Holy Spirit just as we would get to know anyone else. We read about Him, we talk to Him, we spend time in His presence, we learn to yield to His leadership, we ask Him to reveal Himself to us, etc. As a person we learn to know Him just as we would any other person.

If we depend on our own ability to face life's circumstances, we will never tap into the power to become. The power to become all God intends us to be is found in the Holy Spirit. Give yourself wholly to Him. Learn to know Him as a person.

October 20th

THE KINGDOM OF GOD

"He sent them out to preach the Kingdom of God"
Luke 9:2

John the Baptist came preaching the Kingdom of God. Jesus Christ came preaching the Kingdom of God. The disciples were sent and they preached the Kingdom of God. The Kingdom of God with all of its ramifications is the authorized focus of our message. As we go we must be careful to guard our focus. We must preach the Kingdom, not social agendas, self-actualization or denominational dogma.

To preach the Kingdom of God is to preach the universal rule of Jesus Christ over all things, both the redeemed and the non-redeemed. The rule of Jesus Christ is in no way limited to just the church, although the Kingdom's primary instrument to spread the Gospel is the church. The Kingdom of God is an ever expanding Kingdom. As obedient believers in every nation of the earth proclaim the Kingdom in obedience to Christ's command, the Kingdom comes. As it comes, it spreads its rule over individuals, families, governments and all spheres of human activity including law, economics, business, education, science, recreation, sports and media. The Kingdom of God is not limited to just the transforming of individual's lives. As individual lives are transformed and brought under the rule of Christ, what those individuals think and do are transformed as well.

The basis of the great commission of Matthew 28 is the fact that Jesus said all authority in heaven and on earth had been given to Him. From that position of absolute authority in the universe, He is bringing all things into submission to His rule. Through the preaching of the Gospel of the Kingdom of God, He is exercising His authority ever more widely and fully on the earth. As the Gospel spreads, people are converted. As people are converted, institutions acknowledge His Kingdom and His authority is more fully revealed. The Kingdom of God will continue to increase until it is consummated at the second coming of Christ when Jesus delivers the Kingdom over to the Father. The Kingdom will neither be consummated or fully realized on earth before the return of Christ.

What is the focus of your message? Does your life and message reflect complete submission to the rule of Jesus Christ and the acknowledgment of His Kingdom? Has His Kingdom come to you?

October 21st

THE IMAGE OF GOD

"So God created man in His own image, in the image of God He created Him"

Genesis 1:27

Created with purpose and with specific design, man's creation was not the result of luck or the culmination of random thought. We were created to be and to bear the image of God. Most things are made after a pattern. When people set out to make a dress, they do not just start sewing; they first create the pattern that will guarantee the outcome. God Himself was the pattern for man's image. We were created to bear the behavior of God.

Image speaks of more than just the reflection. A reflection can be just a surface change. I can put on a mask and show a new reflection of myself. Image speaks of something from within. To bear the image is to bear the exact representation. To bear the image is to be the manifestation of God inside and out. This is in no way to say that we become little gods. We simply become the manifestation of God by bearing the image of God.

What exactly does that image look like? Paul answers this question in Colossians 1:15. *"He (Jesus Christ) is the image of the invisible God."* Jesus is the perfect manifestation of God. To see what God looks like all we have to do is look at Jesus. Jesus Christ perfectly represents the image of God in a form which we can see, know and understand. We were meant to bear that same likeness but sin came in and man never achieved his destiny. In Jesus we see not only who God is but we also see what man was meant to be. Jesus is manhood as God designed it. He is the perfect manifestation of God and the perfect manifestation of man. Jesus is not simply a sketch of God or a summary of Him. In Him there is nothing left out. He is the full revelation of God and nothing more is necessary. To discover the pattern of our image we need not look any further than Jesus Christ. He is the beginning and the end. He is the sum total of our intended design.

As we behold Him, we become like Him. By virtue of His sacrificial death, the penalty of sin has been canceled and we once again can bear the image and likeness of God. Jesus Christ is the only pattern. By focusing on Him, the correct image is guaranteed.

October 22nd

GETTIN' BUSY

"We hear that some among you are idle. They are not busy; they are busy bodies... as for you brothers, never tire of doing what is right"
II Thessalonians 3:11-13

The older one gets, the more fatigue begins to play a significant role in behavior. What the body could do at 20, it can not do at 40. The abuse the body endured for the sake of the mind's desire is but a memory of years past. Problem is, it takes many years for the mind to catch up to where the body is. So the mind makes a decision on the body's behalf and then wonders why the body rebels through fatigue and sickness. Fatigue comes because we have a 20 year old mind held hostage in a 40 year old body.

Man's answer is usually to stop everything. Not only is this unrealistic; neither is it biblical. Work is a Kingdom expectation regardless of age or level of fatigue. The reason rest is a biblical command is because rest is essential in order to fulfill the expectation of work. Jesus said, *"My Father is always at His work to this very day and I, too, am working."* (John 5:17) Work is a vital aspect of God's character. As we are transformed into the likeness of Jesus Christ, one of the subjects of transformation is our work ethic. He came to get us busy.

The American concept of retirement is not a Kingdom concept. No, this does not mean that we never retire from our careers. It simply means we never retire from our work in the Kingdom. We take our call from the Father and if He is always at work, then we must adopt that same mentality in our practice.

Fatigue is often the result of wrong perspectives and poor time management. The perspective that leaves room for idleness is wrong. This is the thinking that says, "I have worked hard; now I owe it to myself to kick back and relax." Rest, most certainly, but become idle, definitely not. Paul says, *"Never tire of doing what is right."* As Christians, we must learn to find strength and replenishment in obedience. As we learn to obey, the Holy Spirit leads us into those times of rest and re-creation that enable us to continue the work God has called us to do. As we learn to obey, we discern the work that is ours to do and stay out of the work that isn't ours. Consequently, we learn to spend God's energy, not our own.

Times of rest are essential, but we must always guard against idleness. The harvest is plenteous and the laborers are few. It is time to get busy.

October 23rd

THE GRACE OF GIVING

"For I testify that they gave as much as they were able, and even beyond their ability. Entirely on their own, they urgently pleaded with us for the privilege of sharing in this service to the saints"
II Corinthians 8:3-4

What an attitude of giving! The Macedonian churches had such a clear sense of God's desire and the needs of the saints that they saw the act of giving, not as a responsibility, but as a privilege. What was their secret to giving? Paul reveals it in verse 5.

"They gave themselves first to the Lord."

When one has freely given himself over to the Lord, the issue of giving is not a problem, for giving has already been done. A completely surrendered life will result in giving becoming a form of art. That is, it will lead to the perfecting of giving. Paul told the Corinthians to *"excel in the grace of giving."* Do not ever become satisfied with your level of giving, but continue to challenge your current level and press it to the maximum. As everyone takes this attitude, Paul tells us, there will be equality in sacrifice. Different levels of giving, but equal levels of sacrifice for all are giving in obedience to the Holy Spirit as lives that are fully given to Him.

Giving is not something reserved for the rich. The story of the widow's mite reveals that everyone of us is expected by God to excel in the grace of giving. A surrendered life is a life that gives. It is a life that acknowledges the absolute ownership of Christ even in our finances. God owns more than the tithe. He owns it all.

May I challenge you to press yourself beyond your current levels of giving. Yes, God does supply our every need, but He usually does so through the checkbooks of His willing people.

October 24th

THE HEAD AND THE BODY

"Now I rejoice in what was suffered for you, and I fill up in my flesh what is still lacking in regard to Christ's afflictions, for the sake of his body, which is the church. I have become its servant by the commission God gave me..."

Colossians 1:24-25

The apostle Paul carried a passion for the church. He clearly saw the church as the body of Christ and the God-ordained ongoing incarnation of Jesus Christ.

One of the great deceptions of recent times has been the separation of Christ's body from its head. Many profess a passion for Christ as the head of the body, but have little regard for the body itself. They speak praise for the head, but only criticize the body. They confess devotion to the head, but want nothing to do with the body. "Para church" ministries have become normal practice in Christendom. While we applaud the incredible work these ministries have accomplished, we are greatly concerned with the model they have adopted. Para means outside of. A para church ministry is a ministry outside the church. Many times these para church ministries have been started due to the limited vision of the local church leaders. Limited vision is wrong. The answer is to change the limitations, not go outside the God-ordained instrument and start something new.

Paul saw no separation from Christ and His body. Because he saw them as one, he could say without any idolatry, "I have become its servant." Yes, he was serving Christ, but to serve the body is to serve the head. To serve the head and have no regard for the body is to have a misconception of what the body of Christ is. The body of Christ is the bride of Jesus Christ, betrothed and in preparation of maturity. The longer we disregard the body, the longer that preparation process will last. The sooner we, like Paul, become the servant of the body, the sooner we will see the bride making herself ready and that maturity being realized.

Do you carry a passion for the church? Have you become its servant? Allow God to expand your vision for the body of Christ and give yourself in service to your local church.

October 25th

THE FULLNESS OF CHRIST

"For in Christ all the fullness of the deity lives in bodily form and you have been given fullness in Christ"

Colossians 2:9-10

There is nothing static about the Christian walk. The Christian life is a pursuit. What we are in pursuit of is all the FULLNESS of the deity. When do you think we will achieve that pursuit? Do you think we will ever exhaust the fullness of God?

Jesus told in John 14 that His Father's house has many rooms. How easy it is to satisfy ourselves with a little and stop short of the fullness God intends to give. Some of us have just stepped into the entry way and in the finiteness of our thinking, decided this is enough. Compared to the homelessness we were previously in outside of Christ, the grandeur of the entry is enough. But compared to the rest of the many rooms within our Father's house, the entry way is just the beginning.

In the entry way, we have found the room of greeting. We have only been welcomed in. The fullness of the house is yet to be seen. Awaiting us is the kitchen, the room of nourishment and preparation. Awaiting us is the library, the room of study and maturation. Awaiting us is the sitting room, the place of fellowship and conversation. Awaiting us is the ballroom, the place of celebration and festivity. Also awaiting us is the bedroom, the place of intimacy and heart. To stop at the entry is to fall short of the fullness of fellowship Father intends to bring us to.

We have been given fullness in Christ. Not just the entry way, but the whole estate. Every room is ours to enjoy, for in every room is another aspect of Christ's fullness. Have you placed a limitation on your experience? Have you stopped at the entry? The kitchen? The study? If so, let down your guard; the fullness is yours to have and yours to enjoy.

October 26th

THE FATHER'S ACCEPTANCE

"Our Father which art in heaven"

Matthew 6:9

In this passage of Scripture, Jesus not only teaches us how to pray, He reveals the very nature of God. God does many things and in His doing, aspects of His identity are formed. But when it comes to revealing the very nature of who God is, He is revealed as a Father.

It is vital that we carry a correct understanding of the Father. The understanding of who we see God to be dictates how our personal environment is shaped. If our concept of God is a warrior, our environment will become militaristic. If our concept of God is a judge, our environment becomes fearful. But if our concept of God is a Father, our environment becomes family.

Father is God's essence; warrior is his role. Father is God's nature; judge is his role. One is what God does, the other is who He is. Our fellowship with God centers on who He is, not on what He does. Who He is brings us to substance. What He does keeps us in the shadows.

If what God does becomes the basis of our fellowship, our environment becomes strictly performance orientated. If God, the warrior, is our basis of acceptance, we must be constantly warring in order to be in a place of acceptance. If our ability to perform war ever breaks down, so does our place of acceptance. As a result, we find ourselves constantly working for something we already have. We are accepted in God because of Christ's finished work. Our Father decreed our acceptance, not because of what we do, but because of who we belong to.

Works for God are not done in order to be accepted, but because we are accepted. I work because I am a son and my Father has employed me in the family business.

October 27th

SIN SOURS

"Though evil is sweet in his mouth... his food will turn sour in his stomach"

Job 20:12-14

Sin is a deception. It begins as a deception of mind and thought. Its beginnings are deceptively sweet. It makes its appeal and then the heart justifies what the mind wants. The rational mind falls prey to the sweetness of sin's taste and the violation is conceived.

The problem with sin is it cannot be assimilated. Sin cannot relate to the stamp of Christ within. So while sin tastes sweet to the mouth, it sours when it tries to be assimilated into our being. Evil is alien to the way of God. Though our minds would say sin is the easier way; it is not. We are not made for evil. We have been created for the pleasure of God and when we behave contrary to our created purpose, life sours. We have been made for God centeredness. Created and redeemed for love, faith and being reconciled to God's way. Evil, then, is trying to live contrary to the way of God.

Redeemed man is allergic to sin. He cannot assimilate sin into the temple of the Holy Spirit. Living contrary to God's way poisons us. Though it tastes sweet in the mouth, it always turns sour in the stomach. Sin may be pleasurable for a season, but God always has the last word. Sin will never fully satisfy man's desire, it cannot, for man was created to serve God, not sin.

Do not judge a matter by its beginning. Judge it by its end. Though your decisions taste sweet now, what will happen once they are measured by the judgment of God? Sweet or sour?

October 28th

THE WAY

"For since the creation of the world God's invisible qualities—His eternal power and divine nature—have been clearly seen, being understood from what has been made, so that men are without excuse"

Romans 1:20

We live in a universe, not a multiverse. Being a universe everything made has been ordered under one law and one WAY. The very created structure of the universe has been made to respond to the WAY of God. When creation is subject to God's WAY, it lives. When it works contrary to The Way, it dies.

God's WAY is not just a way for the Christian. It is the universal WAY. It is the WAY for the universe. It is the WAY for everyone and everything. If it were limited to just the Christian, it would be "a" way. But it is not just "a" way, but it is "The" WAY. It is the WAY for creation. It is the WAY for man and animal alike.
It is the WAY for every conceivable circumstance known to man. Whatever the situation, God has the way into and the way out of.

"All things were created by Him and for Him." (Colossians 1:16) All things inherently have the stamp of Christ on them. Whether Jesus is acknowledged or not, His stamp of ownership exists in all things.

There is an eternal mark and destiny written inherently upon your life to follow. As you discover that inherent way, life is opened up to you and you move from existence to life. Apart from following the WAY, man is dead, though he lives. The greatest discovery you will ever make is to discover the way and continually walk therein. You belong to the way, inherently. The WAY belongs to you, redemptively. You belong to each other.

October 29th

WHEN YOUR ENEMIES ARE REDUCED TO ONE

"Then the Lord said to Gideon, 'Go in the strength you have ... Am I not sending you?' 'But Lord,' Gideon asked, 'how can I save Israel? My clan is the weakest in Manasseh and I am the least in my family.' Then the Lord answered, 'I will be with you and you will strike down the Midianites as if they were but one man.'"

Judges 6:14-16

When it comes to spiritual warfare, it is not who we are in the strength of our own might, but it is who God causes our enemies to become. Gideon had his focus upon his own inadequacies. He saw that his clan was the weakest and he was the least of the weakest. But God did not choose him for his strength and ability. God knew that even in the weakness of his current state, he was still strong enough, for God has reduced the power of the Midianites to the strength of one man. Gideon saw an entire army, but God saw only one man.

When God goes before us, the strength we currently have is sufficient. Because God was sending Gideon, the strength he currently had was all he needed. All too often we remove ourselves from the battle thinking that we are no match to the difficulty before us. It is at these times that we must hear the word of the Lord to Gideon, *"Go in the strength you have."* Whatever level of strength we possess is enough because our strength is not the issue. When God sends us, He goes before us to reduce the numbers who stand against us to one.

What is it God has called you to do? What obstacle stands in your way? Has your focus been on the obstacle or upon the commission of God? Go in the strength you have and let God reduce the strength of your obstacle to one. You shall surely overcome.

෴

October 30th

THE DRIFT FACTOR

"We must pay more careful attention, to what we have heard, so that we do not drift away"

Hebrews 2:1

This passage of Scripture is written to us as an admonition of evaluation. It is written as a warning against carelessness and neglect. As Christians, we have been born into a battle and we stand the possibility of defeat unless we make constant evaluation of our state and make necessary adjustment.

There is a tendency in each one of us to become disconnected and slowly, subtly and unintentionally, lose what we once had in Christ. The writer of Hebrews concern was not falling away, but drifting away. To drift away is a universal law. Nothing drifts into, it always drifts away from. One does not drift into a deeper relationship to Christ, you drift away from Him. In physical law it is called reversion of type. This is a law stating anything left to itself, without ongoing care, will always return to its former condition. A weeded garden left without ongoing care will soon revert back to a weed patch. In like manner, a spiritual life left to itself, without ongoing care, will not drift into maturity, but will disconnect and revert back to its former condition of sin and carnal living. Without ongoing care it will disconnect. Once we disconnect, the drift begins. The drift is often so subtle, many times we are not even aware we are drifting until we do not know where we are.

For this reason Hebrews tells us *"pay more attention."* More careful means more frequently and in greater degrees. To remain on course, we must increase the time spent in the presence of God whenever that tendency to drift is present. If we are spending an hour a day in the presence of the Lord and still drifting, we must increase it to perhaps 1 1/2 hours or 2. More frequently and in greater degree means exactly that . . . to remain connected and avoid the drift factor requires more time spent in the presence of the Lord. Last year's commitment will not pay this year's requirement.

Are you drifting? Increase the time you spend in His presence.

October 31st

THE CROSS, OUR PROOF OF PAYMENT

"God made you alive with Christ. He forgave us all our sins, having canceled the written code, with its regulations . . . He took it away, nailing it to the cross"

Colossians 2:13-14

It is difficult for the human mind to fathom the depth of God's forgiveness. How could anyone forgive what God had to forgive? Well, God is not just anyone. Forgiveness reveals love in its deepest form, the love of a holy God for a sinful people.

Because it is so hard for our minds to grasp this depth of forgiveness, we often struggle with guilt and condemnation. The mind simply cannot accept that we could be forgiven that easily, so it bombards us with guilt and condemnation. Some try to pacify their guilty feelings in denial. They rationalize their sin, saying there is nothing wrong with what they are doing, "after all it is the '90s." Others make peace with the pressure of guilt and just live with it. But the Bible says we are free from both and need not live with either. God's answer to guilt was neither denial nor accommodation. We cannot deny the debt of sin, for the debt is real. Nor can we give in to the guilt of sin, for the guilt has been removed.

God's answer to the guilt and condemnation of sin was canceling the debt through the sufficiency of the cross. The cross of Jesus Christ so satisfied God's just demands, He simply canceled the debt and declared it legally paid and the penalty null and void.

The action is as if I charged my credit cards to the maximum limit and then defaulted on my payments. But in mercy someone stepped in and paid off all my debts and in so doing canceled the penalties and obligations of my default. Later, as creditors came wanting payment, I would not need to argue my innocence nor fear their threats. All I would have to do is show them my proof of payment and be at peace in my benefactor's mercy.

The blood of Jesus Christ paid our debt and as a result canceled our penalty and obligation. Though the creditors continue to come wanting our installment of guilt, we simply need to show them the cross which is our proof of payment and document of cancellation.

November 1st

TEARING DOWN THE ALTARS

"Tear down your father's altar to Baal. Then build a proper kind of altar to the Lord your God"

Judges 6:25-26

Judges 6 is the story of God's visitation upon Israel after seven years of oppression. Israel had done evil in the sight of the Lord, so the Lord gave them over to be oppressed by the Midianites. After seven years of oppression they cried out to the Lord, and God in His graciousness sent them a prophet with a mission.

If there ever was a day when the church of Jesus Christ was in need of the prophetic voice, it is today. We are in real need of someone anointed of God to inform our minds, stir our emotions and direct our wills.

So it was with Gideon. God heard the cry of Israel and once again agreed to bring them into His plan. But there was a problem. During the seven years of oppression, Israel had allowed compromise and mixture to infiltrate their lives. Though they were commanded to worship God only, they had built altars to the false gods of their day.

Have you allowed altars to be built in your life? No, these are not altars you sing to or altars you bow down to. They are simply attitudes we have adopted and thoughts contrary to the way of God that we have allowed to co-mingle in our thinking. In doing so, they have become blemishes in our sacrifice to God. These altars are sometimes subtle and at other times blatant. They are altars of skepticism and unbelief. Altars of grumbling and fault finding. Altars of unforgiveness and self pity. Altars of bitterness and strife. Proper altars cannot be built until these false altars have been torn down.

The good news is that which took years to build, can be torn down in a matter of minutes. If you allow the Holy Spirit to come in and shine His light on you, He can tear down the false altars that have been built over your life and rebuild a proper altar to the Lord.

November 2nd

SPIRITUAL BIRTH

"Sing, O barren woman, you who never bore a child; burst into song, shout for joy, you who were never in labor; because more are the children of the desolate woman than of her who has a husband"

Isaiah: 54:1

It is out of the barrenness of soul that God announces spiritual birth. Trustfulness is a spiritual birthright and a divine expectation. From the introduction of the dominion mandate to the pronouncement of the great commission, we see God's intention for us is to reproduce what we have been given in order that He might touch more lives.

Out of our barrenness comes a bursting forth. God first impregnates us with promise. The promise of God builds within us a sense of holy anticipation. This holy anticipation leads us into the preparation of heart and spirit. During this time of preparation, God further defines His intention. The clarity of the promise is understood, leading us into tremendous encouragement. Encouragement then leads us into divine intention.

Spiritual birth is just like natural birth. God follows a gestation period. During the gestation process, He matures us and prepares us for birth. It is the time closest to the birth that birth seems the farthest away. Transitional labor is that time right before the baby enters the birth canal and the delivery begins. It is during transition that a woman can become the most discouraged. With pain at its peak and strength all but gone, everything in her wants to quit. But transitional labor is a sign of imminent delivery. Soon the equipment is wheeled in, the doctor prepares and the baby comes. What seemed like it would take an eternity is changed suddenly.

Are you pregnant with vision and Kingdom desire? Are you experiencing the frustration of expectation? Be patient; God will bring it to pass. By submitting to the process, the process will go quicker. Barrenness will become birth. The promised seed will become reality.

☙❧

November 3rd

SPIRIT SENSITIVE

"Do not put out the Spirit's fire"
I Thessalonians 5:19

Wishful thinking teaches us that God is God and He will do what He will do regardless of us. Though this mentality is wishful, it is also irresponsible. Contrary to wishful thinking, the scriptural record shows that, though God is God, and reserves the right to do as He pleases, His desire is often linked to our response and willingness to cooperate together with Him as His dual witness. Though we might be afraid to admit that a sovereign God would willingly limit His actions to finite man, nevertheless, it is true. Our response to God's intention always has and always will affect His desire. God's intention met with man's unwillingness results in jilted desire. God's visitation met with man's pride results in God's resistance. Consequently, the Holy Spirit works with us and trains us to act in a manner that releases Him to do all that Father and Son desire Him to do.

The focus of the Holy Spirit's work is often attitudes. It is our attitude that puts out the Spirit's fire. Whenever the fire of the Holy Spirit is met with an attitude of pride, unbelief, stubbornness, etc., the fire is extinguished. So the Holy Spirit comes to replace those attitudes of pride and unbelief with humility and faith. In His coming, He trains us to be sensitive to the desires so as not to quench Him or put out His fire.

Apparently the Holy Spirit is not as tough skinned as we might think He should be. Jesus enforces this fact in Matthew 12:32 when He admonishes us by saying, *"Anyone who speaks against the Son of man will be forgiven, but anyone who speaks against the Holy Spirit will not be forgiven either in this age or in the age to come."*

Developing a heart that is sensitive to the person of the Holy Spirit and to His leading is essential to spiritual maturity. Let us remain humble before the Lord so we can stay sensitive to His desires.

November 4th

YOUR KINGDOM COME

"... Your Kingdom come, your will be done on earth as it is in heaven"

Matthew 6:10

Is the Kingdom of God something we can expect to experience now or is it just a future event? Is God's Kingdom just a spiritual Kingdom or is it a Kingdom that affects this time-space world? These questions and others have generated much discussion concerning the Kingdom of God. While theologians and novices alike have debated these questions, the Kingdom of God has continued to come. For nearly 2,000 years everyday believers of every tribe, kindred and tongue have prayed the prayer Jesus taught us to pray. *"Your Kingdom come,"* and come it has. The Kingdom of God has come and it will continue to come. The Kingdom of God is now and still yet to be. The Kingdom of God is both present and future, spiritual and physical, here and coming.

The Kingdom of God is the governmental sphere of Jesus Christ. Wherever and whenever the King is recognized and obeyed, the Kingdom has come to that place and person. One of the great deceptions of modernity is the compartmentalizing of our lives. Easy believism has compartmentalized our spiritual and church lives from our physical and social lives. It is inconceivable to think that it would be pleasing to God to bring our spiritual lives under His reign, but to leave our physical and social lives for some future event. God's Kingdom and Christ's rule forcefully advance as believers are truly converted and let their commitment to the King's laws be expressed through the various facets of their lives. The King's reign must influence family, finances, education, law, politics, recreation, business, arts, science, etc. Every sphere of life must come under the governing reign of God's Kingdom.

Before the Kingdom comes to the various spheres of life, it must come into us personally. As we come under God's Kingdom, yielding our will and choices over to the will of the King, the Kingdom has come in our lives. As a growing army of individuals live in obedience to their King, they will influence offices, schools, businesses, clubs and the Kingdom of God will come to that place. As we pray daily *"Your Kingdom come,"* Father's desire is to come to us—to bring His dominion over us and then extend that dominion in this time-space world.

November 5th

RECONCILED TO RECONCILE

"Therefore, if anyone be in Christ, he is a new creation, the old has gone and the new has come. All of this is from God who reconciled us to himself through Christ and gave us the ministry of reconciliation"
II Corinthians 5:17-18

I could never count the number of times I've heard someone say, "I have no ministry." How many times have you asked yourself, "Why am I here? What is my ministry?"

All of us are in various stages of that search. The search to discover why Father apprehended us and what the ministry is that He purposed for us to do. Be it certain that we all have a specific calling, a unique purpose that each one of us has been specially equipped to function in. My focus is not the specific ministry we have, but the general ministry Father has given all of us to do. Paul makes it quite plain in II Corinthians 5:18 that we have all been given a ministry. From the greatest to the least, from the youngest to the oldest, from the mature to the immature, we have all been given a ministry of reconciliation, to be part of a process of reconciling others to God and being reconciled to each other. Though we may do other things, we must all be given to the ministry of reconciliation. Even as we were reconciled to God through Christ, we must carry that same ministry to others.

Herein lies the battle. If our adversary is unable to keep us from being reconciled, he will do all he possibly can to keep us from becoming reconcilers. To be reconciled is a blessing. To become reconcilers is a ministry. If the focus remains on the blessing, reconciliation becomes self-related. But when reconciliation focuses in on the ministry, we then become a personal threat to the kingdom of darkness because we are no longer just consuming, but now we are producing.

We have been reconciled in order that we might reconcile. A life reconciled is short lived. Once it's done, it's done, but a life of reconciling is a perpetual ministry.

If you have not already, I encourage you to embrace your ministry and develop an eye for those in need of reconciliation.

November 6th

SOURCE OF SUPPLY

"Paul an apostle of Jesus Christ by the will of God"
Colossians 1:1

Ambition is a word that has taken a pre-eminent place in current thought and practice. From the days of our youth, we have been trained to make something of ourselves. It has been instilled in us to achieve and strive to be somebody by accomplishing some great task. Human ambition is a benchmark of modern day man. Hard work and diligence and fortitude are godly traits, provided the source is clearly understood. Man is the source of human ambition. Human ambition will never bring us the pleasure of God or take us to our desired end. Paul said, *"To this end I labor, struggling with all His energy which so powerfully works in me."* (Colossians 1:29) Herein we find the source of our supply. Christian achievement is accomplished through exchange. As we exchange our life for His, we are given the energy we need to accomplish God's desire. Divine initiative and human responsibility come together and produce what is needed for accomplishment. The difference between exchange and human ambition is divine initiative.

"Paul an apostle of Jesus Christ by the will of God." Paul's office of an apostle was not the result of personal ambition. Paul was an apostle by the will of God. The office was not something he earned or achieved. Divine initiative chose him and human responsibility responded by embracing the training. An apostle is one who is sent out. They do not go out on their own initiative, but they are sent out by divine decree. An apostle is God's doing, the result of His choice, not man's ambition.

Human ambition stands in direct opposition of the grace of God. Human ambition says, "I will make of myself something great." Grace says, "Apart from Jesus, I can do nothing." Grace acknowledges that a man is not what he has made of himself, but what God has made of him. This does not excuse hard work or make room for irresponsibility. Once God takes the initiative by making His will known, man must respond with the diligence necessary to fulfill God's desire.

"You did not choose me, but I chose you." (John 15:16) What we will become is the result of God's choosing. Accomplishment begins with the discerning of His desire, then the embracing of His supplied grace to achieve.

November 7th

TAKING THE HELM

"The least of these was a match for 100 and the greatest was a match for 1,000"

I Chronicles 12:14

Such was the testimony of the Gadites. The Scriptures describe the tribe of the Gadites as brave warriors whose faces were like the faces of lions. Not only is this descriptive of a tribe of years past, but it is also descriptive of God's desire today. As a result of the indwelling presence of God, the least of us is a match for a hundred and the greatest of us is a match for a thousand.

With those odds, leadership should be a cinch. If the least of us is equal to a hundred, then the least of us should be a hundred more times qualified to lead than anyone this world can offer. Then why is there such a void of leadership?

The void comes due to personal familiarity. Hosea 4:6 tells us that God's people are destroyed from a lack of knowledge. It's not that we don't possess a knowledge of the facts. The fact is we know more now than ever before. What is killing the people of God is what we do with what we know. The world knowledge has to do with having a proper perception. What stands between us and the helm of leadership is a familiar perception of ourselves that causes us to see ourselves after the flesh and not through the eyes of the Spirit. We know it is wrong to see others after the flesh, (II Corinthians 5:16), but what about seeing ourselves after the flesh? When we see ourselves through the perception of the Spirit, we see that at our worst we are a match for hundred and at our best we are a match for a thousand.

As we, the people of God, begin to see ourselves through the eyes of the Spirit, we will find the boldness and courage of the Gadites to take the helm of leadership. Out of the void of leadership, we currently see God raising up a generation that has married the purpose of Esther with the understanding of Issachar. It's a generation that has joined the purpose of, *"for such a time as this,"* to the vision of *"understanding the times and knowing what to do."* Esther alone gives zeal without understanding, but without understanding we misrepresent the Kingdom of God. Issachar alone gives understanding without a sense of Kingdom obligation. When the two are united, "purpose and vision," plus "calling with understanding," we have resolution and godly transformation. When the two are united, someone takes the helm of leadership and knows what to do. The door to the wheelhouse of leadership stands open. With the dominion mandate as our commission, let us go in and take the helm.

November 8th

WINNING RESPECT

"... So that your daily life will win the respect of outsiders"
I Thessalonians 4:12

Respect is essential in order for us to influence the lives of others. Without respect, there is no dominion. Without respect, there is no discipleship. Respect is what gives us a place in people's lives. Respect enables others to let down the walls of self-protection and open themselves up to the deposit of God in their lives.

Control demands respect. When people have to demand respect from others, they have already lost what they demand. Respect cannot be demanded; it must be won. When people live respectful lives, they receive respect in return. Respect is always given, but never taken.

We lose the respect of others when we . . .

1. HAVE NO ONGOING RELATIONSHIP WITH JESUS. Respect begins with having the character and likeness of Jesus Christ. When we are transformed into His image, we will win the respect of those we come in contact with. It is the daily abiding in fellowship with Christ that brings that transformation about.

2. SAY ONE THING, BUT DO ANOTHER. To win the respect of others, we must value our words. When a promise is given or a commitment is made, we must follow through regardless of the cost. Those who value their words and if necessary, swear to their own hurt, are those who win the respect of others.

3. LACK SELF DISCIPLINE. Disciplined people are respected people. Those who have disciplined their lives to run a marathon or complete a doctorate are those who have gained the respect of their peers. When we see people who have disciplined themselves to accomplish their goals we willingly yield to them our respect.

4. CONDUCT OURSELVES AS AN INFERIOR STANDARD FROM THE REST. Respect does not grade on the curve. Respect is won by living up to the standard and expectation of God. Others can, but if we do as others we will lose their respect and as a result lose our ability to influence them for the Kingdom of God. The behavior of others is not our standard of expectation. Our standard is Jesus Christ.

He is our goal. When we live to please Him and seek to become like Him, we will win respect as a result.

Let the likeness of Jesus Christ be your goal. Become like Him and in so doing, you will be respected.

ഗ‌ോ

Pause for thought:

Is your lifestyle and behavior a reflection of Jesus Christ? Do you have enough of Jesus in you for people to respect?

November 9th

SEASONS OF GROWTH

"There is a time for everything, and a season for every activity under heaven"

Ecclesiastes 3:1

God has ordained that His creation follow a predetermined order. He established a time for everything and a season for every activity. Every year, according to God's predetermined design, the seasons come. Spring always follows winter, to be complimented by summer, which always leads us into the fall. The seasons are God's doing and man can not manipulate them or alter them in any way. They are a cycle of life repeated year after year by God's decree.

There are also seasons of growth in our spiritual life. The same predetermined cycle God follows in the natural, He also follows in the spiritual. In our spiritual lives, there is a season for every activity. There is a time to be born and there is a time to die. There is a time to plant and there is a time to uproot. There is a time to tear down and there is a time to build. There is a time to weep and there is a time to laugh. Every activity of God's intended desire has a corresponding season. God does not plant in the summer or prune in the spring. He does not harvest in the winter or fertilize in the fall. His activity with man always works in conjunction with the season in which he currently has us.

Perhaps the most difficult season to understand and embrace is the winter season. Winter is a time of dormancy and unseen results. It can be a time of tremendous depression and gloom if a seasonal perspective is not maintained. Winter is a time of root focus. It is a time wherein God focuses on those issues in our lives that produce fruit, not the fruit itself. The dormant season is a time to develop new strategies that will prepare us for the seasons to come. It is a season to find our rest in God and allow Him to produce in us a root of patience, love, quiet confidence and much needed perseverance for the harvest to come.

Are you in a winter season? Then rejoice; there is a time for everything and a season for every activity. God has ordained your winter, but be assured spring always follows winter. As sure as your winter has come, a harvest will follow.

November 10th

SPIRIT OF ADVENTURE

"'Lord, if it's you,' Peter replied, 'tell me to come to you on the water'"

Matthew 14:28

Our walk with God is designed to be the most exciting game in town. Far more exciting than the temporal pleasures of sin or any other pseudo excitement this world has to offer.

Adventure is a basic need of humanity. We have been created by God with a need to experience adventure. A spirit led life is a life full of spiritual adventure. Encounters with God, demons, heroes, villains, all of these and more are the normal Christian life.

Preparation begins in the "boat," but it is not long before you discover you can only accomplish so much while you are confined to the boat's limitations. Outside the boat you are forced to draw from a deeper level of relationship and anointing. The boat is not the church. The boat is whatever you have fashioned as your comfort zone. Getting out of the boat may mean ministry out from the church, but for most it is bigger than that. It is finding ministry outside your comfort zone.

"Getting out," begins with desire. It starts with living in harmony with that God-given desire for adventure and excitement. All of us have been programmed with it. It is part of our created design. But for most, it has become dormant and is trapped by layers of unbelief and doubt. Surrounding ourselves with spiritually adventurous people will draw that desire to the surface. Once there, we must place ourselves in situations that will call us out. (i.e., volunteer for a position that stretches your current resources) Speak out the next time you find yourself in a conversation contrary to the Kingdom way. Ask the Lord to give you a word for someone you know and is in need of ministry.

Excitement awaits us outside the boat. Spiritual adventure is the inheritance of the saints, for the word of God promises that those who know their God will do exploits. But there is little room for exploits inside the boat.

November 11th

THE GREATEST VET OF ALL

"I saw heaven standing open and there before me was a white horse whose rider is called Faithful and True. With justice he judges and makes war"

Revelation 19:11

It seems only appropriate that as we honor our military veterans, we also honor the greatest vet of all. God is not a pacifist. He is a veteran of many wars. All too often, God and His people are categorically stereotyped as pacifists. The insinuation is: in order to be a good Christian, we must be diametrically opposed to war and any form of violence.

Though one could never support an aggressive, war monger attitude, we could support the fact that while God is committed to peace, He made a lot of war in order to achieve that desired end.

John, the revelator, describes Jesus as one who will rule with an iron scepter. He comes with a sharp sword with which He will strike down the nations. He does not return with a meager peace delegation, rather He comes with the armies of Heaven to make war.

David declares in Psalm 144:1, *"Praise be to the Lord my rock, who trains my hands for war, my fingers for the battle."* David goes on to describe God as a fortress, a shield and a stronghold. He is depicted as a military man, a man of war.

So on this day, as we honor our military vets, we do so with the understanding that Jesus is the greatest vet of all. The consummate Warrior. The soldier's Soldier. The veteran's Vet.

November 12th

THE TOMB BECOMES A WOMB

"What you sow does not come to life unless it dies"
I Corinthians 15:36

In the human mind, there is nothing further apart than the tomb and the womb. The womb represents the beginning and the tomb represents the end. In between the two is a space of seventy plus years representing experience, memories and a multitude of things to separate the two. But in the mind of God, things are a bit different. Though the womb still represents the beginning, the tomb represents a beginning of its own. Often what appears to be the end of man is just the beginning of God.

Though death is the end of life as we know it, it is just the beginning of eternal life. The only finality in death is the finality of our temporal existence. But the tomb of death in this sphere is the womb of life in the eternal sphere.

This truth is not only seen in life and death. Those whose lives are led in Christ find it clearly illustrated in everyday circumstances. The redemptive power of Christ turns the tomb of circumstances into the womb of new life in Christ. Jesus illustrated this in His own life. When His followers placed Him in the tomb, it appeared to be the end. All of their hopes and dreams were dashed in defeat and despair. But that tomb was not the end; it was the beginning. Yes, it was the end of the temporal, but it was just the beginning of the eternal. It also represented the end of sin's captivity and the beginning of freedom for the redeemed.

Life in the Kingdom of God begins in death. Unless the kernel of wheat falls into the ground and dies, it abides alone. In order for us to find all we are to be in Christ, our old man of sin must die. That tomb of death becomes the womb of new life in Christ.

Though the tomb of circumstances surrounds you, look beyond what the natural eyes see. The womb of new life in Christ awaits you.

November 13th

SUPREMACY OF CHRIST

"He is the head of the body, the church; he is the beginning and the firstborn from among the dead, so that in everything he might have the supremacy"

Colossians 1:18

Jesus Christ stands alone. There is no one or no thing that can compare to Him. There is nothing in the heavens and there is nothing on the earth. He is the first and He is the last. He is transcendent, separate in distinction, yet He has willingly chosen to come near and embrace mankind. His coming near does not take anything from His distinction. In fact, His coming adds to that very distinction. The fact that one so supreme and transcendent would come near to man distinguishes Him even more.

We live in an age that seeks to eliminate all distinctions. The distinctions of male and female are slowly eroding away. The concept of unisex has redefined how many see the sexual distinctions of male and female. This redefinition is not limited to just gender distinctions. It is a philosophical shift that seeks to eliminate all distinctions and reduce humanity to a melting pot of nothingness.

Ours is an age of syncretism. Social architects are trying to harmonize and unite many different schools of thought and come up with one superior way. Nothing is eliminated in their attempt. The philosophy is not to eliminate anything, but to reduce it and in its reduction make it palatable to the masses. Their tactic is to reject nothing, for in rejection those who hold to that philosophy are eliminated. So they simply redefine the belief by eliminating its distinctions, but still embracing its verbiage. In doing so, its adherents are lured into a form of their belief, but have lost its very distinctiveness.

In the name of religious toleration, this reduction has come to the church. In order to be open minded, many have had to accept a redefinition of Jesus Christ. Rather than being the only way, they have accepted that He is one of several ways. They have accepted that He is prominent, but not preeminent, for prominence sets Him apart and distinguishes Him for all other man-made attempts. These are not denying Christ, but dethroning Him. Attempt as they may, the cast has already been set. Jesus Christ cannot be redefined. Almighty God has already declared by divine decree that in everything Jesus Christ has the supremacy. We need not look further. He cannot be improved. He cannot be reduced. He cannot be dethroned.

November 14th

A HEART OF THANKFULNESS

"Were not all ten cleansed? Where are the other nine? Was no one found to return and give praise to God except the foreigner?"
Luke 17:17-19

Just how important is a heart of thankfulness? It could be easily said that ungratefulness is one of the most prevalent, yet inexcusable sins of humanity. So much is taken for granted. So much is assumed. So much is done for others without even a word of thankfulness.

Upon seeing this attitude in the nine, Jesus addressed it head-on. He said, *"Were not all ten cleansed? Where are the nine?"* Their lack of gratitude did not surprise Him, but it did disappoint Him. To deal with the problem, He didn't revoke the healing of the nine. Rather than taking from the nine, He chose to give to the one. Upon the returning of the one, Jesus said, *"Rise and go; your faith has made you well."* This word "well" means to be saved and made whole. Implied in the passage is the fact that the nine were just healed. Only the one who returned to give thanks was saved and made whole. No one ever thanks God without receiving even more with which to thank Him. That which we honor, we receive more of.

Cultivating a heart of thankfulness is what keeps God and His works from becoming commonplace. To allow God and His works to become common is to profane the work of God. To profane something is to make it unhallowed and public. There is nothing unhallowed about God or His works. Thankfulness is both an attitude and an act that keeps the works of God holy in our lives. As we offer up the sacrifice of thankfulness, we draw a line that says, "We hallow you for what you have done and do not treat it as common or profane."

Let us never take for granted or call common the holy works and person of God.

November 15th

CHRISTIANITY STARTS WITH CHRIST

"For God was pleased to have all of His fullness dwell in Christ and through Him reconcile to Himself all things"

Colossians 1:19

Christianity, for the most part has become off center. Christianity is Christ. When Jesus ceases to be the central focus, we become off center. Jesus is the alpha and the omega. He is the beginning and the end. He is the fullness of God in bodily form, the exact representation of God. Without Jesus, there is no revelation. Without Him, there is no starting point or central focus.

Some would say their faith starts with God. God is their central focus and their starting point. Though that sounds good in concept, it breaks down rapidly. To start with God apart from the revelation of Jesus Christ is to start with our concept and idea of God, but our ideas of God are not God. We must start with God's ideas and concept of Himself. God's idea of Himself is Jesus Christ. Jesus Christ is Immanuel, God with us. If Christ is ever removed, then everyone has a definition and concept of God. Consequently, everyone has a different starting point and central focus.

In Christ, the transcendent God became eminent. The vague God became clear. Jesus defined in bodily form and human character, the divinity of God. Once Christianity strays from the centrality of Jesus Christ, it becomes lost in programs and secondary issues. Human ideas replace divine mandates. Begin with programs and you will end with man. Begin with Christ and you will end with the fullness of God.

A church off center is destined to crash. A person off center becomes a problem, not a solution. The cross is God's instrument of alignment. In dying to ourselves and embracing the cross, we are removed from the center. Then Christ becomes our starting point and our point of reference.

☙❧

November 16th

IT'S NO PRIVATE MATTER

"Our father which art in heaven"
Matthew 6:9

The very nature of Christianity begins with "Our" not "me." Jesus taught us to pray by framing our disposition with an "Our" perspective, rather than a "me" perspective. Had Jesus begun this prayer with "me" rather than "Our," it would have changed the very nature of the Kingdom. Instead of being corporate and "we" centered, it would have become individual and "I" centered. The word "Our" shifts the entire emphasis from "me" to the Father primarily and to the family secondarily.

Christianity begins with the renunciation of self. The very nature of the Kingdom is self surrender to the Father and to a focus on the "Our." Without a focus on "Our," the rest of the Lord's prayer turns quite self-centered. Give Me, lead Me, deliver Me, forgive Me. The very nature of the prayer would change from corporate to individual.

"Our" is all inclusive. "Our" makes room for every denomination, tongue and tribe. It includes every race or ethnic origin. "Our Father" embraces the fatherhood of God and the brotherhood of man.

Humanism seeks to make religion a private matter. Ask a religious person about their faith and they will promptly reply, "My faith is a personal matter." Since Humanism begins with man, his faith is private to himself. Christianity does not begin with man. Christianity begins with God and then moves to the corporate. Consequently, Christianity is quite public. It is intended to be openly shared.

Is your faith private or has it become a public offering? The freedom to openly share our faith is the greatest adventure we will ever know. Keeping it to ourselves produces death. Giving it away leads to life. The only way we can keep it is to give it away.

November 17th

THE SPIRIT OF ADVENTURE

"So Jephthah fled from his brothers and settled in the land of Tob, where a group of adventurers gathered around him and followed him"
Judges 11:3

The God we serve is a God of adventure. Everything about Jesus is adventurous. From eternity past to the present He has been a Man whose heart we set on adventure. He faced the adventure of the incarnation, the adventure of redemption, the adventure of the resurrection and soon He will face the adventure of the consummation.

Man has been created with a basic need of adventure. Being created in the image of God, we are created with an innate desire to be adventurous. This is why action movies sell so well. We enjoy them because, as we watch them, we vicariously satisfy the God-given need for adventure.

The social architects of our day are attempting to redefine this basic need. Some are uncomfortable with God being a God of war and adventure, so they are attempting to recreate Him in their own image. In 1986, a decision was made by some of the Methodist Church to eliminate any hymn that carried a militaristic theme. I can only assume this was done because their concepts of God and war were not congruent themes. But the Word of God reveals God as a God of war. (Psalm 144:1; Revelation 19:11) He wars to protect His purpose and to defeat the enemy of our souls.

The apathy and cowardice of man has sought to effeminize the character of God and in doing so, we have lost our spirit of adventure. Though man attempts to redefine Him, God is God and He will not be mocked or recreated. C. S. Lewis once said, "God is so masculine, all of creation is feminine in comparison."

God searches for those to whom He can impart His spirit of adventure. He found Jonathan and his armor bearer. He found David and his mighty three. He found the Joshua's, Caleb's and Gideon's. What will He find in you? It is okay. Take a risk.

November 18th

WEARINESS OF SILENCE

"But if I say, 'I will not mention him or speak any more in his name,' his word is in my heart like a burning fire, shut up in my bones. I am weary of holding it in"

Jeremiah 20:9

Have you ever wondered why you often feel the weariness you do? Do you ever sense that feeling of being weary and you just ca not put your finger on the reason? As you examine your life, everything seems to be in order. There is no hidden or unconfessed sin. You spend consistent time in prayer and the Word. To the best of your knowledge all is relationally well between you and others. Yet, there still seems to be a sense of weariness. What could it be?

Jeremiah put his finger on a major cause of weariness in the church today. SILENCE, apathy, passivity, wrongful focus—these and other attitudes like them have silenced the church of its witness to the world. As a result of that silence, God's word has burned within our bones producing a pressure and need of release. It's the buildup of the Word's pressure that many interpret as weariness. It's not the weariness of fatigue, but the weariness of silence.

Rest is the answer to the weariness of fatigue. But rest will not solve the weariness of silence. The only remedy to the weariness of silence is to speak. As we speak His name and testify to the Gospel of Jesus Christ, the pressure that has been building up in silence is released and the weariness dissipates.

Silence speaks loudly. In fact, over time, silence begins to scream. The word of God shut up in our bones screams for release. It screams to be sent out to accomplish what it was sent to do. Whenever God's Word is contained, it searches for a release. It's that searching that produces in us the restlessness and weariness. Once we speak and the word is released, the weariness dissipates.

Have you been sensing a stirring in your bones? Has there been a weariness that you could not put your finger on? Perhaps it is the weariness of silence. Begin to speak His word. Look for opportunities to witness, teach or speak on His behalf. Soon you will see the weariness go.

November 19th

THE TURNING OF OUR CENTERS

"Seek first the Kingdom of God and His righteousness and all these things will be given to you as well"
                                                                    Matthew 6:33

Salvation is much more than just being qualified for heaven. To be saved means we are being saved from the kingdom of self tyranny and progressively coming under the Kingdom of God. God's Kingdom is His government. To seek first the Kingdom is to seek first His government. That is, to seek His way first above the way of self preference and desire.

"We all, like sheep, have gone astray, each of us has turned to his own way and the Lord has laid on him the iniquity of us all." (Isaiah 53:6) Self rule and self government are the root of sin. Man's natural tendency is to seek after and please self. We are predisposed to going our own way. Once we are saved, the Holy Spirit begins to work out our salvation by turning our centers of self interest and causing us to seek after and desire the governmental way of God. The exchange of governments is the first step toward spiritual maturity. Many are saved, but never grow up into all God desires because they never turn their centers by exchanging self government for God's government.

Jesus said, *"I am the way."* (John 14:6) Jesus is not just something we give mental assent to, He is a way we follow. Those who walked with Jesus clearly understood His unique way. So distinct was the government of God that the early church became known as *"those of the way."* (Acts 9:2) The way of Jesus Christ replaced the way of self and it became so evident in the lives of believers that it made a reputation for them that was known throughout the land.

Has your center been turned since you were saved? Whose way are you following? Have you exchanged self government for the government of God? God's desire is for us to discover the way of the Kingdom of Heaven. His desire for us is to seek that way above every self seeking tendency. His promise is, if we seek His way first, then everything else will be added to us. But if we seek everything else, not only will we lose that, but we will also miss "the way" and remain in bondage to the tyranny of self.

☙❧

November 20th

THIEFOLOGY

"Be self controlled and alert. Your enemy the devil prowls around like a roaring lion looking for someone to devour. Resist him, standing firm in your faith..."

I Peter 5:8

Evil is the antithesis of good, and the devil is the antithesis of God. Satan is incapable of doing anything original except lie, cheat and destroy. Most of what Satan does is the evil opposite of what God has originated. Just as God follows a systematic plan we call theology, Satan follows a similar systematic plan called Thiefology. Thiefology is the understanding that Satan does not have creative power or thought. He is completely bent on evil, and his evil bent follows a systematic plan. If the plan can be figured out, we who belong to Jesus, could more readily enforce His victory.

The tragedy over the years has been that Satan has never had to change his plan. The same deception he used with Korah in Numbers 16, he still uses today with extreme effect. The same strategy he used with Absalom, he still uses today. He has never had to change his strategy because it is still extremely effective.

The tactics are few, but quite effective. Unbelief and doubt are primary weapons in our understanding of thiefology. *"Hath God said"* is a tactic he has used since the garden. He comes, and though seemingly innocent, questions and undermines our faith in what God has promised.

The undermining of delegated authority is another widely used tactic of thiefology. The undermining was clearly seen in Absalom, King David's son. The "Absalom spirit" seeks to draw people away from the person God has put into authority and brings them to the person the spirit is operating through. As with Absalom, this spirit makes promises of understanding and accusations of the leader's inability to understand. Anyone who draws people to himself is not being led by the Spirit of God. Someone who undermines authority and exalts himself as the solution is yielding to the tactics of thiefology and missing the heart of God.

Separation is another tactic of thiefology. "Divide and conquer" is his focus of assault. Whether it be unfulfilled expectations, hurtful words or self centered focus, the enemy uses these all to offend the heart. Once the heart is offended, the separation promise is in full bloom. Soon the heart is separated and the mind will soon justify what the heart wants. Once separation takes place an excuse is made, but the excuse is never the issue; it is just an excuse.

Let me encourage you to be alert. Study the Word for the purpose of discerning the patterns of this thiefology. The sooner we become wise to the devil's plan, the quicker we will be able to defeat his strategy.

∞

Pause for thought:

How does unbelief and doubt affect how you act on the promises of God's Word? How do you respond to delegated authority? Have you allowed any separation to enter into your relationships?

November 21st

THE WAY AND NOT THE WAY

"I am the way and the truth and the life. No one comes to the father except through me"

John 14:6

Jesus Christ was not just "a" way. He was and is "the" way. He did not come to point "a" way to eternal life, but He came as the only way to eternal life. Apart from Jesus, there is no other way. Consequently, life sifts down to two realities: The way and not the way. Inherent to every circumstance and situation is the way and not the way. God is not passive and His will is not selective. God is a knowable God who is personally involved in the daily affairs of His children. He has a will and a way for every situation that confronts us.

"Those who are led by the Spirit of God are the sons of God." (Romans 8:14) The choice to be led into the way confronts us in every thought, act and feeling. For every individual and every nation, there are just two issues facing them and their decisions, the way and not the way. Many have perceived God to be a vast space of gray. As situations arise and decisions are to be made, they feel God has given them a bargain and has left the decisions to them. But, man left to his own decisions, only produces death. Man left to make his own way will consistently choose not the way. Proverbs 14:12 says, *"There is a way that seems right to a man, but in the end it leads to death."* Knowing this to be true, God willingly makes known the way in every situation to those who are willing to seek Him for it.

If the simplicity of the way and not the way is not true, then it does not matter; but, if it is true, nothing else matters. If God passively opens up a multitude of choices and does not care what we choose, we are safe. But if He has a will and a prescribed way, we had better follow that way if we want to live.

November 22nd

THE WAY OF INCREASED EXPECTATION

"In the past God overlooked such ignorance, but now he commands all people everywhere to repent"

Acts 17:30

The way of the Kingdom is a way of increased expectation. The deeper we go in God, the less we get away with. The closer we are to Him, the less room there is for behavior that is contrary to His way. Like a guide, the Holy Spirit is constantly leading us and bringing us into deeper waters. The deeper we get in the Spirit, the more is expected of us in return. In order for Christ to increase in our lives, we must just decrease. Consequently, what we were permitted to do in the past may not be permissible in the future. What the Holy Spirit turned a deaf ear to yesterday may be the focus of His attention today.

As we climb the mountain of the Lord, we must lighten our load. A heavy load does not pose much of a challenge at the beginning of the journey. But, as the body fatigues and the altitude increases, the load must lighten. So it is in the Spirit. As we come into the Kingdom, the load of sin and self is heavy. As the Holy Spirit takes us up the mountain of God's purpose, He requires that we discard certain behaviors that weigh us down and impede our progress. If we choose to obey, our burden is lightened and the way is made easy. If we ignore the prompting, the load becomes burdensome and the way difficult. If the command is ignored repeatedly, the journey is stopped.

What might the Holy Spirit be requiring of you? Maybe in your ignorance it was permitted last year, but now you are commanded to repent. Be assured whatever He requires you to repent of, He supplies the grace to obey. Allow those issues to fall off and stay behind. Then your climb up will be that much easier.

November 23rd

THEREFORE GO

"All authority in heaven and on earth has been given to me. Therefore go and make disciples of all nations, baptizing them in the name of the Father and of the Son and of the Holy Spirit, and teaching them to obey everything I have commanded you"

Matthew 28:18-20

Obeying the Great Commission is so much more than the distribution of gospel tracts. The responsibility of obeying the Great Commission is not something that is limited to just those who carry an evangelistic gifting. The church universal was commissioned by Christ to go. Everyone of us individually has been commissioned to herald Jesus Christ as King over all the Earth and the judge over all mankind who commands all men everywhere to repent.

To obey the Great Commission is to proclaim the good news of salvation by grace through faith in the atoning blood of Jesus Christ. Salvation is not achieved through works or by subscribing to a particular church dogma. Salvation is realized through the blood of Christ plus nothing. The Great Commission involves the calling of all believers to make disciples of all nations. Disciples are those who have repented, been baptized and are being trained to obey all of God's commands in the Bible as they apply to us today.

The Great Commission cannot be restricted solely to proclaiming the good news of salvation by grace through faith, without the accompanying call to repentance and faithful obedience to Christ's commands. The deliverance believers enjoy from the condemnation of the moral law does not exempt them from the obligation to obey the law. Obedience to the commands of Christ are not a means to salvation, but are an expression of our love and allegiance to the King of kings.

As those commissioned of God to go, we are to be the sent ones. All too often the sent ones become the stuck ones. Over time, we become comfortable, apathetic and callused. As the disciples in Jerusalem faced this dilemma, God sent a persecution on the church to scatter those who had been sent but had become stuck. The persecution awakened them to their commission and as they went, they made disciples of the nations they touched. Perhaps it is time for you to go. Are you a sent one who has become stuck?

November 24th

TO EVERY MAN

"It is Christ whom we proclaim, warning Every Man and teaching Every Man in all wisdom, that we may present Every Man complete in Christ"

Colossians 1:28

The power of the Gospel of Jesus Christ is all inclusive. There is not a man, woman or child that the Gospel cannot change and transform into the likeness of Jesus Christ. Many have fallen into the pit of hopelessness, thinking that they are beyond help, beyond the possibility of change. But EVERY MAN is within the perimeters of the Gospel's ability to transform.

The love of Jesus Christ is not exclusive. It is not a love that is reserved for a select few. The fact of the matter is that the only thing in this world which is for EVERY MAN is Jesus Christ. Intellectualism is not for every man; all are not thinkers. There are certain gifts that are not granted to every man. Certain abilities limit everyone from achieving heights of talent and expertise. There are those who are blind and are limited from experiencing the wonder of sight. Not every man can be a writer, surgeon, preacher or realize their life long goal. There are talents a man will never possess and privileges a man may never enjoy. There are accomplishments only a few will ever achieve. But to EVERY MAN is given the honor of being called a son of God and partaking in the vast inheritance that is ours in Christ. To EVERY MAN has been given the potential to partake of the divine nature.

You are not outside the sphere of EVERY MAN. You are not beyond the possible realm of change. There is nothing hopeless about your situation. God's intention is to present you complete in Christ. That is to present you whole and free. The glorious hope of the gospel is presented to EVERY MAN regardless of age, gender, nation or tribe. God's love and mercy extend to all in the person of Jesus Christ and sets EVERY MAN free who believes the truth.

○₃₈○

November 25th

UNDEDICATED MONEY

"What was sown among the thorns is the man who hears the word, but the worries of this life and the deceitfulness of wealth choke it, making it unfruitful"

Matthew 13:22

Unfruitfulness is a curse. Everything about God speaks of life and productivity. When the life of God touches something, it comes to life and reproduces. There is a spontaneous regeneration in the life of God.

In the parable of the sower, Jesus warns us of that which chokes the life of God and makes a man unfruitful. The worries of this life and the deceitfulness of wealth are life thieves. They rob us of our ability and our mandate to reproduce and multiply.

Many have said that money is man's number one enemy. But money in and of itself is not man's enemy. The enemy of man's destiny is the delight of being rich. It is the focus that sees money as an end in itself. It is a focus that delights in the thing, rather than in what the thing can do. Undedicated wealth is a life thief. It robs us of Kingdom focus and sets our pursuit on the temporal, rather than the eternal.

Undedicated money becomes a god. When riches become an end in themselves, they take on god-like proportions. Simple money becomes mammon. Jesus said, *"You cannot serve both God and mammon."* (Matthew 6:24) Mammon is a false god that redefines destiny. When mammon is in control of one's life, destiny becomes decay.

Life is what controls your focus. Life is emotion, says the sensualist. Life is pleasure, says the hedonist. Life is money, says the materialist. Life is Jesus, says the Christian.

Money is good, provided it is money that is dedicated to the Lord. Has your wealth been dedicated to the Lord? If not, you are being robbed of your life and are dying by installments. Turn it over to Christ to live.

November 26th

GRATITUDE

"How can I repay the Lord for all his goodness to me?"
Psalm 116:12

What motivates genuine Christians, the world over, to sacrifice, to lay down their lives, to suffer? Faced with the question of what makes Christians tick, unbelievers maintain that Christianity is practiced out of self-serving purposes. For some, unfortunately, this is true. But the true driving force in authentic Christian living is, and ever must be, not the hope of gain, but the heart of gratitude.

Gratitude for what? For all His goodness to us! For His great Love, Grace and Mercy! Ungratefulness causes us to grow dull and forget what we were saved from. We did not receive what we deserved because of Jesus Christ and His shed blood. God gave us His all!

We love because He first loved us. Responsive love, fed by gratitude and expressed in thanksgiving, should flow forth from our being as the ruling passion in our lives. Giving our all to God who has given His all to us.

That which gives God pleasure is the Christian whose heart never ceases to be grateful.

Our acts of thanksgiving are not to be hollow formalities, but genuine expressions in the heart for all of God's giving . . . for all He has done . . . for all that He is.

GIVE THANKS WITH A GRATEFUL HEART!

November 27th

ORIGIN AND PURPOSE

"For by Him all things were created: things in heaven and on earth, visible and invisible . . . all things were created by Him and for Him"
Colossians 1:16

We were not just created *by* God, we were also created *for* God. There is much debate today around the issue of creation. "Creation vs. Evolution" is a topic that gets much conversation. As important as creation is, it is only half of the equation. Once creation is settled, one must also settle the issue of origin and purpose. To know who created us, but not know why we were created, is to stop short of God's intended purpose. The information of creation deals with our sense of security and belonging. The "why" of creation deals with our sense of identity and purpose.

We were created by Him and for Him. This is the starting point of life and existence. Humanism starts man with himself. Though Christians reject the philosophy of humanism, it is easy to be influenced by its tenets. Without a thorough understanding that we were created for Him, we can fall into Christian humanism. Christian humanism still starts man with himself, then it throws in some Bible verses so he will think right. Man can be fully saved and still have the wrong center. Man can be fully saved and still be living for himself. God's desire is to turn our centers so that we will see we were created for Him. *"For thy pleasure we were created."* (Revelation 4:11)

Jesus said, unless we take up our cross and follow Him daily, we could not be His disciples. It is the working of the cross in our lives that turns our center. As the cross principle cuts across our desires, it teaches us to say no to ourselves and yes to Him. It shows us how we so easily interpret God through ourselves rather than interpreting ourselves through God. The cross principle places God in the center of belief and practice and teaches us to revolve around Him. By the cross, we are able to dethrone ourselves and enthrone Jesus Christ as the central focus and master of our lives.

We will never fulfill our created purpose until Jesus Christ is clearly established in the center of our life and of our focus. He is both our origin and our purpose.

November 28th

OBSERVER OR PERCEIVER

"Now these things occurred as examples, to keep us from setting our hearts on evil things as they did"

I Corinthians 10:6

There is a major difference between one who observes and one who perceives. Observing is simply seeing what takes place, but not having any understanding as to why it took place. Perceiving is the ability to see beyond what you see and understand why and how it took place, so as to either prevent it from happening again or repeat it, depending on the nature of its outcome.

Most will go through life only observing. They will see their mistakes; they will see others' mistakes, but they will be helpless to make the necessary changes, for they are only observing those mistakes, not perceiving why and how they took place.

Perceivers ask questions. They ask the Holy Spirit what and how. They examine every situation, asking for discernment, taking notes and then making necessary changes so they don't repeat past failures.

Failure is a servant if we view it with perspective. If perspective is added to failure, then failure becomes a learning experience, but without perspective, failure is failure. Fail once, call it learning. Fail twice, call it advanced learning. Fail three times, call it stupidity. From the third time and on, the power of the Holy Spirit should be able to perceive what needs to be done in order to turn the cycle of failure and change.

"My people are destroyed from the lack of knowledge." (Hosea 4:6) This verse is not speaking of a knowledge of the facts. The fact of the matter is we know more than we ever have. The knowledge the Lord speaks of has to do with perception. The people of God are destroyed due to a lack of spiritually perceiving the facts they know.

Pray: Ask God to make you a perceiver. Study the Word, seek to find its wisdom in relation to the situations in which you find yourself.

November 29th

SEED POWER

"The Kingdom of heaven is like a mustard seed . . . though it is like the smallest of all your seeds, yet when it grows, it is the largest of garden plants and becomes a tree . . . "

Matthew 13:31-32

God builds on the principle of the seed. Very seldom are we ever given anything in its mature or full grown state. The promises of God are given as seed. We receive the seed and sow what is given. As we are faithful to believe that God can cause that seed to grow, it becomes the very thing God had promised.

The Kingdom of God is built upon the smallest of all seeds. In the Kingdom of God, big results are predecated upon small seeds. The smallest seed of faith will produce the largest of results. Freedom from those habits that enslave us begin with the smallest seed of faith. Freedom begins with the seed of proclamation that cries, "I am free." Though it seems so small in comparison to the habit, there is incredible power contained in the seed.

Seed growth is not commensurate to the size of the seed. Seed growth is commensurate to the power of the life contained in the seed. Though the mustard seed is the smallest of all the seeds, with that seed God grows the largest of all the trees in the garden. Often we do not feel like the little seed we possess will ever become much. But the reality of that seed of promise becoming a tree is not predecated upon our feelings. The seed will become a tree because of the life contained within the seed. The power is in the seed, not the gardener. The power is in the dream, not the dreamer. It is the seed giver that possesses the power not the seed holder.

"Abraham believed God and it was credited to him as righteousness." (Romans 4:3) Our responsibility before God is to believe. We do not have the power to change, only to believe we can change. We do not have the power to change our spouse, children or friends, only to believe they can change. Ours is to sow the seed of faith; God's is to grow the seed. When that seed grows, it will become the largest of all plants in the garden.

November 30th

ACCUSATION OR APPEAL

"... to present you holy in His sight, without blemish and free from accusation."

Colossians 1:22

Satan is a deceiver and the primary avenue his deception follows is the avenue of accusation. Revelation 12:10 calls him the accuser of the brethren. This does not just describe what he does, it also describes who he is. By nature he is an accuser. Accusation is his way. Every working moment, whether it be day or night, he is before the throne of God making accusation.

It is in the face of this reality that Paul under the inspiration of the Holy Spirit says, "Oh, by the way, another result of Christ's physical death is you have been set free from all the accusations."

Our freedom is not an end in itself. We have been set free from accusation and that freedom serves a purpose. Primarily that purpose is God affects our relationship to God, and secondarily that purpose affects each other. If God does not bring us into accusation, then we should put away the pointing of the finger and stop accusing each other.

Accusation can be defined as words of truth or lie spoken in a manner designed to tear down and expose rather than edify and redeem. To walk a covenant relationship is to walk in relationships free from accusation. Covenantal behavior says, "If Jesus sets us free from accusation, we had better not enslave one another back into it."

In the place of accusation, covenantal behavior brings us into appeal. Galatians 6:1 says, *"If someone is caught in a sin you who are spiritual should restore him."* Covenantal behavior does not deny the fault, rather it sets the goal as restoration and redemption.

An appeal is designed to reveal the truth and redeem the person. An accusation is designed to conceal the truth and condemn the person. An accusation condemns in that it makes no room for discussion or clarification. It attacks and asks questions later. An accusation condemns in that, once the words are spoken, the death of the tongue is imparted.

Relational offense and wrong doing is inevitable. When offenses come we must exercise our will to stay on the covenant ground of appeal and seek to discern the truth so as to maintain the relationship.

CSRO

Pause for thought:

In what relational circumstances have you been acting out of accusation? How can you use appeal in resolving other people's personal issues?

December 1st

WE SOW—HE GROWS

"Now faith is being sure of what we hope for and certain of what we do not see."

Hebrews 11:1

The promises of God are yea and amen. But often standing between us and those promises is a mountain of unbelief. Our family way is the way of faith. We walk by faith believing not in the seen, but the unseen. Consequently, the focus of satanic attack is to sow seeds of unbelief. These seeds of unbelief come in questions and accusations of doubt. "Did God really say" . . . "Surely this doesn't apply to you" . . . "You will never win in this area."

The devil does not have the power of creation or original thought. All he has learned he has learned from God and then perverted its purpose. Just as God builds by the principle of the seed, so does the devil. He sows a seed of doubt, then systematically over time that seed produces a forest of unbelief, if left unattended.

But God has not left us defenseless. God does not get mad, He gets uneven. In the face of unbelief, He has given us the promise of hope (that's even). If that were not enough, He has also given us the words of faith that commands the removal of the mountain of unbelief (that's uneven). In the face of unbelief, hope gets us even and faith makes us uneven.

The walk of faith begins by our discerning the division of responsibilities. What is our responsibility before God and what is His? All too often we remain in unbelief, because we are trying to succeed in areas He has not given us the responsibility or faith to succeed in. Our responsibility before God is to believe. God's responsibility is to work. Abraham believed God and it was credited to him as righteousness. (Romans 4:3) Our responsibility is to believe God can move the mountain. His responsibility is to move it. Our responsibility is to sow the seed of faith. His responsibility is to grow the seed. We have not been given causative power, only sowing power. We can't cause anything to grow, only believe it can grow. We do not cause our spouses to grow, only believe they can. We don't cause our own freedom, only proclaim we are free. We don't cause our overcoming, only believe we are overcomers.

Our focus as believers is not one of working for what God has promised, but trusting and believing that He is able to complete that which He has begun in our lives.

December 2nd

GOD GETS UNEVEN

"To proclaim the day of vengeance of our God."

Isaiah 61:2

God does not get mad, He gets uneven. God's way of vengeance is quite different than man's way. Man sees vengeance in the sense of hostility and revenge, but God sees it in the sense of justice and mercy. God is love. Because God is love, He executes His vengeance from a position of righteousness, not anger. The result of God's vengeance is we are put in a superior position over our enemies. We are made to be uneven.

The focus of God's vengeance is positive action toward His people, not negative action toward His enemy. He executes His vengeance by setting His kids free, not hammering the devil. He could hammer the devil. He certainly has the power to do so. But what good would it do to hammer the devil and leave us in our various stages of oppression. God's way of vengeance is to get uneven by setting us free and in so doing thwarting the devil's plan to destroy us.

If the father of lies has been feeding us lies, Father does not demonstrate His vengeance by just giving us the truth and in so doing gets even. He then gets uneven by filling us with the joy of the Lord as well. In saving us, Father gets even. In filling us with the Holy Spirit, He gets uneven. In making us conquerors, He gets uneven. In empowering us to do what Jesus did, He gets even. By empowering us to do greater works than Jesus, He gets uneven.

God's heart for His people is not satisfied with just getting even. His heart is so toward us. He has given us the same power that raised Christ from the dead to take us beyond the place of even. We need not be satisfied with just getting by. We have all the power we need to be the overcomers He proclaimed us to be.

It is time we rise up out of unbelief and believe God's promise. His desire is to use us in the execution of His vengeance.

December 3rd

THE DAY OF DEATH

"... And the day of death better than the day of birth"
Ecclesiastes 7:1

The Kingdom of God is indeed a backwards Kingdom. In the kingdom of this world the focus of life is that which is seen. All this world has to offer is the here and the now, so its focus is that which you can touch. But life in the Kingdom of God is quite the opposite. The focus of the Kingdom of God is not limited to this time and space world, so its focus is not on that which is seen or that which is temporary. The Kingdom of God comes to enlarge our focus and train us to focus on that which is unseen and live for that which is eternal.

This is a truth that is dramatically illustrated in the reality of death. The Scriptures tell us that death is the destiny of every man. The question facing man is not will he die but how many times will he die. To die once is to spend eternity separated from God, our loving Father. To die twice, once spiritually and once physically, is to spend eternity in blessed fellowship with our Creator and Redeemer.

Society at large fears death. Because its focus is on the here and now, it fears the eventuality of the end. As christians it is easy for us to become culturized by the world's perspective of death and take on some of its habits of mourning.

Solomon puts death in its proper perspective. To view death from a biblical perspective is to see it as a time of promotion and celebration, not a time of mourning and despair. King David said it this way, *"Precious in the sight of the Lord is the death of His saints."* (Psalm 116:15) Precious in that to be absent from the body is to be present with Christ.

Our habits of mourning the dead are not consistent with what the Bible says about the death of His saints. We need to keep death in its proper perspective. Death for the Christian is not the end, but the beginning. Consequently, we can rejoice when a Christian passes away for they will be in the presence of the Lord.

December 4th

THE GARMENT OF PRAISE

"The garment of praise instead of the spirit of despair"
Isaiah 61:3

Ashes, mourning and despair are all the fruit of the world's philosophy. The longer this philosophy has to mature the more its evil fruit will become evident. The more evident it becomes, the greater is our opportunity to share in the midst of the darkness.

The Scriptures describe praise as a garment, whereas worship is a response that flows from within. Praise is a garment we put on from without. Praise is a decision, not an emotion. We praise regardless of how we feel. You do not have to feel praise. Praise is a garment you decide to put on. You decide to do it regardless of your feelings. In fact, the best time to put on the garment of praise is when you do not feel like praising. When you don't feel warm you put on your coat. Likewise, when you do not feel praise, you put on the garment of praise.

Some never feel praise because they never choose to engage praise when it is happening. Satisfied with spectating, they observe others praising but never do so themselves. To enter into praise you must make a decision to engage. You must decide to focus on the goodness of the Lord, sing, raise your hands, bow your knee, dance or whatever the posture of praise must be.

The result of that decision is worship. Whereas praise is a decision, worship is a response. As we decide praise, God releases worship. Praise is outer, worship is inner. Worship is that spirit of awe that issues forth from within. It comes as a result of God's action. Praise is initiating, worship is responding. Praise is causative, worship is responsive.

As we put on the garment of praise, God gets uneven with our enemies. As we put on the garment of praise, He releases the spirit of worship (that's even). As worship is released it drives away the spirit of despair (that's uneven).

December 5th

POSSESSION BY THE WAY OF PROCLAMATION

"The Spirit of the Sovereign Lord is on me because the Lord has anointed me to . . . proclaim the year of the Lord's favor."

Isaiah 61:1-2

The favor of the Lord begins by way of proclamation. Before God's favor is a possession, it is first a proclamation. The process of freedom begins with our rising up in boldness and proclaiming to our enemies, *"This is the year of the Lord's favor and today is the day of His vengeance."*

Some may think this level of boldness is presumptuous. But our boldness does not stem from our presumption, but from His promise. *"As surely as the earth brings forth its shoot and the garden causes what is sown to grow, surely the Lord will cause righteousness and justice and praise to spring forth."* (Isaiah 61:11)

Our proclamations do not cause the growth. We do not have the power to cause anything to spring forth. God alone possesses the power of growth. But even God can not cause to grow what has not been sown. The proclamation of freedom is simply the sowing of the seed, not the growth of the tree. The proclamation is sowing the seed of expectation so God has something to work with. We sow, He grows.

You might say, "My proclamation does not feel like freedom." It's not freedom. It is just a proclamation of freedom. Like the seed is not the tree, so the proclamation is not the freedom. But without sowing the seed, you will not get the tree. Often the accuser comes after our proclamation of freedom and says, "You fool, you're not free; proclaiming freedom does not make you free." If we listen to his accusation it may circumvent the process of freedom. Our response to his accusation should be, "You fool, I know my proclamation doesn't make me free, Jesus makes me free. My proclamation just sows a seed."

As we proclaim His freedom and favor we set a process into motion. If we do it long enough, it will produce the fruit of divine promise.

December 6th

UNGODLY BELIEFS

"... We take captive every thought and make it obedient to Christ"
II Corinthians 10:5

Presuppositions are the beliefs we hold in life (right or wrong) that form our foundations and determine our direction. These presuppositions become the grid work through which all of life, both in knowledge and in experience is interpreted. When these presuppositions are in harmony with truth, we prosper and walk in the freedom that God desires. When they aren't in harmony with the truth, that truth is rendered void of the inherent powers to set us free.

In John 8:32 Jesus said, *"You shall know the truth and the truth shall set you free."* But if that truth is processed through the grid work of ungodly beliefs, the truth is redefined and in the redefinition it is robbed of its power of freedom. The truth still contains the power, but the ungodly belief redefined the truth and made it to be something other than what it was.

If we hold an ungodly belief that God does not love us and is not for us, the truth of His heart toward us will be redefined to be for everyone else except us. We will believe intellectually that God is for us, but when we attempt to appropriate the truth our ungodly belief will redefine the truth of God's love to be for someone else.

If a wife's ungodly belief is that her husband does not love her, then the truth of his affection will be redefined and left void of effect. When he tells her how much he loves her, she will conclude, "You are just saying that." When he sends flowers to express his love, she will conclude, "You're just doing that because we have had a fight and you want peace." Every attempt of love will be redefined through the grid of ungodly belief.

Ungodly beliefs plague us in forgiveness, relationships, anger, trust. Before we can walk in the freedom of God's truth, we must first identify any ungodly belief we may be enslaved to. Once the ungodly belief is identified, it must be dislodged with the truth of God's Word. When we see the truth of God's Word up against the reality of our ungodly belief, we must make a deliberate choice to choose God's Word and take that ungodly belief captive.

December 7th

FREE FROM ACCUSATION

"But now he has reconciled you through Christ's physical body to present you holy in his sight, without blemish and free from accusation."

Colossians 1:22

The power of accusation is rooted in the fear of punishment if found guilty and convicted. Without the reality of consequence or punishment, accusation is merely empty words.

Satan is described as the accuser of the brethren. Day and night before the throne of God, he brings accusations against the sons and daughters of God. The power of the accusation is the lie. The lie is that his accusation carries with it consequences of punishment. Our fear is if he is right, God may get mad and punish us. The truth of the matter is, he may certainly be right in his accusation. To judge his accusation on factual information would be to determine it to be true. But, God has freed us from that accusation and the consequences of those facts.

Yes, it is true, we are sinners. Yes, it is true there is no one who is righteous. Yes, it's true, in me dwells no good thing. But in Christ, Father has declared me to be a new creation, has freed me from the consequences and punishment of those accusations. Consequently, the fear of punishment no longer exists so the power of accusation is broken.

The only power left in accusation is the power of deception. If the enemy can convince us that his accusations are still effective, then they accomplish his intent. The power of deception is broken through the knowledge of Christ. When we know that in Christ we have been declared free from accusation, then we no longer need be subject to the deception.

Our reconciliation is complete. It is a past tense work accomplished through the cross. Consequently we have been declared holy, without blemish and as a result, free from accusation. Next time the accuser comes, remind him of the truth.

December 8th

THE DEAD NEED NO DEFENSE

"Blessed are you when people insult you, persecute you and falsely say all kinds of evil against you because of Me."
                                                                Matthew 5:11

Accusations are perhaps the devil's number one strategy launched at the church today. Satan is the father of lies and accusation is the avenue these lies take in order to infiltrate the church. Through ignorance and neglect this avenue of accusation has become a super highway.

"But now He has reconciled you through Christ's physical body through death to present you . . . free from accusation." (Colossians 1:22)

Please note the Scriptures do not say Jesus released the accuser. Paul doesn't tell us the accusations will stop, but rather though they come day and night, we have been set free from them. Too much time is spent trying to defend our merit and the inaccuracy of the accusation. Fact is, it does not matter if the accusation is right or wrong, because we have been declared free from it regardless.

We are set free from accusation for one reason and one reason only and that is the completed work of Jesus Christ at Calvary. In Christ we die and a dead man need not worry or argue his defense. He is free from all accusations because he is dead and because he is dead the accusations have no merit.

The strategy of Christ's defense was not to argue the merit of our innocence before the accuser or somehow try to defend our inherent goodness. Fact is, He agreed with the accusations and perhaps added a few of His own. He then pleaded our guilt and personally served our sentence, thereby rendering the accusation null and void. The terms of the settlement did not call for the accusations to stop. But they do make full provision for all liability and punishment stemming from the accusation to be placed on Jesus.

Consequently, we can walk free knowing our lives are hid in Christ and those who are dead need not fear accusations whether they are based on truth or lies. In Christ we are dead and dead are free.

December 9th

DESTINY, NOT HISTORY

"However, I consider my life worth nothing to me, if only I may finish the race and complete the task the Lord Jesus has given me"
                                                                    Acts 20:24

Eternal destiny is a powerful force in the life of the believer. Once we are apprehended by God and get a glimpse of the eternal purpose He has for us, that purpose becomes our force of direction and enablement. Without a sense of eternal purpose, we have no road map for our lives, Yes, the Word of God is our only standard of faith and practice, but the Bible must be personally applied and from its pages we must discern the eternal destiny it has determined for our lives.

We must learn to evaluate our lives on the basis of destiny, not negative history. Destiny is our standard of evaluation, not negative history. When we use destiny as our standard, it forces us into a forward look, not a backward one. It brings us into the hope of our future, not the regrets of our past. When negative history is our judge, we live in constant regret. We are restrained by what could have been and what we should have done. It is important to learn from our history, but history does not carry the same power of motivation that destiny does. Destiny is a forward force. Destiny keeps us inspired and determined. It keeps us focused. Destiny keeps us ordering our priorities correctly. It prevents us from giving ourselves to temporal issues.

Each one of us has been given an eternal destiny. Just as we each have a unique personality, we have a unique destiny. We are a people who have been apprehended for a purpose. *"I press on to take hold of that for which Christ Jesus took hold of me."* (Philippians 3:12) What is the "that" for which you were taken hold of? When a person gets a clear glimpse of their "that," destiny becomes the judge, not history. They become driven by the forward look, not the rear view mirror.

If you have yet to apprehend your "that," pray for enlightenment. Pray that God would give you understanding into your eternal purpose and unique destiny.

০৪৪০

December 10th

THE RUMBLINGS OF EMANCIPATION

"Remember the height from which you have fallen. Repent and do the things you did at first."

Revelation 2:5

The prize is held not for those who begin the race, but for those who finish. The crown in the Kingdom is held for those who persevere to the end. Such is the case in the stewardship of truth and the way in which our heavenly Father has called us to walk. It is not the possessing of this truth that wins us the prize, it is the finishing of that truth.

"Watch out that you do not lose what you have worked for, but that you may be rewarded fully. Anyone who runs ahead and does not continue in the teaching of Christ does not have God." (II John 8-9) Father has given to each of us a particular way to follow, particular distinctives that form our identity and define our way. Our reward is predicated upon our continuing in His way and not forsaking it for an alternative.

This is a phenomenon in the physical family that illustrates the problem of an aborted way. A family is defined in the bans of its name and unique identity. As the children grow, they are trained by that identity and equipped to represent it. As they enter the late teen and early adult years, all they were trained in comes under evaluation and attack. Those rooted in the value of family heritage sink their root down and own the way for themselves. Those whose root has never been planted opt for a different way and forsake their God given heritage.

The spiritual family faces a similar phenomenon. The sovereignty of God gives a spiritual family a particular identity. Over the years, the members of that family are trained and equipped to represent that way. There comes a time in that family's journey when its members begin to evaluate and challenge the family way. Those rooted in family take ownership of the way. Those who aren't rooted opt for an alternative way and justify their decision with all the short comings of the family way.

Destiny is a pre-ordained condition ordained by God. Fulfillment is tied to our ability to preserve that pre-determined way and not choose a man-made alternative. Are you being tempted by the rumblings of emancipation? Your reward is tied to your ability to continue in the teaching Christ has given you. Do not opt for an alternative. Continue in this way.

December 11th

WORLD VIEW

"I pray also that the eyes of your heart may be enlightened"
Ephesians 1:18

The ability to see is a gift. The ability to see correctly is a treasure. Seeing correctly is seeing from the perspective of the One who is truth. What the person sees from the eyes of their heart defines their world view. A person's world view is the grid through which they view life. It is the perspective a person holds through which all of life is filtered. World view consists of those certain things we believe before we believe anything else.

Consequently, if our world view is off, everything that follows will be off too. If the primary things we believe are wrong, then the secondary things that follow will be wrong as well.

Nobody starts their pursuit of truth with an empty palette of perspective. We start with certain presuppositions that color our palette. If your palette perspective is yellow and someone comes speaking blue, you will hear green. But if my palette perspective is red and someone comes speaking that exact blue, I will hear purple. Same truth, different world views, consequently different conclusions.

World view is what we have on our palette of truth. Relative truth or cultural truth are both partial, not primary. Consequently, they will not mix with primary truth and maintain its purity. If you bring the primary truth of the Gospel through a relative or cultural grid, it will not mix. The Gospel is primary and absolute. Therefore, it will mix with or apply to whatever you bring through its grid. Biblical truth on relationships will mix with marriage, friendship, parenting, or whatever relationship you search out.

What shapes your world view? Is the basis of your world view partial or absolute, cultural or biblical? The Word of God is our only standard for faith and practice. Allow its absolute nature to shape your world view.

☙❧

December 12th

FOCUSED ON THE UNSEEN

"So we fix our eyes not on what is seen, but on what is unseen. For what is seen is temporary, but what is unseen is eternal"
II Corinthians 4:18

A famous comedian of the early '70s coined a phrase that became quite popular in its day. This character's famous line was: "What you see is what you get." Though intended to be funny, this phrase is quite prophetic, for in the Kingdom of God, what you see is what you get. More accurately stated, what you focus on determines what you get.

As Abraham's children, we have been called to a walk of faith. The faith walk is a walk of purposeful focus. To walk by faith is to walk with our eyes fixed on what is unseen, rather than only trusting in what our eyes see. The natural man trusts only in what is seen. His perspective and outlook on life are determined by what he is able to discern by what his natural eyes see. If he is able to see his way by virtue of the right circumstances and opportunities, he decides his way accordingly.

But it is not so with the spiritual man. The spiritual man does not base his decisions by what he is able to see with his natural eyes. Though he is grateful when the natural circumstances confirm his decision, they are not the bases of that decision. The spiritual man walks by faith, not by sight. His hope is in the unseen, not the seen. No one hopes for what he already sees. Once we see what we've hoped for, we no longer need hope, for we have the evidence of what we've hoped for; consequently, the hope has become faith. Hope is not for what is seen, but for what is still unseen. Hope's focus is the promises yet to come. Hope's focus is the dream yet to be realized. Hope's focus is the prodigal who has yet to return, the loved one who has yet to repent, the sick who have yet to be healed. Hope is for all those things promised and yet to come.

The hope walk is a walk of focus and perspective. To focus on the seen is to possess the temporary. Though we may obtain it, it soon passes away. To focus on the unseen is to focus on the eternal. Though it may take longer to obtain and though we may be severely tested in the process, once it is ours, it never passes away, for hope's focus is the eternal.

Where does your focus line up? Are you focused on the seen or the unseen? Is your perspective and outlook shaped by only those things you see or do you have enough hope running through you to fix your focus on those things that are unseen?

What you see is what you get. So, determine to see with the eyes of your spirit and in so doing, see the unseen and build upon the eternal.

෴

Pause for thought:

Are you focused on the seen or the unseen? Is your perspective and outlook shaped by only those things you see or do you have enough hope running through you to fix your focus on those things that are unseen?

December 13th

NEW BEGINNINGS

"In the beginning God"

Genesis 1:1

The first four words of the Bible are *"In the beginning God."* These not only record the Bible's first four words, they also make a statement concerning the nature of God. God is a God of new beginnings. He is rooted to the past, He builds for the future, but is always present to declare a new beginning. God does not just create, He is creation. To be in the presence of God is to be in the presence of new beginnings.

Abraham, Moses, David, Peter and Paul all were granted a new beginning. Whether it was lying, murder, adultery or denial, all were forgiven and granted a fresh start. Cain slew his brother, Abel, and judgment was passed on Cain. God cursed Cain and sentenced him to become a restless wanderer. But in the judgment of God, there was the provision for a new beginning. We read that Cain gave birth to a son named Enoch. Enoch walked with God for 300 years and then as the Scriptures say, *"He was no more because God took him away."* (Genesis 5:24) From a cursed, restless wanderer to being transformed into the very presence of God in one generation, that is a new beginning.

Perhaps the greatest testimony of God's heart for new beginnings is the resurrection of Jesus Christ. Imagine how the disciples felt the day following the crucifixion. Imagine the darkness of despair that gripped their hearts. Out of that despair of darkness, Peter denies the Lord three times, and what was already black suddenly got even darker. Little did the disciples know that their darkest day was but the eve of a new beginning. In the midst of their darkness, the sovereignty of God was working and the resurrection of Jesus Christ was just about to shine in their darkness and declare an eternity of new beginnings. The resurrection of Jesus Christ serves to constantly remind us that, regardless of our circumstances, we must always make room for the sovereignty of God. If we stay *"in Christ"* in our attitudes, our trust and in our expectations, there will be a new beginning.

What circumstances does life have you in? Whether it be the circumstances of bad choices, a hurtful past or a victimizing relationship, today can be a day of new beginnings for you. *"If anyone be in Christ, he is a new creation; old things pass away and all things become new."* (II Corinthians 5:17) Regardless of your situation, the sovereignty of God can declare for you a new beginning.

Allow the resurrection hope of Jesus Christ to be imparted to you today. Take that hope as a gift of Father's love and His desire for you to find Him in the beginning.

ଓଓ

Pause for thought:

What circumstances in your life are you ready for a new beginning in?

December 14th

THE SPIRIT OF ELIJAH

"And he will go on before the Lord in the spirit and power of Elijah, to turn the hearts of the fathers to their children..."

Luke 1:17

It was prophesied by Gabriel that John the Baptist would go in the Spirit of Elijah. Just what is the spirit of Elijah? It may have been easier to understand if the angel of the Lord said Elijah himself would come, but what does it mean to go on in the spirit of Elijah? Though the Scriptures do not give us an exact description, I would suggest to you that the spirit of Elijah is the spirit of Fatherhood that seeks after the hearts of Father's children. The heart is the focus of both Gabriel's announcement and the prophetic announcement that Gabriel quotes in Malachi 4. The Holy Spirit comes to us in search of our hearts.

The curse of our day is the curse of, "withheld hearts." Our churches are full of people who will give their money, give their time, some will even give to the point of sacrifice, and yet in all their giving they will withhold their hearts. The longer I am involved with discipleship and the deeper I go into the process, the more I am convinced that the issue is the heart. If fathers are unwillingly to give their hearts and sons are unwilling to receive a heart given, the fruit of discipleship will never be produced. This is why Malachi and Gabriel came prophesying to the heart of man.

The spirit of Elijah is a heart given. The spirit of Elisha is a heart turned. Elisha willingly turned his heart to his spiritual father, Elijah. The mutual turning of their hearts resulted in a double portion anointing being released on Elisha. The double portion anointing requires both a donor and recipient. It requires fathers who are willing to give their hearts to their sons and sons who are willing to turn their hearts to their fathers and receive the heart given. The curse of our day is the inability to give one's heart or the unwillingness to receive a heart that has been given. To receive a father's heart is the willingness to receive the leadership of another and carry the vision God has given that individual. To carry their heart is to allow the deposit of God in them to be deposited to you.

Why has the church lost its voice and become so ineffective over the years? Could it be because we have not seen or believed the importance of the spirit of Elijah being released in the church today? Look what happened to Zechariah when he did not receive the word concerning John coming in the spirit and power of Elijah. Perhaps the silence of the church today is due to the unwillingness of sons to carry the hearts of the fathers and the fathers to impart their hearts to their sons.

※

Pause for thought:

Are you willing to carry the heart of another? Are you willing to see the purposes of God as expressed in another and ask God to release a portion of their spirit into you that you might function in that double portion anointing?

December 15th

ELIJAH'S GREATEST MIRACLE

"Tell me what I can do for you before I am taken from you?" "Let me inherit a double portion of your spirit, Elisha replied."

II Kings 2:9

Have you ever stopped to consider what Elijah's greatest miracle was? Let us face it. This guy was used of the Lord to do some pretty amazing things; three years of drought, calling fire down from heaven, raising the widow's son from the dead and the show down at Mount Carmel. All of these and the rest were truly extraordinary events. But, as amazing as they were, I would suggest that none of them were the greatest of Elijah's miracles. Elijah's greatest miracles was his spiritual son, Elisha, for after Elijah was taken up to heaven in the whirlwind, the double portion of his spirit gave way for Elisha to do twice the amount of miracles that Elijah did.

Elijah was used of the Lord to perform fourteen miracles. Elisha was used of the Lord to perform twenty-eight. The amazing thing is many of the miracles were exactly the same, both in method and outcome. Both struck the water and it parted. Both brought water in times of drought. Both increased a widow's supply of food. Both raised sons from the dead. The raising of the widow's son did have one unique difference for Elisha. Elijah was instructed to stretch himself on upon the boy three times. The boy's life returned in the third time. Elisha was given the same instruction of stretching himself out upon the body mouth to mouth, eyes to eyes and hands to hands. The unique difference with Elisha is the boy's life returned to him on the second try. Elisha carried with him a double portion of Elijah's spirit. I am convinced the boy's life returned after 1 1/2 times. With the double portion of Elijah's spirit, Elisha was able to do what Elijah did with one half the effort, but how do you lay on someone one half time?

Elisha was used of God to perform 28 amazing miracles. Through his ministry lepers were healed, entire armies were defeated and multitudes were fed with a few loaves of bread. After receiving the double portion of Elijah's spirit, Elisha was used to part waters and raise the dead. As amazing as these miracles were, Elisha would have lived and died pushing a plough if it were not for the father's heart of Elijah. Elijah's willingness to invest in a son enabled the ministry God had given him to continue giving, even after he was dead.

To invest in the generation to come is to invest in a gift that keeps on giving. If fathers will take the time to invest in sons, long after they are dead and gone, that father's gift will keep on giving to the generations who will follow after. Elijah's greatest miracle was Elisha. Long after Elijah was taken up into heaven, he continued to part the waters, raise the dead and feed the widows. No he did not do it himself, he did it through his spiritual son Elisha.

So it is with us. We may not change the world in our life time. But perhaps our investment in a spiritual son or daughter will change their world. Perhaps it will be the changing of their world that brings about the spiritual revolution we desire. Let us never underestimate the power of investing in the life of another. Our greatest miracle may be in that son or daughter we now train.

൝

December 16th

THAT THEY MAY BE ONE

"That all of them may be one, Father, just as you are in me and I am in you. May they also be in us so that the world may believe that you have sent Me"

John 17:21

Just how important is the unity of the believers? Is the unity of the church simply a popular teaching or could it be one of the single most important factors facing the body of Christ today?

So much is said today concerning the prophetic events that must take place before Christ returns. Much debate has taken place in regard to the temple in Jerusalem. It has been argued for years as to whether it must be rebuilt and if so, where it must be rebuilt. Prophecy in relationship to Christ's return has captivated the mind of the believer for centuries.

While all of these arguments are important, the most obvious prophetic fulfillment before the church today is the prophetic prayer of John 17, *"that they may be one."* This priestly prayer of unity is not just a popular teaching that makes for a good conference topic. The unity of believers was a direct prayer request of our Lord Jesus. Could God pray a prayer that can not be answered?

It has often been said that expectation determines outcome. Perhaps the sad outcome of Christ's prayer is due to the fact that the church has not expected the prayer to be answered. How easy it is to read this prayer with a robust "amen" but not stop long enough to recognize our personal responsibility in seeing this prayer realized.

If Jesus Christ were to return without this prayer of unity being answered, Satan would have an accusation of unanswered prayer against Him. Satan's accusation would say, "Jesus was strong enough to redeem them, but He does not have the power to unite them." For 2,000 years this accusation has stood. It is time for the church to rise up in answer to Christ's prayer and make every effort to preserve the unity purchased for us at Calvary.

Once we resolve the expectation of unity, we must discern the basis of that unity. Throughout time the church has tried to base its unity on many factors. For some, the basis of our unity has been common experience. Those with a common experience have rallied together only to see them experience change over time, and with the change, their basis of unity erodes as well. Others have come together around a common personality; it has been a gifted leader that has brought a group of people together. But, as with experiences, leaders come and they go. Our unity will breakdown if it is based in that common personality. The same could be said about common doctrine or even common vision. The only solid basis for unity is the reality of our common parentage. Members of the body of Christ are already one on the basis of common parentage. There is only one Father. Every member of the redeemed family of God has one Father. It is the fact that we are all members of the same family, with the same Father, that makes us one. When this hits us by way of revelation, every other issue like experience, vision, doctrine, etc., all pale in significance.

Not only does our unity give the world reason to believe, it also answers the prayer of John 17 and opens the way for Christ's return. Let us make every effort to preserve that unity and hasten His return.

꿇

December 17th

THE WONDER OF REDEMPTION

"Praise be to the Lord who this day has not left you without a kinsman redeemer"

Ruth 4:14

The book of Ruth opens with five funerals and closes with a wedding. It opens with the reality of famine and death but closes with the celebration of restoration and romance. Not all of life's stories have these kind of ending, but chapter four of Ruth serves to remind us that regardless of the focus in previous chapters of life, God always writes the last. The Christian need not fear the future or be anxious of tomorrow for our lives are hid in His sovereign care.

How can we as Christians live in such confident optimism? We face the future from a perspective of hope because of the redemptive power of God. Praise be to God for He has not left us without a Kinsman redeemer.

Old Testament law made provision for what was called the Kinsman redeemer. The Kinsman redeemer was an individuals' next of kin who held the responsibility before God to marry a dead brothers widow in order to preserve the family name, redeem a family member from slavery, redeem land that stood the risk of sale by foreclosure and exact vengeance against a murderer of a family member.

Jesus Christ is our Kinsman redeemer. He gave Himself to us in order that He might redeem us from all wickedness and purify for Himself a people that are His very own. (Titus 2:14)

Redemption is the act of setting free by payment of a price. To redeem someone is to release them by paying the ransom. It is to repurchase what has been previously sold. Though we sold ourselves into sin, Jesus Christ repurchased us by His blood and in so doing He liberated us from any obligation to the sin nature. Whatever our circumstance, whatever our situation, whether it be of an eternal consequence or of an immediate one, the power of God is able to redeem our lives and buy back what may have been lost.

Have you lost ground in the spirit? Are you losing ground in discipline and resolve? Have you lost the spiritual passion you desire? In Christ you have a Kinsman redeemer. In Christ, you have one with the power to buy back what has been lost. He is able to repurchase what was once owned and forfeited by our neglect. No, you do not deserve to get it back, but you did not deserve to own it before it was forfeited.

The wonder of redemption is clearly seen in God's desire to repurchase those practices that were once ours but forfeited through neglect. Do not argue with redemption, just receive it.

ॐ

Pause for thought:

Have you lost ground in the spirit? Are you losing ground in discipline and resolve? Have you lost the spiritual passion you desire? Are you ready to receive His redemption?

December 18th

GOD OF THE IMPOSSIBLE

"For nothing is impossible with God"

Luke 1:37

Christmas brings with it the good news that nothing is impossible with God. The birth of Jesus was surrounded by impossible situations, yet God overcame them all. A virgin was to give birth to a son. Jesus was to survive the unmerciful slaughter of every boy child under two. Jesus was born into the impossible and lives to illustrate the fact that with God, nothing is impossible.

As we celebrate the season, we tend to be distracted from reality. Soon, the cheer of the season wears off and the impossible situations begin to overshadow our thoughts once again. It is in the face of these impossible situations that we ask, as Mary did, "How, how will these things be?"

In Gabriel's answer to Mary, we find our hope as well. *"The Holy Spirit will come upon you and the power of the Most High will overshadow you."* (Luke 1:34) What an exchange. Instead of being overshadowed by impossible situations, we can be overshadowed by the power of the Most High God.

What are the impossible situations you face this holiday season? Are you facing the impossible in your marriage? Has it been impossible with the children? Maybe you are up against the impossible, financially? Is what you are facing more impossible than a virgin giving birth to the Messiah? Whatever your impossibility is, hear the Word of the Lord, *"Nothing is impossible with God, for the Holy Spirit will come upon you and the power of the Most High will overshadow you."*

God is the same yesterday, today and forever. Why not trust His miracle working power for your impossible situation. It worked for Mary and it will work for you, too.

December 19th

MAKING ROOM

"While they were there, the time came for the baby to be born, and she gave birth to her firstborn, a son. She wrapped him in cloth and placed him in a manger, because there was no room for them in the inn"

Luke 2:6-7

No room for Him in the inn. Perhaps the manger and its less than desirable surroundings was not His first place of choice, but it was the only place that would have Him. You see, for various reasons, the place of sophistication and charm, had no room for Him. Maybe they were too dirty from their travels. Perhaps their appearance was below the grade of their regular clientele. After all, what would the guests say if "they" were allowed to stay?

"No room for Him in the inn." Do we have room for Him today? Before you answer that traditional Christmas question with a resounding yes, let me present it from a different angle.

If those Christ sends to us come dirty from their travels, will we make room for them and give them a place to stay? When the appearance of those who are sent are undeniably below the norm, will we without reservation, open our hearts and give them room? When they come and leave behind the hay and droppings of their stable, will we graciously welcome them back?

Though our goal will be to call them into obedience to God's Word, we must never greet them at our doors with unrealistic expectations. Our choice must be to make room for those who are dirty from travel and need Jesus to get cleaned up. I am glad there was room for me, and there will be room for others.

December 20th

THE WAITING GAME

"So do not throw away your confidence; it will be richly rewarded. You need to persevere so that when you have done the will of God, you will receive what he has promised"

Hebrews 10:35

Often the Christian walk is a waiting game. In this walk, progress is not dependent upon human ingenuity. Madison Avenue techniques will produce a form of success, but in the long run they will come up short of God's righteous desire. To succeed in the Kingdom of God, we must learn to wait. We must wait upon the working of the Holy Spirit. As the Holy Spirit moves, we move. Where the Holy Spirit is working, we work. What the Holy Spirit is saying, we say. Until He does it, we wait.

During the waiting period, we can easily lose our confidence. As we wait, the Holy Spirit is often silent. His silence is producing in us greater levels of dependency and trust. His silence is weeding from us attitudes of personal ambition and wrongful motives. But in that silent period, we can also throw away our confidence if we do not keep the proper focus. If, during the waiting period, we turn self reflective, our focus is taken off Jesus and is turned to self. Self is a confidence thief. Once our focus is turned to ourselves, we fall into the deadly game of comparison. We begin to compare ourselves to others. We compare their accomplishments to our own. We compare their gifts to ours. We measure our stature to those who are our peers in the Lord. Comparison is an evil taskmaster. It is a carnal exercise of no redeeming value. Comparison will either error on the side of pride or it will error on the side of insecurity. Pride robs us of God's assistance and insecurity robs us of His confidence.

"Each one should test his own actions. Then he can take pride in himself without comparing himself to someone else." (Galatians 6:4) Jesus Christ and His will is our only standard of comparison. As we compare ourselves to Him and His will, He supplies the grace to become and the patience to wait. You will never measure up to others, but you can become like Christ. Christ is our confidence and Christ in you, your hope of glory.

December 21st

SHADOW OR SUBSTANCE

"Don't let anyone judge you by what you eat or drink or with regard to a religious festival, a New Moon celebration or a Sabbath day. These are a shadow of the things that were to come; the reality, however, is found in Christ"

Colossians 2:16-17

Two thousand years later and mankind is still consumed with shadows and suspect of substance. Man will travel miles in search of a shadow, all the while denying the very substance he has known all his life. Jesus Christ could not possibly be the substance, he reasons; that would be too simple and in fact a bit foolish. But God has chosen the foolish things of this world to confound the wise. He takes great delight in shrouding truth and foolishness in order that He might reveal the wisdom of His plan.

Paul's focus to the Colossians was the fullness of Jesus Christ. He was writing to establish the fact that Jesus was the fullness of God in bodily form and He gave His life as a ransom for us that we might be given that same fullness. Having argued his case for Christ's fullness, Paul contrasts Jesus to the emptiness of ritualism, legalism, mysticism and ceremonialism. He argues that all of these were mere shadows of what was to come, but the substance of what they pointed to was the person of Jesus Christ.

Deception has changed little in the past two thousand years. A quick glance at contemporary man tells us he is still consumed with the shadow. The religious man is consumed with ritualism, legalism and ceremonialism. Humanism is full of new age mysticism and discreet pantheism. Currently we are even seeing a resurgence of angelic icons. Man, outside of Christ, is trapped in the same patterns trying to fill up his emptiness. But none of these shadows are capable of adding one ounce to the emptiness we experience outside of Christ.

Jesus Christ is the fullness that fills our emptiness. Security will not fill us. Peace will not fill us; neither will property, purpose or belonging. Outside of Christ, these are but shadows that point us to the fullness. In Christ we find the fullness of them all condensed into one person.

December 22nd

CONTROLLED BY CIRCUMTANCES OR DIRECTED BY DESTINY

"All of this took place to fulfill what the Lord said through the prophet: 'The virgin will be with child and will give birth to a son, and they will call him Immanuel,' which means, God with us'"

Matthew 1:22-23

Perspective makes an amazing difference. Two people can experience the exact same circumstance and come away with opposite results, all because of perspective.

"All of this took place to fulfill what the Lord said through the prophet." The events surrounding the birth of Christ were quite extraordinary. A young woman who had never slept with a man was pregnant. A young man who had led a devout life was now engaged to a pregnant woman and was being led around the countryside by dreams and angelic appearances. From the natural eye, Joseph's life was being controlled by a set of unfortunate circumstances, but from the spiritual eye, Joseph was being sovereignly directed through every circumstance by the prophetic desire of God.

The degree to which we will fulfill our divine destiny is largely predicated upon the perspective we carry concerning God's sovereignty over the circumstances of life. Mary's pregnancy, Joseph's journey and Herod's killing of the male children were all a must to fulfill God's prophetic plan. Through every circumstance and misfortune, God directed Joseph and Mary as a symphony conductor directs his orchestra. With His watching and caring eye, God directed their lives through every step so as to fulfill what was spoken by the prophets in times past.

As God's prophetic desire unfolds, there are times when we do not understand His ways. As it was with Mary, when she heard of God's desire through Gabriel, we are presented with a choice. The choice is either to panic at the uncertainty or ponder over God's sovereignty. As Mary pondered over God's desire and willingly surrendered to the plan, all that was spoken through the prophets was fulfilled.

God has similar plans for His people today. These plans will certainly include trials and circumstances beyond our comprehension. But as they come, we must embrace them as did Mary: *"I am the Lord's servant; may it be to me as you have said."*

December 23rd

THE THRONE OF GOD

"For unto us a child is born and unto us a son is given and the government shall be upon His shoulders... Of the increase of His government and peace there will be no end. He will reign on King David's throne"

Isaiah 9:6-7

What is a king without a throne? What is a kingdom without a domain? The throne has always been central to the intent of God in the midst of mankind. The Magi came asking, "Where is the One born King?" Jesus was unique in that He was born King. No one died and made Him King. He was King by nature. He was the very definition of King. He was King by virtue of who He was, not because of what He did. His coming announced the end of all self appointed kings and man centered kingdoms.

The throne of God is now found in the hearts of man. The human will is His domain... our choices over which He reigns. The fullness of our salvation is found in direct relationship to the throne of God *"of the increase of His government there shall be no end."* The throne of God is now defined by increasing degrees of expression and practical outworking in our every day choices. As His throne increases in our life, we find ourselves making choices that promote God's way, even if it means death to ours. Our free time becomes His, our thoughts become focused on Him, our actions change, our behavior no longer is the same.

Peace and government come together. As the Christ of Christmas rules in your heart, you can expect peace.

December 24th

NOTHING AS USUAL

"She gave birth to her first born, a son. She wrapped him in clothes and placed him in a manger, because there was no room for them in the inn"

Luke 2:7

No, there was nothing unusual in Christ's coming. He did not come in the fanfare due a king. He did not come in the splendor or majesty one might expect. Though there was nothing unusual in His coming, there was nothing usual once he came. Not only did the coming of Jesus Christ split time from B.C. to A.D., not only did He revolutionize the known world, but Jesus Christ also birthed a culture that for 2,000 years has reshaped every known barrier of race, circumstance or man-made distinction.

According to Isaiah 9, the coming of Jesus Christ established a new governmental system. This govenmental system was a Kingdom that would dwell in the hand of God, not in the will of man. The coming of that Kingdom created a culture that is established as a law base distinct from the law base of man. The Bible creates its own culture and it becomes the new law base for the society to follow. Though this new culture provides for the various distinctions of race, time and geography, the law base of the culture remains the same. Sin is sin no matter what color we are. Love is the language of our culture whether we live in Africa, America, Asia or wherever. Mercy, forgiveness, obedience, worship, sacrifice, prayer—these and many others are all cultural practices regardless of our circumstancial placement, because they are Kingdom absolutes.

What have you allowed to be the primary shaper of your culture? Is it your circumstances? Is it your ethnic placement? Is it your time and geography of birth, or have you allowed the law base of Christ's Kingdom to be your cultural architect and the shaper of your destiny and practice?

ଓଃ୫ଠ

December 25th

HIMPOSSIBLE

"For nothing is impossible with God"

Luke 1:27

It does not matter how you look at the birth of Christ, it was surrounded with impossibilities. There was the certain impossibility of a virgin, named Mary, giving birth to a son who would be the Son of the Most High. There was the impossibility of Joseph having to deal with the relational and social implications of Mary's pregnancy out of wedlock. Couple that with the supernatural guidance of angels and prophetic dreams, both Mary and Joseph were confronted with great impossibilities.

Have you ever considered the impossibility of Gabriel's mission? Imagine getting that assignment: "Gabriel, I want you to go to Nazareth. There you will find a virgin, named Mary. I want you to tell her she is pregnant and she will give birth to a son. By the way, tell her that her son will be God!" Sure, Gabriel was an archangel, but it was still an impossible assignment. When he greets Mary, he seems to have a little difficulty telling her. Rather than just saying it, he greets her with an anesthetic, *"Greetings, you who are highly favored of the Lord."* (Luke 1:28) Even Mary knew something was up with this greeting. An angel is standing before her telling her God really likes her. Mary's response to this greeting was, *"Mary was greatly troubled at his words and wondered what kind of greeting this might be."* (Luke 1:29) Gabriel answers Mary's bewildered look by telling her again she was favored by God and she was going to give birth to a son and she was to name her son, Jesus.

What makes this story so impossible was Mary's impossible response to Gabriel's news. Upon hearing this eternity-changing news, Mary simply responded, *"May it be to me as you have said."* (Luke 1:38) If an angel appeared to you and said you were pregnant with the Son of God, would your response be, *"May it be as you have said?"*

In Mary's response, we discover the answer to impossible situations. The answer to impossibilities is self-surrender. Our way through impossibilities begins as we surrender ourselves to the will of God. Gabriel declared to Mary, *"For nothing is impossible with God."* Without God, nothing is possible. That is, we may do a lot, but it all amounts to nothing.

Though the circumstances we face in life may be impossible, in Christ they are "Himpossible." When a life is surrendered to and yielded over to Christ, everything becomes "Himpossible." This is the assurance we have because we know it is He who is directing our lives and making provision every step of the way.

Mary, Joseph and Gabriel all discovered that it was just as God had spoken. With Him, nothing was impossible for them. With Him, nothing—not even *your* thing, will be impossible.

☙❧

December 26th

ABOVE ALL

"The end of all things is near. Therefore be clear minded and self controlled so that you can pray. Above all..."

1 Peter 4:7-8

Here is the apostle Peter's opportunity to underscore his list of final responsibilities. With the end of all things in view, Peter is urged of the Holy Spirit to define an end time priority list.

"Above all," Peter says, *"love each other."* Of all the issues that warrant responsibility in the final days, love supercedes them all. Above everything else we are to love, because love covers a multitude of sins. The exhortation to love presupposes that in the final days there will be much sin to cover. Relational sin comes as no great surprise to the child of God. The possibility of being hurt relationally is very high in the body of Christ. The Holy Spirit's answer to that hurt is love. Love covers a multitude of sins, including relational sins. Love covers betrayal. Love covers abandonment. Love covers misunderstanding. Love, true God-given love, will cover an offense and not demand justice for oneself or vengeance for the wrong doer.

It is in the face of relational wrongdoing that we discover how selfless we really are. In the midst of relational harmony anyone can be selfless. It's when one has been unfairly treated or maligned, that we discover their depth of selflessness. Selflessness will love in the face of betrayal. In the face of misunderstanding, selflessness will seek to understand, not to be understood. Because love is selfless, it will not seek retaliation or revenge. For the sake of God's purposes on this earth, love will yield all selfish desire to the cross and seek only God's highest in the situation.

Such love exists only in the shadow of the cross. As long as one's focus is self, he will never love with a covering type of love. Love that covers is found only at the foot of the cross. It is found at the place where we die to any need of self-absorption and yield all hurt to Jesus. A view to the cross is the means by which this love is supplied. As we keep our eyes on the cross, seeking the purposes of God higher than our own, a fresh and constant supply of love is released enabling us to cover whatever wrongdoing we may face. A focus on self will only keep us enslaved to the offense and forever subject to the one who may have offended us.

Are there issues in your life that need to be covered? Are there people who have you trapped or circumstances that have you enslaved? Love is your answer. Love will provide the necessary covering enabling you to get free from the person and out from under the situation. The end of all things is near. Therefore, above all else, love. Love those who have wronged you and in order that you might remain free and fulfill the heart desire of God.

○✧○

Pause for thought:

Are there issues in your life that need to be covered? Are there people who have you trapped or circumstances that have you enslaved? How will you love in these circumstances?

December 27th

THE NEED FOR PENETRATION

"The harvest is plentiful, but the workers are few. Ask the Lord of the harvest, therefore, to send out workers into his harvest field"

Luke 10:2

To be sent into the harvest field is to be sent into the harvest field. You can not be sent into something and at the same time remain far from it. To be sent into the world is to penetrate it. It means to go beneath the facade and pierce the walls of isolation and self-protection. To bring forth the fruit of salvation, we must penetrate the surface and reach down to where the seed of the Gospel can take root. Seed, even if it is good seed that remains on the surface and never penetrates the soil, will eventually die. At best, seed that never penetrates the surface remains dormant and never fulfills its created purpose. To live and produce the fruit within, the seed must penetrate the soil and take root. Jesus told us in Matthew 13 that sons of the Kingdom are the good seed. This is why He commanded us to pray for the Lord to send the workers into the harvest. The good seed must go into the soil and take root.

Have you ever noticed how easy it is to remain perimeter people? It is so easy to pass through life and never press beneath the surface. As I was in the gym the other day, working out with my head phones on, the Lord showed me how that was a picture of the spiritual attitude many of us carry. We pass through life with the head phones blaring as if to say, "I'm busy with my own thing, so don't bother me." Consequently, people do not feel the freedom to ask us about our faith because we communicate, "I'm not available."

To impact life, we must penetrate it. To change the world, we must get into it. The Great Commission is a call to engage the people of this world. Without engagement on a personal level, Jesus will remain just a concept if we do not penetrate the facade and engage people wherever they are.

In Acts 1, Jesus commissions the disciples with power, then sends them into Jerusalem, Judea, Samaria and to the uttermost parts of the world. By Acts 8, the disciples had become stuck and their call to penetrate was anything but that. So the Lord had to send a persecution to unstick them so they would once again penetrate the society to whom they had been sent. It is not that the disciples were not doing anything; it is just that most of what they were doing was being done for themselves, and they had forgotten their original commission to penetrate the facades of the lost and be a witness to the saving grace of the Lord Jesus.

Pause for thought:

Are you a perimeter people, or have you pierced the facade and allowed the Holy Spirit to use you in penetrating what you never have before?

December 28th

POWER THROUGH ANTICIPATION

"Those who hope in me will never be disappointed"
Isaiah 49:23

Have you ever stopped to think of the latent power in anticipating God? The power of anticipation can be a driving force. When a people's anticipation is high, faith is released and the entire outcome can be altered. I have often wondered when a special speaker comes to town or a special meeting is held, why is the worship so much better? Why are the people more eager and ready to immediately enter into the presence of God? The reason is simple. It is the power of anticipation. For weeks they have been anticipating God to move in the meeting. They have taken in all that has been said to promote it and now finally the time has arrived. So with great anticipation, they come and when the anticipation in God is released, the power is released as well.

Anticipation is defined as a prior action that takes into account later action, the act of looking forward to, the visualization of a future event. There is power in anticipation because anticipation is a seed that directly influences a future response. The lack of anticipation provides for nothing, but the presence of anticipation is like a burst of faith that lifts us to a high level and opens doors of opportunity that would be otherwise left closed. When the enemy is able to rob our anticipation, he has cut off a supply line of faith.

Faith is the result of something. It is the result of hearing the Word of God. It is also the result of a growing anticipation. For anticipation is nothing more than good old fashioned hope. Hope is the anchor of our soul. It is from hope that faith proceeds. You can not have faith without first having hope because faith deals with the future and hope deals with the now.

Let us allow anticipation to build. Anticipation builds through positive confession and positive expectation. It builds through active confidence in what Father desires to do.

Can you feel the power?

December 29th

SLOW CHANGE COMES QUICKLY

"The Lord is not slow in keeping His promise, as some understand slowness"

II Peter 3:9

Time is relative. What is mid-morning for one in this country is early evening for someone in another country. Placement has everything to do with time. Where we happen to be, determines our perspective on timing.

Once we step into the Kingdom of God, we step into a new time zone. In the Kingdom time zone, time is not as it seems. A day is like a thousand years. Consequently, waiting for the Lord can seem like an awfully long time, but in this time zone, a thousand years is also like a day. Consequently, our wait can seem rather swift.

God is eternal and He stands outside of time. Though the result of His work is measured in time, the origin and source of that work is not. God's plan is timeless and His means are timeless. Consequently, slow change often comes quickly.

"In its time, I will do it swiftly" (Isaiah 60:32) The Lord is not slow in keeping His promises. Once it is time for that promise to be fulfilled, God moves swiftly. What seems to last like a thousand years, is the promise coming to its time. While we wait for the fullness of time, God is using the timing of that promise to test us and mature us. *"For the revelation awaits an appointed time and will not prove false. Though it linger wait for it. It will certainly come and not delay"* (Habakkuk 2:3)

The promise has come concerning change. God's intent in setting us free is clear. Freedom will come and not delay. Freedom will come in its time and when it does, it will come swiftly. While we wait, we believe. While the freedom lingers, we proclaim, "we are free."

Perspective has everything to do with timing. A day in the Kingdom of God is like a thousand years, but a thousand years in the Kingdom is also like a day. This date is our day for change, in its time, it will come suddenly.

December 30th

SUSTAINED TRUTH

"It gave me great joy to have some brothers come and tell about your faithfulness to the truth and how you continue to walk in the truth. I have no greater joy than to hear that my children are walking in the truth"

III John 3:4

It is one thing to receive truth and quite another to walk in what has been received. Our western minds are prone to believe that to hear truth is to know it. Consequently, walking that truth out is often displaced by the need to hear something new. The need for new truth can be a subtle deception. It becomes a compulsive drive that takes us from one teaching to the next without any of the truth actually taking root in our lives and producing the fruit of Father's desire. In this subtle deception, accumulation becomes the goal, not assimilation.

God's desire for His children is not simply the accumulation of truth, but the assimilation of what has been received. Assimilation does not happen at the point of contact. Truth is assimilated over time. Like time released capsules, truth is designed to be slowly released that it might work systematic change in our thinking and behavior. Consequently, our focus must be the sustaining of truth, not just its receiving. To receive truth and not sustain it over time is to lose what we have received.

Sustained truth is guarded truth. As much as Father desires our continuing in the truth we have received, the enemies of our souls desire to see that truth forsaken. One of the ways they accomplish this is by tempting us to abort the truth that has already been received in exchange for something new. Consequently, we are continually dealing with issues that are half grown because they have never been given sufficient time to become fully grown. Maturity in the Kingdom of God is not measured by the volume of truth but by the age of truth. In other words, how long have we continued in the truth we know? Has any of the truth we profess to know been allowed to process us over time and come of age?

Truth is like expensive wine, the older it is, the better it becomes. Aged truth is refined truth. When you hear it, there is a purity in its sound. It goes in smoothly. There is no pride in its delivery. There is less mixture in its presentation. To possess that level of purity in the truth we know, we must continue in what we have. To walk in what we already have must become more important than receiving more than what we are capable of walking out.

Let us guard the truth we have already received and seek to excel in it. Let us focus on sustaining that and let the Holy Spirit focus on what is new.

☙❧

Pause for thought:

Write out the truths that the Holy Spirit has revealed to you, to remind you to guard them and walk in them more fully.

December 31st

TRAVEL OR ARRIVAL

"Jesus said, 'It is finished'"

John 19:30

Imagine the joy to be able to say, *"It is finished,"* as Jesus did. In a day and age when very few things are completed, to finish something is nothing short of miraculous. This is especially true in our pursuit of the Kingdom of God. The Kingdom is a forceful advance. It is ever moving forward and we are running after it. It has been said often that as Christians, we will never arrive. That is, we will ever be in pursuit of the Kingdom and never reach the place of fullness and completion. While that notion is true, is it the truth?

Jesus, being the pattern Son, arrived. Paul, fashioned in the likeness of Christ to be an example and a continuation of that pattern, arrived. Echoing the words of Christ on the cross, Paul writes, *"I have fought the good fight; I have finished the race."* (II Timothy 4:7) Perhaps we could justify Christ's accomplishment by saying He was the Son of God, so, of course, He would arrive, but what about Paul? Paul was just a man as you and I. He possessed nothing we do not. He was graced with no special endowment. The same Holy Spirit that enabled his arrival lives in us to enable our arrival, if we believe it is possible.

Perhaps the reason no one ever arrives is because we have believed the lie that we can not. Certainly, the Kingdom of God is vast. Certainly, the ways of God are limitless. Certainly, man will never figure God out. We serve the God of the impossible, who makes all things possible to those who believe, even the possibility of completing the race God has given us to run. No, we may not exhaust the ways of God. No, we may not complete the search of that which is unreachable, but we can finish our race. We may not solve the issues of eternity, but we can complete that which God has given us to do. As long as the goal is unattainable there is no reason to try, so we pacify ourselves with subnormal living. Once we see the goal has been attained by those who have gone before, we are lifted to a higher level of expectation and pursuit.

Believing we will never arrive, man has satisfied himself with travel rather than arrival. Travel is not the issue in God's Kingdom; it is arrival. The issue is not movement; it is accomplishment. Our example both by Jesus and by Paul is completion. To run the race set before us and finish the course, we can expect to arrive. We can give ourselves to the race and seek a way as to run with the expectation of completion.

Pause for thought:

Are you running as to win or just running? Are you traveling this road of life with a destination in mind or just traveling? If we run, let us run to win, and in so doing follow the example of those who have gone before and finished the race.

Index According To Subject

Living In Prophetic Reality

A Heart Of Wisdom	7
Destiny Not History	376
Focused On The Unseen	379
In Pursuit Of The Part	299
Interpreting The Times	73
Interrupted By Need	285
Looking Down	11
Origin And Purpose	363
Rewarded Fully	144
The Appointed Time	95
Without A Vision, The People . . .	25

Real Evangelism

A New Creation	150
A Sense Of Urgency	112
A Witness Of The Wonder	279
At Peace With God	162
Fruit That Remains	3
Generation Next	258
Having Our Cake And Eating It Too	23
Jesus, The Way	304
Lifesavers	24
Lostology	180
Love For The Lost	148
Making Room	392
Missions Awareness	65
New Beginnings	381
Practice Hospitality	51
Reconciled To Reconcile	339
The Decade Of Harvest	214
The Ministry Of Reconciliation	54
The Need For Penetration	402
The Power To Reproduce Is In The Fruit	46
The Reality of Revival	39
The Same Power	105
Therefore Go	359
To Every Man	360
To Keep It You Must Give It Away	210
Turning Off The Blue Lights	243
When Heaven Parties	212
Who Searches For Whom?	247

Real Holiness

A Call To Obedience	155
A Much Needed Rest	197

Title	Page
A Narrow Minded Bigot	157
A Window And A Mirror	160
An Undivided Heart	42
Backsliding	186
Becoming Offensive With Offenses	194
Breaking The Tyranny Of Unforgiveness	122
Call To Obedience	206
Carnally Minded	60
Change	31
Coming Out	131
Denying Self	47
Free From Accusation	172
Free From Addiction	288
From Shadow To Substance	195
Have They Noticed A Change?	84
Holding Others' Sin	234
In It Or Of It	255
Obligated To Jesus	61
Offend The Mind	49
Overcoming Temptation	147
People Of Distinction	309
Play The Squeeze	301
Playing God	117
Points Of Light	310
Seed Sown Among The Thorns	274
Seeing Through Spirit Eyes	30
Self	33
Sin Sours	330
Swallowed Into Hell Alive	128
Tearing Down The Altars	335
The Curse Of Familiarity	179
The Hope Of Withheld Desire	201
The Spirit Of Disqualification	267
The Taking Of Offense	199
The Unpardonable Sin	115
Thiefology	355
Turned Over By God	41
Undedicated Money	361
Under Control Of The Evil One	289
Ungodly Beliefs	373
Unspoken Profanity	20
When Rebels Stumble	28
When Silence Is The Best Defense	27
When Your Enemies Are Reduced To One	332
You Have Gone Too Far	151
Coming Out	189

Real Intimacy With God

A Passion For His Presence	278
A Photograph Of God	211
A Worship Center	252
Fresh Supply	38
God Is So Big	187
Grace Love	190
If You Build It, He Will Come	221
In And At	176
In The King's Presence	154
Intimacy	303
Limitless Love	10
Observer Or Perceiver	205
People Of His Presence	135
Presenting Ourselves	269
Prison Or Prisoner	270
Ready Your Heart	271
Shadow Or Substance	50
Steadfastly Devoted	295
The Call Of The Highlander	298
The Cancer Of Negativity	198
The Drift Factor	333
The Father's Acceptance	329
The First One Is Free	79
The Fullness of Christ	328
The Image Of God	324
The Importance Of Intimacy	272
The Passion Of His Presence	293
The Quiet Place	291
The Rock Of Personal Discovery	100
The Secret Of Contentment	320
Trust And Obey	196
When God Hides	106
When He Who Is In Comes On	55

Real Leadership

Led Poisoning	306
Taking The Helm	341
A Noble Desire	183
Controlled By Circumstances Or Directed By Destiny	395
Self-Promotion	213

Real Maturity In Christ

New Definitions & New Boundaries	12
Renewal Of Commitment	141
The Garment Of Praise	371
A Call For Justice	119
A Heart of Thankfulness	156

Title	Page
A Heart Of Thankfulness	349
A Past In Our Future	193
A Preceding Word	159
A Servant Named Rejection	249
A Winning Attitude	161
Another Chance, Yes; Same Opportunity, No	163
Before I Die	129
Boasting In Our Weakness	164
By My Spirit	165
Christocentric	219
Consequences	166
Decision Committers	287
Destiny's Name	283
Embracing The Season	167
Engagement	203
Expect Victory	171
Expecting Health	74
Fit For The Glory	263
Fixing And Setting	284
Free From Accusation	374
Freedom Not License	280
From God's Perspective	82
From Potential To Progress	146
Grace Given	173
Gratitude	362
Hidden From Sight	80
Howdy Pilgrim	302
If	145
Inspiration Or Transformation	207
Knowing More Than God	246
Many Fillings	40
Maturity Of Character	286
Moving From Jesse's House	228
Obedience Is Better Than Sacrifice	233
Power Of The Holy Spirit	143
Saying What You Think	13
Shown By God	124
Slow Change Comes Quickly	405
Source Of Supply	340
Sowing And Reaping	83
Spirit Of Adventure	345
Spiritual Birth	336
Subtle Wanderings	260
Tested By Fire	296
The Balance Of Wealth	90
The Blessed Hope Of Eternity	77

The Blood Is Everything	139
The Complete Jesus	45
The Cost Of Playing It Safe	37
The Cross, Our Proof Of Payment	334
The Dead Need No Defense	375
The Forward Look	91
The Grace Of Giving	326
The Greatest Vet Of All	346
The Living Word	140
The Lord Has Gone Before You	290
The Price Of Progress	242
The Servant Of All	321
The Silence Of The Lambs	224
The Spirit Of Adventure - see p370	352
The Waiting Game	393
The Wonder Of Redemption	389
Theology Of A Lesser God	44
Transferable Wealth	253
Travel Or Arrival	408
Treasures Or Stuff	237
What Is Your Name?	87
What They See Is What We Get	63
When Clay Is Good As Gold	209
When The Silence Gets Louder	265
Winning Respect	342
Yeah-Buts and Rational Lies	48
Yesterday's Tomorrow	184
Postponed Defeat	294
Redefining Jesus	281
Seasons Of Growth	344

Real Prayer

A House Of Prayer	70
He Works On Behalf Of Those Who Wait	68
Let It Rain Let It Pour	101
Sufficient Prayer Cover	71
The Power of Corporate Prayer	5
The Prayers Of Desperation	6
The Praying Church	67

Real Spirit Led Living

Observer Or Perceiver	364
Our Engagement Ring	308
Resurrection Power	104
Spirit Sensitive	337
The Curse Of Complacency	317
The Power To Become	322
Uncommon People	292

	When God Comes Down	315
	The Holy Spirit	116
Real Submission and Authority		
	Christianity Starts With Christ	350
	From Search To Worship	314
	Paradigm Shifts	312
	Part Time Or Full Time	311
	Supremacy Of Christ	348
	The Way	331
	The Way And Not The Way	357
Real Warfare		
	Get Ready	4
	Standing Firm	300
	The Arena Of Battle	297
Realities Of Work		
	A Biblical Philosophy Of Work	15
	A Call For Pioneers	133
	A Kingdom Work Ethic	273
	At What Price Success?	244
	Desire And Preparation	85
	Gettin' Busy	325
	It's Never Too Late!	185
	Machine Or Man	22
	No Club Med	168
	Rest On The Run	19
	Success Or Excellence	62
	Summertime Blues	218
	Work	266
Resurrection Reality		
	The Crowning Event	108
	The Incomparably Great Power	99
	Two Strikes Against Me And A Fast Ball On The Way	107
The Real Family Of God		
	A Change Of Focus	153
	A City Without Walls	76
	A Mother's Honor	142
	A New Opinion Of Each Other	158
	A Spiritual Home	14
	Above All	400
	Accusation Or Appeal	366
	Covenant Relationships	26
	Delayed Blessings	149
	Encumbered Expense	251
	From One Man	132
	Grieving The Holy Spirit	174
	Kissers or Cleavers	97

Loose Lips	16
Making Provision For Failure	56
Many Parts, But One Conciousness	29
Proving Our Spirituality	264
Set Into Family	231
Spiritual Placement	59
Supporting Ligaments	181
Taking Suspicion Captive	57
That They May Be One	387
The Cannibalism Of Self	58
The Death Treatment	53
The Head And The Body	327
The Relationship Between Unity And Worship	32
The Separation Tactic	136
Which Family Are You?	86
Zeal For Your House Consumes Me	250

The Reality Of Faith

Even When We Can't See It	191
Faith As A Foundation	134
God Of The Impossible	391
Himpossible	398
Possession By The Way Of Proclamation	372
Power Through Anticipation	404
Receiving The Promise By Grace	313
Seed Power	365
The Caleb Company	268
The Certainty Of God's Promise	170
The Expectation Of Anticipation	261
The Importance Of Faith	75
The Possibility Of The Impossible	289
The Proper Time	316
The Two Sides Of Faith	138
The Way Of Faith	262
We Sows - He Grows	368

The Reality Of Sonship and Discipleship

A Force Of Three	114
A Heart For The Nations	238
Being Led By The Spirit	254
Elijah's Greatest Miracle	385
Empowerment	236
Family	178
From Child To Son	94
From Consumer To Producer	217
He Did It His Way	121
Led By Another's Destiny	305
Nonprofit Or For Profit	21

Originators Or Imitators	215
Planned Parenthood	72
Serving Beyond Ourselves	43
Sons Of The Kingdom	92
Success is Succession	127
The Pattern Son	226
The Pride Of Originality	222
The Rumblings Of Emancipation	377
The Son Given	102
The Spirit Of Adoption	319
The Spirit of Elijah	383

The Reality Of The Kingdom of God

A Spirit Of Willingness	64
A Time For Evaluation	126
A Time For Putting Aside	110
Binding The Strongman	69
Brought Over	34
By What Standard	239
Cost Or Investment	192
Counting The Cost	241
Father's Gift	169
Forcefully Advancing	1
God Gets Uneven	369
He Overcame By Being Overcome	175
It's No Private Matter	351
No Half Way Covenants	229
Nothing As Usual	397
Owner Occupancy Only	318
Prophet And Loss	96
Prophet Or King	78
Selling All	2
Settling The Issue Of Time	232
Strategic Infiltration	17
The Day Of Death	370
The Impact Of One	257
The Kingdom Of God	323
The Priority Of One	88
The Taste Of Authenticity	137
The Throne of God	396
The Tomb Becomes A Womb	347
The Turning Of Our Centers	354
The Way Of Increased Expectation	358
Your Kingdom Come	338

The Word Of God In Reality

Hearers And Thinkers	130
I Don't Understand	52

Inerrancy Of Scripture	177
Memorization And Meditation	307
Over-taught And Under-practiced	256
Seasons And The Word	275
Seed Sown On The Rocks	276
Sustained Truth	406
The Divine Learning Process	36
The Seed On The Path	277
The Source Of Knowledge	8
The Standard Of Revelation	240
Ungodly Beliefs	109
Weariness Of Silence	353
When Truth Is Black And White	35
World View	378

Other Titles By Norman A. Willis:

Unity With A Return

➢ Why did so many New Testament writers speak of the imminent return of our Lord Jesus Christ, yet two thousand years later we still wait? Could it be we are missing something? Is it time we begin asking questions? Is it time we ask ourselves, "What must we do to make ourselves ready?" With John 17:20-23 as his blueprint, Pastor Norm examines these questions and sounds a prophetic call for unity for the sake of Christ's return.

Enemies From Within

➢ In this booklet, Pastor Norm insightfully exposes two enemies that work their carnage from within our own corporate and family circles: the stronghold of familiarity and the cancer of negativity. This booklet will teach you how to identify these enemies and stop their destruction.

Playing God

➢ Tradition has made forgiveness unconditional when in reality Jesus placed a major condition upon it. Jesus stated that to receive forgiveness, we must first extend it. Pastor Norm establishes the fact that to withhold forgiveness is to set ourselves up to "Play God" and as a result, subject ourselves to the torment of unforgiveness and bitterness.

☙❧

For Ordering Information Contact:
Christ Church Publishing
11725 NE 118th St
Kirkland, WA 98034
Phone: (425) 820-2900
Fax: (425) 820-5627
Email: cckirkland@msn.com